1 SAMUEL

Hebrew Bible Monographs, 19

Series Editors
David J.A. Clines, J. Cheryl Exum, Keith W. Whitelam

Editorial Board
A. Graeme Auld, Marc Brettler, Francis Landy,
Hugh S. Pyper, Stuart D.E. Weeks

1 SAMUEL

A NARRATIVE COMMENTARY

Keith Bodner

SHEFFIELD PHOENIX PRESS

2009

Copyright © 2009 Sheffield Phoenix Press
First published in hardback 2008
First published in paperback 2009

Published by Sheffield Phoenix Press
Department of Biblical Studies, University of Sheffield
Sheffield S10 2TN

www.sheffieldphoenix.com

All rights reserved.
No part of this publication may be reproduced or transmitted in any form or by any means, electronic or mechanical, including photocopying, recording or any information storage or retrieval system, without the publishers' permission in writing.

A CIP catalogue record for this book
is available from the British Library

Typeset by Forthcoming Publications
Printed by Lightning Source

ISBN 978-1-906055-10-3 (hardback)
ISBN 978-1-906055-88-2 (paperback)
ISSN 1747-9614

CONTENTS

Acknowledgments	vii
Abbreviations	viii
Introduction	1
1. Title and Text	1
2. Canonical Location	2
a. The House that Ruth Built	2
b. 'In those days there was no king in Israel'	3
c. The Deuteronomistic History	3
3. Major Characters	6
4. Approach	8

A NARRATIVE COMMENTARY

Chapter 1	11
Chapter 2	26
Chapter 3	37
Chapter 4	43
Chapter 5	51
Chapter 6	55
Chapter 7	63
Chapter 8	69
Chapter 9	78
Chapter 10	92
Chapter 11	102
Chapter 12	109
Chapter 13	118
Chapter 14	130
Chapter 15	149
Chapter 16	166
Chapter 17	176
Chapter 18	191
Chapter 19	202
Chapter 20	212
Chapter 21	223
Chapter 22	231

Chapter 23	240
Chapter 24	249
Chapter 25	258
Chapter 26	274
Chapter 27	283
Chapter 28	290
Chapter 29	304
Chapter 30	309
Chapter 31	316
Bibliography	327
Index of References	331
Index of Authors	339

Acknowledgments

This book began with an invitation from John Jarick, and was originally slated for the *Readings* series under his editorship. As it happened, the volume ended up in a different series, but I am grateful for Dr Jarick's continued support. I have retained the *Readings* format and general literary approach. Anyone who has worked with Duncan Burns on the production side of a manuscript can testify to his 'above and beyond' effort and competence, and once more I appreciated his skills. Over the course of the writing, Peter Miscall read considerable portions, as did Daniel Hawk. Graeme Auld and Walter Brueggemann poured forth timely encouragement, and, as always, Barbara Green and Bob Polzin provided meaningful 'dialogics'. The annual exhortations of Professor D.J.A. Clines in the SBL exhibit hall spurred me on to the finish line, and my colleague Barry Smith politely inquired *every week* as to the completion date. Along the way, critical queries were posed by Mark Leuchter and David Vanderhooft, while some long conversations with Jacob Wright were invaluable.

Numerous friends in the venerable Canadian Society of Biblical Studies listened patiently to my papers on many of the topics explored here. Craig Evans extended gracious hospitality on a number of occasions, and I also appreciate the chance to share ideas with the students and faculty members of McMaster Divinity College and Regent College as a visiting professor. Seth Crowell, Mary Beth Clements, Steve Dempster, Greg Maillet, and David MacDonald all deserve an honorable mention, while Ryan Johnson and Mike King were basketball teammates at an opportune moment.

I am eternally thankful for the sacrifice and indefatigable support of my 'Shulammite', Dr Coreen Bodner, who has, along with our three energetic offspring, Victoria, Jeff, and Evelyn, enabled me to affirm the declaration of a great poet: חֲבָלִים נָפְלוּ־לִי בַּנְּעִמִים ('the boundary lines have fallen for me in delightful places', Ps. 16.4).

ABBREVIATIONS

AB	Anchor Bible
CBQ	*Catholic Biblical Quarterly*
DJD	Discoveries in the Judaean Desert
ICC	International Critical Commentary
JBL	*Journal of Biblical Literature*
JHS	*Journal of Hebrew Scriptures*
JSOT	*Journal for the Study of the Old Testament*
JSOTSup	*Journal for the Study of the Old Testament*, Supplement Series
KJV	King James Version
LXX	Septuagint
MT	Masoretic text
NIBC	New International Biblical Commentary
NRSV	New Revised Standard Version
OTL	Old Testament Library
RSV	Revised Standard Version
SOTSMS	Society for Old Testament Study Monograph Series
VT	*Vetus Testamentum*
WBC	Word Biblical Commentary

Introduction

The book of 1 Samuel has engaged readers over the centuries because of its dramatic depths and theological mysteries. Readers are not just attracted to the famous stories such as David's confrontation with the giant Goliath, but other episodes such as the travails of Hannah, the capture of the ark, the birth of Ichabod, and the shade of the long-dead Samuel reappearing on a dark night in Endor, each of which is endlessly intriguing. 1 Samuel is a brilliant and intricate work of literature that often resists easy conclusions and confronts the interpreter with innumerable challenges. In this brief introduction, I would like at least to draw attention to several of these challenges, and discuss a few preliminary matters and questions that we will encounter during the course of our journey. My remarks are limited to and organized around four different areas: *title and text* (the name of the book and its textual traditions), *canonical location* (the placement of the book within the Bible and issues of context), *major characters* (the key personalities), and *approach* (the reading strategy used in this commentary).

1. *Title and Text*

The book we are studying has been saddled with a couple of different titles. Its title in the Greek tradition is '1 Reigns' (or '1 Kingdoms'), the first of four books known as Samuel–Kings in the Hebrew Bible. Some have argued that the division of the books is fairly loose, and based on relative scroll length or some other practical purpose. The title *1 Reigns* has a particular aptness in light of the book's content: the transition from charismatic judgeship to the beginning of dynastic monarchy, with a sustained reflection on leadership. 1 Reigns alerts the reader to the fact that the stakes are high during this stretch of Israel's history, and political decisions and ideas proposed here will have far-reaching implications for the nation. While there is a certain currency in the title 1 Reigns, the Hebrew tradition opted instead for *Samuel* (with further division into 1 and 2 Samuel taking place in the early sixteenth century). This title has nothing to do with authorship, as Samuel the character could not possibly have written either 1 or 2 Samuel. Nor does it primarily have to do with Samuel (Hannah's son) as a dominant figure in the story, who does not even appear in the next installment of the story, 2 Samuel. In my view, the title *Samuel* has to do with a prophetic utterance that Samuel happens to speak: 'your kingdom will not arise', the last judge informs the first king, because 'the LORD sought for himself a man according to his heart' (13.14). This is a story, in other words, about a prophetic utterance gradually finding its fulfillment, and Samuel's declaration guides the plot of both 1 and 2 Samuel.

This commentary is based on the standard Hebrew Masoretic text (MT). However, scholars appreciate that there are difficulties with the MT of 1 Samuel, and there are numerous places in the text where one is unsure of the reading. Translators usually turn to the Greek Septuagint tradition in places where the Hebrew text is problematic. The Septuagint (LXX) is not without its own idiosyncrasies, and at some points offers a substantially different story (the David and Goliath narrative in chap. 17 is such an example; see Auld and Ho 1992: 19-39). While my primary interest is the Hebrew text, I occasionally discuss a variant reading as a window into understanding how the text may have been interpreted in ancient times. Furthermore, the Qumran fragments of Samuel (finally published in Cross 2005) also add another dimension for text criticism that can prove helpful. But, of course, not all readers have the advantage of specialized training in biblical languages. Fortunately there are a host of serviceable English translations. Preferably, the reader of this commentary will have at least two translations handy; since the RSV and the NRSV are readily available, I will assume that the reader is able to consult these two versions. For all that, I tend to translate a fair bit of the text during my analysis—often quite literally—in order to bring out a certain point under discussion. Moreover, I will follow the verse numberings of these English translations (rather than the Hebrew, which has occasional discrepancies) for ease of use.

2. *Canonical Location*

a. *The House That Ruth Built*

In the Greek ordering of the Scriptures—which the Christian Bible follows—1 Samuel is immediately preceded by the book of Ruth. The reader can observe that both Ruth and 1 Samuel begin with a domestic tableau, and various household problems are used to comment on the national situation. Birth of offspring is a key component of both narratives, and in both books important themes of reversal and surprise unfold, as God creatively works in situations where hopelessness seems to abound. Perhaps most importantly, the book of Ruth provides a tacit introduction to David; the house that Ruth builds culminates in David, who is mentioned as the last word of the book.

b. *'In those days there was no king in Israel'*

In the Hebrew canon, however, Ruth is situated in the third section, the Writings. Consequently, in the Hebrew Bible 1 Samuel is preceded by Judges, and is grouped together with the books known as the 'Former Prophets'. 1 Samuel is therefore one segment of a larger collection (Joshua to 2 Kings) tracing the experience of Israel in the land. The book of Judges functions as an introduction to many of the issues raised in 1 Samuel, where the reader notes the subtle foregrounding of Judah and the gradual degeneration of Benjamin. Various locales are shared between the latter part of Judges and early parts of 1 Samuel, such as Shiloh, the hill country of Ephraim, Bethlehem, and Gibeah of Benjamin. Most compelling is the correspondence between the final sentence of Judges—a refrain that occurs some four times in the final five chapters—and the storyline of 1 Samuel. Judges ends with the ambiguous line: 'In those days there was no king in Israel. Every man did what was upright in his own eyes.' Does this suggest that once a king arrives in Israel things will be better? Or worse? The last sentence of Judges thus functions as a transition to the story of kingship recounted in 1 Samuel.

c. *The Deuteronomistic History*

Both Ruth and Judges form a useful literary backdrop for 1 Samuel, and create a different sense of expectation in the reader's mind. For my analysis, though, I will ultimately privilege the book of Judges, and assume that 1 Samuel is part of the larger story of the Former Prophets, or the 'Deuteronomistic History' as it has come to be known in scholarly circles since the formulation of the hypothesis by Martin Noth. In short, this grand narrative is a response to the crisis of life after destruction. In 586 BCE, the Babylonian army invaded Jerusalem, destroyed the temple, and deported a significant number of people. The trauma of this event resulted in new literary creation. It was during this time of exile—as a religious and cultural minority who were captives in a foreign land—that the nation seriously reflected on their faith, in the crisis of Jerusalem's collapse. What do they believe? What went wrong? If they ever get a chance to return to their land, how should they live? There are a number of voices and reflections during this period that are preserved in the Hebrew Bible. The book of Ezekiel is one example, parts of other prophetic books are other examples.

A major compilation during the exile and its aftermath—we imagine—is the epic recounting of Israel's story in the 'Former Prophets' spanning from Joshua to 2 Kings. As I mentioned above, the Former Prophets are often referred to as the Deuteronomistic History, this being because the theology articulated in the book of Deuteronomy informs the subsequent narrative of Joshua to 2 Kings. Our assumption is that these books—Joshua, Judges,

1 and 2 Samuel, 1 and 2 Kings, with the core of Deuteronomy as a necessary overture—form a reasonably unified and cohesive narrative that tells the story of Israel from its *conquest* of the land until its eventual *collapse* at the hand of the invading Babylonians. At the beginning of the story, Israel is *outside* the land of promise, looking in. Addressing the nation, Moses exhorts the people: 'I have set before you life and death, blessing and curse. Therefore, choose life, that you and your descendants may live, to love the LORD your God, to listen to his voice, and to cling on him, for *he* is your very life and the length of your days, so that you may dwell in the land which the LORD swore to your fathers, to Abraham, Isaac, and Jacob, to give them' (Deut. 30.19-20).

In this long sermon of Deuteronomy, Moses challenges the people: if you love the LORD and walk with him in covenant obedience, then you will experience a healthy measure of blessing in the land. By contrast, Moses warns, should the people persist in disobedience, covenant unfaithfulness, and compromise, they will not experience blessing, but ultimately 'cursing'. Expulsion from the land is the epitome of non-blessing. In 2 Kings 25, the people are again *outside* the land of promise. With this theological premise of Deuteronomy the long narrative of Joshua–2 Kings begins: will Israel be faithful and enjoy blessing in the land? Or, in the end, will unfaithfulness prevail, and with it the long passage to exile? This theological challenge is woven into the fabric of the text, and the Deuteronomistic History has a cast of thousands who live through many centuries in time. As Thomas Römer (2005: 24) summarizes, 'The book of Deuteronomy, which is presented as Moses' testimony, appears as the hermeneutical key and the ideological basis for reading and understanding the following history'.

There are a number of major themes the reader can discern in the Deuteronomistic History: the monotheistic ideal (the one God who saved Israel from Egypt, and led them back to the land of promise); the struggle against idolatry; the centrality of Jerusalem; the dynamic nature of Torah; the necessity of avoiding foreign influence; the election of the Davidic dynasty; the prophetic word and its fulfillment (see Weinfeld 1972). Following the lead of scholars such as Robert Polzin, I use the term 'Deuteronomist' simply as a shorthand term for the implied author(s) of the work, in order to stress continuity with Deuteronomy and a coherent plotline throughout the narrative. The various books themselves contain a number of highlights that contribute to this overall story:

(i) *Joshua*. The book of Joshua opens with a speech from God himself, who rallies the new leader with a challenge to believe amid formidable obstacles. The book of Joshua will be about conquest, yet the opening speech is centered on *God's word*, not military strategy. After some qualified success and a few notable setbacks, the second half of the book recounts the allocation of the land to the various tribes (Judah gets the largest share), and closes with a speech from the aged Joshua exhorting the people to stay faithful and not give up.

(ii) *Judges*. After the death of Joshua, the book of Judges begins with a subtle foregrounding of the tribe of Judah and proceeds to illustrate the rollercoaster of Israel's faith. There is a fourfold cycle of backsliding in the book: Israel serves other gods, becomes enslaved to the nations whose gods they worship, and at the end of their rope, they cry out to God, and invariably God rescues them in a surprising way. There is a *south to north* movement over the course of the book, as the various narratives focus on one judge for virtually every tribe. The last chapters of the book include episodes of idolatry and civil war, and the book concludes with the overt mention of 'a king'. This prepares the way for the advent of the monarchy in the nation.

(iii) *1 Samuel*. The birth of kingship is painful—much like having children has its painful moments—and this is the image the author uses to introduce the monarchy. The first 'son' born in this book is Samuel, who in turn becomes the first kingmaker in the nation. The birth of Samuel intersects with the fall of the house of Eli, and a serious crisis arises in chap. 8 when the elders demand, 'Give us a king, like all the nations!' Israel's first king, Saul, is from Benjamin, and his name means 'asked for'. While Saul has his good points, the tribe of Benjamin does not share the same destiny as Judah, and in time David of Judah is secretly anointed as Saul's successor. The book ends with the tragic picture of Saul falling on his sword, a fatal action that might presage the fall of the monarchy itself in Israel.

(iv) *2 Samuel*. The book opens with the account of David's accession over all Israel and the capture of Jerusalem, renamed 'the city of David'. A key moment is chap. 7: David offers to build God a 'house' (temple), but God declines the offer, and instead promises to build David a 'house' (dynasty). This promise of a dynastic line represents a watershed moment in the theological plot of the narrative, a promise that is sorely tested in the days ahead. A turning point for David's career is chap. 11, the Bathsheba *rendezvous* and subsequent murder of her husband Uriah. David has been promised a dynastic house, but now the sword will not depart from that house, as the considerable family dysfunction in the remainder of 2 Samuel testifies. The book ends with a sin, a sacrifice, and the acquisition of land for the eventual 'house' of God.

(v) *1 Kings*. The early events of 1 Kings include the death of David and the succession of Solomon, who purges his opponents and consolidates his throne by means of some extensive building projects: the palace takes thirteen years to build, the temple takes seven years. At the end of his life the narrator discloses that Solomon has a divided heart, and this directly leads to a divided kingdom in 1 Kings 12. There are now two nations: 'Israel' in the north, and 'Judah' in the south. The northern kingdom experiences a rapid flow of fleeting dynasties and one-term wonders, while the southern kingdom is comparatively more stable, with a descendent of David continually on the throne. However, both nations struggle with theological orthodoxy, and the escalating international tensions and frequent confrontations between king and prophet does not augur well for the future of both north and south.

(vi) *2 Kings*. The story of division continues, and the conflicts intensify (both external with other nations, and internal with faithfulness to the covenant). The advancing Assyrian army eventually destroys the northern kingdom of Israel (2 Kgs 17), but the tiny kingdom of Judah continues because of a spectacular divine intervention. The southern kingdom survives for a while, but it is only a matter of time before the Babylonian army (the new superpower on the block) advances toward Jerusalem and destroys the country, sending the people into exile among the various Babylonian provinces (2 Kgs 25). Yet the lamp of hope has not been extinguished, and this is not the end of the story. With the nation in exile, and stripped of the illusions of idolatry and the failed institution of the monarchy, the people of God now have to consider how best to live in radically altered circumstances.

The narrative of 1 Samuel, therefore, is part of the national autopsy performed in light of its monarchic collapse. In all probability, the composition of this narrative was a complicated affair (see, e.g., Sweeney 2007: 3-32), and I should say that numerous scholars of late are contesting the notion of the Deuteronomistic History and abandoning it, much like the Philistines were ready to abandon the ark after it caused so many hemorrhoids. Nonetheless, I use the idea of the History as a heuristic way of making sense of the available data as a cohesive story, and instead of reading 1 Samuel in isolation, it is more profitable to understand the book as one section of wider narrative continuum.

3. *Major Characters*

There are a host of memorable and remarkably drawn characters in the book of 1 Samuel, and we will have occasion to meet them in the pages that follow. But three characters should be introduced briefly here—Samuel, Saul, and David—whose lives intertwine, whose portraits overlap, and who in many respects are defined by each other. I understand these figures to be presented with a high degree of complexity. In the past, many interpreters have viewed these characters as rather flat and somewhat robotic (Samuel being the good prophet, Saul the evil first king, and David his romantic and wonderful successor). In such interpretations, characters are usually read in fairly unequivocal terms: someone is an example either of virtue or vice, and every action of the character is then evaluated within this predetermined framework. My analysis suggests a more provocative set of characterizations by the Deuteronomist, paying attention to the *character zone* that surrounds each of these major figures: that is, the language used around the character, the configuration of dialogue, the postures adopted, direct and indirect evaluations, and the responses to various circumstances.

The prophet Samuel is a multi-layered figure. He is a given a prenatal introduction in the story, and he is the one character who is granted a post-mortem cameo. Samuel emerges as a champion of orthodoxy, yet it must be said that he does not seem to be the most attractive personality. Samuel certainly has major issues with Saul—whom he anoints as king but then fires a week later—and surely one must ask whether or not Samuel is a good mentor for Israel's first king. The prophet Samuel, though, is not the only one to find fault with Saul. As David Gunn (1980: 23) summarizes, 'Saul's reputation has been hardly an enviable one, at least in Christian circles. While Jewish tradition has treated this first king of Israel with some sympathy, Christian tradition has shown him a large measure of hostility.' I will at least attempt to be more even-handed in my assessment of Saul, and not merely assume that he is wholly disposed to evil. A good example would be Saul's sacrificial error in chap. 13. John Goldingay (2003: 583) notes the following:

> The story has a hard time demonstrating that Saul is at fault and an even harder time demonstrating that the magnitude of the wrongdoing justifies the magnitude of the price he pays. This question becomes all the more pressing when we reconsider his story after reading David's, for Saul never commits acts as grotesquely wrong as David's sin against Bathsheba and Uriah, with its horrendous consequences for his family and his people.

To my mind, Goldingay touches on one of the central questions of the narrative: Why does Saul fare so much worse than David? David himself emerges in the story an extremely talented individual with a knack for leadership, sound political judgment, with fine physical endowments and confidence in the God of Israel. Interpreters often clothe David with the expression 'a man after God's own heart', giving him the pious benefit of the doubt in those murkier situations he (often) finds himself in. Yet I will argue that this expression 'after God's heart' has far less to do with David's inner spirituality as it does with God's choice; in other words, 'after God's heart' means 'after God's election'. It is an external rather than internal designation, and has more to do with God's grace than David's works. Consequently, the most intriguing and even surprising 'character' in 1 Samuel is God, who emerges as a 'politically incorrect deity [who] refuses to be tamed' (Noll 2004: 408). In my opinion, readers from all communities of faith can be challenged, encouraged, rebuked, and inspired by the portrait of God that emerges from the pages of 1 Samuel.

4. *Approach*

There have been numerous methods used to read biblical texts in the past: typological, philological, comparative, historical, and source-critical approaches are usually surveyed in introductory handbooks. This commentary adopts a literary approach, a close reading of the text that attends to matters of plot, character, point of view, irony, wordplay, direct speech, ambiguity, spatial and temporal settings, and the role of the narrator. A literary approach has a high degree of interest in the *poetics* of the text, that is, how it works as a piece of literature, and how language is used to convey meaning. For example, in Shakespeare's *Macbeth*, the weird sisters open the drama with the refrain, 'Fair is foul, and foul is fair'. In his opening scene, the main character Macbeth enters the stage with the words, 'So foul and fair a day I have not seen'. There is an intersection of language here in these utterances of central characters that interweave their destinies, and foreshadow plot connections to come. In the same way, Hannah's line in 1.28, 'He is asked for/lent' (or 'He is Saul', הוּא שָׁאוּל), serves to connect prophet and king at the earliest opportunity in the narrative, and alerts the reader to the importance of nameplays that will follow in the story. The literary approach, in brief, reads the story searching for evidence of intelligent design, discerning what Paul Ricoeur once described as 'the intelligible whole that governs a succession of events in any story' (cited in Brooks 1984: 13). In the present academic climate, literary approaches are increasingly eclectic, drawing on scholarship that deploys a range of critical methodologies with the belief that insight can be obtained from many different reading strategies.

A Narrative Commentary

1 Samuel 1

After the tumultuous conclusion of Judges, or after the genealogy of Ruth, the reader is presented with another genealogy—that of Elkanah of Ephraim. While one might think that Elkanah will be a major figure in the narrative, he is gradually displaced as the central character in the story by his barren wife Hannah. This chapter is about openings: the long narrative about the birth of Israel's monarchy opens, just as Hannah's womb is opened to produce the first kingmaker. Hannah's womb opens with the birth of Samuel, who in turn will open the door to the birth of the monarchy in Israel. With great subtlety, the frequency of the verb 'to ask' indirectly introduces Israel's first king, Saul, whose name means 'asked'. From the outset, then, prophet and king are linked in this narrative that introduces kingship to Israel.

1.1-2

The story begins on the domestic front. A certain man named Elkanah is from the tribe of Ephraim ('double fruit'), from the town of Ramathaim ('double height'), and has a 'double wife' marital situation.

In the opening lines of 1 Samuel 1, the meaning of names has some significance. In this respect there is a similarity with the book of Ruth. In Ruth 1, the first character is Elimelech ('my God is king') who leaves Bethlehem ('house of bread') in Judah ('praise') because of a famine, and sojourns in Moab ('from his father'). Elimelech's wife Naomi ('delight') will later change her name to Marah ('bitter'), in part because of the fate of their two sons Mahlon ('sick') and Kilion ('failing'), who both die (not surprisingly, in light of such morbid nomenclature). The beginning of 1 Samuel is similar. Elkanah ('God is creator') loves Hannah ('favor'), but only Peninnah ('branching') bears fruit for this man from Ephraim ('double fruit').

While it is not always the case, there are numerous occasions in Hebrew narrative when the meaning of names bears some weight. As a literary technique, the use of names can be an efficient means of rendering character and individualization. The name can carry a sense of destiny, and character traits can be revealed by the name. At the level of the larger storyline, various points of theme and plot can be conveyed through the use of names, and even theological nuances can be discerned. In 1 Samuel 1, the names in the earlier parts of the chapter serve to build momentum toward a more important play on names: Samuel and Saul. As Moshe Garsiel (1985: 73-75) notes, the connection between the names of Saul and Samuel foreshadows 'their fates tangled together', and draws a comparison between two kinds of asking: Hannah will ask for a son, and the people will ask for a king.

Hannah's barren condition prohibits her from contributing to Elkanah's genealogical line. This is in contrast to Elkanah's other wife Peninnah, who has numerous 'sons' and 'daughters' (1.4). Since there are hundreds of names in the Deuteronomistic History, it is somewhat surprising that there are no names attached to any of Peninnah's offspring. The omission of any names suggests that Peninnah's children will not contribute to the continuity of Elkanah's genealogy in the opening sentence of 1 Samuel, and there may yet be hope for Hannah to experience the favor of God the creator.

Of course, for an exilic reader there is a certain symbolic import to barrenness. Just as Hannah is barren and has scant prospects for the future, so Israel as a people have experienced long periods of spiritual barrenness. Yet there is hope for Hannah, since she is connected to a number of other barren wives who have received a miraculous intervention of divine grace to breathe new life into sterility. Perhaps the same hopes are possible for a nation in exile.

Indeed, Hannah's barrenness puts her in some elite biblical company. Her helpless estate brackets her with Sarah, Rebekah, and Rachel in Genesis. These barren wives became instruments of providence in furthering the promise made to Abraham. And, although this might seem cold comfort to Hannah, in Luke's Gospel the portrait of Elizabeth consciously alludes to this episode in 1 Samuel 1. In the Bible as a whole, then, God has a habit of using barren wives, and their offspring are usually important characters in the narrative. Most recently in the Former Prophets, Manoah's wife is barren, yet gives birth to a Nazirite son Samson ('sunny'). Notwithstanding the rather unsavory contours of Samson's lifestyle choices—from the vantage point of Israelite orthodoxy—he is used by God to alleviate (temporarily) the misery wrought by the Philistines. Should infertile Hannah give birth, one would expect her offspring to have a prominent role in the story. Since the final line of Judges reads 'In those days there was no king in Israel...', the reader may be expecting a prominent character to burst on to the narrative set.

The introduction of Elkanah and his family in 1 Samuel 1 is rather more than it seems at first glance. One recalls that Flaubert's *Madame Bovary* begins with the innocuous scene of a classroom—with a clumsy schoolboy and not particularly profound dialogue—yet there is more to the opening of that novel than meets the eye on first reading, as important matters of plot, character, and theme are subtly foregrounded. So it is with 1 Samuel 1. In the midst of what must be a fairly average household in ancient Israel at the end of the Judges era—with a stress on land and lineage—could it be that more is contained in the introduction to Elkanah than meets the eye?

On the one hand, this rather pedestrian genealogy is a long way from the lists of wars and court officials that will inundate the narrative in the not too distant future. On the other hand, Robert Polzin (1993: 25) argues at length that the opening chapters of 1 Samuel function as a parabolic introduction to the story of the monarchy in Israel, whereby the 'having of sons' is analogous to the 'having of kings'. Just like Hannah is about to give birth to a son, so Israel is about to give birth to a king: '"The having of sons" is the image chosen by the author to convey the complicated story of how Israel came to have kings'. Polzin's parabolic proposal will be further considered in due course. Meanwhile, one could argue that the opening genealogy introduces themes such as *sonship* and *succession* into the narrative. These are themes that will be developed in the larger storyline.

1.3
The subject of the narrative turns to the annual journey of Elkanah to Shiloh. The verbal form used here implies habitual action: year by year. The purpose of this pilgrimage is to worship and sacrifice, indicating a piety on behalf of Elkanah. In fact, it has been argued that he is a Levite, and the controversy is created by the Levite genealogy for Elkanah in 1 Chronicles 6. Despite some valiant attempts by commentators to harmonize, in the end one suspects in 1 Samuel that Elkanah is not a Levite, but rather a northerner from Ephraim, who happens to be regular worshipper. Of course, Elkanah's (eventual) son Samuel will be a controversial figure, and so perhaps this genealogical disagreement is just the first of many tensions.

The object of Elkanah's worship is 'the LORD of hosts', and it is notable that this is the first time in Scripture that this powerful appellation is used. While the name itself is the subject of scholarly inquiry (the suggestion is made that this title reflects divine captaincy, that God is champion of the battle array of Israel), there is less discussion about why, of all places, this name occurs *at this particular* juncture of narrative time and space. My guess is that the name is used here as a reminder of divine sovereignty at the outset of Israel's experiment with kingship, and an expression of God's ultimate kingship. In 1 Samuel Israel will ask for a (human) king 'like all the nations', and this request will influence the rest of the biblical story in ways not anticipated by the elders in chap. 8.

The destination of Elkanah is Shiloh, a city in Ephraim (for the interested tourist, there are directions in Judg. 21.19, 'So they said, "Behold, the yearly festival of the LORD is taking place at Shiloh, which is north of Bethel, on the east of the highway that goes up from Bethel to Shechem, and south of Lebonah"'). In terms of background, Shiloh is a mixed bag: there are some positive events that take place there, but also some murkier moments. On the positive side, Shiloh was an important place of worship in the tribal confederation of Israel. In the latter chapters of Joshua (chaps. 18–21), the people gather to further apportion the land; it is here that the Levites are assigned to their towns and the Reubenites and Gadites head off into the sunrise of their eastern inheritance.

On the more sordid side of the ledger, however, there are some skeletons in Shiloh's closet. I mean this quite literally, as the idol of Micah (the rogue priest hired by the Danites in rather dubious circumstances) is installed in Shiloh: 'The descendants of Dan raised up the idol for themselves. As for Jonathan son of Gershom son of Moses, he and his descendants were priests for the tribe of the Danites until the day the land went into exile. They set up for themselves the idol that Micah had made all the days that the House of God was in Shiloh' (Judg. 18.30-31). Scandalous as it may sound, the possibility exists that Micah's carved image remains in Shiloh even under the stewardship of the house of Eli.

In terms of the present time, the reader is told that the sons of Eli, Hophni and Phinehas, are in Shiloh as priests of the LORD. Nothing more is said, but the significance of these priests in the main storyline will shortly emerge. As Bruce Birch (1998: 974) notes, 'The events that link the fate of these two families will determine the future of Israel'. 1 Samuel 1 moves in such a direction that these two households—representing the immediate past and the future of leadership in Israel—are brought together in Shiloh. Surveying the literary contribution of Eli and his sons to 1 Samuel in general, Graeme Auld (2003: 214) explains that this account informs the reader that houses and dynasties can indeed fall, and that leaders can be displaced by underlings. The tacit introduction of Eli (by means of his sons) sets the Shiloh subplot in motion.

1.4-5

The sacrificial meal results in a distribution of the feastly portions, an annual affair that is part of Elkanah's ritual habit in Shiloh. The many branches of Peninnah's family duly receive their portions—indeed, the unnamed brood of her offspring (of every conceivable gender) is underscored: 'all her sons and daughters'. Historically, the mothers of large families have found mealtime to be a stressful period. For Hannah, the annual feast of Shiloh is stressful, but for altogether different reasons: in contrast to Peninnah's family tree, Hannah has no twigs to nourish. In the distribution of portions, Elkanah certainly does not overlook Hannah—the reader is told that he loves her—and makes sure that she does not go hungry in the midst of the crowd. But what exactly does Hannah receive from Elkanah? A difficulty arises when one compares two translations of 1.4-5, the RSV from 1952, and its successor, the NRSV from 1989:

> On the day when Elkanah sacrificed, he would give portions to Peninnah his wife and to all her sons and daughters; and, although he loved Hannah, he would give Hannah *only one portion*, because the LORD had closed her womb. (RSV)

> On the day when Elkanah sacrificed, he would give portions to his wife Peninnah and to all her sons and daughters; but to Hannah he gave *a double portion*, because he loved her, though the LORD had closed her womb. (NRSV)

Many consumers experienced postwar inflation between 1952 and 1989, but by any measure this is a rather a dramatic increase in Hannah's serving. The trouble stems from the problematic Hebrew phrase in 1.5 (מָנָה אַחַת אַפָּיִם), a construction that has generated a myriad of translations, ranging from a single, to a choice or special, to a double portion. There are a number of ways to construe the evidence, and in the end it seems that one is left with a contextual decision: given the circumstances, what makes the best sense?

While 'double portion' is appropriate in light of Elkanah's love for Hannah as a foil to Peninnah's foliage, I am opting for the sense of 'single mouthful'. This is not simply due to a nostalgic longing for the happy days of the 1950s as opposed to the excessive indulgence of the 1980s, but because I think Elkanah's perspective is the point of view refracted here: 'But to Hannah he would give only a single portion, for Hannah he loved, *but the LORD had closed her womb*'. While Elkanah loves Hannah, and would gladly have given her many portions for many offspring, he can only give her a single serving for herself because *from his perspective* the LORD has closed fast her womb, and she has no other mouths to feed.

1.6-7

One could argue that it does not matter whether Hannah's portion is a single or a double, since the taunting of Peninnah causes her not to eat anyway. No doubt Elkanah's love for Hannah feeds Peninnah's provocation. Notably, Peninnah is not called by her name, but instead is labeled as Hannah's 'adversary'. Ironically, this word is often used to describe the intense anguish of labor pains (as in Jer. 6.24); here it is used to describe the distress brought on by her rival's goading.

The conflict between Hannah and Peninnah alludes to a previous clash among co-wives—one barren and one fertile—Rachel and Leah, the mothers of the twelve tribes. As Birch (1998: 975) notes, 'The themes of barrenness and the rivalry between wives is known from the earlier biblical stories of

Sarah and Hagar (Gen. 16), and Rachel and Leah (Gen. 29–30), where these mothers and their sons also represent the relationships between tribes and people'. It should be emphasized here that infighting among the mothers anticipates tribal conflicts to come in the story. At the end of Judges there is massive conflict between the sons of Rachel and Leah, that is, civil war among the tribes of Israel, with Benjamin nearly eliminated. The advent of kingship in Israel will also produce conflict, and at this point in the story this conflict is symbolically represented in Hannah and Peninnah.

1.8

Peninnah's words accomplish their intended effect, and Hannah is made to 'thunder'. Elkanah too speaks to Hannah, but presumably he is attempting the opposite: 'Hannah', he probes, 'why do you weep? Why don't you eat? Why is your heart afflicted? Aren't I better than ten sons for you?' In this interrogation, some commentators see Elkanah as being tender toward his favored wife, Hannah. He values her person. He too is despairing, but encourages her to look on the bright side, and he modestly commends his own manly virtues as a surrogate for her son-less condition. Other commentators, perchance all too familiar with life in a post-Eden world, hear the words of a husband who really does not understand the frustration of his weeping wife. Offering food is one solution; asking a series of 'why' questions represents a different approach. In fact, in the entire Deuteronomistic History this is the only time that 'why' (למה) occurs three times in rapid succession. Hannah is not recorded as responding to her husband Elkanah here, and some readers will not wonder why.

As mentioned above, there is more to this domestic tableau in Ephraim than meets the eye. With Polzin (1993: 23), one strains to see the deeper levels: 'Is there some political or ideological significance to this simple familial situation, to this intersection of conflicting emotions?' As for Elkanah's words to Hannah in 1.8, there is more than meets the ear. Polzin further intones: 'Specific discourse, repeated themes, even plot structures—all foreshadow selected sections of the monarchic history to come but are rearranged to present an opening meditation on the main ideological problems involved in the institution of kingship' (1993: 71). Indeed, Polzin hears a different accent in Elkanah's speech; he hears in them a parabolic rumbling that will echo throughout the narrative.

Elkanah's speech is *double voiced*, that is, reverberations of these words can be felt beyond their local context of articulation. In the immediate storyworld, these are the words of a husband speaking to his wife—a wife who will shortly ask God for a son. But in the larger context, Polzin hears the words of God speaking to his people—the people who will shortly ask God for a king. Elkanah's words—outwardly those of a frustrated husband—can be paraphrased as: 'O Israel, am I not worth more to you than ten kings?' (1993: 26). The reason Polzin hears the double-voiced accent in Elkanah's speech is because he understands the purpose of the Deuteronomistic History—of which 1 Samuel constitutes a chapter—to be a sustained mediation on the monarchy *in light of its ultimate collapse*. Early (implied) readers of the work, according to this interpretation, would be familiar with exile, and would be encouraged to reflect critically on topics like leadership and theology in a new era beyond the invasion of Babylon. Elkanah's questions may come at the wrong time for Hannah, but, Polzin would argue, at the right time in the narrative.

This is all well and good, but one suspects that Hannah is not aware that her husband is endowed with double-voiced speech accents, so she is probably still weeping at the end of 1.8. Yet, 'to the pure, all things are pure', and a hyperactive purist could argue that something good comes out of Peninnah's unendurable taunting, and Elkanah's quadruple questioning. Such words seem to be the catalyst that drives Hannah to the 'house of the LORD' in 1.9 where she will pray a desperate prayer. It may be that the text invites the possibility that Hannah may not have been driven to desperate prayer unless taunted to the point of holy anger. Since numerous scholars view this narrative as a story for a community that has experienced the barrenness of exile and the taunting of rivals, perhaps something instructive might emerge from these episodes of anguished Hannah.

1.9

It is after the eating and drinking—presumably festivities that she does not partake in based on the Hebrew verb forms used here—that Hannah arises to venture to the LORD's temple in Shiloh. In this temple (or 'palace', as the term הֵיכַל is often translated) Eli the priest is sitting on a chair (or 'upon the throne', as the phrase עַל־הַכִּסֵּא is often translated). Eli's posture is worth remembering: here in his first scene he is sitting on a throne; in his last scene this 'royal stand-in' will also be sitting on a throne before he topples over backwards and breaks his neck in 1 Samuel 4. Shiloh will soon be displaced as the spiritual center of the community; the house of Eli will soon be displaced as the spiritual leaders of the community.

For the time being, Eli the priest is a leader in the nation. The reader has been told in 1.3 that he has two sons, but why is Eli presented here in 1.9 as something of a royal figure? After all, thrones and palaces are metonymic, as Polzin says, 'for royal power and authority', for kings rather than Israelite priests (1993: 23). Such regal ambiance must, like Elkanah's words, carry with it a resonance that will be discerned as the story progresses: 'This initial meeting, ostensibly between Hannah the would-be mother and Eli the has-been priest, has royal overtones that look forward in a number of interlocking ways to the central matter of kingship which forms the subject matter of the entire history' (1993: 23).

Moreover, when Hannah enters into the 'house of God' at Shiloh, she is also crossing the threshold of the 'annunciation type-scene'. With a type-scene in biblical narrative, there is a series of events that will unfold in a pattern that conforms to the reader's expectation. As Robert Alter notes, there are three ingredients to the annunciation type-scene (1999: 3; cf. 1981: 47-62). First, the report of the barren condition of the wife (in 1 Sam. 1, this is intensified through the 'fertile rival wife' subplot). Second, there is a promise of the birth of the son delivered by a messenger of God (here there is a slight parody, with Eli *getting things wrong* as demonstrated below). Third, there is marital intimacy that results in divine favor culminating in the birth of the promised child, who is invariably a prominent character in the narrative. 'As we shall see', Alter concludes, 'the middle motif is articulated in a way that is distinctive to the concerns of the Samuel story' (1999: 3).

1.10-11

Within the temple precincts of Shiloh Hannah is described as 'bitter' of soul. The term for 'bitter' (מָרָה) recalls the infamous place in Exodus 15 where the 'bitter' water causes Israelite grumbling. Also Naomi acrimoniously changes her name: 'Don't call me Naomi (pleasant)' she says to the towns-people, 'call me Marah (bitter), for the Almighty has made me bitter' (Ruth 1.20). It is in this bitter state that Hannah weeps (again) and makes a vow. Perhaps surprisingly, Hannah has not been afforded one syllable of direct speech to this point in the story. One guesses that the author has been building momentum toward this moment. This hunch seems confirmed when the reader finally hears the first words out of Hannah's mouth after years of soundless sorrow: she says 'O LORD of hosts'. It is remarkable that Hannah is the first character in the Bible to address God by means of this unrivaled epithet.

The content of Hannah's vow contains a long 'if...then' conditional utterance. She pleads with God to remember her by giving her male seed, and if he does so, then she will 'give him to the LORD all the days of his life'. Some commentators hear an echo of Jephthah's vow in Judges 11 here, where that judge makes a rash vow and his daughter becomes the unwitting subject. To my mind, a more immediately instructive example from Judges comes from chap. 13, where Manaoh's barren wife is also the subject of an annunciation type-scene. Scholars have observed that the opening words of 1 Samuel correspond to the opening words of Judg. 13.2, the story of Samson. In Judges 13, the agent of the LORD tells the woman that her son will be a Nazirite (for the background of the Nazirite vow, see Num. 6, where, among other things, the votive is to abstain from wine and haircuts).

In 1 Samuel 1, it is Hannah who volunteers this consecration, with 'razor' being the most concrete evidence that—should God open her womb—her male child will be a Nazirite. The Greek tradition at 1.11 (preferred by the NRSV) has an amplification: '…I indeed dedicate him to you *until the day of his death, and he shall drink no wine nor strong drink*, and no razor shall come upon his head'. In non-bacchanalian fashion the Greek Hannah dedicates her offspring as a teetotaler, much like the angel of the LORD directs for Samson in Judges 13. However, the Masoretic Hannah dedicates her future offspring 'all the days of his life', whereas her Hellenistic counterpart says '*until the day of his death*'. Whether this mortal phrase strikes a faintly ominous note or is simply an idiomatic turn is beyond my ken; the character zones of Manoah's wife and Hannah intersect at this point, so the reader is left to ponder the connection between their sons.

1.12-14

In terms of the larger storyline, it is significant that Hannah asks God for a son. Again, the opening chapters of 1 Samuel serve as an introduction to the complex problem of Israel and kingship, and the author has chosen 'having sons' as an image for 'having kings'. Hannah makes a request in chap. 1, and the people also will make a request in chap. 8. As Polzin (1993: 25) observes, 'No other specific requests are made of the LORD in these chapters, so that there is a solid basis in the text for suggesting that the story of Hannah's request for a son is intended to introduce, foreshadow, and ideologically comment upon the story of Israel's request for a king'. Furthermore, at the risk of discovering a chiastic structure where none exists, it does seem that a nice balance will emerge in 1 Samuel 1–3: Hannah speaks to God about the (future) obedience of her son, and God will speak to that son about the (past) disobedience of Eli's sons.

Speaking of Eli, as Hannah is mutely quaking in prayer, the priest is sitting on his throne watching her mouth. By Eli's reckoning, she is obviously not a Nazirite who has abstained from the fruit of the vine, and in the KJV he lyrically rebukes, 'How long wilt thou be drunken? Put away thy wine from thee!' Most readers will notice some hierodule humor here: while Hannah is vowing that her son will be a sanctuary servant and that she will abstain from wine, Eli accuses her of being a wine-bibbing woman! This is the second time in the story that a male character does not fully comprehend Hannah's actions. Elkanah earlier asks Hannah why she does not eat, and now Eli grills her as to how long she will be drunk. Intoxication aside, in the context of the type-scene Alter comments on Eli's role: 'Compared to the angels and men of God who deliver the good news in other annunciation type-scenes, the priest here plays a peripheral and slightly foolish role. This oblique undermining of Eli's authority', Alter (1981: 86) concludes, 'is of course essentially relevant to the story of Samuel: the house of Eli will be cut off, his iniquitous sons will be replaced in the sanctuary by Samuel himself, and it will be Samuel, not his master Eli, who will hear the voice of God distinctly addressing him in the sanctuary'.

Eli's error is revealing on two fronts. First, it certainly does not say a great deal for the spiritual life of Shiloh: here is a woman praying with great travail of spirit, and Eli's default assumption is licentious behavior. Shiloh, once a place for national assembly, is not having the best run of form. Maybe there is an implicit censure here; maybe there are other errors taking place within the vicinity of the Shiloh shrine. Second, perhaps more subtly, Eli's clerical error tells us something about him: he can see. When Hannah is praying, Eli is recorded as 'watching her mouth', which implies that his visual faculties are functioning. As we will see, there is a gradual diminution of Eli's eyesight as the narrative unfolds. At this point Eli sees, as Peter Miscall (1986: 13) observes, 'but he does not hear'. This is important, because there is a thematic link between physical eyesight and spiritual discernment that will be prominent later in the story. Curiously, this is not the last time in 1 Samuel that someone will be guilty of misjudgment of the basis of mere outward appearance.

1.15-16
It is often the case that people accused of drunkenness vehemently deny the charge. In Hannah's case, the denial is legitimate. She tells Eli in no uncertain terms that she has not been pouring *in* spirits, she has been pouring *out* her spirit! Hannah tells the sedentary Levite that she is 'stubborn of spirit' (a more literal rendering than the NRSV's 'deeply troubled'). This strange self-description is thematically appropriate: if the having of sons is anything like the having of kings, Israel will be stubborn in their request for a king just like Hannah is stubborn in her request for a son. Hannah wants to be a mother, and she asks Eli not to accuse her of being a 'worthless woman'. It is preferable to translate this phrase literally as 'daughter of Belial', since Eli's sons Hophni and Phinehas will later be described as 'sons of Belial' (2.12).

1.17
Eli deserves some credit for admitting his mistake, and his blessing of Hannah kindly counterbalances his earlier blunder. At the same time, Eli's benediction has an unintended irony: 'Go in peace', he blesses, 'and may the God of Israel grant your request (שׁאלה) that you have asked (שׁאל) of him'. The irony is that Eli is blessing Hannah in her 'request', and she is going to give birth to a son who will announce the doom of Eli and his sons. The irony is magnified because Hannah neither uses the noun 'request' nor the

verb 'ask', yet Eli supplies them, and Eli has not even heard that Hannah wants a son because she was speaking 'in her heart' and no sound was heard. As Birch (1998: 975) notes, 'Eli's language in this speech introduces the first two of seven uses of the verb "to ask" (שאל) in this chapter. Instead of the "petition you have made", this expression should be rendered "the asking you have asked".'

The occurrence of 'ask' is a significant moment in the story, since this is the root that forms the name 'Saul'. J.P. Fokkelman (1993: 51) intones,

> Shortly the root (שאל) is to become the most important key word in the whole section. This verb, i.e., 'to ask', has the task of linking and contrasting, in an extraordinary fashion, the two most important people in I Sam. 1–12, the prophet Samuel and king Saul! Without having the faintest idea of their impact Eli has uttered words which touch upon the secret of the future.

Just as Elkanah's speech in 1.8 carries a double-voiced edge, the same seems to hold true for Eli in 1.17. Thus Elkanah and Eli have more in common than two males who issue rhetorical questions to Hannah about culinary matters. Their speech accents become thematic conduits in the narrative. According to Polzin's (1993: 26) dialogic imagination, '...the story proper, as it works itself out principally in the dialogues between Hannah and Eli on one hand and Hannah and Elkanah on the other, becomes a programmatic inner dialogue in which the Deuteronomist expresses many of the conflicting ideological issues involved in the establishment of kingship in Israel'.

1.18

The longest dialogue and extended scene in the chapter draws to a close, and, fittingly, Hannah gets the last word. Despite using only four words, there are two components to her parting words to Eli. First, her use of 'favor' (חֵן) forms a nice wordplay with her own name (חַנָּה), anticipating the favor that barren Hannah is about to receive from God. Second, her last word to Eli—'...*in your eyes*'—is notable. Hannah's speech is an affirming one that reflects Eli's finest hour in the story. From this point on, however, Eli's eyesight will gradually grow dim, until extinguished in 1 Samuel 4.

Hannah's words in 1.18 may be straightforward enough, but her subsequent departure takes different routes in the RSV and NRSV. Upon leaving the sanctuary, everyone agrees that 'she eats', an action that, as Robert Gordon (1988: 76) comments, 'signals her confidence that her request has been heard'. But after this, Hannah's paths diverge: in the RSV, 'the woman went her way and ate, and her countenance was no longer sad', but in the NRSV (following the LXX), 'the woman went *to her quarters*, ate *and drank with her husband*, and her countenance was sad no longer'. When one considers Eli's prior arraignment of Hannah and her denial of drunkenness, it may seem unlikely that she departs from the sanctuary and imbibes with Elkanah. The Greek tradition is puzzling here, in light of Hannah's avowal that her Nazirite son '*shall drink no wine nor strong drink*'. Regardless, it should be emphasized that, as an antithesis to 1.7, Hannah now eats, indicating an interior change that is reflected in her outward countenance. I am inclined to translate the last clause as 'her face was not *as it had been* again'. Hannah's next visit to Shiloh, one suspects, will involve no weeping.

1.19-20
Hannah's non-downcast departure is an effective transition away from Shiloh and back home. After 'they arose early and worshipped', they make their way their house at Ramah; the place name has been shortened to Ramah after beginning as Ramathaim. The sequence of four plural verbs (they rose early, they worshipped, they returned, they came) conveys a sense of solidarity between Hannah and Elkanah, and anticipates their intimacy, as 'Elkanah knew Hannah his wife'. The key moment, though, is attributed to God: the LORD 'remembers' Hannah, which corresponds to her prayer in 1.11. The beginnings of the answered prayer of a barren Israelite must be one of the central theological points that emerges in 1 Samuel 1.

'In every good story', Walter Brueggemann (1990: 11) reminds us, 'we are not told too much too soon'. God remembers Hannah, but patience is still required. The NRSV renders the start of 1.20 as 'In due time', but the literal phrasing is a more labored expression: 'At the finished circuit of the year, Hannah conceived, and gave birth to a son'. Hannah indeed gives birth, but this is only the start of the reader's post-natal labor in the remainder of 1.20. While many scholars are happy for Hannah, they are less willing to dole out congratulations about her naming speech following the birth of her son: 'she called his name Samuel, because from the LORD I asked him'. The problem, these scholars point out with Eli-like perspicuity, is that the name 'Saul' is more visually apparent in these consonants. This must be a clue, so the reasoning goes, that what we are dealing with is a misplaced birth narrative here for a king, because Saul's name is more readily formed from the root 'ask', not Samuel.

'It takes ingenuity', Peter Miscall (1986: 14) concedes, 'to explain the play on *sha'al* as offering a legitimate etymology for the name Samuel (*shemu'el*)'. Among the interpretive options here, commentators have seen either a misplaced birth narrative for Saul, or an intentional wordplay that connects the names Saul and Samuel. If one assumes the latter option, then, as with other speeches in this chapter, Hannah's words mean more than at first glance. Hannah's naming speech contains the root שאל, which in turn echoes with Eli's (prophetic) utterance, further hinting at the importance of this root in the story to come. Rather than confusion between the birth of

Samuel and the name of Saul, Polzin (1993: 25) views this integration of the names as integral to the Deuteronomist's purpose:

> One attempt at integration would be to imbue the details of the story of Samuel's birth, a familial story, with sociopolitical overtones, that is, to assume that the implied author is foreshadowing and putting into context a complex account of the LORD's decision to give Israel a king by prefacing that account with an account of the LORD's decision to give Hannah a son. The birth of Samuel, in all its complex detail, introduces and foreshadows the birth of kingship in Israel.

Samuel's delivery into the story world creates a complex wordplay with the name 'Saul', and at the very least this signals that these two major characters will be together for a considerable amount of narrative space. Hannah's use of the consonants in the name 'Saul' in her speech is no accident, and, as Graeme Auld (2003: 214) recaps, this usage becomes a useful thematic marker: 'Just as the story of Eli and his family alerts us to the fate of royal dynasties which will come and go in the story to follow, so Hannah's account of Samuel's name reminds us that the fates of Samuel and Saul were desperately commingled, and that Saul, too, was asked for and desperately wanted by his people'.

1.21-22

Rural life goes on for our fruitful family of Ephraim, and at the appropriate season, it is again time for the annual journey to worship. Elkanah duly goes up to Shiloh with 'all his house' to offer his yearly sacrifice, and to fulfill 'his vow'. One recalls the vow that Hannah made, but struggles vainly to recall something similar for Elkanah. Perhaps he made one—given the amount of fighting in his household, a vow is not implausible—but the reader is not told. Regardless, there is a slight misdirection when we are told in 1.21 that 'all' of Elkanah's house journeys with him to Shiloh, because it is now revealed that two members of this house remain in the hometown: Hannah and her son, for whom she has 'asked'. The excuse, Hannah posits, lies in the need for nursing: 'Until the lad is weaned and I will bring him, that he may appear in the presence of the LORD and live there forever'. A grammatical purist may object that Hannah's excuse contains some awkward syntax; a rationalist may give this new mother the benefit of the doubt, and point out that nursing a newborn can drain one's eloquence. All would agree that the delay in Samuel's dedication probably stems from the mother's reluctance to give up her new child, so long in the asking. The NRSV has an extra assurance (following the Qumran fragment) in Hannah's excuse—'I will offer him as a nazirite for all time'—but one suspects that the 4QSam Hannah is protesting too much.

1.23

Elkanah's speech to Hannah has two parts. 'Do what is good in your eyes, wait until you have weaned him...' is affirming enough, but the remainder of Elkanah's utterance is more enigmatic: '...only, may the LORD establish his word'. This is a somewhat puzzling statement, such that some scholars prefer the Greek rendering, '...may the LORD establish that which comes out of your mouth'. As with 1.8, Elkanah's words here in 1.23 mean something more than he intends, and thus there is a symmetry between his two speeches to Hannah. Since these are the only occasions that Elkanah speaks in the story, such an interpretation is not far-fetched. In fact, several recent scholars note that the terms Elkanah uses ('the word of the LORD'; 'establish') will turn out to be a important keywords in the wider narrative. Peter Miscall (1986: 14-15) has a useful summary of Elkanah's contribution here:

> What is the word (*dabar*) that he is to establish, to raise up (*yaqem*)? What could Elkanah have in mind? What can we as readers make of the wish over and above Elkanah's intention? Is his wish to be taken as intending an implicit promise made by the LORD through the birth of Samuel? If so, what is the promise? Taken as referring to the immediate context, we are left in the dark as to the reference of 'his word'. But 'establish' (*qum*) and 'the word of the LORD', separate or together, play significant roles in 1 Samuel and are put into play by Elkanah's enigmatic wish... Although the referent of Elkanah's wish is not determinable, the wish does set in motion a consideration for words, particularly the LORD's, and their establishment or lack of establishment. Elkanah's wish is pregnant, since its range of meaning and effect extends far beyond its context.

1.24-28

The end of Samuel's weaning marks the beginning of the last scene of the first chapter. At whatever age, Hannah's son is weaned and they proceed to Shiloh. There is some mild controversy over what accompanies them on their trip. Some translations read 'three bulls' (MT) while others read 'a three year old bull' (LXX). Both the RSV and NRSV opt for the Greek reading, presumably because 'the bull' (singular) is sacrificed in 1.25. All bull aside, Hannah also brings a skin of wine to Shiloh. According to Num. 15.8-10, this is entirely appropriate. But in light of all that has happened, Hannah's transporting a skin of wine injects of moment of levity into the weighty event of Samuel's nazirite dedication. The skin of wine reminds the reader that her son is not to partake of such beverages, and when she presents both the lad and the wine to Eli, there must be an ironic moment: you accused me of drunkenness, now I present to you the object of my prayer (a son who will not drink wine) along with a skin of wine. Eli had earlier accused Hannah of drunkenness while she is asking for a son—now Eli becomes a surrogate father for that answered prayer.

There are two levels to Hannah's long speech to Eli. On the one level, the presentation of the lad to Eli is expressed with slightly awkward syntax, and nicely captures the sense of excitement in Hannah's words to Eli. She provides a reminder that this is the child for whom she 'asked', and gives a solid testimony of the LORD's answered prayer. Hannah also provides a rationale for the lad's dedication. On another level, the reader is again confronted with the name 'Saul' in Hannah's words. If the root שאל is used previously, and if the name 'Saul' is hinted at earlier by Eli and by Hannah, there is no mistaking it here. In fact, Robert Bergen (1996: 73) notes that four different forms of the root שאל occur in Hannah's speech, culminating in the last one, which is impossible to miss. When Hannah says, 'as long as he lives, he is given to the LORD', she actually says, 'as long as he lives, he is *Saul* to the LORD' (הוּא שָׁאוּל לַיהוָה). This brings the introduction of kingship to an apt conclusion in this opening chapter. 'In other words', as Polzin (1993: 26) summarizes,

> the story in chapter 1 about how and why God agrees to give Hannah a son, Samuel, is an artistic prefiguring of the larger story in 1 Samuel about how and why God agreed to give Israel a king. It is in the light of these and other thematic, emotive, and ideological connections within the larger story line that the etymology spoken by Hannah makes artistic sense; the story of Samuel's birth *is* the story of Saul's birth as king of Israel. Saul's destiny, like his name, explains Samuel's. When Hannah says, 'For I asked for him (שְׁאִלְתִּיו) from the LORD', she speaks also about Saul (הוּא שָׁאוּל) and the royal history his reign inaugurates.

The final line of the chapter is ambiguous. A literal rendering of the Hebrew text would read, 'and there he worshipped the LORD', but it is not clear who the 'he' is. The RSV translates line 'And they worshiped the LORD there', while the NRSV follows the Greek rearranging of the text, and opts for 'She left him there for the LORD'. Fokkelman understands the object of the phrase—'and there he bowed in worship to the LORD'—to be Eli, while several other commentators understand Elkanah as the worshipper. Mary Evans (2000: 17) claims that Samuel (having absorbed 'his call to worship God with his mother's milk') is the one who bows, whereas the Qumran fragment apparently figures Hannah as the subject (thus 'and she bowed there to the LORD'). It is a good thing that *somebody* is worshipping, because such action does not seem to happen (at least as far as the leadership goes) all that frequently in Shiloh, as is evidenced in the next chapter.

1 Samuel 2

This equal-opportunity chapter begins with a woman singing a song of praise to God, and ends with an oracle of doom from an itinerant man of God. In between is a long account of the abuses of the sons of Eli, as contrasted with the growth of young Samuel. Hannah's maternal care—symbolized in her annual gift of a garment—is compared with Eli's ineffective paternal care, as illustrated in his unsuccessful rebuke of his sons. Eli is told that an alternative dynastic line will succeed his, and as a sign, his two sons will both die on the same day. Eli's best days are behind him, not before him.

2.1

The first segment of 1 Samuel 2 is often referred to as 'Hannah's song'. The dedication of the 'asked for' son results in an overflow of praise from the once-barren wife, now an exultant mother. Some time ago, Brevard Childs mentioned that Hannah's song is the interpretive key for 1 and 2 Samuel, and a host of theological themes and ideas are presented in these words that appear later in the story. The song highlights reversal and transformation, replete with examples of the strong becoming weak, and the weak made strong: the fighter, the full, and the fertile have their fortunes reversed, while the barren and the broken are blessed by God. It may be that in these stanzas is a call to hope for a nation in exile, to have their barren situation transformed by the LORD of hosts, as invoked by Hannah centuries earlier. A number of stories emerge from these lyrics: the joy of a formerly sad mother, the triumph of a (future) king, and the implied author's subtle critique of Israel's request for a king. One might ask: If the birth of a son serves as an introduction to the birth of the monarchy in Israel, then what is the contribution of this song to the larger storyline?

Hannah's prayer is long and complex, with a number of elements that are difficult to interpret. The central challenge for the reader is to ascertain the purpose of the song in the overall architecture of the narrative. As Auld (2003: 215) remarks, 'The lack of a close fit between the poem and its immediate literary context can be differently evaluated'. While some commentators have searched diligently for the redactional fault lines between the poem and the surrounding narrative, other commentators have seen poem and prose as part of an intentional design. In the latter category, Polzin (1993: 30) is instructive:

> We hear in the song not one but at least three voices, each with its own perspectives and multivoiced accents, each cooperating with the other two to form, in Bakhtin's terminology, a 'polyphonic composition' that is both harmonious and dissonant, transparent yet opaque, looking backward and forward, full of thematic variations on themes already met or soon to be encountered'

The three voices Polzin discerns are: Hannah (as a jubilant mother), the persona of the king (triumphant, much like a once-barren mother), and the voice of the implied author (the Deuteronomist, whose voice may be more subdued and melancholic, with warnings of impending rain on the triumphal parade of Israel's monarchy).

This song places Hannah in the great tradition of female vocalists in the Bible. Within this elite group are Miriam, Deborah, and Hannah; as many commentators observe, Hannah's song anticipates the Magnificat of Mary (Lk. 1.46-55). In fact, it is possible to argue that early scenes in Luke's Gospel poignantly allude to this stretch of 1 Samuel. As part of this venerable company, then, one expects that the particular words ascribed to Hannah are carefully weighed. To be sure, the verbs 'rejoice' (עָלַץ) and 'celebrate' (שָׂמַח) are a common set of parallels terms that, as Lyle Eslinger (1985: 103) notes, appear in biblical poetry (see Pss 5.12; 9.3; and 68.4):

> In all cases, the verbs describe the joyful response of humble worshippers of Yahweh, who exult in the strength of their God. Also associated with all occurrences are statements about the futility and wickedness of man's pride and efforts at self-help, whether done in defiance or ignorance of the deity.

In the early lines of the song it is not difficult to hear Hannah's story emerge. For example, the struggle with Peninnah is alluded to on several occasions. As Robert Gordon (1986: 79) remarks, 'The mention of *enemies*, who make frequent appearance in the Psalter, invites us on this occasion to recall the description of Peninnah as Hannah's "rival" (*ṣārātāh*) in 1.6'. Other images, though, are more puzzling to decipher. Why does Hannah use the term 'horn' at the beginning and at the end of the song? While 'horn' forms a poetic *inclusio* to the song by virtue of its re-appearance in 2.10, many translations (such as both the RSV and NRSV) eschew the literal term 'horn' for the metaphorical rendering 'strength' or the like. But one should be cautious about fully abandoning the horn metaphor. As Bruce Birch (1998: 981) explains, the horn image is used elsewhere in the Hebrew Bible as a sign of both national victory and in respect to God's giving of offspring: 'The special significance of this image in Hannah's song is that what begins in v. 1 as the raising of Hannah's horn concludes in v. 10 with the raising of the king's horn. The power of God, which can make the barren woman rejoice in a child, can also transform threatened tribal Israel into a kingdom'. The image of the horn, then, unites the poem and serves to symbolize both the story of Hannah and, though more obliquely, the larger story of Israel as a nation. The reader is further invited to discern these interwoven stories as the poem continues.

2.2-5

The references in the poem to food and barrenness serve to re-accentuate Hannah's story in 1 Samuel 1. Yet some of these images also lend themselves to the multiple stories in the poem. The reference to 'those who were full' in 2.5 is a case in point. While the banquet scene of Shiloh is evoked—with the many portions for Peninnah and comparatively less for Hannah—Robert Gordon sees another layer of meaning: the full ones 'falling on hard times' anticipates the speech of the man of God at the end of the chapter, pronouncing doom on the 'full' house of Eli and forecasting the rise of an alternative priestly dynasty. If Gordon is on the right track, then the double use of 'Tall!' in 2.3 assumes a heightened significance. The NRSV renders the first part of 2.3 as 'Talk no more so very proudly', but a more literal translation would read: 'Do not multiply your speech, O Tall one! O Tall one!' Even a cursory glance ahead in the story of 1 Samuel reveals that 'tall' is a big issue in this narrative. Physical height can be, at the very least, illusory, and breed a false sense of security. Saul's outstanding attribute is that he is taller than all the people, and Goliath's height instills great fear in the fighting ranks of Israel. Yet both will fall down (forward) at different times before the end of 1 Samuel. By analogy, kingship will be a problematic institution if it is built on the principle of *outward appearance*, and the goal of the Deuteronomist in this stretch of narrative is to illustrate that reliance on such perception is fallacious.

Along with Hannah's story, then, one can hear the story of kingship emerge in these lines. If the accents are faint early in the poem, by the time the crescendo of Hannah's song occurs, the 'king' is explicitly intoned. Thus there are elements in this poem that only make sense in light of the monarchial story imbedded in the song of the once-barren woman: 'The royal climax of Hannah's song appears out of the blue, completely irrelevant to Hannah and her situation until we understand the story of Samuel's birth as a finely orchestrated overture on the birth of kingship in Israel' (Polzin 1993: 31). The gradual movement in the song celebrates a divine propensity to confound expectations. This is Hannah's experience, as she who was taunted by the 'full' now gives birth to 'seven', while the fertile one fades away. In the larger Deuteronomistic History stretching until the end of 2 Kings, a similar situation will unfold in Israel's landscape: the proud will be brought low, as dynasties collapse and new ones are formed by former servants.

Consequently, it is appropriate that 2.4 includes a reference to the 'bow of the mighty'. In Hannah's song, this bow is transformed into a useless implement. But its presence anticipates another song, the lament of David in 2 Samuel 1. David's requiem for Saul and Jonathan, the reader is told, is 'written in the Book of Jashar (scroll of the upright)', and is chanted by a new king in memory of a fallen old king. The rich interplay of language between these songs imparts to the reader that such reversal of expectation should provide a sober accompaniment to Israel's experiment with kingship. Joel Rosenberg (1987: 124) provides a cogent summary of Hannah's song as it anticipates the direction of the narrative:

> This exuberant psalm expresses the historical outlook both of biblical tradition in general and of Samuel in particular: YHWH is invoked as the God of surprise, bringing down the mighty, raising up the downtrodden; impoverishing the wealthy and enriching the pauper; bereaving the fertile and making barren the fruitful—always circumventing the trappings of human vanity and the complacency of the overcontented. The many turns of personal and familial fortune in the ensuing chapters are an elaboration of the compressed strophes of Hannah's song. Indeed, the ensuing narration makes clear that Hannah's triumph and Samuel's entry into priestly service coincide with the house of Eli's fall from divine favor.

2.6-10

It should be emphasized that at key moments in the books of Samuel—near the beginning, middle, and end of the scroll—there are songs that capture some of the main theological themes of the surrounding narrative. Recent commentators have argued at length that such a design is intentional, and the imbedded song act as something of a chorus for the larger storyline. Just as Hannah's song in 1 Samuel 1 merges with the lament for Saul and Jonathan in 2 Samuel 1, so Hannah's song also shares language with David's hymn in 2 Samuel 22, forming a theological *inclusio* for the entire scroll. In other words, in 1 Samuel 1 Hannah sounds a lot like David later on in 2 Samuel 22, and thus 'the voice of a triumphant king merges with that of an exultant mother' (Polzin 1993: 33). As we have seen, Peninnah's taunting causes Hannah to '*thunder*' in 1.6. Notably, Hannah then sings, 'The adversaries of the LORD shall be broken to pieces; against them he will *thunder* in heaven', just as David will later celebrate his own reversal of fortune by singing, 'The LORD *thundered* from heaven, and the Most High uttered his voice' (2 Sam. 22.14). Furthermore, just as the image of the *horn* begins and ends the song of Hannah, so David sings that God is 'horn of my salvation' (2 Sam. 22.3). 'The entire song', Walter Brueggemann (1990: 17) remarks, 'is about a "raised horn", which means visible elevation to worth, dignity, power, prestige, and well-being'. Through shared language such as this, the movement from barren wife to exultant king is poetically connected, and the links between the barren wife who gives birth to a kingmaker is tied with the future king himself.

By poetically capturing the change from powerlessness to praise in Hannah's song, in many ways the story of the nation is hinted at. Mary Evans (2000: 20) comments that in this story of an exultant mother, there is a sustained reflection on both power and powerlessness that points to the story of Israel, a story that

> moves from the kingless, oppressed, and usually powerless nation seen in Judges to the liberated and unified nation provided through David and (if Samuel and Kings are seen as a whole) on to the powerful nation found in the reign of Solomon, before moving back to the oppressed and powerless nation of siege and exile.

The story of Israel thus emerges in this song about *transformation*—replete with examples of how God intervenes in powerful ways to change a host of situations. Hannah's experience parallels that of Israel as a nation: as in 2:8, the nation of Israel has been lifted 'like the needy from the ash heap' to 'inherit a seat of honor'. Yet there is an implicit warning in the song to avoid the pitfalls of pride and arrogance that can easily result in a spectacular fall. Hence the song calls for trust in the LORD, who will guard his faithful: 'Human efforts to secure one's destiny will not prevail apart from trust in what God is doing. In Hannah's song, all of the ways of human power can be reversed through the power of God: military force, wealth, family. It is God's power that endures' (Birch 1998: 982). This slightly melancholic accent is where Polzin hears the voice of the Deuteronomist—always hovering in the background—casting a somber hue to the exultant tones of once-barren mother and triumphant king. In the context of this narrative about the advent of kingship, there is both an implicit reminder about a more powerful sovereign, and a word of warning from an author acquainted with the grief of exile.

2.11-18

As Hannah's long prayer comes to an end, Elkanah then departs (presumably with Hannah, childless once more), with the lad left in Shiloh. The next major phase of the story takes place in the same spatial setting of Shiloh. A virtual surrogate father, Eli is the superintendent of the newest temple acolyte, apparently left in his care by the parents from Ephraim. Hannah's prayer represents the high point of spiritual life in Shiloh in two ways. First, one gets the feeling that there is not a great deal of prayer that happens among the leadership, so this is as good as it gets. Second, Hannah's prayer represents something of a literal high point as well, since a repeated theme in the song is how the mighty—perched on high—will fall, and how the arrogant will be humbled. This situation is about to unfold, and provide a dramatic illustration of corrupt leadership being brought low.

On the way to being brought low, 1 Sam. 2.11-17 is a section that features some further interplay of language with the preceding prose about Hannah, and with her song as well. On the prose side, we recall that 1.13 Hannah implores Eli not to reckon her as a 'daughter of Belial' (בַּת־בְּלִיָּעַל). As mentioned above, the irony is that Eli himself has sired two examples of the real thing, since the narrator now discloses that Hophni and Phinehas are 'sons of Belial' (בְּנֵי בְלִיָּעַל). As one of the worst epithets in the entire Hebrew Bible, to be called a 'son (or daughter) of Belial' is to be classified with the criminal and the underworld. Furthermore, in Hannah's song she extols, 'the LORD is a God of knowledge', yet antithetically, the sons of Eli 'do not know the LORD'. As Miscall (1986: 17) notes, 'Matters in 1 Samuel have so far progressed according to the "proper order" to the extent that the good, Hannah and Elkanah, have been rewarded; we can therefore expect that the wicked will perish in darkness'. To invoke an motor-racing image, Hophni and Phinehas are in pole position for such perishing.

The 'Belial' qualities of Hophni and Phinehas are set in relief when the everyday practice of Shiloh is observed. While the 'custom' of normal sacrifice is adumbrated by the Deuteronomist, on the temporal plane there is a merger between past and present. The normal procedure *would have been* that the priest accepts anything that the lad pulls out of the sacrificial vessel, but *as it now stands* there is a corrupt use of this priestly hook (or fork), as the priest's lad demands fresh (i.e. not yet sacrificed) meat for their portion. This use of the priestly fork is illegal, as Gordon (1986: 82) explains: 'The priests' subsistence at Shiloh depended more on "pot luck", perhaps in the belief that the hand of God decided the trident's catch'. Such luck, however, was not to be risked by Hophni and Phinehas: they instruct their 'lad' (נַעַר הַכֹּהֵן) to grab the raw meat before it is 'corrupted' by any sacrificial boiling. It has been noted that the implement 'the hook of three teeth' is not otherwise attested in the Hebrew Bible. Walter Brueggemann (1990: 28) refers to the fork as 'bigger-than-regulation'. Perhaps, then, the fork is an Elide innovation aimed at increasing the priestly portion, and as such, personifies their flippancy.

There is, however, one lad who is exempted; that young Samuel is off the hook from this corrupt use of the fork is clear by means of the contrasting use of this phrase: *before the LORD*. The author is careful to explain that young Samuel is a lad who is ministering *before the LORD* (2.18), whereas the reader is told that the sin of the young men is great *before the LORD* (2.17). Accordingly, one is led to think that the 'lad of the priest' is a generic designation, whereas Samuel 'the lad' is a specific person who has not fallen into the corruption of the sons of Eli. If the having of sons is anything like the having of kings, Eli is going to face his share of parental problems.

2.19-21

Just as there is a contrast emerging between the son of Hannah and sons of Eli, so there is something of a contrast between the parents as well. The short scene of 2.19-21 provides a vignette about Samuel's parents, and a snippet of their life after depositing Samuel with the priest. Their annual journey to sacrifice in Shiloh continues, and Hannah brings a gift for the growing youngster year after year. The gift is practical enough—a little robe (מְעִיל)—except that the lad is already, so we are told, gird in a 'linen ephod'. The mother's gift of a robe carries a certain symbolic import in the narrative. On one level, Samuel's clothing symbolizes his distinction (and different fate) from the other servant lads of Hophni and Phinehas. But on another level, it is significant that another key figure in 1 Samuel will be clothed in a robe: the king. It would probably be a slight stretch to suggest that Hannah has royal ambitions for her miraculous son. The easier route is to follow what the Deuteronomist is doing with the mother's gift, and the anticipation of the storyline to come: '...the dressing of him in a garment that will later come to be characteristic of contested kingship, will clothe the struggle between prophet and king' (Green 2003: 110).

It is better to give than to receive, but the pious parents—having given their son—also receive the priest's blessing on an annual basis. It took a long time for Hannah's womb to be opened, but the dedication of Samuel is by no means the end of her child-bearing career. Whether it is Eli's blessing or a strictly divine initiative is not specified, but now that Hannah's womb has been opened, a flood of offspring burst forth. There are five further children, although none of them are named. Perhaps this is meant to imply that Samuel—the only one of Elkanah's many children to have a proper name disclosed to the reader—will be the one responsible for continuing Elkanah's genealogy. Further, perhaps this hints that Samuel will have sons of his own.

While benevolent enough, the language of Eli's blessing is difficult to render into English. The NRSV translates the blessing in 2.20b as, 'May the LORD repay you with children by this woman for the gift that she made to the LORD'. A more literal rendering of the second part might be '...in place of the asked one that he asked of the LORD'. Regardless, Eli's blessing is more than it seems, especially when one considers the double occurrence of the verb 'ask', again appearing in the speech of Eli. This must serve to reinforce the irony that Eli's leadership and the era of the Judges will come to an end as the people ask for a king, a king that is 'asked' of Samuel, who himself is the son whom Hannah asks for.

2.22-26

Numerous commentators point out that the rise of Samuel corresponds (or is set over and against) the fall of the house of Eli. The priest Eli is old and his best days are behind him; Samuel is young and growing in favor. The focus on the families in 1 Samuel 1–2 is evident, as the stories of Hannah the mother and Eli the father are interwoven in the narrative. The point is raised above that the destiny of the nation is involved in the lives of these two families. It is a rather fierce irony, therefore, when 'Eli pronounces a blessing for [Hannah's] faithfulness even as his household is falling under a curse for its lack of faithfulness' (Birch 1998: 986). The reader is told that Eli is 'very old', and that he hears what his sons are doing. Whether this is intended to mean that Eli does not have a long history of parental discipline or he just now is acquainted with the evils of Hophni and Phinehas is not clear, but the use of 'old' hints that time is not on Eli's side.

The catalogue of transgressions is summarized in one action: laying with the hostesses who serve 'at the doorway of the tent of meeting'. In general terms, Walter Brueggemann (1990: 22) refers to the crimes and misdemeanors of Hophni and Phinehas as a 'cynical use of priestly power'. In specific terms, it is notable that particular wrongdoing of laying with the hostesses is targeted. J.P. Fokkelman (1993: 128) notes the intersection of language between 'hostess' and the title 'LORD of hosts' as used in 1.3 and 1.11:

> The choice of the word [hostess, צבאות] is incriminating as well because it engages in a play on words with the famous title 'Lord of hosts' (יהוה צבאות) which was mentioned, a short while ago, for the first time in the Bible. The priests abuse, therefore, a veritable host of women who themselves only have a mind to serve God, being in his presence to this end. This is a sacrilege whose insolence is of outrageous proportions.

Furthermore, the spatial setting of the sin invokes a reference to the book of Joshua, in the days when Shiloh was enjoying a good run of form as the place of national assembly: 'In Joshua, the inheritances of many of the tribes were distributed at Shiloh "at the door of the tent of meeting" (Josh. 19.51)' (Miscall 1986: 10). So now, the door of the tent of meeting is a place of corruption, and through this linkage the degeneracy of the Shiloh sanctuary since the days of Joshua is dramatically underscored, and the line of Eli is directly responsible.

It is the delinquency of his sons with the hostesses that Eli 'hears' via a report circulating among God's people. That Eli is acoustically sensitive and can 'hear' is important, because his eyesight has been gradually dimming. Moreover, Eli will shortly hear a prophetic word of judgment against his house that will make the ears 'tingle'. Notably, the sin of the sons is filtered through the ears of the father, who proceeds to call the lads to account. The character of the rebuke is somewhat indirect: the rhetorical question 'why' followed by the summation, '...not good is the report I am hearing'. Eli's capstone in this rebuke is a long 'if...then' utterance that one guesses is a warning, rendered in the NRSV as, 'If one person sins against another, someone can intercede for the sinner with the LORD; but if someone sins against the LORD, who can make intercession?' The sons, however, are not willing to 'hear' their father, the one who has 'heard' the report of their misdeeds. The reason that they do not hear in 2.25 is theologically arresting, and variously translated in the RSV as 'for the LORD desired to put them to death', and the NRSV as 'for it was the will of the LORD to kill them'. It is no more comforting to translate the line literally as 'for the LORD delighted to cause them to die', and it is interesting to note the diversity of ways that translators seek to avoid the literalness of this line.

The contrast between the sons of Eli and Samuel cannot be more apparent than in 2.26, when Samuel is imbued with an uncommon destiny as an antithesis to the corruption of Eli's dynastic sons. It is striking that the LORD visits Hannah in 2.21, and she is blessed with offspring; in 2.27-36 an anonymous man of God is about to visit Eli, and announces the destruction of his offspring and the redundancy of his priestly line.

2.27-36

In a long indictment against the house of Eli, the anonymous man of God begins with the 'rhetorical question' strategy just as Eli does with his recalcitrant sons. In the prophetic realm, however, the unnamed man of God is more effective. Eli comes across as being fairly mild with his sons, as it were. The man of God who delivers the oracle of 2.27-36 is not the least bit mild. Commentators have noted that the oracle contains three different kinds of time reference: the past, the present, and the future. With respect to the past, the man of God delineates the priestly responsibility bestowed by the LORD: in the house of Pharaoh, the house of Eli's father receives God's revelation, and from all the tribes, they are chosen 'to be my priests'. Moreover, it is the house of Eli's father to whom God gives all the 'fire offerings' of Israel. The abuse of this privilege is the subject of 2.13-17, and now becomes one of the many present condemnations of the man of God. Indeed, Eli appears to be guilty of partaking of the stolen offerings, and is included in the judgment. Since the reader learns in 1 Samuel 4 that Eli is 'heavy', it is surely ironic that his portliness is due to the illegal offering apportionment. Further, when Eli is described as 'heavy' (כבד) in 1 Samuel 4, it forms a wordplay with 'honoring' (כבד) his sons in 2.29. The man of God has the last word in the wordplay: 'Far be it from me—for those who honor (כבד) me I will honor (כבד), and those who despise me will be lightly esteemed'. The purpose of this wordplay is thematic within the larger narrative. W.G.E. Watson (1986: 246) cites 'reversal of fortune' as one of the expressive functions of wordplay in the Hebrew Bible. Here, the term כבד dramatically underscores Eli's fall from grace.

The most comprehensive of the three components of this speech pertains to the future. Eli is old, but he is to be the last of a dying breed—there will be no more old men in the house of old Eli. The eyes of Eli are singled out with a full-orbed reference: not only will his eyes fail, but he will grieve as his sons Hophni and Phinehas will die on the same day as a 'sign'. The vacuum created by the virtual destruction of Eli's house will be filled by 'a faithful priest', for whom will be built a lasting house. Graeme Auld (2003: 215) mentions that at this point 'the story deftly anticipates two themes from 2 Samuel: the remnants of Saul's family watching the establishment of David, and the older priestly families giving way to Jerusalem's Zadokites'. When one glances ahead to 1 Kings 2, the notice about the fulfillment of the prophetic word seems foolproof. Of course, the reader is not the only one to notice this displacement; here in 1 Sam. 2.36 the man of God explains that at least one remnant of the house of Eli will survive long enough to beg these new office holders for a scrap of food. In the context of the oracle, this must represent just desserts: the remnant of the corrupt dynasty is now left begging for bread because the ancestors 'made themselves fat' by stealing the offerings of Israel. The punishment certainly appears to fit the crime, just as Hannah's poetic justice intones: 'Those who were full have hired themselves out for bread' (2.5).

The humiliation of Eli's house is made complete through an anagram in the final line of the oracle. The NRSV renders the last words of the scion of Eli's house as 'Please put me in one of the priest's places, that I may eat a morsel of bread' (2.36). But as J.P. Fokkelman (1993: 151) observes, the verb 'put me' (ספחני) forms an anagram with the names Hophni (חפני) and Phinehas (פינחס). As one recalls, the Deuteronomist uses the anagram of judgment elsewhere, as 'Achan' (עכן) and 'Canaan' (כנען) in Joshua 7 (see Hawk 2000: 120). In the present example of 1 Sam. 2.36, the irony lies in the fact that Hophni and Phinehas are not accorded any direct speech in their narrative. Yet their hungry descendent is left begging for bread by using an anagram of their name.

'In these verses', Robert Gordon (1986: 84) summarizes,

> there is set forth the rationale for the disinvestiture of the house of Eli and its eventual replacement by the Zadokite family which, after the rustication of Abiathar to Anathoth for his complicity in the Adonijah rebellion (1 Ki. 2.26f.), exercised a priestly monopoly in the Jerusalem temple for as long as the monarchy and state lasted.

The speech of the man of God in 2.27-36 is quite obviously the longest direct speech in the book thus far, and one guesses that part of the purpose must be to foreground in the reader's mind the *genre* of prophetic speech at this important moment on the eve of the monarchy. The oracle of the itinerant man of God here in 1 Samuel 2 serves as a powerful reminder of prophetic accountability in leadership, and such a theme will recur in numerous ways in the story in the days ahead. Not only does this speech introduce the theme of 'the prophetic word and its fulfillment' as articulated by Gerhard von Rad, but this is also a kind of preview of how prophets will confront kings in the Deuteronomistic History. It is surely not coincidental that more often than not the prophet will bring a message that pertains to the toppling of a dynastic house. Furthermore, the man of God arrives at this northern sanctuary of Shiloh, and in Kings, prophets will often have further issues with northern sanctuaries and corrupt leadership. Other priestly lines (e.g. in the era of Josiah) will be similarly dealt with, and consequently, this speech represents a preview of the forthcoming narrative.

1 Samuel 3

There is no identifiable shift in spatial setting between chaps. 2 and 3, and neither is there any indication that a great deal of time has elapsed. After the long speech from the anonymous man of God that concludes 1 Samuel 2, this next chapter presents an extended scene where Samuel, in the temple precincts of Shiloh, hears the voice of God that he does not recognize, and under the odd tutelage of Eli, eventually is privy to a further word of judgment about Eli's house. The opening chapters—beginning with the opening of Hannah's barren womb and her song of praise—highlight Samuel's birth and growth to maturity as a prophet to the nation, in a studied contrast to the house of Eli, which is falling as fast as Samuel is rising. This present episode is a new chapter in Samuel's life: the birth of prophet now gives way to the birth of a new kind of prophetic activity. 1 Samuel 3 represents an important transition, as the young Samuel is a temple lad at the outset of the chapter, and a prophetic man at the end. It is surely not by accident that at the outset of the people's request for the king, God's call of the prophet is foregrounded.

3.1-3

On several occasions in the narrative so far, the reader is informed that Samuel is 'ministering' to the LORD under the aegis of Eli's leadership. The purpose of such emphasis is to contrast Hannah's son with Eli's sons; the latter 'do not know the LORD, whereas Samuel is growing in both divine and human favor. The reader is told that 'the word of the LORD was rare in those days; vision was not bursting through'. Since this is a strange statement in light of the very long oracle of the anonymous man of God in the preceding chapter, it must be that that the term 'rare' (יָקָר) actually means 'precious' or 'costly'. Appropriately, this is the first time that this term 'rare' occurs in the Bible. In this usage, the 'word' seems to be differentiated from 'vision' as separate modes of divine communication. As Graeme Auld (2003: 214) mentions, 'In the story of the divine call to Samuel (ch.3), we encounter a more dense concentration of significant words relating to prophecy than anywhere else in the Bible'. J.P. Fokkelman further notes that the opening line of this chapter presents both 'audio' and 'visual' terms for prophecy, and in a sense, both occur in this episode: Samuel will hear, and God will appear. Furthermore, a number of terms (reveal, know, hear) are recycled from the oracle of chap. 2, and reinvested in the present context: a second pronouncement of doom on the house of Eli.

The next sentence signals a point of temporal transition: from 'in those days' in v. 1 to 'on that day' in v. 2 suggests that the times are about to change in Shiloh. The bulk of 1 Samuel 3 narrates the events of one long night and its morning sequel. At this time Eli is 'lying down in his place'. Eli's posture is oft-noted in the narrative, and rarely does he seems to do anything that involves movement; recall that he is introduced as 'sitting' on his throne in chap. 1, and he will depart by falling backwards from the same sedentary position. Of course, he is not so young in years, and rather corpulent (as the reader learns in 4.18), so such immobility is not exactly surprising. On the same topic of inertia and Eli's introduction, not only is he laying down, but now his eyes are dim and he cannot see. When Eli is first introduced in the narrative, he is 'watching' Hannah's mouth as she prays. While he incorrectly assays her as a drunken women, there seem to be little problem at least with his eyesight. By the end of his life, he will be totally blind. This raises the larger issue of sensory perceptions in this chapter, as Polzin (1993: 49) reflects: 'The opening exposition is full of language about the diminution of sight and light—no frequent vision, eyesight growing dim, not being able to see, a lamp not yet extinguished—metaphoric language pointing to a conspicuous lack of insight exhibited largely, but not exclusively, by Samuel'. Samuel will have a problem on the acoustical side of things, while Eli has problems in the area of the visual.

While there is a certain darkness that shrouds the sanctuary at Shiloh, in 3.3 the 'lamp of God' serves to provide a moment of illumination. Numerous scholars draw attention to several texts in the Torah that refer to lamps, but it seems that the Deuteronomist is shedding light on something else through this image: elsewhere in Samuel and Kings it is the *Davidic kingship* that is referred to as a lamp (see 2 Sam. 21.17, where David's men are quoted, and note also the narrator's comments in 1 Kgs 11.36 and 15.4, and 2 Kgs 8.19). One wonders how an audience that understands the Babylonian captivity would see this reference to the 'lamp', and whether it contains a flicker of promise in a time of deep shadows. It is difficult not to look ahead in the narrative, especially when the 'ark of God' is also mentioned in 3.3. The ark has only had a couple of cameo appearances since the heady days of the walls of Jericho (see Josh. 6), but will be in the spotlight of 1 Samuel 5–6.

3.4-10

'There is deep irony', notes A.F. Campbell (2003: 55), 'in the old rejected priest instructing the inexperienced young man who will replace him how to receive God's word announcing evil against Eli's own house'. Young Samuel has been around for quite some time in the narrative—so it seems—but has not yet been accorded any direct speech. That deficiency, as it were, it about to be remedied. Moreover, the reader is also privy to God's voice as well, but exactly when God speaks is the subject of a little text-critical drama. For example, in 3.5 the Hebrew text reads, 'And the LORD called to Samuel', but the RSV and NRSV both follow the LXX, and prefer the proper name 'Samuel' twice repeated as a divine utterance. However, I would contend that the name Samuel is not actually spoken as direct speech until the climax of the scene in 3.10; that is, there is an intentional delay in hearing Samuel's name. What follows is my translation of this transaction of dialogue in 3.4-10:

> And the LORD called to Samuel, and he said, 'I'm here'. And he ran to Eli, and said, 'I'm here, for you called to me'. He said, 'I didn't call. Return, lay down!' And he went, and lay down. The LORD continued, calling Samuel again. Samuel arose and went to Eli, and said, 'I'm here, for you called to me'. He said, 'I didn't call you, my son. Return, lay down!'
>
> (Now Samuel did not yet know the LORD, and the word of the LORD had not yet been revealed to him.)
>
> And the LORD continued calling Samuel a third time. He arose and went to Eli, and said, 'I'm here, for you called me'. Then Eli understood that the LORD was calling to the lad. Eli said to Samuel, 'Go, lay down, and if it should happen that he calls to you, then you should say, "Speak, LORD, for your servant is hearing"'. So Samuel went and lay down in his place. And the LORD came, and was standing, and called as previously, 'Samuel! Samuel!' And Samuel said, 'Speak, for your servant is hearing'.

American baseball has a well-known rule: three strikes, and batter is out. Such draconian legislation obviously does not apply in this ancient Near East context, as the lad Samuel gets four chances to hear the pitch of the divine voice. There is an uncommon poignancy to God 'standing' before the young man, since such theophanies do not 'break through' all that often in the Deuteronomistic History. This is the first 'call narrative' of a prophet in quite some time: 'Samuel in a horizontal position and needing an almost blind priest to identify the LORD for him may tell us something about the Deuteronomist's first reference to a prophet since the time of Gideon (Judg. 6.8)' (Polzin 1993: 50). Numerous parallels emerge between this episode and another 'call narrative' in 1 Samuel 16; salient points of comparison will be discussed when that point is reached in the present analysis. Meanwhile, there is a crucial datum omitted. Eli directs the young Samuel to say, should the voice call again, 'Speak, LORD, for your servant is hearing'. However, Samuel neglects to use the divine name, and simply says 'Speak, for your servant is hearing'. Commentators are divided over this omission. Some argue that the omission is not of much consequence; after all, Samuel does not yet 'know the LORD'. Others suggest that this omission entails a measure of 'disobedience', and is not altogether dissimilar to the disobedience that will cost Saul his kingship in 1 Samuel 13. In light of 'hearing' and 'obedience' being key themes in the narrative, this issue ought to be kept in mind.

3.11-14

The ear-tingling message of doom—the second in as many chapters spoken against the house of Eli—contains an intriguing analepsis. In the divine message to Samuel, the announcement is made that Eli's house will be punished, 'for the iniquity *that he knew*'. This is interesting in light of the unfolding characterization of Eli. Some commentators are inclined to argue that the portrait of Eli is one of an inept, yet essentially well-meaning old priest. Though he makes a mistake with Hannah, he makes up for it with words of blessing on numerous occasions. When he hears of his sons activities, he attempts to reason with them. As W.G. Blaikie was wont to observe, 'Eli was memorable for the passive virtues. He could bear much, though he could dare little' (quoted in Gordon 1986: 90). However, the revelation here seems to imply that he has known about the iniquity, yet not 'weakened' his sons. Indeed, Eli certainly seems to have partaken of the sacrificial loot, since we find out in the next chapter that he is corpulent. But the verb 'weaken' (both RSV and NRSV translate as 'restrain') forms an ironic boomerang with 3.2—Eli's eyes are 'weakening', and he has not 'weakened' his sons. There also is a scribal euphemism in 3.13. The Hebrew text literally reads 'for his sons were blaspheming themselves', with the understanding the divine name should be here (other instances of scribal euphemism include Job 2.9 and Gen. 18.22; cf. Alter 1999: 18). Recalling a key theme of Hannah's poem, there is some further poetic justice: the household of Eli have made themselves corpulent through stealing God's sacrifices, *ergo*, sacrifices will never atone for them.

3.15-18

Whether out of habit and a sense of duty, or to avoid his master's eye (as it were), Samuel spends the morning opening the doors of the house of the LORD—a house that has been freshly visited by the LORD himself, speaking judgment against the house of Eli. For the second time in the chapter, Samuel hears his name called out, and he answers with his now customary 'Here I am'. Eli commands Samuel to tell him the news, and puts Samuel under the threat of divine judgment, which is mildly ironic, since that is exactly what the news pertains to. Samuel then tells Eli, though this is reported indirectly, 'everything' and 'hid nothing from him'. This will not be the last time that Samuel is the bearer of ill tidings about a dynastic house—he will have similar news for Israel's first king, much like this old judge. Several scholars note that in the Deuteronomistic History there are a number of dynastic houses that come crashing down from glorious heights and are reduced to begging bread. It happens with the house of Eli. It will happen with Saul's house, as his last descendant of note, Mephibosheth, is reduced to eating bread at David's table. It will happen with the Davidic house as well, as the last king of Judah is under house arrest and eating at the table of the king of Babylon. The mighty will indeed fall before the long narrative of Joshua to 2 Kings comes to an end.

At the end of the speech of the anonymous man of God in chap. 2, there is no response recorded from Eli. Here in chap. 3, by contrast, he does respond to Samuel's message, albeit brief and not altogether lucid: 'He is the LORD', Eli says, 'what is good in his eyes, let him do'. The mention of God's 'eyes' is interesting, in light of Eli's incremental blindness. Furthermore, there is an echo of the last line of Judges here: 'In those days there was no king in Israel, and each did what was upright in his own eyes'. The one who will anoint Israel's first king has just delivered the bad news to the last of the line of old judges.

3.19-21

1 Samuel 3 concludes in a tidy fashion. As Fokkelman observes, Samuel himself makes the transition from נַעַר ('lad') to נָבִיא ('prophet'), and the word of LORD—rare at the beginning of the chapter—becomes spacious by the end. In terms of this new prophet, it is possible to argue that Samuel is one of the most extensively narrated characters in the Hebrew Bible, since we meet him before he is born and experience his presence beyond the grave. In the story so far we have seen the birth of the prophet; now we have the birth of a new era in the prophetic movement. The reader is told in 3.19, 'And Samuel grew, and the LORD was with him and let none of his words fall to the ground'. Commentators have slightly different views on the referent of 'his' in 'let none of *his* words fall to the ground'. Some infer that it is Samuel, the initial subject of the sentence, while others see God as the subject, i.e., God does not let any of *his own* words fall to the ground. If the latter is the case, the first instance would be the words of judgment spoken against the house of Eli, poised to find (partial) fulfillment in the next episode. Brueggemann's 'exilic' reflection (1990: 27-28) merits some attention:

> This narrative, in concert with Israel's most profound faith, finds it credible to have God assert, 'Behold, I am doing a new thing'. The narratives of Samuel want to assert that conviction, but they must do so in the midst of a difficult public crisis. God's new thing is not a grand religious act but an invitation to a fresh, dangerous social beginning. All around the innocence of this narrative

there were undoubtedly threats, bargains, and cunning calculations. In the midst of all these seductions, however, there is a season of naïveté when a young boy can receive a vision, an old man can embrace a relinquishment, a surprised mother can sing a song, the ears of the conventional can tingle, and life begins again. A new beginning means a terrible ending of some other arrangements. As we shall see, Samuel subsequently grows vexed and irascible about those endings, but not now, not here. This new beginning requires facing candidly all that has failed, and this narrative does that without flinching or deceiving.

Of all the available images, the Deuteronomist chooses the 'having of sons' to introduce the complicated story of the 'having of kings'. In 1 Samuel 1–3, the reader is shown a number of sons, and the narrative of kingship is introduced through poem and prose. The disestablishment of a dynasty is also a complex affair; now that judgment has been pronounced on the house of Eli, it will unfold in both the short and the long term of the narrative. The unfolding of judgment, one should stress, does not happen in an altogether predictable fashion, and, as is the case in the house of Eli, unfolds with a certain drama. Judgment is not always immediate. It may be delayed. Consequently, the drama of judgment of Eli's house foreshadows the future falling of other dynastic houses throughout the Deuteronomistic History. Moreover, this is not the last time in Samuel that a father will be blamed for the excesses of his sons (see Auld 2003: 214). The latter career of King David is marked with such parental struggles.

The 'having of kings' is also a story about the 'having of prophets', and from this point on king and prophet will always go together. As we will see, God will condescend to the people's request for a king. As a check and balance, the office of the prophet is correspondingly elevated. However, as 1 Samuel 3 graphically illustrates, it is not always easy to hear the voice of God. Further, this chapter represents a turning point in the history of Shiloh: on the eve of its destruction, Shiloh becomes a place from which the 'word of the LORD' emanates. In the past, Shiloh has been a center for sacrifice, and become corrupted. At the end of 1 Samuel 3, it is now a center where the word of the LORD departs with centrifugal force: 'What had been the ritual center under the leadership of Eli has now become the center for the prophetic word under the leadership of Samuel' (Birch 1998: 993). Such a point needs to be highlighted because even though there is no record of its destruction by the Philistines in 1 Samuel 4, in all likelihood the city is invaded and demolished. But this is far from the end for Shiloh: 'Here the blind old prophet Ahijah was appealed to in vain by Jeroboam's wife on behalf of her son' in 1 Kings 14 (Ewing 1949), and Shiloh functions as an illustration in the famous temple sermon of the prophet Jeremiah (Jer. 7).

1 Samuel 4

Thus far in the narrative the reader has seen a remarkable divine capacity for overturning the status quo: both the barren womb of Hannah and the leadership of Eli's house are subject to dramatic reversals, and Hannah gives birth to the prophet who is an instrument for speaking the divine word against Eli and his sons. Chapter 4 presents a shift in both the spatial setting and the central characters in this next phase of the narrative. The scene shifts from inside Israel to the external conflict with the Philistines, and the characterizations move from a focus on two families in the Shiloh environment to events on the national stage. Despite these changes, some of the key themes of Hannah's song—such as the arrogant abased, and the abased faithful raised high—very much continue in this next phase of the story. 1 Samuel 4 is a chapter with three parts. In the first part, the nation of Israel suffers defeat at the hands of the Philistines. As a countermeasure, they summon forth the ark of the covenant to accompany them on the field of battle. The strategy does not pay off: they suffer an even greater defeat, the ark is captured, and Hophni and Phinehas are killed. The second part of the chapter revolves around the announcement of defeat in the city of Shiloh, and the resultant uproar of the city. The third part of 1 Samuel 4 focuses on two individual recipients of the news—Eli and his daughter-in-law—and their responses to the report of the defeat and the exiled ark. Eli falls backwards and dies. Likewise, his daughter-in-law dies in childbirth, bearing a scion to the house of Eli who is born under a sentence of doom. The ark is taken from Shiloh, and will never return there.

4.1

In the past scholars have often seen 1 Samuel 4–6 as constituting the 'ark narrative'. For a variety of reasons, so the theory goes, this unit represents a very old tradition that is eventually stitched into the surrounding text. More recently, a number of scholars have seen 1 Samuel 4–6 as intrinsically connected with the surrounding prose, and they question the notion of this material as an independent composition. These scholars understand 1 Samuel 4–6 to function as a parable of *exile* and *return*, pointing to such terms as an interpretive key to this section of the narrative. For an 'exilic' audience, the Philistines probably function as a cipher for a foreign antagonist and captor, an oppressor and subjugator of God's people. 1 Samuel 4–6 thus occupy an important position within the overall schema of the Deuteronomistic History, and make an important theological statement in this stretch of narrative that introduces the monarchy into the Israelite national consciousness. Equally significant, these chapters illustrate that the sovereignty of God extends even beyond the borders of Israel.

There is some controversy over the beginning of the chapter. Some translators understand the first sentence—'And the word of Samuel came to all Israel'—to conclude chap. 3, while others understand the sentence to introduce the events of chap. 4. Since the 'word of the LORD' to Samuel in chap. 3 mentions the destruction of Hophni and Phinehas and the marginalization of Eli's house, a useful way to understand the opening sentence is as follows: 'And the word of Samuel was for all Israel: now Israel marched out to battle against the Philistines...' That is, the word that Samuel receives is now about to start working itself out on the wider international stage, by means of conflict with the Philistines. It is slightly odd that the word of Samuel begins this chapter, but Samuel himself makes no further appearance in the chapter. While the absent prophet in 4–6 is one of the pillars of the independent 'ark narrative' theory, there are other explanations for why the Deuteronomist does not focus on Samuel here. Chapters 1–3 present a parable whereby the having of sons is akin to the having of kings; likewise, chaps. 4–6 are equally important in the story of Israel's leadership, as it presents a narrative of exile and return after the dramatic collapse of a ruling dynastic house. Both of these narrative threads are brought together in chap. 7, where the prophet—now acting as national leader and judge—again is central.

The second part of 4.1 has its own issues: 'Now Israel went out to battle against the Philistines; they encamped at Ebenezer, and the Philistines encamped at Aphek'. On the surface, it sets the scene for the conflict between Israel and the Philistines, but it is not entirely clear who the aggressor is in the battle. Do the Philistines initiate, or is it 'the word of Samuel' that ignites the hostility? In the absence of any obvious cause, one recalls the general animosity between the two nations in the Samson era, with the Philistines enjoying the upper hand. Since the Philistine camp is located in Aphek, an Israelite city, the Philistines seem to be the initiators. In terms of the place names, J.P. Fokkelman (1993: 198) notes that Ebenezer and Aphek will enjoy some significance later in the story. Ebenezer is prominent in 1 Samuel 7 as the site of Israel's successful campaign against the Philistines, while Aphek once more will be the Philistine base where the battle is launched that seals Saul's fate in 1 Samuel 29.

4.2-5

The confrontation begins, and Israel is defeated by the Philistines, losing 4000 soldiers in the battle. Upon regrouping in the camp, the Israelite response to this loss is voiced by 'the elders'. The last time the elders of Israel speak is in Judg. 21.19, where they ask—in light of the disaster of Benjamin—'What shall we do for wives for those who are left, since there are no women left in Benjamin?' Notably, the next time they speak will be in 1 Sam. 8.4, where they ask for a king. Here, the elders begin by asking why *the LORD defeated* Israel on this day. While the elders are quick to ascribe divine sovereignty as the cause of their military setback, their solution is somewhat novel: 'Let us take from Shiloh the ark of the covenant of the LORD for us. Let it come into our midst, and it will save us from the grip of our enemies'. Since the ark has not been on active duty—apart from a few cameo appearances—since the battle of Jericho in Joshua 6, it is hard to know the impetus behind the elders' rationale. One may have expected the elders to seek 'the word of the LORD' from Shiloh, since 3.21 refers to the ubiquity of the divine word at Shiloh through the prophet: 'The LORD continued to appear at Shiloh, for the LORD revealed himself to Samuel at Shiloh by the word of the LORD'. Instead, the elders choose the ark. The exceedingly long title that accompanies the ark in 4.4 ('the ark of the covenant of the LORD of hosts, the one seated among cherubim') perhaps augurs well for the elders' decision, but high hopes are best held in abeyance. For the reader, there is a slight rain on the parade: the custodianship of Hophni and Phinehas, presumably carrying the ark, represents a deflation after the long title that denotes celestial power. Since the man of God has prophesied that both sons of Eli will die on a single day, one wonders if *this* will be the day. The camp of Israel, however, is not as pensive, and the camp exhales a mighty war shout. The shout is so loud that 'the earth resounded', indicating that the elders' choice is popular.

4.6-9

If the Israelite reaction to the ark's arrival is a confident war shout, the Philistine response is far less sanguine. A whole sequence of Philistine actions is recited in 4.6-7, as they hear, say, know, and fear. Their response to this 'theological' crisis involves the exclamation, 'nothing like this has happened before', yet they then proceed to allude to the Exodus experience of Israel. It is interesting, to say the least, that the Philistines are recorded as 'quoting' Israel's Egyptian encounter, yet commentators are usually quick to point out two slight inaccuracies (from the viewpoint of Israelite theology). First, as one would expect in a pluralistic society, the Philistines refer to 'these mighty gods', implying that their Israelite neighbors are, like all Canaanites, polytheists. (As an aside, one hopes that it is merely coincidental that in 1 Sam. 7.3 the prophet will command Israel to put away all the 'foreign gods' closeted in their midst.) Second, the Philistine reference to 'every sort of plague *in the wilderness*' has raised some eyebrows; strictly speaking, the plagues occur in Egypt itself rather than in the wilderness, as such, but the point is not lost.

It has been observed that Israel seeks a religious solution to their crisis, while the Philistines, by contrast, chose the path of *added human resolve* as a response to this problem. Their stated motivation is the avoidance of slavery: 'Take courage, and acquit yourselves like men, O Philistines, lest you become slaves to the Hebrews as they have been to you; acquit yourselves like men and fight'. There is not a clear instance where Israel as a nation are said to be slaves of the Philistines, but the notion of subservience may be obliquely supported in Judg. 15.11, when the men of Judah ask Samson, 'Do you not know that the Philistines are rulers (מֹשְׁלִים) over us?' At the same time, there may be a bit of hyperbole in this speech of the Philistines, to provide extra motivation for the battle. One has to be careful not to always take Philistine discourse at face value.

4.10-11

The Israelite strategy of bringing the ark to the battlefield is not successful; in fact, there is more than a sevenfold increase of casualties. The deaths of Hophni and Phinehas surely signals the beginning of the *word* unfolding against the house of Eli, as on this 'one day' both sons are slain. Not only do the Israelites lose the battle, they also lose the ark. There is a keyword that connects the two times the ark is 'taken': in 4.3 the elders say 'let us take' (נִקְחָה), and in 4.11 the ark is 'taken' (נִלְקָח). It has been argued by several scholars that the Philistines are not the direct agent, as such, and the sense that God allows it to happen is reinforced by the niphal passive verb (נִלְקָח). This entire result must be completely counter to the elders' expectations (and the expectations of the Philistines, for that matter). As Brueggemann (1990: 32) notes, 'The result of the second battle shows that Israel's trust and the Philistines' fear have been misplaced'. If so, it is mildly ironic that history will eventually repeat itself, though with the parties reversed: in 2 Sam. 5.18-21 it is the Philistines who bring their gods onto the battlefield with a negative effect: 'The Philistines abandoned their idols there, and David and his men carried them away'. Again, the expectation is reversed. David and his men, we should also note, suffer no ill effects after taking the Philistine gods.

4.12-16

The next major phase of 1 Samuel 4 reverts back to the spatial setting of Shiloh, as a messenger arrives in the city 'on that day'. The man seems to run right past Eli, stationed at the side of the gate; perhaps in his grief and haste he overlooks the blind priest. In light of the messenger's condition—torn raiment, and earth on his head—such failure is excusable, especially since he is bearing the ill tidings of the death of more than 30,000 soldiers. Furthermore, the tribal identity of the messenger merits some reflection: he is a 'man of Benjamin'. As Peter Miscall observes, there is a long association of Shiloh and Benjamin: Shiloh 'was the site for the distribution of the land to separate tribes, including Benjamin, but it was also the site for the 'preservation' of Benjamin in Judges 21. Benjamin seized virgins from there during 'the yearly feast of the Lord' (Judg. 21.19; 1 Sam. 1.3)'. Indeed, one could say that it is because of the annual festival of Shiloh that Benjamin *still even* exists as a tribe here in 1 Samuel 4. The birth of Benjamin (Gen. 35) is alluded to at the end of this chapter, and so it is striking that the herald—whose news drives the wife of Phinehas into premature labor—is from the tribe of Benjamin.

Eli's posture in 4.13—'sitting upon the throne'—is exactly the same as his introduction in chap. 1. If this posture has royal overtones in chap. 1 as Polzin argues, then Eli's reign is poised to come to an abrupt end here in chap. 4. 'In my end is my beginning', writes T.S. Eliot, and Eli's line is about to become a wasteland. Not only is Eli sitting, but he is also 'watching', or 'anxiously peering' (מְצַפֶּה) as the verb can be translated. Eli is ninety-eight years old and 'his eyes were standing still so that he could not see', and hence the image is of a blind man eagerly watching, but oblivious to the word of judgment now unveiling before his sightless eyes. It is worth observing that the term for 'standing still' (קָמָה) is the same verbal root used in 1 Sam. 1.23, when Elkanah says to Hannah 'may the LORD establish his word', that is, may he cause his word to stand' (יָקֵם). Consequently, Eli's eyes now physically symbolize the divine word spoken against him gradually beginning to realize fulfillment as he sits on his throne for the last time in the narrative.

As the man of Benjamin runs past the anxiously peering priest, the reader is told that Eli's heart was 'trembling' for the ark of God. While one may wonder about Eli's opinion on whether or not the ark should have ever been taken out of Shiloh and onto the battlefield, it seems strange that his heart is not trembling for *his sons*, in light of the prophetic word spoken against them. Regardless, the news of the man of Benjamin causes uproar in the city that the blind Eli, appropriately, hears: 'And Eli heard the sound of the outcry, and said, "What is the sound of this tumult?"' The man of Benjamin must have better ears than Eli has eyes, because immediately he comes over to Eli and reports the news. Since Eli is unlikely to notice the torn clothes and earth on the head, the man explains that he has just fled from the battlefield. 1 Samuel 4.16 then provides Eli's last word of direct speech in the narrative, as he asks, literally, 'What is the word, my son?' Eli's last speech is ironic because the 'word' of the messenger is actually the 'word' of the man of God in chap. 2 now unfolding, and also because Eli calls him 'my son', and the messenger's word concerns the death of his two sons. Things will steadily grow worse for Eli as he hears the rest of this report.

4.17-18
The man of Benjamin finally shares the news with Eli, and his slightly awkward syntax no doubt reflects exhaustion and nervous haste. Whether he is saving the worst for last or framing the message with a sense of chronological order, he mentions the ark as the last item in this chronicle of woe. The man of Benjamin is called a 'messenger' by the NRSV, and 'he who brought the tidings' by the RSV. However, a bold translation of the Hebrew term הַמְבַשֵּׂר would be 'the bearer of *good news*'. It would be difficult to construe this news as 'good' from Eli's viewpoint, notwithstanding the Belial activities of his sons. But this is certainly not the last occasion that such messengers carry 'good news' in 1 and 2 Samuel, and as Polzin points out, the verb 'to bring (good) news' almost invariably occurs in the Deuteronomistic History when the news is good for David or the Davidic royal house. To consider but one example—the case of Absalom—the verb 'to bring (good) news' occurs five times. The report of Absalom's death is bad news for David the father, yet simultaneously is good news for the political stability of David the king. Likewise, the news of Hophni and Phinehas is bad news for Eli the father, but paves the way for the advent of kingship and the (eventual) inception of the Davidic house. Consequently, the 'good news' of Eli anticipates later developments in the story. The bad news is that Eli's house will have a lot in common with David's house: 'The crashing death of Eli in 4.18 foreshadows and embodies the Deuteronomist's graphic evaluation of the institution that Israel at first thought would bring good news and glad tidings; the news mostly results in death and destruction' (Polzin 1993: 61).

At the risk of belaboring the obvious, Eli's response to the report of the ark's capture is theatrically stunning: the mention of the ark triggers a backwards fall, with the terminal velocity resulting in a broken neck for the aged priest. While the reader has known for some time that Eli is old, it is rather new information to discover that he is 'heavy'. It is entirely possible that Eli's portliness is a direct consequence of eating the sacrificial meat before the fat is burned off (see 1 Sam. 2.15-16). Hence there is irony when Eli is described as 'heavy' (כבד), since this echoes the high-cholesterol charge of the anonymous man of God who interrogates Eli in 2.29, 'Why do you look with greedy eye at my sacrifices and my offerings which I commanded, and honor (כבד) your sons above me by fattening yourselves upon the choicest parts of every offering of my people Israel?' The same term will reappear in the requiem of Phinehas' wife at the end of the chapter, when she mourns the loss of Eli and the ark and says, 'Honor (כבד) is exiled from Israel'. The notion of 'honor being in exile', as Robert Gordon (1986: 97) notes, is poignant within the larger context of the Deuteronomistic History: 'The appositeness of the reference will not have been missed by those of a later generation who suffered the loss of their temple and the inconvenience of deportation following the Babylonian depredations'.

The captivity of the ark is used as an instrument in fulfilling the divine word spoken against the priestly house of Eli. At the same time, the final sentence of 4.18 informs the reader that Eli 'had judged Israel forty years'. Commentators often discuss this note, although it is usually assessed in terms of its contribution to the debate about the compositional history of the ark narrative. From a literary viewpoint, a purpose of this obituary might be to indicate that Eli should be included among the Judges of Israel, the last of which was Samson. In light of this detail about the considerable length of Eli's judgeship, it would now appear as though the chaos of Judges 17–21 takes place under the aegis of Eli's leadership, or at the very least, seemingly overlapping with his tenure. As a result, Eli's legacy is further besotted, since it is under his stewardship that Israel experiences further disintegration that culminates in the final sentence of Judges: 'In those days there was no king in Israel; every man would do what was upright in his own eyes'. As for the sanctuary at Shiloh, its best days are now over. Graeme Auld (2004: 174) argues that the fate of Shiloh in these opening chapters anticipate the fate of Jerusalem: after the exile(s) of the ark, neither Shiloh nor Jerusalem have anyone sitting on a throne.

4.19-22

The news of the ark's capture sends Eli plunging to his death, but the battle defeat has further collateral damage for the growing family of Eli's doomed line. The final scene of 1 Samuel 4 features the wife of Phinehas on her deathbed, giving birth to an Elide with a gloomy future. Since a number of terms and dialogues are important within the chapter, here is my translation of the final scene in this chapter:

> Now his daughter-in-law, the wife of Phinehas, was pregnant and about to give birth. When she heard the report that the Ark of God had been captured, and that her father-in-law had died (along with her husband), she doubled-over to give birth, for her labor pains threw her into a convulsion. As the time of her death drew near, the women standing over her said, 'Don't be afraid, for you've given birth to a son!' But she did not respond, and did not even take the matter to heart. She called the lad, 'Where is Honor?', stating, 'Honor is exiled from Israel' (concerning the capture of the Ark of God and her father-in-law and husband). She said, 'Honor is exiled from Israel, for the Ark of God is captured!'

For the second time in 1 Samuel there is a birth under difficult circumstances. In chap. 1, Hannah is formerly barren, but gives birth to Samuel, and celebrates the event with both a naming speech and (in her song of chap. 2) lyrics that celebrate the boy's future. Eli's daughter-in-law also gives birth, but by naming the child Ichabod (literally, 'Where is honor?') and twice exegeting the name as 'Honor is exiled from Israel' the mother does not entertain high hopes for her son. Hannah has a son, a husband, and is about to embark on a fruitful career as a mother of six. By contrast, Eli's daughter-in-law is a dying widow, giving birth to an orphan who has little by way of prospects for vocational fulfillment. The anonymous man of God has announced that one man will be left in Eli's house who will have to beg for bread from the 'assured priest' whose family will eclipse the Elides. Hannah annually clothes her son in a garment of promise, whereas the widow Phinehas takes no comfort from the women standing around her who say, 'Don't be afraid, for you've given birth to a son!' When the dying mother asks 'Where is the honor', one is reminded of the words of 1 Sam. 2.30: 'those who honor me I will honor'. Eli honors his sons more than God, and his daughter-in-law reaps the grim consequences.

It has been observed that the birth of Ichabod here in 1 Samuel alludes to the earlier birth of Benjamin in Gen. 35.16-18: '…Rachel was in childbirth, and she was hard in her labor. At her hardest point in her labor, the midwife said to her, "Don't be afraid, for also this one is for you a son!" And as her life was going out, for she died, she called his name "Ben-oni", but his father called him "Benjamin".' The irony of the present situation is not lost on the reader: a man of Benjamin brings news that will induce a premature birth, a birth that in turn alludes to the birth of Benjamin himself. Furthermore, the house of Benjamin—which has had a poor run of form, given its near extinction in Judges—will find itself the tribe of Israel's first king. So, as 1 Samuel 4 comes to an end, there are two 'survivors' that receive mention: a man of Benjamin who brings the good news, and a descendant of Eli whose birth resembles that of Benjamin. The more distant future is also hinted at with the use of the verb 'exile', perhaps prefiguring another exile in the days ahead. Barbara Green (2003: 145) provides a provocative summary:

> The unnamed man of Benjamin is the more crucial survivor of the piece, and his character will be developed later, from a different genre. In addition to his tribal status, which suggests him as the survivor and royal successor to the Elides, he is fled from the battle—alone among those not slaughtered, his clothes (neither cloak nor ephod here) disordered, his head marked by the disaster he announces. He is looked for by a blind man and greeted as his son; his news brings death to the mother and outcry from the people. The analogue for the defeat of Judah and leaders detailed at the end of 2 Kings, the shocking deportation of citizenry into foreign captivity, is difficult to miss.

1 Samuel 5

The dying words of the daughter-in-law of Eli are: 'Exiled is honor from Israel, for the ark of God is captured'. The loss of the ark causes stress for a number of Israelites, but it also will cause stress for those responsible for its capture, the Philistines. Notably, the Philistines allude to the Exodus in chap. 4, talking about the plagues which 'those mighty gods' caused the Egyptians. Little do they know, but they are on the threshold of experiencing 'the heavy hand of the LORD' against them. 1 Samuel 5 is a short chapter divided into two parts. Part one takes place inside the precincts of Dagon's temple, while part two takes place in assorted locations within the Philistine pentapolis. In both parts, the ark of God wreaks severe havoc in the deepest recesses of its captors' anatomy.

5.1-2

As Eli's widowed daughter-in-law is delivering her child of no hope, the prizewinning Philistines deliver the ark to the temple of Dagon in Ashdod. As it turns out, the Hebrew syntax of 5.1 suggests an issue of *simultaneity*, that is, there is a general sense of chronological correspondence between the events of the latter part of chap. 4 and the beginning of chap. 5. Roughly, the birth of Ichabod happens around the same time as the deposit of the ark in the temple of Dagon at Ashdod. In Josh. 13.3, Ashdod is mentioned as one of the cities of the menacing Philistine pentapolis. Within the more recent stretch of the Deuteronomistic History, one recalls that there is, or was, a temple of Dagon in Judges 16 located in Gaza. In that story, Samson himself is a 'trophy' that is brought, but counter to the captors' expectation, Samson creates a vast amount of trouble for those Philistines gathered in the temple that day, especially since it comes crashing down all around them, and their lives are abruptly terminated. In the present context, the ark seems to be a trophy in the same genre as Samson. The ark, therefore, is not the first Israelite symbol that will be deposited in a Philistine shrine; nor is it the last, as Saul's headless corpse will be taken to a Philistine temple at the end of 1 Samuel.

5.3-5

With the ark safely deposited in the temple of Dagon, it would appear the people of Ashdod go to sleep content and at ease. However, during the night there seems to have been an unfortunate incident: 'When the Ashdodians rose early on the next day, behold, Dagon was falling down on his face in front of the ark of the LORD' (note the Hebrew participle 'falling', נֹפֵל). Surely this must be an accident, and Dagon is rightfully 'put back in his place'. Israelite readers may discern some legal humor here: contained in the ark is a tablet that says 'you shall have no other gods before me'—yet Dagon is another god, and he is *before* the ark! Again, this situation may just be an unlucky accident, a mere coincidence.

In the cold light of the following morning, though, the accident theory is looking less likely: not only is Dagon 'falling' before the ark, but Dagon has also experienced some very serious dismemberment. The hands and head of the decapitated Dagon seem to have made it as far as the threshold of the temple. It is as though Dagon was attempting to flee (from his own house!), yet the torso is pulled back, but the hands remain—because the 'hand' of the LORD is heavy on the hands of Dagon. For those who are curious, *this* is the reason why 'the priests of Dagon and all who enter the house of Dagon do not step on the threshold of Dagon in Ashdod to this day'. While commentators have proffered a host of theories as to the purpose of this temporal dislocation, one wonders if this momentary 'fast forward' to the present might be to illustrate—for early readers of this text—that here is a temple that survives with a memory of judgment.

This scene in chap. 5 resonates with the preceding chapter: Eli falls backward because of the ark, and Dagon falls forward because of the ark. In 1 Sam. 2.10 Hannah sings, 'The adversaries of the LORD shall be broken to pieces', and Dagon and Eli—otherwise unlike in so many ways—can probably testify to the veracity of Hannah's lyrics. Indeed, just like Israel misjudges the value of the ark in battle, so the Philistines misjudge the ark as well. Dismembered Dagon suffers mightily because of his adherents' misjudgment, and the situation is poised to get worse.

5.6-10

The next section of 1 Samuel 5 moves outside the confines of the Dagon temple into broader Philistine territory. Concomitantly, the reader moves from the physical damage of Dagon to the physical damage of the Philistines themselves. Just as the verb 'to be heavy/to honor' (כבד) is significant in chap. 4, so it continues here in chap. 5, as the hand of the LORD is heavy (כבד) against the Philistines of Ashdod. Not only is there a general mood of 'heaviness', but nasty 'tumors' are also leaving their mark. Understandably, the aggrieved folks of Ashdod seek a solution: they call together a group of politicians, 'all the lords of the Philistines'. But as is often the case, the political solution is not without controversy. In this case, the controversy is a textual one. Compare the RSV and NRSV of 5.8:

> ^{RSV} So they sent and gathered together all the lords of the Philistines, and said, 'What shall we do with the ark of the God of Israel?' They answered, 'Let the ark of the God of Israel be brought around to Gath'. So they brought the ark of the God of Israel there.

> ^{NRSV} So they sent and gathered together all the lords of the Philistines, and said, 'What shall we do with the ark of the God of Israel?' The inhabitants of Gath replied, 'Let the ark of God be moved on to us'. So they moved the ark of the God of Israel to Gath.

Notice that in the RSV (corresponding to the Hebrew MT), it is the Philistine leaders who suggest that the ark ought to be sent to Gath. One may quibble that this is a rather provincial solution: simply send the troublesome ark to another Philistine city, and let it become someone else's problem. By contrast, in the NRSV it the *inhabitants of Gath themselves* who seemingly volunteer to assume responsibility. It is unclear whether their motive is one of sacrificial service and devotion to the Ashdod cause, or whether they are being arrogant and cocky. Either way, there must be an element of confidence to the Gathites, such that they are prepared to entertain this troublesome guest. Hence, when both the RSV and NRSV are considered, in both cases one senses a disinclination for the Philistines to relinquish the captured trophy. It is as though returning the ark to Israel is tantamount to an admission of defeat.

This is not the last time in 1 Samuel that the reader will encounter Gath or one of its citizens. Indeed, Goliath himself hails from Gath, and he is a rather confident chap. So, perhaps there is something in the water that breeds the self-assured type. However, in this case the confidence—if it be such—that they can handle the ark is misplaced, since there is a great panic in the city, and again, tumors appear in unpleasant places. Incidentally, the precise nature of these 'tumors' has long discomfited the scholarly community. Some scholars understand the bubonic plague at work here, while others believe that hemorrhoids (the Hebrew term is 'related to an Aramaic word meaning "strain at the stool"') are causing the Philistine unease (Klein 1983: 50). The latter is the way the KJV translators understand the pain: 'the hand of the LORD was against the city with a very great destruction: and he smote the men of the city, both small and great, and *they had emerods in their secret parts*'. The strategy of moving the ark to Gath—whether by default or by design—is not looking very good at this point in the story.

5.10-12

The internal problems of Gath eventually result in the ark of God being shipped to yet another Philistine city, the city of Ekron. Whether the people of Ekron are willing to have the ark come to them, or whether the mayor of Gath simply exports the problem to someone else is not specified in the narrative. By any account, the city suffers greatly. Not only is deadly panic, but once more the hand of the LORD is heavy (כבד) along with the all too familiar hemorrhoids. Fortunately, Ekron's citizens have the political wherewithal to call together another committee meeting of the five 'lords' of the Philistines, the same group that is called on in 5.8. In fact, this group of five is gaining considerable experience in dealing with Israelite predicaments. One recalls in Judges 16 that this group of five approach Delilah with a plan for subduing their nemesis, Samson. In the present case, though, there is no solution proffered by the five lords. Remarkably, the Philistine politicians are not recorded *any* direct speech whatsoever; the only thing recorded is a demonstrable increase in hemorrhoids such that 'the cry of the city went up to heaven'.

1 SAMUEL 6

Since the heavy hand of the LORD has shown no signs of abating, the situation of the ark's captivity is becoming increasingly desperate for the Philistines. Both Eli and his daughter-in-law have severe reactions to the news of the ark's captivity, and the news induces premature death. The ark, however, has been rather unfazed during its Philistine 'exile'. Less happy, no doubt, are the Philistine captors, as all their people 'from the smallest to the greatest' are struck with panic and agonizing tumors. Furthermore, the strategy of simply sending the ark to another (Philistine) city is completely ineffective. Not only is each successive city struck with the same posterior malady, the Philistines are probably running out of cities as well. 1 Samuel 6 brings the ark's sojourn outside of Israel to a close, and this chapter is structured in two parts. The first part of the chapter deals with the question of how best to the return the ark to its place, and indeed, to determine if it is itself the cause of all this calamity. To that end, a test is devised for determining such, and returning the ark. The second part of the chapter culminates in the return of the ark to Israelite territory. All is not pacific once it returns, however, and there is further damage caused by the ark *within the boundaries of Israel*.

6.1
When re-reading 1 Samuel 5, there is something of a turning point in the story at 5.11. It is here that the citizens of Ekron say 'Send away the ark of the God of Israel, and let it return to its own place'. As Barbara Green (2003: 149) observes, this is the virtual opposite of what the elders of Israel say in 4.3, when they deliberate, 'Let us bring the ark of the covenant of the LORD here from Shiloh, that it may come among us and save us from the power of our enemies'. The last stages of the ark's captivity are now beginning to be narrated, and the opening sentence of chap. 6 informs the reader that the ark is within the Philistine nation for 'seven months'. It is not clear if this temporal note is a round calculation of total time, or if it describes a delay between the words of the people of Ekron and the events of chap. 6 that are about to unfold. In the grand scheme of history, seven months is probably not a vast stretch of time. However, given the 'emerods in the

secret parts' of the Philistine physiology, the emphasis in 6.1 seems to be that a considerable stretch of time has elapsed since the capture of the ark at the battle of Ebenezer. Bruce Birch (1998: 1010) notes that there may be a more symbolic dimension to this chronological reference: 'In the light of the prominent exodus language and imagery in this chapter, we are reminded of the seven days of the first plague against Egypt in Exod 7.25'.

6.2
Desperate times, it is said, call for desperate measures. When the tumors first break out in chap. 5, the Philistines call upon the politicians. Even though the advice of the Philistine overlords is less than satisfactory, they are still consulted even as late as 5.11, though on this occasion the Philistine politicians do not speak a word of direct speech. Since it is not a familiar occurrence for politicians to keep silent, one guesses that they are running out of ideas, as the strategy of Philistine politicians only results in further posterior discomfort. So now, in chap. 6, it is at the climax of desperation that the Philistines do not summon the politicians, but rather call out the religious professionals.

In particular, two kinds of clerics are petitioned: priests and diviners. The category of 'priest' seems quite generic here, and presumably these priests are of the same cloth as those whose descendants are careful not to tread on the threshold of Dagon's house at Ashdod, as memorialized in 5.5. The second category of 'diviners' is more murky, as this specific kind of practitioner is outlawed in Israel according to Deut. 18.14. It is to both kinds of clerics that a pair of questions are posed: 'What shall we do with the ark of the LORD? Tell us what we should send with it to its place'. That the prize of war must go is not in doubt; the issue is with *what* shall it be sent, and ones senses here a note of humble submission that has not been discerned hitherto. Notably, the people use the divine name 'LORD' (יהוה) that so far has not been directly used by a Philistine in direct speech. Such language underscores that—as far as the general populace is concerned—the ark has moved from a political to a religious problem. Unlike other exchanges, these two queries are not rhetorical questions. After seven months of straining at the stool, the time has come for serious information flow.

6.3-6
Theologians, on those occasions when they happen to be consulted in grand affairs of state, are sometimes accused of unnecessarily complicating matters. In this case, the proffered instructions are rather complicated to say the least, and fraught with rhetorical questions, qualifiers, admonitions, and provisional scenarios. Yet no Philistine complains about the line or length of the advice. Indeed, the Philistines have other issues to deal with (such as the

bothersome tumors), and the priests and diviners are afforded the highest proportion of direct speech in the 'ark narrative' of 1 Samuel 4–6.

The advice of the priests and diviners has two components: the first component involves some general spiritual counsel, while the second component pertains to the practical course of action and technical advice. They begin with a conditional utterance: *if* you plan to send the ark of the 'God of Israel' away, *then* it cannot be sent away empty. The recommendation of a guilt offering implies a need for compensation, a tacit acknowledgment that wrong-doing has been committed. The reader also notices that it is the Philistine priests and diviners who say 'you must give honor (כבד) to the God of Israel'. The use of the exact same root 'honor/glory/ heavy' (כבד) that is so prominent in earlier portions of 1 Samuel must operate in the present context as a further indictment of the house of Eli, since God's 'honor' (כבד) is not a priority for Israel's senior priestly leadership. Foreign priests and diviners are directing their citizens to give honor to God, which is exactly what their clerical counterparts in Israel are *not* doing.

On the technical side, the priests and diviners submit the idea of 'models' as a guilt offering. The issue of these models has elicited considerable speculation from commentators, who, in the past, have tended to look at comparative religious practice and the use of effigies in the ancient Near East. Yet these commentators have also been hesitant to reflect on exactly what a golden hemorrhoid looks like, and for such reticence we are in their debt. The Deuteronomist, so it would appear, has little interest in describing such an image. What is surprising, though, is that the people are also instructed to make models of 'five gold mice'. To this point in the story, at least in the Hebrew text, mice have not been mentioned. While there is an infestation of rats in the Greek text as early as 5.6, thus far the ravaging vermin have not featured in the story. At the risk of being lured into a text-critical mousetrap, it seems safe to conclude that the revelation of this important detail captures the sense of confusion that pervades the entire Philistine society, and afflicts every member: added to the embarrassment of hemorrhoids is an invasion of mice that have brought further disaster upon the captors of the ark. The reader only now discovers that the Philistines have been plagued with *external* as well as *internal* crises.

It is striking that the priests and diviners—like their colleagues in 4.8—invoke memories of the Exodus and conduct a short seminar in Israelite historiography. Commentators have noticed an abundance of Exodus language in this stretch of text, as terms such as 'send' (שלח) and 'make a fool' (עלל) are keywords in both narratives. Peter Miscall (1986: 32) nicely summarizes the cogency of the Egyptian reference: 'The Philistines again draw a lesson from the events of the Exodus, the necessity of respecting the Lord and his power; it is a lesson that Israel is reluctant or unable to draw'. At the same time, however, it should be noted that the priests and diviners are careful to stress the second-person 'you' in the equation: 'perhaps he will lighten his hand on *you* and *your* gods and *your* land' (6.5b, emphasis added). Since one would assume that the priests and diviners occupy the same land, and worship the same deities, it might be expected that they would say '...*us*, and *our* gods, and *our* land'. As A.F. Campbell (2003: 79) observes, these priests reveal 'a remarkable capacity for distancing themselves from their clients'. So, while the priests and diviners are characterized as somewhat of a foil for the Elides, they are not without their own unique set of problems. Moreover, since 'small and great alike' are inflicted with the tumors, it would seem that even the priestly leaders of Philistia are not exempt from the hemorrhoid issue.

6.7-9

For industrialized societies in our present consumer age, it is fairly common to take a new car for a test drive. In the pre-industrial society of which the Deuteronomist is writing, the *test* drive in 1 Samuel 6 is of rather different order. The priests and diviners suggest that their compatriots devise a test to see if it really is the hand of God against them, or if the whole outbreak of hemorrhoids (and rats) has happened in one big run of bad luck. To that end, the people are instructed to load the ark and the box of models onto a new cart, to be pulled by two nursing cows that have recently given birth and never been yoked. The key element of test involves the movement of the cows, and whether or not they walk straight to the Israelite town of Beth-shemesh. Ancient bookmakers would no doubt have put long odds on this happening. In the first place, nursing mothers prefer to be with their young 'sons' (the name given, rather than 'calves'), as Hannah's conduct in chap. 1 will attest. Furthermore, cows that have never taken the yoke would probably not be excited about this career change later in life. One guesses that it would be hard to teach an old cow new tricks, especially when the cow's udder is dripping with unpasteurized milk. In the rather unlikely event that all this should happen, then it is '*he* who has done *us* this great harm', and the priests now include *themselves* in the equation. One gets the impression that the priests and diviners would not be upset should the experiment fail; if it succeeds, it might not be good for business. As Polzin (1993: 64) notes, 'Israel may be defeated in spite of its possession of God's ark and the ark itself may be seized, but all this is not to imply that God has lost any of his power over other people's gods'.

6.10-12

The 'men' dutifully execute the instructions of the clerics by hitching the two nursing cows to the wagon, while the 'sons' are penned up 'in the house'. The ark is loaded on the cart along with the grim cargo of the golden hemorrhoids and golden mice, and the test commences. The expected peregrination of the nursing cows would *not* be straight up the road, especially equipped with unfamiliar yoke, penned up sons, and udders full of milk. Yet in the event, this is precisely what happens. The unswerving march of the cows is highlighted through a verb ('and they were straight on the road'), and they do not swerve 'to the right nor to the left'. One is reminded of Deut. 28.14, where Moses exhorts the children of Israel not to 'turn aside from any of the words which I command you this day, to the right hand or to the left'. The cows retain the straight path of 'obedience' even though there is no visible driver of the cart. The detail that the cows are 'lowing' might even suggest that they are being driven against their will—and perhaps their better instincts, as it turns out, since they are on the road to slaughter.

6.13

According to the book of Joshua (15.10), Beth-shemesh is a border town within the territory of Judah. Border towns are always vulnerable when the neighboring country is hostile, but there are some advantages. In this instance, the advantage of residing in Beth-shemesh is that its inhabitants will be first to glimpse this extraordinary procession of the ark's return. The event takes place during the regular occupation of wheat harvest; while the Philistines have been subject to highly irregular activity, life goes on in Israel. There is a certain vividness to the Hebrew text of 6.13: 'Now Beth-shemesh was reaping the wheat harvest in the valley. They lifted up their eyes and saw the ark, and they rejoiced at the sight.' This phrasing nicely captures the sense of amazement, and, admittedly, the parade from the Philistine border would a rather odd combination of sight and sound: lowing cows towing a wagon loaded with the ark of the covenant and a box of hemorrhoids, all under the (surely incredulous) surveillance of the five Philistine overlords. While the NRSV renders the last part of 6.13 as 'they went with rejoicing to meet it' (following the Greek text), there are good reasons for retaining the Hebrew text 'they rejoiced at the sight' (as in the RSV). The notion of *visual perception* is important in the narratives of Eli: his sight fails him, and this seems emblematic of his lack of spiritual discernment. The same theme is continued here: while the people of Beth-shemesh are rejoicing at the 'sight' (ראה) of the ark's entry into their border town, many will soon suffer for 'looking' (ראה) into the ark, and the same verb is used to draw the connection.

6.14-18

Given the sheer number of odd things that happen with the return of the ark, it would be a challenge to conclude that 'mere chance' is the reason why disaster befalls the Philistine nation. There is one further detail in the ark's return that would strike the Israelite reader as interesting: of all places, the cows just happen to stop in a field belonging to one Joshua of Beth-shemesh. Several commentators note the symbolic connection between the mention of 'Joshua' here in 1 Samuel 6 and the host of Exodus allusions in this narrative. The period of the Exodus draws to something of a close with the appearance of 'Joshua' as the successor of Moses, and, fittingly, the foreign sojourn of the ark draws to a close in the field of someone with the same name. It might seem appropriate, given the reference to Joshua and the Exodus story, that in 6.15 the Levites make an appearance. However, such a group appearance of the Levites has not happened for a long time in the story, and will not happen again for quite some time. Such infrequency has led a number of scholars to conclude that this verse must be a later insertion to the text. Be that as it may, this Levite cameo might have the utility of illustrating the importance of *handling* the ark at the end of its exile. If so, the Deuteronomist is underscoring the issue of proper care and stewardship vs. the improper care and recklessness. The latter has been exemplified by both the house of Eli and the Philistines, and will be the experience of Beth-shemesh in a moment (see 6.19).

All the activity of the Levites—indeed, the whole adventure—takes place under the watch of the overlords, who are pictured as 'seeing it' in 6.16. There are a number of things the five Philistine overlords see. They see rejoicing (the antithesis of their recent experience with the ark), sacrifice (the opposite of their guilt offering), and they also see the result of their *test* drive, and probably conclude that indeed it is the hand of the LORD that has been heavily upon them. The several repetitions of the number 'five' in this stretch emphasizes the comprehensiveness of the 'striking': small and great alike, priest, diviner, and overlord—none are untouched by the heavy hand. The Philistine overlords also notice the sacrifices on 'the great stone' (if this is the correct reading of the difficult Hebrew text), a monument that remains as a witness 'to this day'. Thus the stone in Joshua's field is a reminder of return, just as the threshold stepping in Ashdod in 5.5 is a witness 'to this day'. The departure of the five overlords brings a measure of closure to the ark's Philistine captivity, sojourn, and release—but even though the exile of the ark has ended, the Deuteronomist's story is far from finished.

6.19-21

1 Samuel 6.19 is a verse that is burdened with controversy. While there is little doubt that a number of Israelites die, the reasoning is subject to considerable variance, as illustrated when the RSV and NRSV are compared. The NRSV renders the first part of 6.19 as follows: 'The descendants of Jeconiah did not rejoice with the people of Beth-shemesh when they greeted the ark of the LORD; and he killed seventy men of them. The RSV, by contrast,

renders this way: 'And he slew some of the men of Beth-shemesh, because they looked into the ark of the LORD; he slew seventy men of them'. Graeme Auld (2003: 218) summarizes the problem experienced when the ark re-enters Israelite territory:

> But there were casualties among the people because of divine displeasure. The ancient texts give quite different reasons: either one clan did not join in the celebrations (LXX), or some people looked into the ark (MT). The upshot is that the Israelite people of Beth-shemesh, not unlike the Philistines of Ashdod and Gath, want to be rid of it.

A further textual problem involves the precise number of casualties. While both the RSV and NRSV list 'seventy men' as the death toll, the Hebrew text actually reads 'seventy men, fifty thousand men'. The problem is compounded by the fact that the LXX also includes these numbers, and thus one needs more than a sleight of hand to pull a text-critical rabbit out of this hat. Historians are skeptical that 50,070 people actually resided in Beth-shemesh at this point in time, as it would be a vast and sprawling ancient Near Eastern metropolis, somewhat out of keeping with the pastoral setting of the story itself. Of course, the reader is entitled to conclude that the textual controversies are somewhat miniscule compared with the theological controversy of the 'striking' *within* the boundaries of Israel—at least in the MT and LXX, more Israelites are struck by God because of the ark than numerous wars with the Philistines. Could it be that the ark is no respecter of persons? In light of this event, the presence of the ark can obviously be a burden to Israel and the Philistines alike. The deaths in Beth-shemesh produce a key line in this stretch of narrative: 'Who is able to stand before the LORD, this holy God?' James Ackerman (1991: 1-24) understands this to be an important theme of the wider narrative, and to that end it is wise to bear this episode in mind, as this is not the last time that death will be associated with handling the ark (see 2 Sam. 6).

One assumes that Shiloh is not an option for returning the ark. Indeed, Shiloh will not feature prominently again as a spatial setting in the Deuteronomistic History. While other biblical traditions (such as Jer. 7 and Ps. 78) are cited as evidence that Shiloh is destroyed, the text of 1 Samuel does not elaborate. Perhaps the reader is meant to infer that this place of worship is destroyed by the Philistines in the aftermath of the battle of Ebenezer, yet is intentionally omitted to keep focus on the captured ark, the ark that will never return there again. From this point onward, there are other sanctuaries and places of worship, such as Nob (see 1 Sam. 21–22), that are highlighted in the story. Notably, Ps. 78.60 reads, 'He forsook his dwelling at Shiloh, the tent where he dwelt among humanity'. To my mind this fits with one of the themes of 1 Samuel: God 'moves' from one place to another, just as he moves away from the priestly house of Eli. The point is not so much the destruction of Shiloh; rather, the power of the illustration lies in God's *abandonment* of the site. Shiloh and the house of Eli are the past; something new will happen in the future. The same might be said for royal houses later in the story.

Honesty, we are often told, is the best policy. During the many vicissitudes of human history, the policy of honesty has been difficult to maintain, especially when a society is plagued. It is noticeable that the Philistines—upon experiencing mice and other irritations—adopt the strategy of transferring the ark from one region to the next.

In the second half of 6.20, the people of Beth-shemesh ask a further question: 'To whom shall he go so that we may be rid of him?' They are about to take a page out of the Philistine playbook, and send the ark to another region: but will they be honest about why they are sending it? It is difficult always to get the voice inflection right when reading Hebrew prose, but there certainly does *not* seem to be any lamentation when the people of Beth-shemesh send a message to another city in 6.21: 'So they sent messengers to the inhabitants of Kiriath-jearim, saying, "The Philistines have returned the ark of the LORD. Come on down and take it up to you!"'

A charitable reading of the text might conclude that, at the very least, the folks of Beth-shemesh are being economical with the truth. There could be a positive spin ('the Philistines have returned the ark!'), but the salient detail about the seventy (or 50,070) cadavers is omitted. But then, the place where they are sending this message—Kiriath-jearim—itself has a penchant for 'inaccurate précis'. To be sure, in Joshua 9 the reader of the Deuteronomistic History discovers that Kiriath-jearim is a city within the Gibeonite federation—the same Gibeonites who engraft themselves into Israel by means of deception. Thus, there is a certain historical retribution here: just as the Gibeonites (including Kiriath-jearim) have a tendency to deceive, so the people of Beth-shemesh send the ark to this city under (arguably) misleading circumstances. 1 Samuel 6 thus ends on a note of invitation, but the reader will have to wait until the next chapter to find out how the invitation is received.

1 Samuel 7

To this juncture in the story, two central narrative threads can be observed. First, chaps. 1–3 provide an overture for the book by means of an extended 'parable', whereby the having of sons is the image chosen by the author to introduce the complicated story of Israel having kings. Just as it is a challenge for parents to raise male offspring, so it will be a challenge for Israel *as a nation* to rear royal offspring. It is in this first narrative thread that two families are introduced: Elkanah's son Samuel is called to be a prophet, while words of judgment are spoken against Eli's house in general and his sons Hophni and Phinehas in particular. The second narrative thread is presented in chaps. 4–6, where the sons of Eli are killed in battle with the Philistines, and the ark of covenant is captured. During this second section of 1 Samuel, the ark wreaks havoc in Philistine territory before it is eventually returned to the land of Judah. 1 Samuel 7 occupies a point where these two narrative threads converge, and this pivotal chapter functions as a last meditation on judgeship and theocracy before the advent of kingship—from which there is no turning back. After a long hiatus, it is here in chap. 7 that Samuel re-emerges as a dominant character. There are two main events in this chapter: an elaborate ceremony of national repentance at Mizpah, and another battle against the Philistines. As a counterpoint to the previous battle in chap. 4, Israel is far more successful here in chap. 7, and a state of contrition is one obvious difference in the Israelite consciousness. The chapter concludes with a summary of Samuel's judging career, and ends on a note of peace, or at the very least, an absence of overt hostility.

7.1-2

At the conclusion of the previous chapter, there is an ambiguous invitation from the people of Beth-shemesh: they invite the residents of Kiriath-jearim to 'come on down' and fetch the ark, recently returned by the Philistines. As they conveniently exclude the fact that 50,070 have recently perished, the reader may be somewhat suspicious about their enthusiastic invitation. Now, at the beginning of 1 Samuel 7, there is a measure of closure as the people of Kiriath-jearim indeed come, and bring the ark up to 'the house of Abinadab on the hill'. The people of Kiriath-jearim then 'sanctify' Abinadab's son

Eleazar to 'watch over' the ark. Such actions have prompted some commentators to speculate that Abinadab and his family are Levites, but such lineage is not given in the narrative. If such levitical ancestry were the case, one might expect that such a detail would be provided by the Deuteronomist. In the absence of such clarification, the point of 'Kiriath-jearim' must lie elsewhere.

For the first time in a long narrative stretch, the family of Abinadab seem to be the ones who exercise proper care of the ark—at least, to the best of their (perhaps genealogically limited) abilities. There are two things that happen contrary to expectation: first, the people of Kiriath-jearim accept the invitation to receive the ark, and, second, for the first time in a long time, nothing bad happens when the ark comes to town. A reader may be surprised that the people of Kiriath-jearim (with their Gibeonite roots) handle the ark so well, in light of the recent disaster of Beth-shemesh (a city in Judah, perhaps with priestly roots; see Josh. 21.8-16). Given the fate of Gibeon, the ark residing in the Gibeonite city of Kiriath-jearim has a certain appropriateness; recall the penalty imposed on Gibeon for their deception: 'But Joshua made them that day hewers of wood and drawers of water for the congregation and for the altar of the LORD—even to this day—in the place that he should choose' (Josh. 9.27). Indeed, before the temple is built, 'Gibeon' is recorded as the site of a great high place (1 Kgs 3.4). At a minimum, then, the ark's lodging here in Kiriath-jearim functions as a 'warm up' for the Gibeonites later tasks. It also provides an instance of further foreshadowing, since this is not the last time the ark will reside with non-Israelites. There is a similar interlude when the ark lodges in the house of Obed-edom the Gittite in 2 Sam. 6.10-12.

After doing tremendous damage throughout the Philistine nation over the course of seven short months, the ark now sits still—with no recorded causalities—for a long twenty-year period. It is fitting that the ark hibernates in Kiriath-jearim, since it will be out of the picture for quite some time (see 14.18). The de-emphasis of the ark is complete when it leaves the (comparatively) high profile locale of Shiloh for Kiriath-jearim, a place that A.F. Campbell (2003: 36) labels 'an insignificant rural outpost'. The ark's 'suspended animation' ends in 2 Samuel 6, a narrative that resumes a number of themes previously encountered here. But 'twenty years' is a long time, and in the present context of 1 Samuel 7, this chronological notice that indicates a long passage of time serves to accelerate the plot, and take the reader to a new point in the story. There is a spiritual renewal (of sorts) during this time: while the ark of the LORD is in the 'house' of Abinadab, the 'house' of Israel 'wailed' (נָהָה) after the LORD. Commentators are unsure of the exact nuance of the verb 'to wail' or 'to lament' here, but whatever it means, it is surely better than 'forgetting' the LORD (as in Judg. 3.7). This state of 'mourning' (another translation option) means that the people are probably going to be more receptive to the words of Samuel in what follows.

7.3-4

The notice of 'twenty years' in 7.2 might also remind us that Samuel has not been seen or heard from in quite some time. At the end of chap. 3, the reader is told that the entire country 'from Dan to Beersheba' knows that Samuel is a prophet. After a long absence, now Samuel resurfaces with a cartload of prophetic conviction. His first words to the house of Israel contain a conditional utterance: '*If* you are returning to the LORD with all your heart...' While Samuel is not necessarily questioning the spiritual renewal in 7.2 of 'wailing', there is surely no harm in verifying their sincerity with some concrete tokens of repentance: 'then turn aside the foreign gods and the Ashtaroth from among you'. One is reminded of the earlier conditional phrase in 2.30, 'those who honor me I will honor, and those who despise me shall be treated with contempt'. The meaning of Samuel's utterance, of course, is that 'foreign gods' have been close at hand for quite some time. The implication, it seems, is that while Dagon is falling prostrate before the ark and ends up headless, Israel is guilty of idol worship. One suspects that the prophet would not see the comical side of this narrative situation.

The second half of 7.3 presents some further directives from the prophet: 'Establish your heart toward the LORD and serve him alone, and he will rescue you from the power of the Philistines'. Such an imperative seems to be a straightforward case of command and compliance. If Israel's heart is steadfast, the nation will be delivered from the clutch of the foreign adversary, much like the schema in the book of Judges. Here in 1 Sam. 7.4 Israel does not procrastinate: the people turn aside 'the Baalim and the Ashtaroth, and served the LORD alone'. Since both male and female genders are assumed with the mention of Baal and Asherah, the consensus is that fertility religion is the background of this reference, a form of cultic activity that usually involves sacred prostitution. The worship of such deities, according to Joyce Baldwin's statistics, would have Israel 'breaking the first and second commandments' (1988: 79). Such a calculation is patently not inaccurate, but one guesses that Baldwin may actually be providing a very conservative estimate; there are probably more than two commandments violated when the game of fertility religion is played. But Baal worship is not a very original sin, as there have been numerous struggles with 'foreign gods' and 'Ashtoreths' before, and earlier figures of authority in Israel have called for their expulsion. For example, Joshua implores the people to 'turn aside the foreign gods that are in your midst' in his farewell address (Josh. 24.23), and in response to a speech from the LORD himself in Judges 10, the people 'turned aside the foreign gods from their midst and served the LORD'

(10.16). The pattern has been that Israel turns aside from such activity for a period of time, but over the long term the same proclivities tend to resurface. In the present case of 1 Samuel 7, Israel is compliant with the prophet's directives, but it remains to be seen if the long-term cycle of idolatry is broken.

7.5-6

Samuel presumably is satisfied with the state of contrition, at least for the moment, and the 'turning aside' of the illegitimate deities seems preparatory for a national assembly of repentance. In 7.5 Samuel calls for a gathering of all Israel at 'Mizpah'. As Fokkelman (1993: 311) notes, 'Mizpah was part of narrative space in the finale of Judges'. Mizpah is the place in Judges 20–21 where the people assemble for matters of decision and the swearing of oaths. Furthermore, the reader of the Hebrew text notes a wordplay between Mizpah (מִצְפָּה) here in 1 Sam. 7.5 and the earlier verb in 4.13, when Eli is 'anxiously peering' (מְצַפֶּה). The wordplay provides a further point of connection between the various scenes so far in 1 Samuel. Another connection with the Eli narrative is invoked through the verb 'pray' (פלל); the motivation for gathering at Mizpah, as Samuel explains, is so he can pray for Israel. As Graeme Auld (2003: 218) notes,

> Samuel's offer to 'pray for' Israel to Yahweh (v.5) may provide the clue to the relationship of these passages. His offer appears to encourage the people's admission (v.6) that they have 'sinned'. And that verbal link reminds us of Eli's warning question (2.25) whether there is anyone who can pray for the one who has sinned against Yahweh. Samuel now claims to be such a one.

The ceremony of pouring out water is otherwise unattested, but (along with fasting) the idea seems clear enough: water is absolutely essentially commodity for life, yet here it is sacrificially poured forth as an offering to God. In the early chapters of 1 Samuel there is a great deal of cultic abuse. By contrast, this ceremony is a genuine sacrifice, with no apparent corruption. One gets the impression that the key issue here—in this long preface to monarchy—is not so much the ark of the covenant being back on Israelite soil, but rather a response to the holiness of God.

7.7-11

If the word 'Mizpah' has something to do with 'watching', then it is somewhat ironic that Israel's ritual of repentance at Mizpah does not go unobserved. The narrator discloses that the Philistines 'heard' of the spiritual assembly at Mizpah, and they gather their own military assembly and come up against Israel led by none other than the Philistine 'overlords' who have already been encountered in the narrative. It is not entirely clear why the Philistines initiate this conflict, but plainly they are not invited guests, and are intent on crashing the party. The Israelites are not—it should be emphasized—the least bit prepared for war. It would appear that in the face of this looming conflict, the Israelites cannot win if left to their own devices, and their position is a helpless one: when the people of Israel hear of the Philistine advance, they are 'afraid'. Faced with this imminent crisis, the words of the Israelites have a tone of desperation: 'Do not stop crying out to the LORD our God on our behalf, that he may rescue us from the power of the Philistines'. There is no call for bringing forth the ark from Shiloh that 'it may save', but rather there is a reliance on the prophet's mediation.

At this moment, it is Samuel who listens to the people. Previously in this chapter, it is the people who listen to the prophet and repent; now, there is an inversion, as the prophet listens to the people and prays. There is no call for the ark, but only a simple sacrifice and a prayer from the prophet. The prayer is immediately effective, as the LORD 'answered Samuel'. The syntax of the Hebrew text indicates that just as Samuel is offering the sacrifice, the Philistines commence hostilities and the battle begins. Based on the precedence of chap. 4, a reader could be forgiven for thinking that the odds are stacked against Israel. This must be the reckoning of the Philistine overlords. The last time these five leaders are mentioned, they are watching the ark returned by the cows to Beth-shemesh. The Philistine overlords might have wished they were back home, as the second half of 7.10 records a stunning reversal of expectation: 'but the LORD thundered with a great voice on that day against the Philistines. He confused them, and they were struck before Israel.' Not only is the unlikely Israelite victory a surprise, but the divine thunder must be meant to highlight the supernatural component: God is fighting for Israel. Samuel himself is not pictured as a military leader here; on the contrary, he is the one who makes intercession for the people, and it is certainly a successful mediation. In the previous battle of 1 Samuel 4, the Israelites flee; now, the Israelites are running again, but this time they are running *after* the Philistines, and not before them.

7.12-14

The name 'Ebenezer' forms an *inclusio* around the battles in 1 Samuel 4 and 7, as the prophet takes a stone and sets it up 'between Mizpah and Jeshanah, and he called its name "Ebenezer" and said, "Thus far the LORD has helped us"'. Most commentators point out that the two battles take place in different locales, which is a fairly easy point to concede. The significance surely lies in the symbolic name that Samuel gives to this place that reverses the disaster of chap. 4. Indeed, Peter Miscall notes that this battle in 1 Samuel 7 'repeats' the battle of Ebenezer in chap. 4: this battle has a number of parallels with the previous one, except that the result is the complete opposite (1986: 37). It has also been argued that 7.13-14 are out of place at this particular point in the narrative, and many have puzzled over the placement of these lines here. Robert Gordon (1986: 108) supplies a useful summary:

> The somewhat idealized picture of domestic stability and of territorial integrity is manifestly intended to demonstrate the sufficiency of the old theocratic order which is about to be called into question. To that end, no account is taken of Philistine garrisons in Israelite territory (cf. 10.5; 13.3), nor of the confrontations between Israel and the Philistines that were a feature of Saul's reign (cf. 14.52).

Alternatively, it has been argued that the temporal reference 'all the days of Samuel' pertains to the formal period of Samuel's judgeship, a period that ends with the inauguration of the monarchy. Regardless, at this point in the story one wonders if the Deuteronomist is painting a deliberate picture of a tranquil Israel on the eve of the request for a king. To be sure, 7.13-14 have a socio-political importance because the specific request for a king in the next chapter will surface in an atmosphere that has a distinct absence of overt hostility. In other words, it cannot be war that provides the impetus for the request for a king.

7.15-17

The chapter ends with a summary report of Samuel's lifelong vocation as a judge. Every year he makes a trip through the Bethel–Gilgal–Mizpah circuit where he 'judges' Israel. At the conclusion of this annual excursion he returns to Ramah (not Shiloh), the home of his parents, and the place where he evidently has his permanent residence. At Ramah as well he acts as a judge, and it is here that he builds 'an altar to the LORD'. The last judge prior to Samuel is Eli, the priestly leader who dies. Samuel is now pictured as one who inherits Eli's mantle of leadership, and indeed, it can be argued that this chapter presents Samuel at his finest. Moreover, as the chapter as a whole is surveyed, things go well for the nation. As Gordon (1986: 106) further remarks, 'In short, everything is under the control of Yahweh and his chosen representative. To ask for a king in these circumstances would, it is implied, be an impertinence'. Despite this chapter being a very fine hour for the prophet Samuel, he is about to be displaced as the central leadership figure in national life.

1 Samuel 8

The various narrative threads of 1 Samuel together lead to this event: the climactic moment (thus far in the story) when Israel asks for a king. Noticeably, there is an absence of apparent hostilities, and the request for a king takes place during a time of relative calm. After a general introduction that highlights Samuel's age, his dynastic impulse and the corruption of his sons, the remainder of this chapter seems to take place on one fine day. There are four main events that unfold. First, the elders present their case and request to the prophet. Second, the prophet's reaction is highlighted by the Deuteronomist, as well as some direct speech from the LORD himself. Third, Samuel presents a long discourse on the 'judgment of the king', and this speech represents the bulk of the chapter and perhaps even its dramatic center. Fourth, the chapter closes on a note of *unfinalization* as Samuel dismisses the people and they all return to their homes.

8.1-3

For the second time in the story, the reader is told that a major leader in the nation is 'old'. In 2.21 we learn that 'Eli is very old, and he heard about all that his sons were doing to all Israel'. There is a similar construction and similar language at the beginning of chap. 8: Samuel is old, and he appoints his sons as judges for Israel. Eli's two sons Hophni and Phinehas are totally corrupt, and their conduct does not reflect well on their father. While Eli's family has enjoyed a long dynasty as priestly leaders in Israel, this privileged house is in rapid decline, and soon will be begging for bread. Samuel's two sons—the sympathetic reader hopes—would be different, but immediately after the Deuteronomist introduces Joel and Abijah, there is a disappointing disclosure in 8.3: 'But his sons did not walk in his ways: they swerved (וַיִּטּוּ) after unjust gain, they took bribes, and caused justice to swerve (וַיַּטּוּ)'. The welfare of the nation is compromised through this kind of fraudulence and judicial corruption, and such practices are warned about in the Torah (see, e.g., Deut. 16.18-20).

It is impossible to know if Samuel is aware of Joel and Abijah's conduct, and equally, it is not clear why they are way down south in Beersheba, of all places. Some commentators wonder if these men—who are behaving badly—are a poor reflection of Samuel's parenting. While this issue might be worth thinking about—and surely the antecedent example of Eli comes to mind—I am not sure that this is the main point. There are a number of poor fathers in the story, and more to come (David, for instance), but the Deuteronomist seems to be doing something else here. This detail about Samuel's sons expands on the question raised in the earlier narrative thread in chaps. 1–3: If having kings is like having sons, what happens when kings have sons? Contained here is the surmise that dynastic leadership creates more problems than it solves. The very fact that Eli's sons are corrupt (coupled with the unsuccessful dynastic appointment of Eli's protégé Samuel) is intended, so it seems, to underscore this point. Barbara Green (2003: 181) has a sobering observation: 'Corrupt dynastic sons lie at the base of the royal tree'. Time will tell, but it may be that the text bears this thesis.

8.4-5
After the general introduction of Joel and Abijah that continues the father–son theme, the next scene features the elders of Israel gathering themselves together and approaching Samuel at Ramah (where the prophet's 'house' is located; see 7.17). One recalls that the last time we heard from the elders is 4.4, when collectively they have the bright idea of bringing the ark onto the battlefield. Perhaps they have learned their lesson, and the present case will involve a better scheme. Perhaps they have a plan to send back the ark to the Philistines, and further afflict their foes with 'tumors' et al. Any such hopes are quickly dashed. The elders approach Samuel in 8.5, and begin their speech by pointing out what the reader (and conceivably Samuel as well) already knows: 'Behold, you are old'. It may have been prudent to begin by saying 'Behold, you are wise', or 'Behold, you have judged us well'. But hindsight, unlike the eyes of Eli, is rarely dim. In addition to telling Samuel that he is old, the elders also tell him, 'your sons do not walk in your ways'. Whether Samuel is previously aware of his sons' dishonesty is now immaterial; he is, at the very least, now aware of the charge.

It is possible that these two incontrovertible facts—Samuel's age and the corruption of Joel and Abijah—are a pretext for a request. Such a supposition appears confirmed when the elders implore the prophet: 'now, appoint a king to judge us, like all the nations'. Abrupt as it may sound, the elder's request for the appointment of a king is not entirely original or without precedent in Israel. Within the pages of the Former Prophets, one recalls the series of unfortunate events in Judges 9, including the precipitating moment in 9.6 when Abimelech is crowned: 'And all the citizens of Shechem came together…and made Abimelech king, by the oak of the pillar at Shechem'. As Robert Gordon (1986: 106) notes, this is a not a high point in the history of Israel's leadership: 'Monarchy was not indigenous to Israelite society, and it is surely no coincidence that Abimelech, the engineer and, initially, the beneficiary of the short-lived Shechemite experiment in monarchy, was Gideon's son by a Canaanite concubine'. One might have expected that the grim example of Abimelech's brief reign of (t)error might serve as something of a warning, but it does not: 'appoint a king for us', the elders ask, 'like other nations'. While the elders seem to be implying that politics is a ruthless game—and Samuel's advanced age and shady sons count against him—one still wonders if this is a rather expedient *excuse* for their request. Is this simply one more rebellion, though conveniently founded on a reasonable grievance? The Deuteronomist seems interested in inviting reflection on this matter.

8.6

Samuel's reaction to the elders' demand represents an important moment in his characterization. So far, Samuel has appeared as a powerful leader, but the various shades in his personality have yet to emerge. The fact that Samuel has corrupt sons is probably the first signs of a more complex character, with all the strengths and shortcomings common to the well-developed personages in biblical literature. Since the Deuteronomist now chooses to filter the story of the advent of kingship through the eyes of Samuel, it behooves the reader to pay attention to such matters of characterization. In 8.6, Samuel's inner reaction is presented as the elders submit their request: 'Now the thing was evil in the eyes of Samuel, because they said, "Give us a king to judge us". And Samuel prayed to the LORD.' The first question that emerges is: Why specifically is the matter evil in the eyes of the Samuel? It seems that there are two options: either Samuel is displeased for *personal* or for *theological* reasons.

To begin with the latter scenario, it is plausible that the prophet is angry for theological reasons. After all, Israel is supposed to have unique status as 'a kingdom of priests and a holy nation' (Exod. 19.6). Even Gideon—despite a litany of personal issues with ephods and concubines—recognizes that God is Israel's head: 'I will not rule over you, and my son will not rule over you; the LORD will rule over you' (Judg. 8.23).

So it is perfectly legitimate for Samuel to be upset for theological reasons, but if this is the case, then the part of the elders' speech that should particularly annoy him would be the phrase 'like the other nations'. Yet, the part of the speech that is highlighted and filtered through his perspective is 'Give us a king to *judge* us'. Moreover, there is a slight word change: the elders use the verb 'appoint' (שִׂים) in 8.5, whereas Samuel's repetition in 8.6 uses the verb 'give' (נָתַן). Of course, these terms are interchangeable enough not to warrant much suspicion, but the subtle change in wording implies that 8.6 is given to the reader from Samuel's point of view.

Consequently, one guesses that the matter is evil in the eyes of Samuel for *personal* reasons in the first instance. As Peter Miscall (1986: 47) notes, 'Samuel deeply resents the people's demand that he exercise his authority to demote or even remove himself by appointing another leader, a king, especially one who will govern or judge (*shapat*) the people as he has been doing'. Virtually every reader of this narrative should be able to sympathize with Samuel's plight. To be declared vocationally redundant is surely not an easy thing to manage. It is to the prophet's credit, therefore, that his first response is to 'pray'. Such an intercessory reflex runs in the family, since on numerous occasions Samuel's mother is the subject of same verb. Previously, Hannah prays for a son who is destined for leadership; now that son prays about the new leadership paradigm rapidly emerging. Furthermore, Samuel's mother once prayed 'He will give strength to his king'; ironically, a king is exactly what the elders have just asked her son for.

8.7-10

For the second time in the story, the LORD speaks directly to Samuel. On the first occasion that God speaks to Samuel in 3.11-14, the speech contains a stern word of judgment spoken against the house of Eli. However, on this present occasion in chap. 8, the divine word is rather different. Samuel may have been expecting God to condemn the institution of kingship, but just as the ark in Philistine territory probably did not conform to local expectation, so God's word here in 8.7-9 contains a few surprises.

In an optimistic contrast to 3.11-14, the word to Samuel here begins in an almost pastoral tone. If the reader has been wondering whether Samuel's reaction to the elders' demand for a king is 'evil in his eyes' for personal or theological reasons, then God himself provides the answer in 8.7: 'Listen to the people's voice, to everything they've said to you. Indeed, its not *you* they have rejected; rather, it is *me* they have rejected from being king over them.' After assuring Samuel that *he the prophet* is not the central issue here, God proceeds to give Samuel a lecture in Historical Theology 101: 'this rejection of me', to paraphrase the divine speech, 'is really nothing new, it is a continuation of the pattern ever since I brought them out of Pharaoh's clutches in Egypt. Now you, Samuel, with your personal rejection here, have an idea of what I have experienced for centuries.'

Even more surprising than this pastoral chiding of the prophet is the divine willingness to accede to the demand for a king. While the LORD does acquiesce to the elders' less-than-sagacious request, he instructs Samuel as follows: 'So now, listen to their voice, only solemnly testify against them, and tell them about the judgment of the king who will reign over them'. The difficult phrase is 'judgment of the king' (מִשְׁפַּט הַמֶּלֶךְ), rendered in both the RSV and NRSV as 'the ways of the king'. Joyce Baldwin (1988: 85) remarks that the phrase can also be translated as the *justice* of the king, and 'there could be an element of satire in the word play, especially in the light of what follows'. Once this phrase—which hitherto has not appeared in the Hebrew Bible—is translated, it still remains to determine what exactly it means. Numerous commentators point to Deut. 17.14-20 as the background text, and this hypothesis seems sensible.

The context of Deuteronomy 17, we recall, is the long speech of Moses to the children of Israel on the threshold of entering the land of promise. Moses has been well acquainted with this group for some time, long enough to know that the days will surely come when they will ask for a king. If this is to be the case, Moses deliberates, then the king must act according to certain guidelines, a number of which Moses then articulates. Specifically, commentators point to Deut. 17.18-20 as containing the heart of the matter: 'And when he sits on the throne of his kingdom, he shall write for himself in a book a copy of this law, from that which is in the charge of the Levitical priests; and it shall be with him, and he shall read in it all the days of his life, that he may learn to fear the LORD his God, by keeping all the words of this law and these statutes, and doing them; that his heart may not be lifted up above his brethren, and that he may not turn aside from the commandment, either to the right hand or to the left; so that he may continue long in his kingdom, he and his children, in Israel'. Even a casual reading of this text in Deuteronomy suggests a number of restraints and prescriptions, and the centrality of the 'copy of this law'. The reader of 1 Samuel 8 may anticipate this kind of detail in the next speech of Samuel to the people. The audience for this speech, as 8.10 makes clear, is 'the people who were asking (הַשֹּׁאֲלִים) from him a king'. The reader of the Hebrew text observes that participle 'asking' contains the root consonants of the name Saul, the first king and what the people are asking for.

8.11-18

'In those days there was no king in Israel, and each man did what was right in his own eyes'. The last line of Judges describes the anarchy in the pre-monarchial days, yet Samuel's testimony in 8.11-18 will imply that, without using these exact terms, the king will do what is right in *his* eyes. As Peter Miscall (1986: 51) reflects, in these days of 1 Samuel 8 there is going to be a king in Israel, but the matter is evil in the eyes of the prophet. Statistically, the longest prose speech so far in the book is courtesy of the itinerant man of God in chap. 2, as he unfolds his lengthy judgment and prognostication of doom on the wayward house of Eli. While this prose record may not finally be broken until Samuel's speech in chap. 12, the speech of 8.11-19 functions as a serviceable warm-up. In fact, scholars often see similarities between the two speeches of Samuel in chaps. 8 and 12, but a lot of water has to go under the bridge before the reader arrives at the latter speech. Meanwhile, 8.11-18 has a political drama of its own that merits some attention. Since there a certain extemporaneous flavor to this speech, I will venture the following translation of Samuel's address:

> He said, 'This will be the judgment of the king who'll reign over you: he'll take your sons and appoint them to his chariots and horsemen, and they'll run before his chariots. Some he'll appoint for himself as unit captains of thousands and unit captains of fifties, others will plow his fields and gather his harvest, or make weapons for his war and accessories for his chariot. He'll take your daughters as aestheticians, cooks and bakers. He'll take the best of your fields, vineyards and olive gardens so he can give them to *his* servants, and ten percent of your seed and vineyard production he'll allocate for his officers and staff. He'll take your servants, your maids, your select chosen men, and your donkeys, and they will do his work. Ten percent of your flocks will be his, and you'll all be his slaves. And one day you *will* cry out because of the king whom you've chosen for yourselves, but on that day the LORD *will not* answer you.'

The prophet is instructed by God to delineate the 'justice (or judgment) of the king', which, as mentioned above, is a somewhat elusive phrase at this point in the story. As Bruce Birch (1998: 1028) comments, 'The phrase seems to indicate some formal standard for the behavior of kings. Both 1 Sam. 10.25 (using a similar phrase) and Deut. 17.17-18 imply a written document to which kings were accountable. Both of these passages, however, imply that the document was some sort of restraint on the abuse of kingship, whereas Samuel's speech in vv. 10-18 provides a catalog of abuse.' On the whole, the installation of the king seems very expensive for the average Jo(seph) in Israel, as military conscription, high taxes, real estate misappropriation, cronyism, patronage, sponsorship scandals, and slavery seem costly indeed. Samuel's description of the king's 'justice' certainly does not paint a flattering picture, and some commentators have the distinct impression that the speaker is not a little sore on the subject. All this corruption, ironically, reminds us of other corrupt leaders, such as Samuel's sons, 'who turn aside after bribes', a detail that commences this very chapter and serves as part of the excuse for the elders' request for a king. The speech has a fairly bleak conclusion. In the previous chapter, Samuel 'prays' and God hears. By contrast, he says now, people will cry out and God will *not* hear.

From the vantage point of the wider Deuteronomistic History, a reader has to concede that kings can certainly be guilty of abusing their privileges. In 1 Samuel 22 Saul warns his Benjaminite colleagues that their property and military interests are threatened by the advance of 'the son of Jesse'. Further, King Ahab will appropriate the vineyard of his neighbor Naboth in 1 Kings 21. Even the 'runners' that Samuel mentions appear later in the story, as Robert Gordon (1986: 110-11) notes: 'The employment of "runners" is a form of vanity particularly associated with young charioteers like Absalom...and Adonijah'. One is reminded of Anthony Trollope's words: 'When a man has nailed fortune to his chariot-wheels he is apt to travel about in rather a proud fashion' (*Framley Parsonage*, Chapter VIII). So, on a number of levels, Samuel's speech does form a preview of what many royal personages will do, and such facts are unwise to deny. At the same time, the reader is obliged to ask whether Samuel is giving the whole story. Robert Polzin (1993: 85-88) argues that only one side of the kingship enterprise is provided here, and that the prophet's bias *against* kingship emerges. In other words, Polzin and other commentators wonder, for instance, about the absence of the advice in Deuteronomy 17, where the king is required to make a copy of 'the law'. Along these lines, Lyle Eslinger (1985: 270-71) maintains that Samuel's approach here is not to *prescribe* the justice of the king, but rather to *describe* the profound 'disadvantages of the monarchy'. Such reflection is important at this crucial stage of the narrative, and it would seem evident that Samuel does not have a high view of kingship in the least. While numerous scholars in the past have equated the opinions of Samuel with those of the Deuteronomist, such a merger may be imprudent. The words of a character in a story are not necessarily synonymous with the views of the implied author, and this caveat should be borne in mind as our analysis continues.

8.19-22

All of Samuel's passion and rhetorical resources has little efficacy as his speech concludes, and an intractable 'no' from the constituency is the response. Notably, there is a complete absence of serious dialogue about Samuel's legitimate concerns, and there is no serious theological reflection about the impact of kingship on Israel as a unique nation. The people refuse to listen to Samuel, and their 'no' is punctuated with a reaffirmation of their desire to be like the other nations, with the added *résumé* item that the king should also fight their 'battles'. It is possible that this supplementary mention of warfare is an emotional appeal to the baser kinds of tribal sensibilities, and is far more like a sound byte than intelligent political discourse. A generous reader could even argue that Samuel is *intentionally* telling only one side of the story in order to persuade the elders of Israel that their request is madness. But if this were the case, it is a moot point, since the people are not willing to listen. Just like Hophni and Phinehas do not listen despite Eli's warning in chap. 2, a similar situation unfolds here in chap. 8, as the people do not listen to Samuel's warning.

While the refusal of the people to listen to Samuel may carry the day as the last word in the request for a king, Samuel is not finished speaking: 'And Samuel heard all the words of the people, and he spoke them in the ears of the LORD' (8.21). The dialogue between Samuel and God suggests that the prophet is far from peripheral—in fact, the prophet is central. The experiment of kingship may not be a complete failure if this dialogue can continue. God evidently hears when Samuel speaks 'in his ears', but again God is willing to accommodate the request of elders: 'Listen to their voice', the LORD commands Samuel, 'and cause a king to reign over them'. Once more, the divine reaction confounds expectation, and God's willingness to go along with this decision is much like a longsuffering parent when a child stubbornly makes a foolish demand.

After God instructs his prophet to cause a king to reign over them, in the final line of the chapter Samuel says to the people 'Go, each man to his city'. This abrupt dismissal can be read in one of two ways: either Samuel is sending the people home so the selection process can begin, or, for reasons only obliquely hinted at, he is deliberately obfuscating. As Graeme Auld (2003: 218) remarks, 'Whether in his final order that the people should disperse (v. 22b) Samuel is really obeying the Deity or only seeking to forestall his will is an open question'. There are readers who will have some sympathy for the prophet: his leadership is rejected, and the people are plunging recklessly down a road that leads to exile. Still, God has unequivocally commanded it, and the prophet is a man under orders—regardless of personal opinion on the matter. Bruce Birch (1998: 1029) balances a number of issues by concluding that Samuel views the request for a king 'as a personal affront and is not immediately responsive to the people's needs or God's command'. Further, Diana Edelman (1991: 42) provides a useful assessment:

> Samuel's sending everyone home in response to the divine command comes unexpectedly, introducing ambiguity. Has he not obeyed God because he is upset about his personal loss of leadership? Is the narrative audience to understand him to be stalling because he fears Israel's inability to remain faithful to the stipulations of kingship? Or are we to conclude that Samuel is merely awaiting more specific divine initiative in the selection and announcement of a suitable candidate?

One recalls in the opening chapter that Hannah—out of overweening attachment to her child—procrastinates the weaning and elicits a comment from her husband (1.23). In a not dissimilar way, God is committed to his offspring, and is willing to submit to this request. But God will do so on God's own terms. The elders have previously asked for the ark to be brought onto the battlefield in chap. 4, only for the ark to be captured. Yet in the ark's captivity there is surprise and reversal, and a very clear manifestation of sovereignty in the narrative. So might it be with this request: God can take an unwise decision and transform it. For a community in exile, leadership decisions of the past clearly affect the fate of the nation, and so 1 Samuel 8 would have currency for a readership that has experienced the trauma of such events. The monarchic option, as we will discover by the end of 2 Kings 25, was not a successful choice or exercise of leadership by the elders. Within the overall plan of the narrative, 1 Samuel 8 seems designed to present an opportunity to reflect soberly on kingship as a leadership paradigm on the eve of its installation. As Robert Gordon (1986: 105) comments,

> For an institution which promised so much, the Israelite monarchy turned out to be a costly failure... And yet, if the monarchy is a monument to human weakness, it is also a symbol of divine grace, for Israel may put her disobedience behind her and look confidently ahead if only she will maintain covenant obedience to her God.

It is this thread of grace that we will be interested in discerning in the pages ahead.

1 SAMUEL 9

There is an inevitability—if nothing else, based on two speeches by God himself in 8.7 and 8.22—that Israel's request for a king will be granted. Such a figure will no doubt be afforded a high degree of narrative prominence, the beginning of which is the subject matter of 1 Samuel 9. Notably, both the prophet and king have been 'asked' for at different times and in different ways in the story. It is thus not overly surprising that chap. 9 has a host of connections with chap. 1. Indeed, through the root 'ask'—deployed numerous times in chap. 1—the reader may be led to believe that the fates of king and prophet are deeply interwoven. It is here in 1 Samuel 9—at long last—that prophet and king come face to face. 1 Samuel 9 is organized in such a way that the meeting between ensconced prophet and fledgling king is the central event. What begins as a mundane search for some lost female donkeys results in an unexpected discovery. Despite some scholars who have argued that the first few episodes of chap. 9 are folkloristic and disconnected, I am suggesting otherwise—namely, that the various scenes in the story (the genealogy, the unintended question 'What is a prophet?', the 'aborted' type-scene, the royal search for the prophetic word, and the sacrificial meal) all bring to the table important themes that will resonate throughout the narrative. The relationship between king and prophet will be an uneasy one in 1 Samuel 9–15, and numerous tensions are foreshadowed in the scenes surrounding their first meeting.

9.1-2

Even a superficial glance at the beginning of 1 Samuel 9 reveals a narrative strategy that is different from chap. 8. In chap. 8, the central action takes place during a long stressful day: the elders request a king, Samuel demurs with an exhaustive yet ineffective restraining order, and the events culminate with Samuel sending everyone home. Chapter 8 thus ends on a note of ambivalence, with people summarily dismissed by the prophet: 'Go, each man to his city'. The initial tone of chap. 9 is antithetical: it steps back in time, so to speak, with a genealogy. In fact, the beginning of chap. 9 closely resembles chap. 1. Notably, Kish (the father of Saul) is introduced in the exact same manner as Elkanah (the father of Samuel) in chap. 1. As Barbara Green (2003: 196) observes, there is another narrative coincidence: when the genealogical lists are tabulated, Samuel would be the 'sixth son' of the list in chap. 1 (Elkanah, Jeroham, Elihu, Tohu, Zuph, and Samuel). Similarly, Saul would be the 'sixth son' of the list in chap. 9 (Kish, Abiel, Zeror, Becorath, Aphiah, and Saul). The reader does not necessarily need a 'sixth sense' to infer that prophet and king are further linked. Just as the root 'ask' (שאל) is used numerous times in chap. 1 to foreshadow the connection between Samuel and Saul, so now in chap. 9 this genealogical linking confirms the shared destiny of these two characters whose lives are deeply intermeshed. Both of these 'sons'—Samuel and Saul—are 'asked for', and together they will make a lasting contribution to the institution of kingship in Israel.

There are two other features of Kish's introduction that merit reflection. First, Kish is described as a 'man of valor' (גבור חיל), a Hebrew expression that means either a man of property or an accomplished warrior. The former sense is probably intended here, but even so, one can expect that the *son of Kish* will be a man with landed interests or a warrior. Second, and more ominously, Kish is from the tribe of Benjamin, a fact that is underscored *twice* in 9.1. Near the end of Judges, the tribe of Benjamin is compared to 'Sodom', and nearly eliminated. Accordingly, one can certainly argue that Benjamin carries a certain stigma, and specifically the town of Gibeah in Benjamin (see the horrific episodes of Judg. 19–20). The reader soon discovers that Gibeah is Saul's hometown (1 Sam. 10.10). It seems prudent to agree with Moshe Garsiel (1985: 78-84) that although Saul will be sympathetically portrayed in these opening episodes, there is also a less than positive ambiance that envelops his *character zone*, and such an ambiance is infused throughout the forthcoming narrative.

Perhaps most importantly, Kish has a son. The name of the son is 'Saul', and his name ('asked') immediately connects with chap. 8 when the elders are 'asking' for a king. There is ample focus on the outward characteristics of this son. Saul is tall, an attribute that will be emphasized in the forthcoming narrative. On this head and shoulders factor, Robert Alter (1999: 46) remarks: 'Saul's looming size, together with his good looks (טוב), seems to be an outward token of his capacity for leadership, but as the story unfolds with David displacing Saul, his physical stature becomes associated with a basic human misperception of what constitutes fitness to command'. Indeed, hearing this physical detail in light of Hannah's song, to be 'tall' can be perceived as a negative endowment: 'Do not amplify your speech, O tall one, O tall one!' (1 Sam. 2.3). 'To be tall in the narrative of 1 Samuel', as Barbara Green (2003: 203) intones, 'is risky, inviting a fall'. Graeme Auld (2003: 219) has a useful summary of these opening verses of the chapter:

> The father of Saul is introduced (v.1) in terms very similar to those of the father of Samuel (1.1), and this is just the first of several comparisons and contrasts the text very economically suggests we should make. Saul's name

means 'asked for', and of course Samuel was asked for by his mother. Like Samuel, too (2.26), he is described as 'good'. The Hebrew word rendered 'young man' can also mean 'choice', of high quality, and that reminds us awkwardly that the house of now rejected Eli was once 'chosen' by Yahweh (2.28). More immediately, it recalls Samuel's warning (8.18) that the people would have cause to complain of the king they had 'chosen' for themselves.

9.3-4

If v. 1 establishes Kish as a 'man of property', then v. 3 indicates that Kish has taken a loss, as his 'female donkeys' are missing. This vanishing act sets the stage for the first dialogue of 1 Samuel 9, as Kish speaks to his son Saul. There has been a previous occasion in the narrative when a father speaks to his sons: when the commands of Eli to his sons Hophni and Phinehas fall on deaf ears. Now, Kish entreats his son: 'Take one of the servants with you, and arise, go, seek the female donkeys'. No reply from Saul is recorded, but 9.4 documents the geographical contours of the journey to find the donkeys: 'So he passed over the hill country of Ephraim, through the land of Shalishah, without finding. Then they passed over the land of Shaalim, but there was nothing. He then passed over the land of Benjamin, without finding'. The wordless obedience of Saul contrasts with the previous conduct of other 'dynastic' sons, notably the sons of Eli (who are called 'sons of Belial') and the sons of Samuel (who are dishonest judges in Beersheba). In my view, this is part of the sympathetic side of Saul's characterization. He is from Benjamin, but this stigma is far from *his* fault, and he is an obedient son, in contrast to Hophni, Phinehas, Joel, and Abijah. These points in Saul's favor need to be raised, since a tragic dimension of Saul's portrait will emerge in due course.

This is the only formal appearance of Kish in the narrative, although on several occasions he will be referred to by other characters. The most important utility of Kish's speech is that it provides a context of paternal command to illustrate the filial obedience of Saul, even to the point of earnestly seeking the donkeys throughout somewhat obscure topography. Despite some earnest attempts by scholars to pinpoint the exact route of Saul and his companion, Lyle Eslinger notes the difficulty of reading this geographical itinerary in a realistic fashion (1985: 289-90). While Diana Edelman (1991: 43) suggests that 'Saul's trek through the southeastern portion of the Ephraimite hill country in search of the she-asses seems to serve as an anticipatory tour of his future kingdom and thus should function to foreshadow plot developments', it may be that the otherwise unattested locations of Shalishah (שלשה) and Shaalim (שעלים) are highlighted because they form modest wordplays on the name 'Saul' (שאול). If Saul's tour through minor-league villages anticipates his kingdom, then one might ask about how impressive this kingdom will be.

9.5

A turning point in the story occurs when Saul reaches the land of Zuph, as this locale is the spatial setting for his first moment of direct speech in the story. It is significant that Saul's first words take place in the obscure land of Zuph because of the intertextual connection with 1 Samuel 1: the only other place where the term 'Zuph' occurs in the entire Deuteronomistic History is in the genealogy of Samuel in the opening chapter. Saul, it would appear, is drawing near to the orbit of Samuel, and his ironic first words ('Come, let's go back') are spoken in Samuel's neighborhood. J.P. Fokkelman (1993: 8) develops this point, and feels that it is not accidental that the clan of Zuph and the land of Zuph are only mentioned in 1 Sam. 1.1 and 9.5:

> It is not by chance that the territory of the Zuph clan occurs once again, directly after the introduction of another father, at the beginning of chap. 9. The farmer's son Saul scours 'the land of Zuph', trying to find the she-asses of Kish; the attempt seems fruitless, but in the meantime he has already got close to the seer Samuel, who himself has the task of being on the lookout—for the future king.

The mention of Zuph provides yet another example of the connection between prophet and king. Unknown to Saul, the search for lost property is actually bringing him ever closer to another son who was 'asked for', and this meeting is where the plot of this chapter is moving. Saul is journeying toward Samuel—a character with a shared background—and thus Saul's future is intimately tied up with someone who has a preternaturally overlapping past.

As for the content of Saul's first words spoken in the land of Zuph—'Come, let's go back, in case my father ceases from the donkeys and worries about us'—several components of his character are revealed in this utterance. Robert Alter's (1999: 47) comments are suggestive: 'According to the general principle of biblical narrative that the first reported speech of a character is a defining moment of characterization, Saul's first utterance reveals him as a young man uncertain about pursuing his way, and quite concerned about his father'. Alter continues: 'But as this first dialogue unfolds, it is Saul's uncertainty that comes to the fore because at every step he has to be prodded and directed by his own servant'. To be sure, similar accents of hesitation and uncertainty—for a variety of reasons—will recur in Saul's discourse as the narrative continues. Furthermore, there are two levels to Saul's first words. On one level, Saul is simply commenting about their ineffective journey, and suggesting that he and his servant turn back out of concern for his father. But on another level, Saul's words 'Come, let's go back' are surely ironic in that there is *no returning* from this journey that leads to kingship. I would suggest that this intentional literary strategy will continue as 1 Samuel 9 continues: there will be other occasions where Saul's words mean more than he intends.

9.6-7

Saul's first words are directed to the servant lad who accompanies him on the fruitless quest through Ephraim ('double fruit') for the lost donkeys. In 9.3, Kish instructs Saul to 'Take one of the servants with you'. Saul is obedient to his father, but he chooses a rather talkative servant lad, and this character becomes Saul's interlocutor in his first speech in the narrative. If it was up to Saul, he and his servant lad would have turned back (and alas, life would have been different for the son of Kish). But it is not up to Saul, and from *kingship* there is no turning back. Hence, Saul and his servant lad are destined to continue their journey, in no small part because of the servant lad's rather voluminous speech: 'Behold, please, there is a man of God in this city, and the man is honorable—everything he speaks really happens. Now, let's go there, perhaps he will tell us our journey that we should walk upon.' For a servant lad, Saul's companion is remarkably well informed, knowing the minute specificities of the 'man of God'. The reader immediately recalls the 'man of God' who erupted on the scene at the end of chap. 2 and spoke doom for the sons of Eli. Perhaps this man of God will have better news for the son of Kish. The man is 'honored', according to the servant lad's testimony, and the same root (כבד) is a key word in the description of the fall of the house of the Eli.

The servant lad's testimony about this man of God triggers Saul's double query: 'But how can we go? What can we bring (וּמַה־נָּבִיא) the man?' For the second time in the chapter, Saul's words mean *more* than he intends. Several commentators have observed that Saul's question, 'What can be bring?', has two layers of meaning, since the same words (מַה־נָּבִיא) can also be read as 'What is a prophet?' As Robert Polzin (1993: 93) notes,

> What is most significant about this initial question in the initial dialogue of this chapter is its double meaning. Besides its obvious import in context, the phrase also expresses the main question of this and the following chapters: given that Israel is to have a king, what is the manner of the office that God has chosen to keep him in line?

That Saul would 'ask' such a question is surely ironic in terms of the larger storyline: from beginning to end, questions surround Saul's *character zone*. These are the first questions Saul—whose name means 'asked'—asks in the narrative, and there are many more to come. In the present context, there is a certain narrative poignancy to Saul ('asked') asking for the prophet: the people ask the prophet for a king, now the soon-to-be-anointed king asks 'What is a prophet?' On the one hand, this question raises the issue, as Polzin argues, about the prophet's role in the monarchy. Thus, it is communicated to the reader that this is a story about the office of the prophet *as much as* it is a story about the call of the king. On the other hand, as Fokkelman (1993: 283) suggests, the question previews Saul's own 'prophetic ecstasy' shortly to come in chap. 10. The question 'what is a prophet' anticipates the more ominous (or at least enigmatic) question 'is Saul among the prophets?' At a minimum, it must be that this question 'What is the prophet?' provides further illustration that Saul and Samuel are deeply entangled in this narrative.

9.8-10

The role of the servant lad in this episode has a curious parallel in 1 Sam. 16.18, where 'one of the servant lads' (אֶחָד מֵהַנְּעָרִים—the same language as Kish uses in 9.3) speaks up and provides information about a son of Jesse. In both of these episodes—1 Samuel 9 and 1 Samuel 16—a servant lad knows or suggests something that Saul does not seem to know, and in both cases the information is vital to the plot. Just as the servant lad in chap. 16 says some remarkable things about the son of Jesse, so the servant lad in chap. 9 has an ace up his sleeve as *there is found* (niphal passive verb) a coin in his pocket—a bit of profit for the prophet. Perhaps this is a further example of what Ferdinand Deist (1993: 7-18) refers to as 'coincidence as a motif of divine intervention' in 1 Samuel 9, or a further link in what David Gunn calls 'the chain of fortunate coincidences' (1980: 61). There are a host of seeming accidents that keep the plot moving, as though Saul is inexorably drawn toward the prophet despite his inclination, 'Come, let's go back!' This could partially explain the reason for the parenthetical aside (nestled in the middle of this dialogue) about the 'seer' in 1 Sam. 9.9. Although some scholars are convinced that 9.9 is out of place, there are grounds for suggesting that its placement here is highly appropriate, not least because of the connections with chap. 16 (see Miscall 1986: 64). A key issue in both chapters is 'seeing': God tells the seer that he has 'seen' the misery of his people in 9.16, while in 16.6-7 God's 'seeing' is contrasted with the faulty 'seeing' of Samuel the seer. Hence, 9.9 is far from a mere antiquarian notice, and despite the seemingly innocuous nature of this discourse, important themes in the larger storyline—themes that are revisited in 1 Samuel 16—are encapsulated in the language.

9.11-14

> Now just as they were going up the hill toward the city, they found some girls coming out to draw water, and they said to them, 'Is the seer here?' They answered them, and said, 'Yes, he's right in front of you! Hurry! Now! Indeed, today he has arrived at the city, for today there's a sacrifice for the people at the high place. Just as you enter the city, you'll find him before he

> goes up to the high place to eat, for the people won't eat until he comes for *he* will bless the sacrifice after thus the invited ones will eat. So now, go up, indeed, him today you'll find him!' And they went up to the city. Now just as they were entering the midst of the city, behold, Samuel was coming out to meet them, to go up to the high place.

Despite the awkwardness of the maidens' speech to Saul and his servant lad, I have translated their discourse quite literally. In a recent study, Gary Rendsburg (1999) has presented a case for 'Confused Language as a Deliberate Literary Device in Biblical Hebrew Narrative'. Among his numerous examples of this device, Rendsburg cites the maidens' response to Saul and his servant lads here in 1 Sam. 9.12-13. Rendsburg notes: 'in their excitement over seeing the tall, handsome Saul, the girls prattle all at once, creating a cacophony of voices represented by the language of the text'. While some English translations smooth out the text to make it appear that the maidens speak in unison, there are unpredictable changes in pronouns in the Hebrew text: 'They answered them (וַתַּעֲנֶינָה אוֹתָם), and said, "Yes, he's right in front of you (לְפָנֶיךָ)! Hurry (מַהֵר)! ...indeed, him today you'll find him (כִּי־אֹתוֹ כְהַיּוֹם תִּמְצְאוּן אֹתוֹ)!' Shimon Bar-Efrat (1989: 97) attributes this irregularity to all the maidens chatting at once: 'the separate voices are not noted explicitly, but it is possible to discern them intermingling with one another... The reader gains the impression that this is not one answer but many, given by different maidens, all trying to respond and supply information.'

To my mind, this discordant symphony of female voices reveals that Saul is entering into the realm of the 'type-scene'. In very general terms, a type-scene involves a character undertaking a sequence of actions or undergoing certain experiences that unfold in a somewhat predictable pattern. There are a number of different type-scenes that scholars have identified in biblical narrative, such as the deathbed speech of the dying father, the barren wife, and the call of the prophet. This episode of 1 Sam. 9.11-13 provides an example of the betrothal type-scene of the maiden at the well (other instances include Gen. 24, Gen. 29.1-12, and Exod. 2.16-21, and John 4 in the New Testament). There is a standard pattern to the betrothal type-scene: a potential hero is traveling away from home, there is a well of water, a fair maiden, some conflict and its resolution, and a consummation of a flirtatious dynamic.

In 1 Samuel 9 Saul (the potential hero) is traveling away from home, and encounters a group of maidens coming out to draw water. However, it can be observed that the type-scene in 1 Sam. 9.11-13 does not come to its expected resolution. Instead of some further interaction with one of the maidens, v. 14 reads: 'And they went up to the city. Now just as they were entering the midst of the city, behold, Samuel was coming out to meet them, to go up to the high place.' Instead of a nice relationship with a fair maiden, Saul instead gets the prophet Samuel. Consequently, this has been labeled as 'an aborted type-scene'. Of course, one could demur that in the next chapters Saul has a grown son, so why does he need a type-scene here? Hence, there must be other reasons why the Deuteronomist would activate these ingredients.

In the present context, the aborted type-scene is important for at least three reasons. First, the aborted type-scene becomes symbolic of Saul's reign—Saul's kingship is aborted much like this type-scene. Within the larger context of 1 Samuel this aborted type-scene provides something of a miniature summary of Saul's career. Robert Alter (1981: 60-61) notes, 'the deflection of the anticipated type-scene somehow isolates Saul, sounds a faintly ominous note that begins to prepare us for the story of the king who loses his kingship, who will not be a conduit for the future rulers of Israel, and who ends skewered on his own sword'. Glancing back to the opening chapter, Peter Miscall (1986: 55) comments that a 'deflected betrothal' is appropriate for a character who has a 'deflected birth story'. But glancing forward, one observes that many other projects Saul commences in the story are aborted, and hence the 'aborted type-scene' dovetails with Saul's overall characterization, and foreshadows the end of his reign before it even begins.

Second, I would submit that the aborted type-scene is used by the Deuteronomist because it is an emblematic image of the disastrous marriage between Israel and kingship. The aborted type-scene thus draws attention to some of the wider implications of Israel's experiment with kingship and the 'husband' language of 1 Samuel. As Jon Levenson (1985: 70-80) has already argued, kingship can represent an alternative embrace for Israel, an embrace that will ultimately result in exile. So, in addition to the argument that this aborted type-scene is significant because it is symbolic of Saul's personal problems, it also signals the disastrous impact of Israel's forsaking of her covenant partner in favor of dalliance with kingship..

A third purpose for this aborted type-scene is that it continues the network of allusions to Genesis, specifically the allusions to Rachel. The struggle between Hannah and Peninnah in 1 Samuel 1 evokes memories of the conflict between Rachel and Leah in Genesis 29–30, and anticipates the tribal conflict caused by the birth of kingship. As discussed in my analysis of chap. 4, the birth of Ichabod evokes memories of the death of Rachel in Genesis 34, and in the next chapter Saul himself will journey near 'Rachel's tomb'. Rachel dies in childbirth, giving birth to Benjamin, Saul's eponymous ancestor. One guesses that these allusions to Rachel contribute to the larger storyline by stressing the northern provenance of Saul and the notion of death in childbirth: if the having of sons is like the having of kings, then the fate of the northern kingdom will be as a premature death. As Peter Miscall (1986: 55) remarks,

> The echo of former meetings at a well of water, a symbol of life, particularly the meeting of Jacob and Rachel, is subsequently weakened by Samuel's prediction that Saul is to 'meet two men by Rachel's tomb in the territory of Benjamin' (1 Sam. 10.2); 'tomb' tips the ambiguous symbol of Benjamin toward the pole of misfortune and death. It invokes the memory that Benjamin's life is at the expense of the death of others, whether his mother or the inhabitants of Jabesh-gilead.

Saul seems to be on the wrong end of a number of converging intertextualities at this point in the story.

To reiterate, the aborted type-scene functions in this context as a powerful technique of *foreshadowing*. In terms of definition for foreshadowing, I am following the standard definition of J.A. Cuddon in *The Penguin Dictionary of Literary Terms and Literary Theory*:

> The technique of arranging events and information in a narrative in such a way that later events are prepared for or shadowed forth beforehand. A well-constructed novel, for instance, will suggest at the very beginning what the outcome may be; the end is contained in the beginning, and thus gives structural and thematic unity. (Cuddon 1999: 326)

The entire scene of 9.11-14—the deflection of the betrothal type-scene in favor of a meeting with the prophet Samuel en route to the 'high place'—foreshadows the aborted nature of both Saul's career and the larger institution of kingship among the northern tribes. Curiously, the maidens mention the (otherwise gratuitous) facts about 'sacrifice' and 'waiting' for the prophet's arrival—the very pretext on which Samuel rejects Saul in 1 Samuel 13. It is ill-omened that Saul should first be told about Samuel as he is going up to the 'high place'; later in the story, David will eulogize Saul's death with the lyrics, 'Your glory, O Israel, upon your high places is slain' (2 Sam. 1.19).

9.15-17

By means of a narrative flashback, the perspective of this scene shifts to the prophet. In this scene the question of *who* will be Israel's first king is answered. It will be Saul of Benjamin, a man who at least has the right name ('asked') for the job. The harder question is *why* Saul is chosen. Bruce Birch points out that no *rationale* is provided for the choosing of Saul, only that Samuel is told 'a man from the land of Benjamin' will be sent, and 'you will anoint him leader over my people Israel'. For Meir Sternberg (1985: 96), the purpose of the aside is establish that 'Samuel left to his own devices might not have selected Saul', while others have suggested that there is a subtle polemic against the House of Benjamin, as the LORD enunciates to Samuel, '...a man from the *land of Benjamin*' (e.g. Sweeney 1997: 517-29). As mentioned above, in light of Judges 19–21, to be from Benjamin is to be marginalized. For my analysis, the major point here is that Samuel is being sent a man from Benjamin who is to be anointed as leader. One gets the impression that the prophet is not enamored about kingship to begin with—when a Benjaminite is added into the mix, the prophet's humor presumably is not improved. Quite plausibly, this is the expositional purpose of the long flashback, followed the temporal relocation back to the present. These lines in 1 Sam. 9.14-17 frame the first encounter and lay the groundwork for the first impressions between the 'seer' and the 'seen'. As we will see in a moment, this first encounter between Saul and Samuel anticipates a tenuous relationship replete with misunderstanding, theological tensions, and perhaps even personality conflict.

For the first time in chap. 9, the proper name 'Samuel' appears, and he is unequivocally the one (seer, man of God, prophet) who will tell Saul and his servant lad their way: 'all the coincidences and intimations of the narrative about the journey are confirmed by Yahweh's explication to Samuel' (Gunn 1980: 61). When Samuel dismisses the people at the end of chap. 8, we do not know how he intends to proceed with the kingship matter. However, God takes the initiative, and it would appear that *even before* Saul begins his search, *he* is the one sought. Just as Saul is prodded and directed by his servant lad in 9.5-9, now Samuel is prodded and directed by God himself in 9.15-17.

9.18-20

> And Saul drew near to Samuel in the midst of the gate, and he said, 'Tell me, please, where is the house of the seer?' Samuel answered Saul, and said, 'I'm the seer. Go up before me to the high place, for you're eating with me today. Then, I'll send you off in the morning, and everything that's in your heart I'll tell you. As for those donkeys lost three days ago, don't set your heart on them, as they've been found. For who is the object of all Israel's desire, if not you and the entire house of your father?'

First impressions, I was once told, are often misleading. Saul's first impressions on Samuel seem to linger for quite some time, and there are further ways that the uneasy tension in Saul's and Samuel's relationship is foreshadowed through the dramatic irony of their inaugural meeting. The meaning of their names is apparent: Saul 'asks' while Samuel ('heard of God') has his ears opened by God. Drawing near to someone in the gate (unknown to Saul it is Samuel himself), Saul's first utterance to Samuel is telling: 'Tell me, please' (הַגִּידָה־נָּא). Scholars often note the play on the verbal root נגד: Saul (the future נגד, 'ruler') asks Samuel to נגד ('to tell, declare') him where the seer's house is. In light of the previous instructions of the maidens, it is somewhat puzzling why Saul should ask this (apparent stranger) in the midst of the gate: 'Where is the *house* of the seer?' The maidens certainly do not advise Saul to enter the town and ask directions to the house of the seer. On the contrary, they implore Saul—albeit replete with awkward syntax—to 'go up' and they will find the seer. Saul seems to be told that seer *has already arrived*, implying that the seer is a visitor to the city. There is a humorous serendipity in the fact that Saul is speaking with the 'seer' himself. Still, it is somewhat unclear, why Saul should inquire as to the seer's house, unless he is exhibiting a tendency to go beyond (or deviate from) instructions. This strangely anticipates how Saul might relate to the various instructions of Samuel: just as he has trouble following the directions of the girls in the type-scene (slightly going beyond instructions), so it will be the same with Samuel's instructions.

It is rarely advisable to put one's foot in one's mouth. Albeit unintentionally, Saul's question—'Where is the *house* of the seer?'—is not the ideal opening line for this conversation. Given Samuel's hostility to the monarchy in general and sense of personal rejection in particular, this question is liable to be misinterpreted by the interlocutor. When Saul asks 'Where is the house?' he presumably means 'domicile', and Samuel could have been mildly amused at this piece of dramatic irony—Saul the Benjaminite is asking him (Samuel) for directions to his own dwelling. Unfortunately for Saul, the semantic range of the Hebrew word 'house' (בית) includes 'dynasty'. An alternative, therefore, is that this question could be misheard as 'Where is the dynasty of the seer?' Of course, Samuel could be a charitable exegete, and understand that the tall Benjaminite intends for 'house' to mean 'domicile'. But given the tenor of his response to Saul—especially his caustic words such as 'to whom is all the base desire of Israel directed'— such a reading should not be automatically assume. It could be that Samuel's anger is increased (as in 8.6) in light of the fact that he himself will have no *dynastic house* precisely because of the institution of the monarchy, the inaugural figurehead of which is asking this impertinent question. For my analysis, the main purpose here is not Samuel's exegesis, but rather the further level of irony in that *neither* Samuel nor Saul will spawn a dynasty. This question thus points forwards and backwards, illustrating the (inherent) difficulties in siring a dynasty. While it looks back with a subtle reflex to the 'house of Eli' and the assurances of its abolition, it also looks forward and highlights the antithetical nature of the dynastic promises of 2 Samuel 7 and the endurance of the Davidic house.

9.21

The seer does not sound pleased with this state of affairs, and it must be slightly overwhelming for Saul. In response to Samuel's double-query ('And for whom is all that is desirable in Israel? Is it not for you and for all your father's house?'), Saul's response is a lot like Gideon in Judges 6. Like Gideon, Saul (the tallest man) claims to be from the weakest clan of the smallest tribe: 'Aren't *I* from Benjamin? From the smallest tribe of Israel? From the tiniest of all the clans within Benjamin? Why would you speak to *me* like this?' As we recall, Kish is described as a 'man of wealth' (גִּבּוֹר חָיִל) in 9.1, but Saul stresses the marginal status of Benjamin among the tribes of Israel. In Saul's return question to Samuel—'Why do you speak to me like this?'—he betrays little inkling of the kingship. Samuel's speech in chap. 8 forewarns the people about the massive accumulation of material goods by 'the king'—such actions seem distant from the son of Kish, at least at this point in the story. In his cultural reading of this material, Philip Esler (1998: 226) discusses 'a God who subverts the local honor code' by choosing 'a son from the lowest family among Israel's lowest tribe'. This will later be seen, Esler says, in the choice of David. So, when Saul asks 'Why would you speak to *me* like this?', there is the theme of God's *unlikely* choosing that comes to the fore, as well as yet another 'unanswered question' in the narrative. I would stress that this communication pattern between Saul and Samuel—unanswered questions, strange commands, almost caustic remarks—will continue throughout the story.

9.22-24

Without responding to Saul's question, Samuel proceeds to take Saul and his servant lad into some sort of chamber, presumably at the high place. Saul is somewhat in the dark—the reader is more aware that something is going on—although the maidens did mention that a sacrifice was to take place. As it is, the sacrifice takes on the flavor of a 'coronation supper', as Robert Gordon (1986: 115) notes, reminding us that to this point in the story, the only other episode with such a high concentration of the terms 'eat' and 'sacrifice' occurs in chap. 1. Peter Miscall (1986: 58) comments, 'The text recalls Samuel's birth story, through the theme of eating and drinking and, at the same time, anticipates both the later banquet to which Jesse and his sons will be invited and Saul's final meal at Endor'. On the topic of meals, in chap. 1 Hannah is the frequent subject of eating, and J.P. Fokkelman (1993: 405) notes a resonance between Hannah's portion and Saul's meal in chap. 1: 'One way of formulating the link is this: just as the life and the calling of Samuel are determined by Hannah (the woman of the personal portion), the life and destiny of Saul are now laid down by Samuel who marks the moment of ceremonial ratification by having a special portion set down'. After seating Saul at the head of the 'invited ones, about 30 men', Samuel then gives instruction to the cook about this special portion. The direct speech in 9.24 is awkward, and it is not clear who is speaking. Most translators assume it is Samuel (e.g. RSV and NRSV, following the Greek) but the words 'Samuel said' are not in the Hebrew text. I am tempted to think that the *cook* speaks these strange words, and I would render the verse as follows:

> The cook carried in the special leg and all that was on it, and set it down in front of Saul. He said, 'Look, that which has been reserved is now set before you. Eat, for it has been kept safe for you until this appointed hour, saying, "I'll invite the people".' And so Saul ate with Samuel on that day.

9.25

Although God has commanded that Saul is to be anointed (9.16), the event has not yet taken place. The expected anointing does not take place at this special gathering. Instead, the reader is confronted with the strange utterance of the cook, the ritual meal, and a reminder (at the beginning of 9.25) that the scene occurs at the 'high place'. The second half of 9.25 is subject to variety of different translations. A literal rendering of the Hebrew text would be, 'and he spoke with Saul upon the roof', but the NRSV (following the Greek) reads: 'a bed was spread for Saul on the roof, and he lay down to sleep'. In terms of the larger storyline, a *private* conversation in an obscure location fits better with the motif of secrecy that is accompanying Saul's journey toward the kingship, yet still there is no anointing of Saul. For Diana Edelman (1991: 50), the prophet's actions raise several questions: 'Why has he not chosen to anoint Saul during the occasion of the sacrifice, which seems to have been called in his honor. Is he still trying to cover up God's move to kingship by secretly designating the candidate? Is the meal a 'test run' to see how the invited guests will react to Yahweh's candidate, before his actual designation? Has God given Samuel more specific commands that we have not been informed about?' Of course, if Samuel and Saul are talking, one wonders what they are talking *about* under the cover of falling darkness. While there is no overt hostility recorded between prophet and king, such hopes of lasting intimacy are a false dawn.

9.26-27

The temporal setting for the final scene of this chapter is the break of dawn on the next day, which is the first day of Saul's new career. Samuel issues an imperative ('Arise, that I may send you'), and there will be many more commands issued before this lengthy interaction (which carries into the next chapter) is over. 9.27 is a somewhat awkward line, but I would render it as follows: 'As they were going down toward the outskirts of the city, Samuel said to Saul, "Speak to your servant lad, so that he passes on ahead of us". He then passed ahead. "As for you, stand still now, so that I can cause you to hear God's word".' The place of the servant lad's dismissal is carefully documented—the outskirts of the 'city'—but no more. Scholars have tried to guess what city it is, but there is no mention in the text. There is an air of secrecy, and not even the city is named. This stands in contrast, as has been noted, with the anointing of David in 'Bethlehem', a spatial location that is mentioned numerous times in chap. 16. Meanwhile, Samuel wants Saul to wait and hear 'the word of God'. This is the first occasion—but certainly not the last—when Samuel will proclaim to Saul the divine word. Perhaps *this* is the reason why Samuel is so keen to have the servant lad 'pass on ahead': Samuel wants secrecy, and we have already seen that this servant lad talks *way too much*. This is a rather light note, to be sure, in a relationship between prophet and king that will be utterly devoid of humor in the days ahead.

1 Samuel 10

The relationship between Samuel and Saul will be a strained one in the days ahead. Such tensions were apparent in the preceding chapter, and the first exchanges between ensconced prophet and fledgling king serve to foreshadow their tense relationship. While the strains will be further evident as the narrative continues, the main event in chap. 10 is the anointing of Saul and his first experiences subsequent to the anointing. The chapter is structured in two parts: both Samuel and Saul are the main characters, yet there is a different emphasis in each part. The first part has Saul in focus, yet Samuel is there also. The main events of part one include the long catalogue of Samuel's instructions and sign language, the fulfillment(s) of the signs and Saul's prophetic activity, and two questions from Saul's inquisitive uncle. The second part has Samuel in focus, yet Saul is there also. The main events of part two include the national assembly at Mizpah (with the drawing of lots and Saul's hiding), and the chapter closes on a negative note with an undercurrent of discontent from the sons of Belial. As Robert Polzin (1993: 101) argues, this chapter is a crucial one for Saul: 'By means of a brilliant set of interlocking compositional and thematic features, the history of Saul's reign is foreshadowed, his insurmountable problems deftly indicated, and his mysterious rejection already suggested'. My analysis will be alert to these various signals throughout chap. 10.

10.1

Outside the city, with the servant lad dispatched ahead, the narrative continues with Samuel taking a 'vial of oil', pouring it on the head of Saul, and kissing him. In 9.16, Samuel is commanded by God to anoint Saul, and at long last, the anointing takes place. Several commentators have pointed out, however, that the anointing instrument is abnormal. In chap. 2 Hannah sings, 'the LORD will give strength to his king, and exalt the horn of his anointed', and indeed, both David and Solomon will be anointed with 'the horn of oil' later in the story. Yet here, Hannah's son gives Saul the vial treatment. A quick glance at a concordance reveals that there is only one other anointing with a vial of oil in the Bible: Jehu son of Nimshi in 2 Kings 9, who drives like a madman. By the end of his career, as we will see, Saul will have *less* in common with the kings of Judah and far *more* in common with various northern kings and their short-lived reigns. If this is a somewhat deficient anointing in chap. 10, it fits with Saul's 'aborted type-scene' of chap. 9, and does not augur well for his tenure as Israel's anointed.

If the anointing with a vial of oil (as opposed to a horn) is the least bit controversial, then Samuel's words are more so. Samuel's words are usually contentious when the meaning is straightforward; how much more so when there are some text-critical issues! A literal rendering of the Hebrew text of Samuel's words in 10.1 would read like this: 'Is it not because the LORD has anointed you over his inheritance to be leader?' However, the NRSV prefers the Greek reading, and renders the speech: 'The LORD has anointed you ruler over his people Israel. You shall reign over the people of the LORD and you will save them from the hand of their enemies all around. Now this shall be the sign to you that the LORD has anointed you ruler over his heritage...'

As it stands, the Hebrew prophet asks an enigmatic and baffling question, whereas the Greek prophet utters a very clear and helpful statement. The extra material supplied in the Greek version certainly adds some flavor, and Samuel is far more loquacious about Saul's royal calling. He is also far *less* ambiguous than has been his wont thus far, and that in itself raises some suspicions. In my view the NRSV is well-intentioned, but the additional data skews the characterization of Samuel in a direction that *the overall narrative* is at pains to resist. Samuel's words in 10.1 are important to consider because, as the speech progresses, there is an exhausting catalogue of details that both the reader and the son of Kish will struggle to keep straight.

10.2

Samuel's post-anointing speech continues with an extensive report of what Saul will encounter after leaving the prophet. By any measure, there is a vast portion of sign language here. As one reads through the entire Deuteronomistic History, this is the highest concentration of such 'signs', and it is a comprehensive inventory (the story of Gideon is the closest parallel). The first thing that will happen to Saul as he departs from Samuel is that he will find two men beside 'Rachel's Grave' at the boundary of Benjamin in Zelzah. The death of Rachel—the mother of Benjamin—has already been alluded to in chap. 4 by means of the birth of Ichabod. It is faintly ominous that further mention should be made of the mother of the tribe of Benjamin who loses her life in child birth: if 'having kings is like having sons' and the mother of Benjamin dies in the process, it could symbolize the premature death of this later Benjaminite, the firstborn of Israel's kings.

The mention of Rachel lends a maternal image to the story, but there is a paternal reference as well. At the spatial setting of 'Rachel's Grave', the two men whom Saul finds will have news for him: 'The donkeys have been found—that you went to seek—and behold, your father has forsaken the matter of the donkeys and is worried about you [plural], saying, "What will I do about my son?"' These words echo the very first recorded speech of Saul himself in 9.5, when he says to his servant, 'Come, let's go back, in case my father ceases from the donkeys and worries about us'. The two men will go a step further and actually quote the direct speech of Kish—quite a feat of prophetic prediction. Barbara Green (2003: 207) comments that the question reiterates the 'father–son' motif and is yet another unanswered question in this stretch of text: 'The question, coming where it does in the story of the making a king of Kish's son, rings...urgently... As tends to be true of questions in this section, it gets no clarifying response; the question, not the answer, is important. Does Kish regret the taking of his son, fear it? We will never know.' In a moment (10.11), all who knew Saul previously will say of him 'what has happened to the son of Kish', yet before this Kish *himself* says 'What will I do about my son?' Like Samuel's father Elkanah (who says 'only may the LORD establish his word' in 1.23), the words of Saul's father Kish mean more than the speaker(s) may realize. Kish says 'What will I do about my son?', suggesting that uncertainty clouds the future of his son.

10.3-6

According to Samuel's forecast, Saul will meet two men at Rachel's Grave, but as he passes away from there and arrives at the Oak of Tabor, three men will find him as they are 'going up to God at Bethel'. The three men will not be empty handed, as one will be carrying three kids, another carrying three loaves of bread, and another carrying a skin of wine. These three men will 'ask' Saul if there is peace, and present him with two loaves, that he should take from their hand. The signs outlined in vv. 3-4 are challenging to interpret, and are perhaps best read simply for their sheer predictive power. Some have connected the Oak of Tabor with Gen. 35.8 ('And Deborah, Rebekah's nurse, died, and she was buried under an oak below Bethel'), but the allusion in this case is hard to confirm. The key point is that Saul is to receive a gift. In his long indictment of chap. 8, Samuel said that the king will 'take' many things, but here the king is given bread from three men going up to worship at Bethel. This is yet another echo of Saul's previous words in 9.7: Saul says that they are 'out of bread' and have nothing to give the man of God—now the man of God says he will be *given* bread by three men going up to God.

After receiving the bread, Samuel tells Saul that he will arrive at Gibeath-elohim, meaning 'the hill of God'. The main attraction of Gibeath-elohim, Samuel says, is a Philistine outpost, yet there is no further elaboration of its significance. Instead, Samuel continues, as Saul enters into the city he will encounter a band of prophets 'coming down from the high place' and prophesying to the accompaniment of musical instruments. As the band plays on, Samuel says, 'the spirit of the LORD will come mightily upon you, and you shall prophesy with them and be turned into another man'. The mention of the Philistine garrison is understandable, since in 9.16 God says that the new leader will 'save my people from the hand of the Philistines'. So, hints of the forthcoming conflict with the Philistines are given here. But why Saul should engage in prophetic behavior is something of a mystery. Earlier, Saul (unwittingly) asks: 'What is a prophet?' This might be another unanswered question in the narrative, but Saul will soon be having a personal experience of prophetic activity. James Ackerman (1991: 20) raises the right question: 'We wonder why Samuel sends him into a prophetic group where he is overwhelmed by religious charisma when there is a Philistine outpost demanding military charisma in the same village'. Glancing forward in the story, the next figure to receive the 'onrushing of the spirit' is David—yet David does not enter into any prophetic activity. This will be, however, after David is anointed with *horn of oil* and after the spirit of God turns aside from Saul (1 Sam. 16).

10.7-8

At the crescendo of Samuel's speech there is a transition from sign language and predications to instructions and imperatives. Saul may not be aware of it, but vv. 7-8 are crucial for his reign. I would render the lines as follows:

> Now it will be when these signs come to you, do whatever you find at hand, for God is with you. And you will go down before me to Gilgal, and behold, I'll be coming down to you in order to present the offerings and sacrifice the peace offerings. Seven days you will wait until I come to you, and I will cause you to know what you should do.

Numerous readers have been struck by an apparent tension between the instructions of lines 7 and 8. For J.P. Fokkelman (1993: 423), Samuel's instructions are not clear: 'Thus what is created in the reader's mind is the odd impression of friction between acting unconditionally and acting conditionally. This must have had a slightly confusing or misleading effect on Saul.' For Diana Edelman (1991: 54-55), the 'ambiguous' words of Samuel might reflect his ambiguous motivations, while Robert Gordon (1986: 118) wonders if these verses proscribe a test for the fledgling monarch: 'is there a Tree of Knowledge in the midst of Saul's Garden of Eden?' As Robert Polzin (1993: 99) observes, 'Saul is commanded on one hand to do whatever his hand finds to do (v. 7), yet he will (have to?) wait until Samuel shows him what to do (v. 8)...' More seriously for Polzin, 'These two verses epitomize the entire section of chap. 8–12, foreshadow the tragedy of Saul's kingship, and implicate Samuel in the Deuteronomist's explanation for Saul's downfall' (1993: 106). Whether or not one agrees with the above commentators about the tensions between vv. 7 and 8, it is inescapable that

10.8 (the command to wait at Gilgal) is a crucial command for Saul's reign. We will return to this controversial command and the 'seven day' waiting period in due course.

10.9-12

> As it happened, just as he turned his shoulder to go from Samuel, God changed him with another heart, and all these signs arrived on that day. They came there to Gibeah, and behold, a band of prophets to meet them, and the spirit of God rushed upon him, and he prophesied in their midst. Then, all who knew him in times past saw, and behold, he was prophesying with the prophets! Each person said to the other, 'What is this that has happened to the son of Kish? Is *even* Saul among the prophets?' And a man from there answered, and said, 'But who is *their* father?' Hence, it became a proverbial saying, 'Is *even* Saul among the prophets?'

In the words of Graeme Auld, this is a scene that does not easily give up its secrets. Not surprisingly, this scene has been subject to a variety of interpretations: some view the scene as pro-Saul, others as anti-Saul, while still other commentators simply avoid the scene altogether. Among those who have come up with more provocative interpretations, Moshe Reiss (2004: 37) wonders if this scene represents Samuel's attempt to 'be the father' of Saul, and thus exercise control over the king. James Kugel (2003: 49) points to the incongruity of the situation, as though the crowd is saying 'What's someone like *him* doing with people like *them*?' In terms of the question—'Is *even* Saul among the prophets?'—Robert Polzin argues that Saul should never have been sent to mingle 'among the prophets' at all. The question, for Polzin (1993: 101), 'expresses a central problem with the reign of Saul, a reign in which there was a tragic mix-up of theocratic roles'. The office of the prophet and the office of the king should be separate, lest a conflict of interest arise. For Barbara Green (2003: 209) the issue is not so much Saul's behavior but rather the *association*—the fellowship of the king, as it were—that drives the scene, and hence 'who is their father' once again raises the topic of dynasty: 'Prophets are not dynastic; that particular call is not inherited. Kings are not typically prophetic. So the speech of the people here offers access to our focal topic: What, how is a king to a prophet?'

Kish is quoted as saying 'What will I do about my son?', and now a local man poses the (again unanswered) question, 'But who is *their* father?' Once more, the father–son motif is raised in the narrative. My guess is that this scene continues to explore the following issue: divine empowerment is not a hereditary privilege. We have seen dynastic issues starkly illustrated previously in the story, as the hereditary promise to the house of Eli is annulled. Dynastic houses of 'fathers' come and go, and Samuel himself has already failed to established a hereditary judgeship. If this is one of the themes of

1 Samuel 1–15—that houses can come and go—then we will see this continue *throughout* the Deuteronomistic History. The house of Eli's 'father' has been rejected; it remains to be seen what will happen to the house of Saul. Of course, this is not the last time that Saul will be featured among the prophets. This event has a sequel, and will have to be reappraised in light of Saul's presentation in 1 Samuel 19.

10.13-16
After Saul finishes 'prophesying', he arrives at the high place where he has an encounter with one of his relatives—an uncle—who comes to him and asks, 'Where did you go?' Despite this scene in vv. 13-16 appearing rather straightforward, it has been subject to considerable scholarly debate, and some have argued that that text needs to be emended. No doubt many of us have relatives we would like to see emended, but in my judgment this section is intelligible enough as it stands, and contributes to the unfolding plotline.

In 10.11, all who knew Saul previously ask the question 'what is this that has happened to the son of Kish?' In the very next scene, a brother of Kish—Saul's uncle—enters the stage. Saul has just been anointed king (albeit strangely), and Samuel has recently warned what the king will do for those close to him. Now Saul's uncle arrives on the scene, and he would seem to be a prime candidate for the kind of patronage that Samuel describes at length in chap. 8. In this scene with his uncle, however, Saul does not look particularly ambitious. There is yet another set of questions as the uncle inquires where they went, and we note the slightly awkward syntax of Saul's reply: 'To seek the donkeys, and we saw that there was not, and we came to Samuel'. Perhaps Saul is hesitant (as in his first recorded words, 'Come let's go back') or wisely circumspect (as may be advisable with an uncle), but he certainly does not give a whole lot away in this transaction of dialogue. Just as Saul uses the baggage to hide later in the chapter, so he uses language to hide from his uncle here.

The uncle wants to know the content of Samuel's words, and based on Saul's evasive response, one guesses that the uncle's question is more than it seems. Saul's response tells part of the story ('He certainly told us that the donkeys had been found'), yet the narrator reveals that this was a selective answer: 'But concerning the matter of kingship, he did not tell him what Samuel had said to him'. So, if Saul *were* to tell his uncle about the matter of the kingship, what exactly would he say? Peter Miscall (1986: 62-63) has some useful comments: 'Saul knows something about the matter of the kingship. But what? And what about himself as king? The 'word' concerns kingship, not king. Does Saul have any greater clarity on the speeches and events of chaps. 9 and 10 than we do?'

It is notable that this is the first time that the root for 'king' (מלך) has been used within the orbit of Saul's *character zone*. Thus far such terms as 'ruler' or 'leader' have been used instead of 'king', and there seems to have been a deliberate avoidance of the term ever since the elders ask for 'a king'. Consequently, that the term 'the kingship' (הַמְּלוּכָה) would be deployed in the context of Saul's conversation with a close relative is surely significant. Saul's uncle, as numerous commentators have pointed out, is 'Ner' the father of Abner (based on the datum of 1 Sam. 14.50). Abner, as we glance ahead in the story, will be Saul's military commander and a figure who undeniably will have a vested interest in Saul's kingship. Abner is a character who will be portrayed as ambitious and powerful in Saul's house. Furthermore, there is a wordplay present, since the Hebrew word for 'uncle' (דוד) is remarkably to similar to the proper name 'David' (דוד). As Barbara Green observes, this cryptic dialogue anticipates or previews how Saul will interact with another 'דוד' in the narrative, as Saul's conversations with David are often evasive or fraught with circumlocutions. Indeed, Green suggests that the 'uncle' here represents the voice of a usurper or 'a next claimant' to the throne. So, as with other conversations in 1 Samuel, this one means a good deal more than it appears on the surface.

10.17-19
As there is no indication in the narrative that any length of time passes between vv. 16 and 17, it would seem that after Saul departs from his uncle, Samuel then summons the people to the LORD at Mizpah. We recall that this is not the first occasion where Mizpah has featured as a spatial setting. In chap. 7, Mizpah is the site of Samuel's finest hour in the narrative, as he convincingly demonstrates the power of the LORD's sufficiency for dealing with the adversaries of Israel. As Bruce Birch (1998: 1047) notes, the purpose of 1 Samuel 7 is to illustrate that kingship is not needed to deal with the Philistine threat. Thus, it is probably not a coincidence that Samuel chooses to assemble the people at Mizpah once more: it recalls that moment of victory and the prophet's role, underscoring that a king is a superfluous choice. Furthermore, Graeme Auld (2004: 205) mentions that Mizpah will feature as a spatial setting later in the Deuteronomistic History, where it is an important administrative center *after* the fall of Jerusalem and the political collapse of kingship (2 Kgs 25.22-36). Samuel's words about kingship, in this present setting of Mizpah, are unequivocally negative.

In the previous scene, Saul does not reveal to his uncle that Samuel has anointed him. In this present scene at Mizpah, Samuel does not mention it either. Samuel begins his speech with an orthodox recitation of God's saving acts on behalf of Israel, including the rescue of this 'kingless' people from various 'kingdoms' who presumably have earthly sovereigns. Samuel then turns to the present state of affairs: 'But you, today, have rejected your God, he who saves you from all your evils and distresses, and you said "No! Indeed, a king you will set over us!" So now, station yourselves before the LORD by your tribes and your thousands.' This is a short précis of events where the prophet focuses on the iniquity of the request itself, and so the matter of his *own sons'* iniquity as the pretext for the request is not addressed. Instead, Samuel commands the tribes to assemble themselves for a lot-casting ceremony. On the couple of other occasions where such a ceremony occurs in the Deuteronomistic History (see Josh. 7 and 1 Sam. 14) it is not a happy or festive moment: the ceremony is designed to uncover guilt. Even though Samuel knows that Saul is God's choice for Israel's king, the lot-casting is certainly a more somber way of introducing him. The narrative does not state whether the idea for the ceremony proceeds from God or Samuel.

10.20-24

The drama of the lot-casting ritual results in the tribe of Benjamin being chosen, and finally, Saul the son of Kish. The ritual is successful enough, but a crisis emerges: at the climax of this very serious ceremony conducted by a very serious prophet, Saul himself—like the donkeys of chap. 9—cannot be found! One is hesitant to think of this as a moment of deutero(c)omic relief, but it certainly throws a monkey-wrench into the delicately meshed gears of Samuel's ceremony. While it may be surprising that Saul is hiding, the procedure of lot-casting is designed to identify offenders and 'individuals whose behavior was detrimental to the common good' (Gordon 1986: 120). So, under the circumstances, Saul's hiding is understandable. One recalls Saul's first words ('Come let us go back') and wonders if this is a non-verbal equivalent. I suppose the possibility exists that Saul is hiding from Samuel; in the future, such action will not be possible.

Even though Saul has been chosen by lot, he cannot be found, so the people have to make further inquiry: 'Has a man come here yet?' The irony is not lost on the reader: the people are forced to 'ask' God to tell them the location of the king whom they have 'asked' for, whose name means 'asked'. In response to their question, the LORD tells them, 'Look, he has hidden himself [or, has been hidden] by the baggage'. This is not the most glamorous commencement of a royal career, but at least Saul is physically impressive. For the first time, in fact, Saul is publicly acclaimed by the prophet: 'Do you see the one whom the LORD has chosen? There is none like him among all the people.' While this can be construed as an affirmation, it is conspicuous that Samuel avoids the word 'king'. It is left to the people to therefore say: 'The king lives!'

10.25-27

In 8.11, in the wake of the request for a king, Samuel outlines the 'custom' or 'judgment of the king'. It is a catalogue of (potential) abuses. Now at Mizpah, Samuel tells the people the 'custom' or 'judgment of kingship', but his words receive no further specificity: 'he wrote (it) in a book and rested (it) before the LORD'. A host of scholars have pointed to Deut. 17.18 as the most natural intertext, since the following prescription is listed there: 'And when he sits on the throne of his kingdom, he shall write for himself in a book a copy of this law...' So, instead of Saul making the copy of the law for himself, Samuel is the one who does the writing. Barbara Green (2003: 213) observes that 'Saul stands with his hands at his side as the prophet takes on the kingly task'. Will Saul ever have 'access' to this copy that is rested before the LORD? In light of Samuel's writing activity, it is fitting that *Samuel* is the one who subsequently dismisses the people from the assembly at Mizpah—much like he dismisses them at the end of chap. 8. Saul has been acclaimed as king, but it would seem that Samuel is still in charge and exercising authority.

Everyone then departs from Mizpah and goes home, including Saul himself, whose destination is 'his house at Gibeah'. For the first time in the narrative, the reader learns without a doubt that Saul's hometown is Gibeah, a place that has a disreputable past. Judges 19–20 recounts the horrific account of the Levite's concubine—events that take place at Gibeah—and the resulting civil war that nearly eliminates the tribe of Benjamin. It is in these latter chapters of Judges—with Gibeah as the epicenter of theological disaster—that the phrase emanates: 'In those days there was no king in Israel; each man did what was upright in his own eyes'. Now, Israel's first king returns to his house in Gibeah as the lot-casting ceremony concludes with the ringing shouts of 'The king lives!'

Saul does not return to Gibeah unaccompanied, but along with him go 'valiant ones whom God had touched in their heart'. This retinue is not quite the same as the group that Samuel describes will 'serve with his chariots and horses and run before his chariot', but perhaps this scenario will unfold later in the story. As it stands, this company that joins Saul seems a rather positive moment for the freshly acclaimed monarch. But there is negative undercurrent, as there is another group whose hearts God has *not* touched. They do not go with Saul, and are labeled as 'sons of Belial'. Elsewhere in 1 Samuel, 'sons of Belial' is an epithet reserved for the nastiest category of (royal) opponents, such as Hophni and Phinehas, and Sheba son of Bichri (2 Sam. 20). The complaint of these sons of Belial involves skepticism for Saul's saving capacity: 'What, will *this one* save us?' Not only do they register this protest, but they also 'despised him, and brought him no gift'. Saul's response to these rascals is notable: 'But he was as one being deaf'.

Again, this places Saul in a favorable light, and it is hard not to have some sympathy for Israel's first king here. The question, 'How can this one save us?', is also a transition to the next episode, which introduces the threat posed by Nahash the Ammonite, where an opportunity is presented for Saul himself to answer the question posed by the sons of Belial who question his capacity to save.

1 SAMUEL 11

Having been acclaimed as king—despite the rumors of discontent—Saul returns home to Gibeah as Samuel dismisses the assembly at Mizpah. Those who despise Saul are asking, 'What, will *this one* save us?' This will be one of the few *answered* questions in the narrative, at least in this chapter. 1 Samuel 11 has four scenes. First, Nahash the Ammonite has camped against Jabesh-gilead; he is threatening to gouge out their (right) eyes, and the only hope for Jabesh-gilead is a deliverer from Israel. Second, messengers bring the bad tidings of Nahash, but Saul hears of it, and, filled with the spirit, energetically responds to the crisis. The third scene presents the offensive launched against Nahash, while the fourth scene of the chapter is the aftermath of battle and the ensuing dialogue. It is fair to say that Saul appears in a rather positive light throughout these scenes, and the chapter ends on a more jubilant note than has been the case hitherto.

11.1

The chapter begins with Nahash the Ammonite 'camping' against the eastern Israelite town of Jabesh-gilead, most likely with hostile intent. The Ammonites, one recalls, are distant relatives of Abraham, and Genesis 19 relates the not-so-splendid beginnings of this nation: Lot flees from the sulfur of Sodom and takes refuge in a cave with his two daughters, who are both concerned that no men are present with whom they can be fruitful and multiply. The daughters get Lot drunk, and nine months later, young Ammon (the name Ben-ammi means 'son of my people') and his cousin Moab ('from his father') enter this breathing world. The Ammonites are often antagonistic toward Israel, and Jephthah of Gilead fights against them in the book of Judges.

The town of Jabesh-gilead also features in the last chapter of Judges, and, coincidentally, the tribe of Benjamin is connected. In Judges 21, for whatever reason, the inhabitants of Jabesh-gilead fail to assemble at Mizpah to take vengeance on Benjamin for the outrage of Gibeah. As a penalty, the entire town is wiped out, with the exception of 400 virgins who become wives for the surviving Benjaminites. So, the town of Jabesh-gilead was instrumental for preventing the disappearance of the tribe of Benjamin.

1 Samuel 11

Further, as Bruce Birch (1998: 1054) notes, there must be unique ties of kinship between these two cities. Jabesh-gilead must have enjoyed a resurgence of population at some point, since now Nahash the Ammonite is encamped against them.

When comparing the RSV and NRSV at this point, there is a substantially different text in the latter. In 10.27–11.1, the RSV follows the MT, whereas the NRSV incorporates additional material found in the LXX and the Qumran fragment:

> Now Nahash, king of the Ammonites, had been grievously oppressing the Gadites and the Reubenites. He would gouge out the right eye of each of them and would not grant Israel a deliverer. No one was left of the Israelites across the Jordan whose right eye Nahash, king of the Ammonites, had not gouged out. But there were seven thousand men who had escaped from the Ammonites and had entered Jabesh-gilead. About a month later, Nahash the Ammonite went up and besieged Jabesh-gilead…

There are numerous scholarly arguments about this extra material, but in my view the Hebrew text is acceptable as it stands, and has a certain literary currency. Some have argued that Nahash would be in need of an introduction, since he has not previously appeared. However, the name Nahash means 'snake', and usually people that bear such names need no introduction. Furthermore, in the Hebrew text of 1 Samuel 11 Nahash is never referred to as a 'king', which is slightly ironic in light of Israel's recent acquisition of a monarch. Nahash bursts onto the scene and camps against the city, and his presence is sufficient to make the inhabitants of Jabesh-gilead go out and surrender: 'Cut a covenant with us and we will serve you'.

11.2-3

From the perspective of Jabesh-gilead, the response of Nahash to their idea of a covenant is less than encouraging: 'By this I will cut a deal with you', says the Snake, 'when every right eye is gouged out of you, and I make it as a disgrace over all Israel!' Students of comparative linguistics may note some syntactic affinity between the speech patterns of Nahash and certain Pirates of the Caribbean. The NRSV, though, smoothes out the reading by inserting the pronoun 'I': 'I will gouge out…' This makes Nahash unambiguously the 'gouger', whereas the possibility exists in the Hebrew that Nahash is implying some self-inflicted ophthalmology, which is unpleasant. Either way, these are harsh terms. The elders of Jabesh diplomatically sidestep this gruff reply and creatively modify the terms of their surrender: 'Relax from us for seven days, so we can send messengers throughout the boundaries of Israel. And if there is none to save us, then we will come out to you'. There is a historical irony: when the tribes are mobilized in the Gibeah of Benjamin episode, Jabesh-gilead does not respond; but now, they hope that someone will respond to their messengers. Perhaps the elders think—in light of the massive casualties of Judges 21—that the other tribes 'owe them one', so to speak. Since there is no recorded reply of Nahash, one suspects that he somewhat arrogantly believes that no 'saving' aide will journey to Jabesh-gilead. From his point of view, the 'messengers' idea might actually serve to enhance the embarrassment. As it is, Nahash will not be afforded any further direct speech in the narrative.

11.4-5

The elders ask for a seven-day respite. Seven days can be a long time, as Saul will painfully discover in chap. 13. But a lot of water has to go under the bridge before that day, and meanwhile, this episode is 'Saul's finest hour' (Miscall 1986: 66). The messengers of Jabesh-gilead duly arrive at 'Gibeah of Saul', where they speak the word about the 'eyes' in the 'ears' of the people, and there is collective weeping. The town of Gibeah—with all of its sordid past from the book of Judges—is now renamed Gibeah of Saul, but it remains to be seen if any reversal of shame is possible. As discussed above, the town of Jabesh-gilead was instrumental for preventing the disappearance of the tribe of Benjamin. Now it is time for Saul of Benjamin to return the favor.

But first, where is Saul? All the people are weeping, but there is still one person absent. In the previous chapter—during the lot-casting ceremony—Saul was hiding among the baggage. Now, he is busy plowing the field when the messengers of Jabesh-gilead arrive. The narrative perspective immediately shifts to focus on the best hope for the messengers, despite his present occupation: 'But behold, Saul coming from the field behind the oxen!' Samuel warns in chap. 8 that the king will 'take' the best of the fields, but here Saul seems simply to be farming. Saul asks the obvious question, 'What is with the people, that they weep?' In response, the messengers recount to him the words of the men of Jabesh.

11.6-7

> And the spirit of God rushed upon Saul when he heard these words, and his wrath was greatly kindled. He took a pair of oxen and hewed them in pieces. He sent [them] throughout the entire territory of Israel by the hands of the messengers, saying, 'Whoever does not come out after Saul and Samuel, so will it be done to his oxen!' And the dread of the LORD was upon the people, and they came out as one man.

At 10.27, Saul is 'as one deaf' to the internal dissenters. Now at 11.6 he 'hears' about the external threat to Jabesh-gilead, and the spirit rushes on him and he burns with anger. Commentators often point out the throwback to Judges as the spirit comes on him in power, and echoes of Judges will continue here. The messengers of Jabesh-gilead do not leave Gibeah of Saul empty-handed, as Saul's action is to hew the oxen in pieces, and send the pieces throughout the boundary of Israel by the hand of the very same messengers who brought the news about Nahash. This is not the first time Gibeah has been involved in such a severance package. In Judges 19, the Levite does the same thing to his concubine, and there is a deliberate allusion between 1 Samuel 11 and that episode in Judges. In terms of the narrative 'past', J.P. Fokkelman (1993: 470) helpfully points out a series of contrasts: the episode in Judges is the internal perpetrator of domestic violence, whereas Nahash is a foreign aggressor. Saul is thus helping to rehabilitate the soiled past of Gibeah. But in terms of the narrative 'future', Barbara Green (2003: 215) wonders if Saul will ever be able to transcend his origins. In the long term, the rescue of Jabesh-gilead by a man of Benjamin will exact a price: 'the people of Jabesh draw the king as temporarily effective but very costly—even destructive, over time, and they sketch a pattern of relationships that ruinously entangle. The people of Jabesh draw Saul as a wounded healer, or better, perhaps, as a lethal surgeon, offering help that may not be affordable.' Perhaps the situation involves both elements: Saul can partially rehabilitate Gibeah's past, but 'can this one save' in the long term? Saul will indeed 'save' in the short term, but the combination of Jabesh-gilead and Gibeah still carry too much baggage of division and civil war.

As far as Saul's characterization in this episode, it is symbolically appropriate that he hews the pair of oxen he was plowing with: from this point on, Saul will not be going 'home' in the same way again, and he will never again engage in the pastoral activity of agriculture. Further, Saul's first words since being acclaimed king in the preceding chapter are an effective rallying cry: 'Whoever does not come out after Saul and Samuel, so will it be done to his oxen!' This is the only 'appearance' of Samuel until the end of the chapter, and he appears only by proxy in the words of Saul. It is a puzzle as to why Samuel is not more visible; it has been suggested that Samuel's *absence* is another reason why Saul is so successful in this episode. Saul's words result in a remarkable show of unity: unity in terms of confessed solidarity between prophet and king, and unity among people as they march as 'one man'. Such unity—on both fronts—will not dominate the narrative landscape again.

11.8-10

A considerable number of troops assemble at Bezek, with soldiers from 'Israel and Judah'. While it seems positive enough here, it is also subtle reminder that—in his finest hour—Saul is not from Judah, and the nation will not always be so unified.

The same messengers who had brought the bad tidings of Nahash are now re-deployed with happier information, as they are covertly instructed to inform the residents of Jabesh-gilead: 'Tomorrow you will have salvation (תְּשׁוּעָה) when the sun grows hot!' Earlier at 10.27 the sons of Belial are murmuring 'What, can *this one* save us (יֹשִׁעֵנוּ)?' Now the same root is delivered to the besieged residents of Jabesh-gilead, and it is no doubt welcome news for those who prefer attached retinas. Armed with this intelligence, the inhabitants of Jabesh-gilead approach Nahash again. Having successfully procured a respite of seven days, they try the same strategy of 'buying time' once more: 'Tomorrow we will come out to you', they say, 'and you can do to us whatever is good in your eyes'. There is an obvious wordplay when they say 'do to us whatever is good *in your eyes*' when Nahash is threatening to have every *right eye* removed. To this proposal there is again no recorded response from the Snake, who no doubt misses a further irony: the proposed damage to the *right* eyes of Jabesh-gilead will be obviated by man from Benjamin, the tribe of the *right* hand!

11.11

On the next day Saul divides the army into three 'heads', another pattern familiar from a couple of battles in Judges (e.g. 7.16; 9.43). In this prelude to battle Saul displays both logistical skills and military aptitude, abilities that have not been apparent based on what we have seen so far. For a fellow who was hiding among the suitcases in the last chapter, this is rather impressive transformation. Several commentators note the condensed report of the battle. There is a considerable buildup to the battle, but only one line is devoted to its description: 'They came into the midst of the camp during the morning watch, and struck Ammon until the heat of the day. The ones who remained scattered, and no two of them remained together.' The focus is squarely on the complete victory that occurs, exactly as Saul guaranteed to Jabesh-gilead, during the heat of the day. As J.P. Fokkelman aptly remarks, 'The sun's rising symbolizes the victory and ensures the good visibility of the defeat. The week which Nahash had permitted is full and turns out quite different to what he had foreseen' (1993: 475).

11.12-15

The final scene in this eventful chapter presents the aftermath of victory, and while there is a shift from action to dialogue, the themes of negotiation and diplomacy continue. Verse 12 is a difficult line both to translate and interpret, but I would render it as follows: 'And the people said to Samuel, "Who is the one who said, 'Saul will reign over us'? Hand over the men, so we can put them to death!"' Their demand seems to refer back to the sons of Belial at the end of the previous chapter, the ones who mutter against Saul and bring him no gift. The quotation is not quite accurate, and indicates the people's own hermeneutic at work as they lodge their grievance with Samuel, and demand a moment of retribution. 'And yet', comments Graeme Auld (2003: 220), 'we may note with a wry smile that the people take this complaint to the very one who had been most doubtful about kingship at all!' Samuel has only been referred to by Saul in this chapter, and this is his first formal appearance. It is curious, therefore, that *Saul* is the one who intervenes with words of pardon: 'Saul quickly steps in to correct the possible misinterpretation. He credits the victory to Yahweh, the supreme commander, at the same time acting in his capacity as human leader to declare a day of amnesty for wrongdoers' (Edelman 1991: 65).

It is not altogether clear what would have happened had Saul not intervened. His words are somewhat in contrast with his previous utterance in this chapter. When he burns with anger upon hearing the report of Nahash, he proclaims (with considerable authority) a call to arms. Now, with equal authority, he pronounces a call to mercy. These words square with the general tenor of the narrative: Saul displays good leadership, but it is God's enabling spirit that ultimately procures the victory, and hence Saul shows wisdom in this acknowledgment. Again, Saul uses the term 'salvation' (תְּשׁוּעָה), once more hearkening back to the sons of Belial, and providing a final answer to their grumbling. We should emphasize that Saul is merciful here, but he will not always be shown mercy when he makes an error.

After a brief narrative sabbatical, Samuel is now the central character once more. On the heels of the king's clemency, Samuel then speaks in his customary imperative: 'Come, let us go to Gilgal, and there let us renew the kingship'. On the basis of these words we can conclude that the dialogue is transacted in Jabesh-gilead, which is notable, for then Saul's finest hour and words of mercy clearly take place on the *other side* of the Jordan. Samuel's idea to return to Gilgal is far from arbitrary. This is one of the places for his annual judicial circuit (7.16). Not only does this put Samuel on his 'home turf' and firmly in charge, but also, as Fokkelman (1993: 483) notes, this spatial setting becomes a most appropriate location for Samuel to talk at length about his own unimpeachable career as judge. At Mizpah Samuel conducts the lot-casting ceremony, and at Gilgal he will make a major speech. In the words of Walter Brueggemann (1990: 90), 'Samuel's characteristic mode of leadership is always to call a meeting in which he himself is dominant and controls the discussion'.

The final line of the chapter brings some closure and looks forward in the story. The sequence of events appears straightforward enough—the people go to Gilgal as Samuel instructs, make Saul king 'before the LORD', sacrifice and rejoice greatly—but there is a faintly ominous note that is sounded amid the festivities. Indeed, there are sacrifices of 'peace offerings' (שְׁלָמִים) at

Gilgal, but this reminds the reader of Samuel's command to Saul at 10.8, '…go down before me to Gilgal, and behold, I will be coming down to you in order to present the offerings and sacrifice the peace offerings (שְׁלָמִים). Seven days you will wait until I come to you, and I will cause you to know what you should do'. Gilgal is the place and the offering is the issue that will be decisive for Saul's future. These sacrifices in chap. 11 are in the cause of rejoicing; the sacrifices in chap. 13 will be a cause of rejection.

Overall, it is appropriate that 1 Samuel 11 should end on this slight note of ambivalence. In a host of respects the narrative is very favorable to Saul, yet this 'finest hour' is punctuated with unsettling moments of foreshadowing. For Robert Polzin, it is not by accident that Israel's first 'abortive' monarch comes from Gibeah, and the 'aura of urban reciprocity' between Jabesh-gilead and Gibeah point to the upcoming tragedy of Saul's kingship: 'For now, in his hour of glory, the failure of Saul's coming reign is also already foreshadowed by the town God chooses for the man of Gibeah to deliver' (1993: 115). Saul's saving of Jabesh-gilead also anticipates his funeral, since in chap. 31 those citizens of Jabesh-gilead previously rescued by Saul (with both eyes intact) rescue his corpse from the Philistine temple and fast for seven days. For Peter Miscall (1986: 67), 'Saul's greatest moment is marred by anticipation of his death'. And finally, the 'renewing' of the kingship at Gilgal is the same spatial setting of Saul's fall from grace in chap. 13 when he is denounced by Samuel.

1 Samuel 12

Of the many intriguing characters in the Deuteronomistic History, few are subject to as many opinions among commentators as the prophet Samuel. Even the most superficial survey of secondary literature reveals a vast number of interpretive positions. This surely has to do with the *office of the prophet* as much as it has to do with *character of Samuel* in the narrative. For some interpreters, the *office itself* requires that the *prophet himself* be above fallibility, and *ergo*, the prophet will always be the one in the right. For other readers, the office of prophet is—like any other position of spiritual leadership—a divine calling that is subject to all the complexities of life in a fallen world. No doubt many an early reader had a similar kind of experience with the characterization of Samuel, and one assumes that the goal of the Deuteronomist is to present Samuel as a highly complex figure. As we have seen, Samuel has some impressive qualities and a high degree of orthodoxy, but also suffers the pain of rejection by the elders of Israel and some personal issues with kingship.

For a number of reasons, chap. 12 is significant for Samuel's characterization. The main event of this chapter is a long speech that includes several trajectories: a discourse on his individual honesty as a judge, a long recitation of Israel's past behavior and current events that culminate in the request for a king. After a brief interlude of thunder and lightning, the chapter concludes with a final admonition, some encouragement, and a dire warning. Throughout my analysis I will keep in mind the comments of Robert Polzin (1993: 116). Even if one does not agree with all of Polzin's assessment, his remarks nonetheless merit careful reflection:

> Samuel will consolidate his control over the people and Saul in chapter 12, yet his memory there of the events of chapter 11 will turn out to be deficient in a self-serving way. By then old and gray, he will recall that the people, not himself, had insisted on a king during the events surrounding the siege of Jabesh-gilead. The narrator, confident that the reader will pick up the discrepancy, thereby highlights Samuel's conveniently faulty memory. Samuel's speech in chapter 12, as we shall see, is markedly defensive; this self-righteous tone of a prophet who protests too much is another of the narrator's subtle but effective means of highlighting Samuel's self-interested actions with respect to Saul and the kingship. Details such as this constitute the author's abiding picture of Samuel throughout these chapters.

12.1-2

Since there is no mention of a change in time or place, we assume that the spatial setting for chap. 12 remains in Gilgal, and the temporal setting is in the immediate aftermath of the 'rejoicing' of 11.15. That our present chapter begins with Samuel's spoken word is appropriate, since the vast majority of this chapter is the longest speech of Samuel's career. He begins by saying to all Israel, 'Behold, I have listened to your voice, to all that you have said to me, and I have caused a king to reign over you. So now, behold, the king walks around before you, but I am old, and I am gray, but my sons, behold they are with you, and I have walked around before you from my youth until this day.' Sometimes in a major political speech, what a figure *does not* say is just as important as what a figure *does* say. Samuel indeed tells the people that he has listened to them, but does not mention God's acquiescence to their request, God's commandment to give them a king, the divine sending of Saul, or even Saul's selection through the lot-casting ceremony. Instead, Samuel continues by pointing to the person of the king, and contrasting his own aged estate. The prophet also emphasizes the presence of his own sons.

Samuel's reference to his sons is puzzling. The reader knows that Joel and Abijah are 'rogues, low men, and two of the greatest scoundrels unhung' (as Dickens might say). Samuel also knows that his sons are integrity-challenged, since the elders have informed him: 'your sons do not walk in your ways' (8.3). So why are his sons singled out for so much attention at the outset of his speech? Robert Alter (1999: 65) wonders if this is Samuel the judge's last dynastic impulse, a 'wistful' glance at an alternative to kingship. For Barbara Green (2003: 188), the reference to the sons at this point coheres with earlier themes in the narrative:

> Samuel makes the presence of his sons part of his claim to innocence and adequacy. That is, the narrator shows us the blindspot of Samuel and the exotopic angle the elders have in regard to the dynastic sons but fails to have any exploit it. Blindness in regard to one's children is not necessarily willful, but in this narrative it is a dangerous faultline, made more tangible in the peoples' silence.

To further both of these points, I would suggest that the *sons* are a component in the larger characterization of Samuel. The 'last judge' is here configured as a parabolic comment at the end of this (long) kingship renewal ceremony in Gilgal. Samuel is a case study in the difficulty of change and transition. He is yesterday's man, but he still has much to contribute, and as such he embodies the conflicting interests of a shift in leadership paradigm. Green's 'blindspot' is a helpful image in light of the larger argument, whereby the 'having of kings' is akin to the 'having of sons'. Samuel can clearly see the weakness of kingship, but what about the corruption of his own sons? This is a central problem with dynastic leadership. My guess is that it is no accident—in light of the compositional plan of 1 Samuel—that the first thing to be rejected in chap. 13 is Saul's *dynastic possibility*.

12.3-11

Everyone agrees that Samuel is considerably more upright than his sons, and as far as his own record as judge, he cannot be accused of perverting justice. As Walter Brueggemann (1990: 90) notes, 'Samuel is on sure ground. He may be cantankerous, quarrelsome, and authoritarian, but no one can say he is using his office for his own benefit.' Nonetheless, Samuel's tone self-vindication has struck some readers as strange. For example, Diana Edelman (1991: 69) comments, 'Once again, Samuel's unclear motivation throughout the transition to kingship are highlighted, especially in light of his personal affront in 8.6 and his failure to begin direct proceedings to create a king according to Yahweh's command in 8.22'. Here in chap. 12, the key word Samuel uses at the beginning of his speech is 'take', and it is also a key word in chap. 8. There, Samuel says the king will 'take', whereas here, by contrast, he claims never to have 'taken' anything. Since Samuel draws pointed attention to the 'king who walks around' in 12.2, one guesses that the situation is not favorable to Saul, and he is pictured as the one who will do the 'taking'. But the links with chap. 8 are deeper than this, as Barbara Green (2003: 187) summarizes:

> The series of five questions Samuel fires off in 12.3 catch both the spirit and the specific language of 8.11-19. By drawing here on the list of royal behaviors listed earlier, but to distance himself by exaggeratedly parodic questions and to demand that the people and God agree with him, Samuel makes a sharp contrast between the practices of himself and those of the king he has previously described (8.11-18).

The speeches of 12.1-6 do not, it must be said, represent the most interesting dialogue in the Deuteronomistic History; the people are rather passive and compliant, and not very creative as interlocutors with the last judge and his very intense speech. Samuel's inquiries sound like rhetorical questions ('Whose ox have I taken? Or whose donkey have I taken?', etc.), but the people must think he expects an answer, so they respond with the same voice of unanimity as when they asked for a king. Some older commentators believed that this was a 'prophetic law suit' of sorts, so I suppose such a Q & A session in such a context would be expected to unfold along such lines. At any rate, we are now ready for the next major portion of the speech, and I would render it as follows:

> The LORD, who appointed Moses and Aaron, and who brought up your fathers from the land of Egypt! So now, stand still, and I will judge you before the LORD, with all the righteous acts of the LORD that he did with you and your fathers. When Jacob entered Egypt, your fathers cried out to the

> LORD, and the LORD sent Moses and Aaron, and they brought out your fathers from Egypt and settled them in this place. They forgot the LORD their God, and he sold them into the hand of Sisera, general of the army of Hazor, and into the hand of the Philistines, and the king of Moab, and they fought against them. They cried out to the LORD, and said, 'We've sinned, for we've abandoned the LORD and served the Baals and the Ashtorahs—now then, rescue us from the hand of our enemies, and we'll serve you'. And the LORD sent Jerubaal, Bedan, Jephthah, and Samuel. He rescued you from the power of your enemies on every side, and you lived securely.

There is an extemporaneous flavor to this speech, as witnessed by the double mention of Moses and Aaron, as well the not-strictly-chronological recitation of events from Judges. The history is telescoped, but it is certainly hard to deny—as even a casual reading of Judges will verify—that God is consistently faithful to his people despite their consistent unfaithfulness. The point of this abridged history, it would seem, is to suggest that *judgeship* as a system of leadership has been satisfactory and need not be abandoned for the *kingship* model, although it is true that Samuel's brief summary here does not present any of the 'problems or complexities of the actual experience of judgeship', as such (Hamilton 2001: 242; Jobling 1986: 51). Of all the judges, only four are mentioned by Samuel, including himself. The Greek translators have 'Samson' instead of 'Samuel' at 12.11, but then, the Greek translators did not have all the advantages of postmodern readers, as our Western politicians frequently refer to themselves in the third-person, usually with deep humility. Accordingly, Samuel has himself stand in an unbroken chain of deliverers from Moses and Aaron unto that day in Gilgal. Bedan is otherwise unattested in the book of Judges, and despite a bevy of speculations, one is unsure what to do with this name in the end. Bedan is either a textual error, or someone we do not encounter in the Judges narrative.

12.12-13

The most difficult part of Samuel's speech now arrives. This stretch is hard to interpret because it stands in opposition with what we have read previously in the narrative. In chap. 8, as we recall, the elders approach Samuel and ask for a king, based on the reasoning (or excuse) that he is old and his sons are corrupt judges. There is an absence of any hostility or foreign adversary in the wake of the very successful campaign of chap. 7. Yet now, Samuel's words in 12.12-13 provide a different construal:

> And when you saw Nahash, king of the sons of Ammon, come against you, you said to me, 'No, but a king will reign over us!' But the LORD your God was your king. So now, behold, the king whom you have chosen, whom you have asked for. So behold, the LORD has given a king over you.

There is a palpable tension between the narrator's account of events in chap. 8 and Samuel's description here. Antony Campbell summarizes the discrepancy as follows:

> In chs. 8–11, Israel's demand for a king is motivated by the bribery and injustice attributed to Samuel's sons; victory over Nahash is preceded by Saul's kingship (10.24) and celebrated afterwards by the kinship's renewal (11.14). However the text is understood, neither the kingship nor its "renewal" is portrayed as a response to the threat posed by Nahash.

Of course, with some nimble gymnastics it is possible to harmonize the accounts, and defenders of Samuel often do so. I suppose that the longer Greek text of 10.27 (plus the Qumran fragment, as reflected in the NRSV) could be helpful here, since it presents a case for a lengthier threat of Nahash. Otherwise, there is a problem with Samuel's account, and numerous commentators have attempted to resolve this dilemma. For Lyle Eslinger (1985: 403), Samuel's inaccurate précis is part of the author's larger characterization strategy:

> By avoiding the real reasons and occasion for the request, Samuel exposes his own sensitivity to it (cf. 8.6f). The discrepancy between the request as described in ch. 8 and ch. 12 is a relatively simple matter of a disparity between the way it was, and the way a deeply involved character would like everyone to believe it was.

For Barbara Green (2003: 218), 'Samuel seems caught in his own issues, as it were, which distort—that is, affect—how he deals with those between whom he mediates'.

While it may seem that these commentators are being hard on the prophet, their analysis is important in terms of the Deuteronomist's purpose at this point in the story. For the first time in the Hebrew text, Nahash is referred to as a 'king', and *this foreign king* thus becomes—in Samuel's account—the motivation for Israel's request. Thus, Samuel's 'defective reminiscence' of the motivation behind the request for a king serves to highlight the rejection of God's kingship by the people, and simultaneously, it serves to remind us of Samuel's own sense of personal affront and rejection by Israel's leadership. This is consistent with the tensions in Samuel's literary characterization thus far, and by no means is it over. As mentioned above, this long stretch in 1 Samuel is *as much* about the office of the prophet *as it is* about the office of the king. The Deuteronomist here is offering a sustained meditation on the difficulty of mediating the prophetic word, and this complication is embodied in the career of the Samuel.

12.14-18

After the controversial recounting of the Nahash threat as pretext for the request for a king, Samuel returns to the theme of repentance. He warns the people: if they fear the LORD, serve him, listen to his voice and do not rebel, then 'both you and the king who reigns over you will be after the LORD your God'. As a corollary, if they do not listen, then God's hand will be against them 'and against your fathers'. The language here is not dissimilar to 7.3, where the prophet challenges the people to return to the LORD and turn away their foreign gods—and if they serve the LORD alone, then he will deliver them from the grip of the Philistines. Samuel's speech and actions in chap. 7 are a high point of his career, and similarly here: when Samuel returns to the theme of 'return', he is very impressive indeed. No one can quarrel with his theology of repentance, and thus, it is easy genuinely to identify with those interpreters who are aggressively pro-Samuel, because this is undeniably solid stuff and Samuel has history on his side (see Bergen 1996: 144). Israel is wandering astray by asking for a king, and the prophet Samuel seems to be the only one who sees the folly. So, the prophet's account of the Nahash affair is immediately balanced with this orthodox call to repentance, and it strikes me as integral to the Deuteronomist's presentation of Samuel. Peter Miscall (1986: 72-73) has a useful discussion of the 'two poles' of Samuel that are evident in the narrative:

> At one pole is the authoritative and stern prophet who declares his innocence and the people's guilt. They have requested a human king and have thereby rejected their true king, the Lord. Samuel's denunciation is severe but not unyielding. The people and their king will have a future—to be determined by their obedience to the Lord's word. This is the 'good' Samuel, the Lord's and the people's established prophet and leader. At the other pole is the authoritarian, harsh, and bitter leader who is forced to appoint his own replacement. He does it with resentment and acrimony. The people's request is evil, because it is a rejection of him. His denunciation of them is more personal polemic than divine word.

As we are evaluating Miscall's comment, it is fitting that a storm is brewing on the narrative horizon. Samuel reminds his audience that it is the season of wheat harvest—hopefully a dry time in the ancient Near Eastern calendar—but rain is imminent. The prospect of rain during the harvest betokens economic loss, reminding us again of Samuel's warning in chap. 8 that the king will 'take'. In the larger narrative schema, it is apt that Saul—fresh from victory over Nahash in what will be his finest hour—now gets soaking wet from the wind and the rain, as clouds will always lour upon the house of Saul. It is equally appropriate that Samuel is the conductor of this thundering orchestra. J.P. Fokkelman (1993: 525) has a brilliant point of connection with Hannah's poem in chap. 2:

In her programmatic song Hannah had indeed said: 'the Highest thunders in heaven, the Lord judges the ends of the earth'. I make this connection because Samuel is, at the same time, so stubborn as to omit an entire stave. He is not in the mood for implementing his mother's two final bars and to strengthen Saul by repeating: 'May He give strength to His king, and may He raise the horn of his anointed one'.

It would be ideal if everyone took the warning with immense seriousness. Before too long, it will be too late. This may be the perfect storm, but not a moment of perfection in Israel's story.

12.19-22

In a response that is reminiscent of the Judges narrative, the people confess their sin of 'asking' (שאל) for a king, and cry out to the prophet to pray for them. Of course, if the confession is really like the book of Judges, then it will probably not produce a lasting repentance. But the key thing for my analysis is the reaction of the prophet: Samuel's response is swift and represents the prophetic office well. Samuel represents a voice that the nation *needs* to hear—the prophetic warning with the classic accents of Deuteronomy and stress on covenant faithfulness. Such voices, as Israel's past and future will testify, can be hard to hear. In Samuel's case, yes, there is a personal edge, and no doubt this can make the truth harder to swallow—but such can be the voice of tradition in any generation: the speaker may be unpalatable, but the words need to be heeded. After commanding the people not to fear, he exhorts them to keep serving God wholeheartedly. He then adds: 'and do not turn aside after the vain things—that cannot benefit nor save—for they are vain'. Notably, the term 'vain things' (תהו) is the same word used in Gen. 1.2 for 'formless void' ('and the world was *unformed* and *unfilled* [תהו ובהו]') to denote the chaos and emptiness of the primeval earth. Here in 1 Samuel 12, the term 'vain things' refers to both the vacuum of idolatry and also, one suspects, the resulting chaos of abandoning God's kingship. In 12.22 Samuel also comments on Israel's electoral status. Notwithstanding the request for a king, God will remain faithful to his covenant partner: 'For the LORD will not forsake his people, on account of his great name. Indeed, the LORD is determined to make you a people for himself.' When we reflect on Samuel's long career, he has witnessed many vicissitudes in national life: from the fall of the dynastic house of Eli and the failure of his own attempts to established hereditary judgeship, to the great victory at Mizpah in chap. 7. The prophet has accumulated considerable wisdom, and knows well the madness of this request for a king. To abandon the LORD, according to the prophet's sage counsel, is a return to primeval emptiness and unreality.

12.23-25

Samuel's speech in chap. 12 is often labeled as his 'farewell address'. True, this is his last major speech, but he will nonetheless be around and active for a long time yet, and the speech is not over. As Walter Brueggemann (1990: 95) comments, 'The speech may have ended with that positive summons [of v. 22]. The summons would be an appropriate closure to a restored relation. But this crusty voice of tradition is relentless.' In 12.23 Samuel implies that he has no intentions of retiring: he will not cease praying for the people, and he will teach (from the root for 'Torah') them the way that is good and upright. Though his sons are not upright, Samuel will strive to teach the people. The final lines of this long address include one more warning: fear the LORD, Samuel exhorts, in light of the great things that he has done for you, 'but if you continue to do evil, even you and your king will be carried off'. As Graeme Auld (2003: 220) points out, within days of the beginning of kingship, Samuel talks about its end: 'Samuel renews the warning of Moses (e.g. Deut 29.25-28), but his fresh anticipation of the end of the monarchy, uttered just as kingship begins, is all the more poignant'. When this speech as a whole is evaluated, it is much like the characterization of Samuel himself: some personal crustiness mixed with some highly orthodox theology that Israel needs to hear in these first days of the monarchy.

This is a convenient moment to pause and take stock of a dominant figure in the narrative so far: we have known Samuel from his birth to this climactic speech to the nation when he is old and gray. We have seen the contrast with the negative decline of sons of Eli and the positive growth of Samuel amid the corruption of Shiloh. We have seen Samuel's impressive leadership—the country acknowledges that he is a prophet, and a high point must be chap. 7. But we have also shared his struggles: his rebellious sons (who do not walk in his ways) are introduced *just before* the elders make him feel personally rejected and ask for a king. God himself comforts (or rebukes) Samuel with the words 'it is not *you* they have rejected, but *me* they have rejected from reigning over them' (8.7). No doubt our interpretive task would be easier if the stern prophet was presented as absolutely flawless, but as we have seen, there is rather more ambiguity. Why does the Deuteronomist present Samuel as such a multifaceted character?

It might be helpful for a moment to compare the portraits of Samuel and Saul, prophet and king. With respect to Saul's characterization, Barbara Green (2003: 113) asks: 'Can a human character be a cipher for a more institutional problem?' I will argue that this is indeed the case for Saul: Saul as a particular king represents the northern experience of kingship in general. Thus, Saul's personal story mirrors the national history. A growing number of scholars are arguing that Saul *is* a preview of kingship in Israel, and that his aborted reign presages the fate of kingship among the northern tribes. So, assuming that an individual character can be understood as a cipher for 'collective experience', at the end of chap. 12 it is also possible to view the prophet Samuel as a cipher. Just as Saul will represent the northern experience of kingship, so Samuel the prophet represents the pain, the struggle, and the difficulty of parenting when sons are rebellious. Samuel's words, 'I will not stop praying for you', are both a commitment and a challenge to the people, but Israel has no interest in abandoning the project of kingship. Samuel represents the (cranky) voice that is hard to listen to, the voice that speaks annoying words of truth. This has an applicability that the Deuteronomist wants readers to take seriously: such voices are a part of every Israelite generation, and wisdom is learning to listen to such voices.

1 SAMUEL 13

The book of 1 Samuel begins, in the aftershock of Judges, with the line 'In those days there was no king in Israel'. The miraculous birth of chap. 1 does not produce Israel's first king, but rather the nation's first king-maker. The institution of kingship must therefore coexist with the prophetic office, and from the outset we have seen that the relationship between king and prophet is a strained one. Now, after Samuel's long speech comes to an end, a new chapter begins, but the previous tensions remain. As Bruce Birch (1998: 1068) summarizes, 'Chapter 13 is a narrative of Saul's external conflict with the Philistines and internal conflict with Samuel. Saul does not succeed in overcoming either of these conflicts, and they eventually bring him to a tragic end.' This chapter is divided into several interlocking parts. After an introductory section and several scenes of skirmish with the Philistines, the hostilities intensify to the point that Israel is hard-pressed, and the troops are defecting. Saul remains at Gilgal, but Samuel does not arrive, and Saul offers the sacrifices. Immediately, Samuel enters the scene with scathing words of denunciation, announcing that Saul's kingdom will not be established because he has not 'kept what the LORD commanded'. After Samuel departs, the conflict with the external foes does not abate, and this eventful chapter draws to a close with a report about the absence of blacksmiths and weaponry in Israel. It is becoming evident that Saul resembles the many 'first born' sons in Genesis. Just as things do not go well for the first born in Genesis, so Israel's first born king fares no better.

13.1

A brief survey of the Deuteronomistic History reveals a standard formula for the king's age and length of reign. While chap. 13 opens with a regnal formula for Saul, it is strikingly corrupt. In the sage judgment of S.R. Driver (1913: 97), the Hebrew text 'as it stands is deficient'. The NRSV captures the deficiency by rendering the verse: 'Saul was…years old when he began to reign; and he reigned…and two years over Israel'. The text critic does not have the usual Greek default here, since the entire verse is lacking in the LXX, and help only comes from the Latin Vulgate and other traditions. Consequently, the reader is left wondering what to do with this troublesome line. Graeme Auld (2003: 220) summarizes, 'The Hebrew text begins the regular age formula but supplies no number; then the two years it does offer for the length of Saul's rule seem impossibly short, though powerfully suggestive of impermanence'. In this chapter, very little goes right for Saul, and the opening verse is a bad start. One might expect the regnal formula to be a rather straightforward matter, but it is not. The reader is not ultimately given Saul's age or his length of reign, and this omission oddly foreshadows the rejection of Saul in the chapter. After this corrupt start, the events of this chapter will only get worse for Saul, and thus the text-critical problem at the outset functions as a symbolically apt introduction for a king whose dynasty will not endure.

13.2-3

In 1 Sam. 7.13 there is a report of a suppression of the Philistine threat: 'So the Philistines were subdued and did not again enter the territory of Israel. And the hand of the LORD was against the Philistines all the days of Samuel.' While the Philistines have been mentioned in passing and alluded to on several occasions, this is their first formal appearance since the decisive defeat under Samuel's undisputed leadership in chap. 7. The Philistines may be 'subdued' in chap. 7, but they remain a thorn in Saul's flesh throughout his days.

The first event of chap. 13 is the division of the troops, and immediately one notices the reduced numbers. Saul chooses three thousand soldiers, a substantially smaller number than the 330,000 mentioned in 11.8 during the attack on Nahash the Ammonite. Whether this anticipates Saul's reversal of fortune in this chapter is undecidable, but one-third of the troops here are 'with Jonathan in Gibeah of Benjamin'. Later in the chapter, and again in 14.1, Jonathan is referred to as Saul's son, but here there is no word of introduction. One assumes Jonathan is Saul's 'heir apparent', yet the absence of any introduction is fitting, since the possibility of a dynastic line for Saul is nullified here in this very chapter. Jonathan's first action in the narrative is to defeat a Philistine garrison. This apparently brave and ambitious act portrays Jonathan as a capable enough leader, but this chapter will not be kind to Saul's 'house', and Jonathan will never inherit the mantle of national leadership. At the same time, Jonathan's initiative here foreshadows a number of his future endeavors in the narrative. In the aftermath of Jonathan's strike, Saul sounds the trumpet, saying 'Let the Hebrews hear!' It is not common for Israelites to refer to themselves as Hebrews, but Saul's use of the term anticipates those 'Hebrews' (עברים) in 13.7 who are reported to 'pass over' (עבר) the Jordan in 13.7.

13.4-7

The trumpet is sounded and Israel is rallying, but the Philistine forces are more than equal to the task, and produce superior numbers of troops and equipment. As numerous commentators have pointed out, it is the Philistine army that holds a decisive technological advantage. In 8.11, Samuel warns that the king 'will take your sons and appoint them to his chariots and to be his horsemen, and to run before his chariots'. That day has yet to arrive for Israel; only the Philistines have the chariots here, and the situation looks bleak for Saul. It is not often that the Deuteronomist breaks into figurative language. When one finds metaphors or similes used by the narrator, the reader is on red alert. Verse 5 is such a case: 'The Philistines gathered to fight with Israel: thirty thousand chariots and six thousand horsemen. The army was like the sand on the lip of the sea for multitude.' In this ominous description one senses a deliberate narrative strategy to show Saul between a rock and a hard place. Speaking of which, that is where his men are hiding, and the situation worsens with the report that many of the Israelite troops disappear into 'caves, thorn-bushes, rock crags, tombs, and cisterns'. Other 'Hebrews' (עברים), instead of hiding, simply 'pass over' (עבר) the river Jordan into eastern lands.

The few soldiers who remain with Saul are trembling, yet Saul does not flee. The mention of Gilgal in v. 4 reminds us of Samuel's commands in 10.8, 'And you shall go down before me to Gilgal; and behold, I am coming to you to offer burnt offerings and to sacrifice peace offerings. Seven days you shall wait, until I come to you and show you what you shall do' (RSV). The syntax of v. 7b indicates that Saul is holding out for the prophet's arrival: 'as for Saul, he was *still* at Gilgal, with the army trembling behind him'. Saul's conduct here suggests patience in the face of lengthening odds. Even the most hard-hearted reader would have to have some sympathy for the king's desperate plight. The reader discovers at the end of this chapter— an intentional analepsis—that Saul's beleaguered troops do not even have weapons! It would be convenient for the king to have the prophet's assistance at this moment, and hopefully Samuel is *en route*, just as he assured Saul he would be.

13.8

Most readers would agree that the host of Philistine chariots and soldiers as numerous as 'sand on the seashore' would pose a considerable challenge for Saul, even after the military brilliance of chap. 11. The biggest challenge for Saul is not, however, the Philistine horde nor the desertion and timidity of his own troops; rather, it is Samuel's command in 10.8 to 'wait seven days (שִׁבְעַת יָמִים תּוֹחֵל) until I come to you'. Here in 13.8, the prophet is a no-show, and Saul might rightly be wondering where the *sheol* Samuel is: 'And he waited seven days (וַיִּיחֶל שִׁבְעַת יָמִים) for the appointed time of Samuel, but Samuel did not come to Gilgal'. There are a number of commentators who say—straight-faced—that Saul did not wait 'long enough', a notion that is absurd, since it violates the plain sense of the narrative. Saul waits for seven days, but Samuel does not come to Gilgal. The situation does not improve when the troops—at least, the few who are still left with Saul—begin to 'scatter'. Previously, this word is used in 11.11 after the victory against the Ammonites: those 'who survived were scattered, so that no two of them were left together'. This will not, one suspects, be a repeat of Saul's finest hour.

13.9-10

> And Saul said, 'Bring near to me the burnt offering and the peace offerings'. And he offered the burnt offering. And just as he finished offering the burnt offering, behold, Samuel came. And Saul went out to meet him, to bless him.

In general terms, the worship of God through *sacrifice* is usually a good thing in the Hebrew Bible. In this specific case, however, the sacrifice is not a good thing for Saul. Moments after offering the sacrifice—the Hebrew text underscores the immediacy through the particle 'behold' (הִנֵּה)—Samuel arrives! The timing of Samuel's entrance is incredible. Indeed, Saul has only offered the 'burnt offering', and is perhaps about to offer the 'peace offering' when the prophet finally shows up. Is Samuel's arrival a mere coincidence, or is it intentional? Is the prophet testing the king, and has Saul done something wrong by offering the sacrifice? Some commentators argue that Saul is out of bounds, and performing an act that only a levitical priest should do. But Samuel is not a Levite either, strictly speaking. Besides, later kings such as David and Solomon offer abundant sacrifices without censure from any quarter (and are guilty of far worse crimes and misdemeanors, incidentally). Other commentators have accused Saul of panicking under pressure, thus revealing a lack of faith. Such a notion, though, is fallacious. Based on his conduct in chap. 11, Saul is anything but impious (recall how he spares his opponents and gives credit for God for the victory over the Ammonites in 11.13). I would ask: after offering the sacrifices, is Saul conscious of any error at this point? Verse 10 ends with Saul going out to meet Samuel, 'to bless him'. Walter Brueggemann (1990: 99) comments, 'Saul's action appears to be properly and guilelessly deferential'. The language of blessing, however, will not be reciprocated.

13.11-14

Statisticians often tell us 'the numbers don't lie'. Human speech is often difficult to gauge, but still, the 'numbers' can be helpful. As Peter Miscall points out, Samuel speaks two words in 13.11, and Saul's rejoinder is twenty-seven words. I am not suggesting that Saul's voluminous speech is an overcompensation, but it is a long reply to the prophet's very short inquiry, 'What have you done?' (מֶה עָשִׂיתָ). Samuel, one guesses, knows exactly what Saul has done, so his question is not a request for information as such. For his part, Saul's explanation sounds as desperate as his situation with the hard-pressing Philistine chariots. He begins by sharing his perception of the situation: 'Because I saw that the army had scattered from me, and *you*, you had not come at the appointed time of days, and the Philistines were gathering themselves at Michmash'. He proceeds to point out Samuel's failure to arrive at the appointed time. This is a charge that Samuel will never answer nor clarify. Neither Saul nor the reader ever finds out why Samuel does not arrive at the appointed hour.

Saul then shares his own inner thought process during the mounting pressure of the Philistine forces and the prophet's tardiness: 'I thought, "Now the Philistines will come down to me at Gilgal, and the face of the LORD I have not entreated"'. Saul's testimony ends with a verb 'to force', the same action of Joseph in Gen. 43.31 and 45.1 when he 'restrains himself' before his brothers: 'And I forced myself', Saul says, 'and I offered the burnt offering'. In 1899, the critical commentator H.P. Smith was convinced that Saul acquitted himself reasonably enough, and given the circumstances, Israel's first king does reasonably well: 'It is difficult to discover anything in the text at which Samuel could justly take offence'. But regrettably for Saul, H.P. Smith is not the one who needs convincing. Samuel is the judge and jury in this case, and he now responds with his verdict in 13.13-14:

> Samuel said to Saul, 'You have been foolish. You have not kept the commandment of the LORD your God, that he commanded you. For now the LORD would have established your kingdom over Israel forever. But now, your kingdom will not arise. The LORD sought for himself a man according to his heart, and the LORD commanded him to be ruler over his people, because you have not kept what the LORD commanded you.'

When Saul explains his actions to Samuel, there is abundant specificity, and the justification—the Philistine actions, Samuel's action (or lack thereof), and his own—corresponds to the details of the situation. By contrast, Samuel's response is not specific: he speaks in general terms about enormous issues. To begin with, Saul has been 'foolish'. Other uses of this word are not overly instructive: in Gen. 31.28 Laban accuses Jacob of being 'foolish' by stealing away and not allowing Laban to host a farewell party, and in 2 Sam. 24.10 David will confess his 'foolish' behavior of numbering the people. For Saul, the foolishness is that he has not kept *the commandment of the LORD*, in this case equated with the word of Samuel himself. It is not altogether clear what 'commandment' Saul has violated: waiting too long or not waiting long enough, presumptuous sacrificing, or not 'doing what his hand finds to do'. Had Saul kept the commandment, things would be radically different: he would have an eternally established throne. But now, after a rather short reign, the king is out of luck, and his kingdom will not arise.

As the speech of Samuel continues, it is revealed that not only will Saul's kingdom not arise, but he will be replaced—or rather *has been replaced*—by another. Just like the aborted type-scene is a bad omen for Saul, Samuel's words here imply that Saul's dynastic possibility has been *already* rejected. It is striking that the prophet implies that *if* Saul had kept the commandment of the LORD, then an eternal kingdom would have been his. In the event, however, Samuel says that Saul did not keep the commandment; consequently, it has been given to another. As Robert Alter (1999: 73) explains: 'Though this would have to be a veiled prediction of the advent of David, in naturalistic terms, the incensed Samuel is in a way bluffing: fed up with Saul, he announces to the king that God has already chosen a successor—about whom Samuel himself as yet knows nothing whatsoever, nor has he even had time for a communication from God that there will be a successor'. I am not prepared to quibble over the term 'bluff', but this certainly fits with a larger pattern of anticipations and affirmations. Saul will hear comparable lines in the future (see 1 Sam. 15.28; 28.17). Notably, Abner son of Ner will adopt a similar strategy of 'prophetic' utterances about David to enhance his own status at the expense of the house of Saul later in the story (see 2 Sam. 3.18; cf. the words of the northern tribes in 2 Sam. 5.2). At the same time, there are moments when Samuel 'the seer' has uncanny insight into future events, such as the many signs and 'donkey report' of 10.2-6. Perhaps this utterance about Saul's successor is in the same vein.

The most unsettling part of Samuel's speech is the possibility that Saul *could* have had an eternal kingdom, a proposition that does not quite fit in with the larger storyline of Judah being the tribe that has the most royal hints. One need not linger, I suppose, on such a contingency, since Saul has been told that he has failed, and that God has chosen someone else 'according to his heart'. It is often thought that this phrase—Alter is right, surely, that it refers to David—has to do with some special inner quality. However, a number of recent scholars have compared other uses of this phrase, and note that the emphasis here lies with God's freedom in regards to matters of election (note the same phrase in the next chapter, 14.7; cf. Ps. 20.5; Jer. 3.15). The summary of John Goldingay (2003: 557) is worth citing:

> Other occurrences of such phrases imply this need not suggest he is a king who shares Yhwh's priorities or way of thinking. It simply identifies David as the king whom Yahweh personally chose and made a commitment to. For theological as well as practical reasons the people will thus have a hard time removing this king whom they anointed. He is more like a lifetime president than one who needs periodic reelection. Yhwh is committed to David independently of commitment to the people as a whole.

In other words, the kind of rejection speech that Samuel delivers here will *not* mark someone who is chosen according to God's heart.

It would be much easier if the Deuteronomist simply labeled Saul's actions as 'evil'. This is the case in the final line of 2 Samuel 11: 'But the thing that David had done was evil in the eyes of the LORD'. However, here in 1 Samuel 13 there is no such opprobrium from the narrator, only the immediate context and the words of the characters that the reader has to evaluate. The matter has proven highly difficult for the commentator, as there is a considerable range of opinion on Saul's guilt, and Samuel's role in the affair: some say that Saul unequivocally is the sinner, while others imply that Samuel is guilty of prophetic regicide. Some say that Samuel should have been a better mentor, while others point out that David will do a whole lot worse than Saul yet not experience the same kind of rejection. Consider first the words of Cheryl Exum (1992: 27):

> It is not altogether evident wherein Saul's disobedience lies: he did wait the seven days required by Samuel, and only then made the offering because his army was scattering and because he feared the Philistines would attack before he entreated Yhwh's favor. Faced with the dilemma of choosing between competing and mutually exclusive courses of action, each with its own validity, Saul offers a sacrifice rather than wait any longer for Samuel. The choice is his, but necessity forces his hand. Samuel's failure to keep the appointment on time, followed by his arrival just as Saul finished offering the sacrifice, suggests something beyond mere chance. Moreover, his accusation, 'You have not kept the commandment of Yhwh', sheds no light on precisely what Saul had done wrong, especially since the narrative records no instruction from Yhwh but only from Samuel (10.8). In fact, Samuel had earlier given Saul confusing instructions. After anointing Saul, Samuel tells him 'do (*'aseh*) what your hand finds to do for God is with you', but then admonishes him to wait seven days 'until I come to you and tell you what you should do (*ta'aseh*). Now he demands an accounting, 'What have you done (*'asita*)?'

Turning to another reader, a poignant voice in the era of post-Holocaust literature unquestionably is Elie Wiesel. In addition to a host of novels, Wiesel has also explored numerous rabbinic legends and biblical texts, with an emphasis on character studies. In one such study, Wiesel (2003: 167) reflects on the career of Israel's inaugural monarch, and unfolds a powerful reading of the Saul story. On the issue of the prophet's 'tardiness', Wiesel inquires:

> Why was Samuel late? Why did he make his king and his people wait for such a long time? If he had an unexpected obligation to meet, a call from God for instance, why didn't he dispatch a messenger to inform the king of the emergency? Whatever the reasons on either side, Samuel's reaction to Saul's alleged haste does seem a bit unreasonable.

For Bill Arnold (2003: 200-201), the fault lies principally with the king: 'On the surface of the narrative, Saul's offense is a failure to wait for Samuel's arrival before consecrating battle. But more generally, this is tantamount to disobeying Yahweh's instructions as given through Samuel (see 13.13), which in turn exposes Saul's larger problem.' Of course, Saul's later actions will serve to enhance Arnold's claim. While one could argue that problems afterward stem from Saul's lack of good mentorship, Arnold does raise a provocative point here at this early point in Saul's career:

> He fails to accept the structure of authority established for him by Yahweh and his prophet Samuel at the time of his appointment (13.14). This unfortunately is a pattern that will be repeated in chap. 15. Thus, Saul's guilt derives from his determination to usurp power rightly belonging only to Yahweh and his servant Samuel.

Bruce Birch (1998: 1072) has a slightly different appraisal of the situation in 1 Samuel 13:

> Is the punishment announced by Samuel out of proportion to the offense? The text does not answer all of our questions. We are inclined to respond to the personalities at play here. Saul seems well meaning and concerned for his people. Samuel seems angry, temperamental, and reactionary. The modern reader is inclined to feel that he is overreacting.

But then Birch raises some points that move beyond the personality conflict of Saul and Samuel:

> We should probably not underestimate the depth of the issues involved in the transitions taking place with the establishment of kingship for the first time in Israel. How much power are kings to have?... Samuel is not an attractive personality in these stories, but the issues are more than a clash of personalities.

Each of these commentators underscores some poignant issues that the text raises, and there is a certain plausibility to each scenario to each of the reading positions articulated above. In my view, there is more here than simply a judgment on Saul personally, nor is this a triumph for Samuel—after the sting of rejection in chap. 8—in personal terms. Keeping in mind the wider direction of the Deuteronomistic History, the central judgment of chap. 13 falls on *kingship as an institution*. Here I am following a hint from David Gunn (1980: 40) when he suggests that the cause of Saul's rejection lies not so much in his actions of chap. 13, rather more in 'something he represents'. This possibility is also raised by A.F. Campbell (2003: 141): 'Placed as it is at the start of kingship in Israel, Samuel's judgment does not fall on Saul alone but on kings as a whole'.

It is surely no accident that the first thing to be rejected is Saul's dynastic possibility. Just like Samuel is unable to form a hereditary judgeship, so Saul does not have the prospect of an enduring royal house—a certainty that is ironically underscored by means of the early introduction of Jonathan in this very chapter without any genealogical reference to his father. The point here, in a nutshell, is that *Saul will not be allowed to choose his successor*, and that reality seems to have been established even before Samuel arrived. Rather than a reigning king's decision, the successor will be 'after God's heart', that is, the decision will be a matter of God's freedom and not 'the will of an earthly father'. As one glances ahead in the story, it is the dynastic issue that marks the difference between the northern kingdom of Israel and the southern kingdom of Judah. The south will have dynastic stability, whereas the north never will enjoy the same experience. In a parabolic way, Saul's kingship will resemble the northern experience, whereas David's kingship will resemble the southern experience. This is represented through the term 'established' (כּוּן). Samuel says to Saul, 'For now the LORD would have established (הֵכִין) your kingdom over Israel forever', but by contrast we read 'And David knew that the LORD had established (הֱכִינוֹ) him as king over Israel' with respect to David in 2 Sam. 5.12 (see also 2 Sam. 7.12-13). Samuel's words contain far more anticipations that any reader can imagine at this moment.

In the same scene where Saul's kingship is rejected, we are reminded of the efficacy of the prophetic word. Precisely because Samuel is a complicated character (and the circumstances surrounding Saul's transgression are murky), there is an emphasis on one of the larger theme within the Deuteronomistic History: that the prophetic word will find its fulfillment. Perhaps Saul lacks confidence in the prophetic word—under the circumstances it is hard to tell, and even if so, a generous reader would point out that Samuel is not on time—but there is a bigger judgment here: that of not heeding the prophetic word. Even if the circumstances are murky, so the Deuteronomist is saying, it is the prophetic word that will invariably find its fulfillment in the narrative. Samuel may be unpleasant and we may be sympathetic to the king's plight, but the prophetic word has a long-term currency that cannot be ignored. The first king has the hardest test. The rest of the kings do not have to fail in the same way, because the institution as such has already been weighed and found wanting. Of course, the conflict between king and prophet here in 1 Samuel 13 foreshadows later conflicts between king and prophet, and the prophet always has the last word.

'Is Saul a sinner', asks Peter Miscall (1986: 88), 'an ineffectual bungler, or a good leader who is being pushed toward disaster?' Regardless of how commentators come down on this decision, all would agree that Saul certainly did not apply for the job of Israel's *first born* king. In the book of Genesis, the first born son is usually a loser: from Cain to Manasseh, the first born has a difficult run of form, and innumerable scholars have pointed out that God consistently thwarts the principle of primogeniture throughout the book of Genesis. Saul is Israel's first born king in a pattern 'just like the nations'. So, in a reversal of *royal* primogeniture (akin to the pattern in Genesis), Saul fails just like any first born son. Saul's failure is not a great deal worse than Reuben, Zerah, or the arm-crossing of Jacob to choose Ephraim, but just as 'the older will serve the younger' according to Genesis 25, so Samuel reports that Samuel's successor has already been 'appointed' (or 'commanded'). It would probably be too bold to suggest that all the reversals of primogeniture in Genesis anticipate the rejection of Saul in favor of David, but it is a very tempting argument.

In Saul's beginning, the end of kingship is announced. Indeed, Israel will not have formal kingship after the trauma of exile, and thus Saul's aborted kingship and dynastic sterility foreshadows the end of the monarchy as such. The rejection of Saul's house, however, should not come as a complete surprise. Such developments have been anticipated from the early days of 1 Samuel with the dismissal of the house of Eli. Recall the prophetic words of 1 Sam. 2.35: 'I will raise up for myself a faithful priest, who shall do according to what is in my heart and in my mind. I will build him a sure house, and he shall go in and out before my anointed one forever'. Just as Eli's priestly line is replaced, so Saul's royal line is succeeded by one 'after God's heart', a matter that is at the heart of the issue of succession.

13.15-18

After the rejection speech, Samuel turns on his heel—so it seems—and departs, leaving Saul with no opportunity for a rejoinder. The prophet's word is final and irrevocable, so I suppose there is no need for an extended dialogue. If Samuel's rejection speech is clear enough, his post-speech destination is not, since there is a text-critical issue in 13.15. The Hebrew text reads: 'Then Samuel arose and went up from Gilgal, to Gibeah of Benjamin'. However, the NRSV (following the Greek) renders the verse: 'And Samuel left and went on his way from Gilgal. The rest of the people followed Saul to join the army; they went up from Gilgal toward Gibeah of Benjamin'. One is not sure why Samuel would go to Gibeah of Benjamin (Saul's hometown), but then again, one is rarely sure of Samuel's whereabouts in this chapter.

Regardless of Samuel's destination, his abrupt departure is quite a deflation after the stunning rejection of Saul, and this is the end of the prophet's direct participation in the narrative until chap. 15. Of course, Samuel is not the only one to depart from Saul: vast numbers of Israelite soldiers have also abandoned the (now-rejected) first king. After Saul musters the troops, the reader is told that the number of these soldiers is in the range of 'about six hundred'. This whole report is slightly odd: Jonathan is still there, but it is mildly surprising that there is no immediate battle. In the end, it seems that Saul's sacrifice accomplishes very little. Not only does it provide a cause for his rejection, but the troops still scatter even though he offers the sacrifice. It does not even seem as though there is an ensuing battle, which the reader may have expected on the basis of 13.8-9. There does follow a report about Philistine troop movements, but this is not a typical battle report. Instead of a combat scene, the narrator reports that Philistine 'raiders' branch out in three different directions, presumably to attack and pillage Israelite settlements. The description of 'three heads' of these raiding parties reminds us of Saul's great victory in chap. 11, when Saul divides his army into 'three heads' (11.11). Moments after Saul's rejection, we are reminded of his *successful* strategy and the many soldiers in the great victory over the Ammonites; this must rub some salt into the royal wound.

13.19-22
This paragraph is a parenthetical aside in which the main storyline is interrupted and new data is imparted: 'Now there was no metalworker that could be found in the entire land of Israel, for the Philistines thought, "Lest the Hebrews make swords or spears for themselves". All Israel would have to go down to the Philistines if anyone wanted to sharpen a plowshare, hatchet, axe or sickle.' The literary technique of *delayed exposition* happens elsewhere in 1 Samuel. For example, in chaps. 21 and 22 it is a key feature of the narrative design, as new facts are revealed at a later point in the story that cause a 're-reading' of the earlier scenes and dialogue. In this context at the end of chap. 13, the delayed exposition reveals that Saul's odds were even *worse*. We now discover that the same soldiers who were hiding in 'caves and in holes and in rocks and in tombs and in cisterns' (13.6) had no weapons! Equally embarrassing, these same soldiers—who presumably are farmers when there is no war—had to get every 'plowshare, hatchet, axe or sickle' sharpened by these same Philistines who were now attacking them. But this is not the only *corner on the market* that Saul has to contend with, as Victor Hamilton (2001: 244) remarks: 'If the Philistines have a monopoly on weapons production so that Israel has to go to them for supplies, Samuel has a monopoly on the commandments of God so that Saul has to go to him. What the Philistines possess metallurgically, Samuel has theologically.'

It is remarkable that in this chapter the reader is given abundant information on some points, yet not *near enough* information at other points. We know, for instance, that the Israelite soldiers were hiding in 'caves and in holes and in rocks and in tombs and in cisterns', and we know the exact price that the Philistines charged for sharpening 'plowshares, mattocks, axes, and sickles'. The reader is even given an interior view of the Philistine consciousness in 13.19, but we are not told why Samuel fails to show up on time. As Peter Miscall (1986: 89) comments, 'Any narrator who knows what the Philistines charged for sharpening plowshares and axes should know whether Samuel and Saul are together at the same place and whether Saul wanted to respond to Samuel's denunciation'.

13.23
This eventful chapter ends with a detail about a further troop movement ('Then a Philistine garrison marched out to Micmash pass'), thus setting the stage for the next phase in the narrative. On the purpose of 13.23, Joyce Baldwin (1988: 106) implies the Philistines are stationing a further guard-post, and the tiny Israelite forces are hemmed in: 'The Philistines further threatened Israel by setting a garrison at the pass of Micmash, beside the ravine that separated the armies, and the tension in the story mounts'. Any victory of Israel, one suspects, will be wholly due to divine intervention, since only Saul and Jonathan 'his son' have any weapons. There is almost a 'business as usual' tone to the final line of the chapter. The king is rejected, but the conflict with the Philistines goes on. Indeed, Saul's barren reign will continue for many more chapters, plagued with Philistine conflict dogging him until the very end. Saul's odds of beating the Philistines are slim, but his chances of surviving Samuel's prophetic indictment are even worse.

1 SAMUEL 14

For a chapter that was all about warfare, chap. 13 featured very little description of actually fighting. While Jonathan strikes a Philistine outpost early in the chapter, Saul himself does not lead the troops into battle—instead he is caught up in ritual affairs of sacrifice. The situation is not dissimilar in chap. 14: Jonathan again initiates conflict, and Saul again is agitated about ritual matters. Samuel does not feature in this chapter, but instead a member of Eli's doomed priestly line is present. Saul has been told that he will not have an 'established' kingdom, implying that his house has no future. Yet 13.22 indicates that Jonathan is Saul's son, and Jonathan is the protagonist of this chapter. In royal terms, Jonathan is not a character endowed with great expectations. A son with no future, we nonetheless see Saul's son presented favorably in these scenes. Chapter 14 is divided into several parts. The opening sequence focuses on Jonathan's initiative in commencing hostilities, and as the battle spreads out, the scene shifts to the camp of Israel and the victory against the Philistines. The middle section of 1 Samuel 14 hinges on Saul's oath and its aftermath, culminating in a confrontation between father and son. In the previous chapter, Saul is rejected (ostensibly) because of a cultic error. It is surely no accident that in this chapter, cultic activity abounds. Jonathan is found guilty in a lot-casting ceremony, but his life is spared. The chapter moves toward a conclusion with a summary of Saul's military actions and familial relations. In a number of ways, chap. 14 foreshadows what the remainder of Saul's days will be like.

14.1

1 Samuel 14 begins with a phrase 'It was the day' (ויהי היום), and this is presumably the same day that the Philistine garrison 'goes out' at the end of chap. 13. Although the phrase is rendered by the NRSV rather generically as 'One day', Joseph Blenkinsopp (1964: 426) defends the translation '*the* day' as follows: 'The time factor is all-important. The entire action takes place in the course of a single day, beginning no doubt in the morning and ending with the dramatic scene of the condemnation and redemption of Jonathan as the shadows were lengthening.' To be sure, the first character mentioned is

Jonathan, and on this occasion he is called 'the son of Saul'. Recalling that Saul's house will not endure, it is counter-intuitive that the rejected king has a rejected son who will be the catalyst for an Israelite victory against considerable odds. Although Jonathan is first introduced in chap. 13 as a man of action, he is not afforded any direct speech in that chapter. As mentioned in the above analysis of 1 Samuel 9, a figure's first words can be an important moment for characterization, as Saul's initial speech ('Come, let us go back') illustrates. Here, Jonathan's first recorded words are: 'Come, let us pass over...' Not only does this reinforce the idea of Jonathan as a risk-taker, but the verb he uses, 'pass over' (עבר), evokes memories of the defections in the previous chapter, as a large number of 'Hebrews' (עברים) go AWOL and 'pass over' (עבר) the Jordan (13.7). This wordplay is important because it anticipates a reversal in this chapter: through Jonathan's endeavors in 1 Samuel 14, those 'Hebrews' who previously 'passed over' will return to the camp of Israel (see 14.21).

The final clause of 14.1 reports a measure of secrecy in Jonathan: 'But he did not tell his father'. The motif of secrecy is a vital component of the plot in 1 Samuel 14, and it also produces a reflex to chap. 10, where Saul does not 'tell' his uncle about the matter of the kingdom. It is hard to know if Jonathan's secrecy signals an estrangement between Saul and Jonathan, or whether the secrecy is merely logistical. Still, in view of the larger narrative there may be hints of the former: 'Are we to see this lack of communication between father and son in the light of their subsequent turbulent relationship? Even in the present chapter filial respect and paternal affection are not overwhelmingly present' (Gordon 1986: 136). Jonathan's covert offensive in this chapter begins in 'the day', but in light of the numerous references to 'night' in this chapter, it is notable that the episode begins with Saul in the dark.

14.2-3
As Jonathan begins his 'passing over' to the Philistine garrison, the camera angle shifts to Saul, who is 'sitting under a tree' in the outskirts of Gibeah. Saul's sedentary position here is worth remembering, since the king will be presented in this posture again later in the narrative. For instance, in 19.9 Saul will again be 'sitting', this time with spear in hand, and poised to strike his musical son-in-law. In 22.9, Saul will be 'sitting', and brooding with his servants around him. In the present context of chap. 14, there is a situational irony: Saul violates Samuel's command by *taking action* in chap. 13, whereas now there is a notable *lack* of action as Saul is 'sitting' and seemingly paralyzed (cf. Edelman 1991: 86). At least Saul is not alone, since 600 men are with him, but this number represents a considerable drop from previous chapters.

In addition to the 600 men, there is another member of the king's retinue: 'Ahijah son of Ahitub, Ichabod's brother, son of Phinehas son of Eli, the priest of the LORD in Shiloh'. At the very least, this long description of Ahijah and his pedigree evokes a host of narrative memories: Ichabod's widowed mother dies in childbirth with the lament 'glory is exiled from Israel'; Phinehas is killed and the prophetic word spoken against him finds fulfillment; heavy Eli falls backwards from his throne and plunges to his death; and Shiloh is displaced as a sanctuary and eschewed as a spatial setting.

Ahijah's attendance on Saul thus assumes a heightened significance here, as two rejected lines are now together in one place: two generations lost in space, with no time left to start again (as Don McLean would sing). The reader is unsure whether Ahijah the priest has been in Saul's presence before, but surely it is no coincidence that *right after* the royal rejection in chap. 13, Saul is pictured with the rejected priestly line! As David Jobling (1976: 368) opines, 'this first mention of an Elide after the disasters which befell Eli's family in chap. 4 triggers the response 'rejected by Yhwh'. Lest the point be missed, it is reinforced by the odd and needless genealogical reference to Ichabod, Ahijah's uncle, picking up on 4.21-22, and reminding the reader that 'the glory has departed'. His own royal glory gone, where else would we expect Saul to be than with a relative of 'Glory gone'?' Having been denounced by Samuel, Saul is now pictured with the doomed house of Eli. Since a message of rejection was also delivered to the Elides through Samuel in chap. 3, it is sadly fitting that these two houses are linked here in chap. 14.

While there is no stated reason as to why Saul is with the priest, one suspects that the previous chapter affords a clue: in chap. 13 Saul makes a 'ritual' error, and is now trying either to compensate for that error, or make sure it is not repeated. The latter speculation gains some credibility when we discover that Ahijah—the Elide priest—is not empty-handed: he is 'lifting up an ephod'. Several commentators note a symmetry: Jonathan has a 'lifter' of weapons (נשא כליו) while Saul has a 'lifter' of the ephod (נשא אפוד). In Exodus 28–29, the ephod is worn by the high priest and is used to ascertain the divine will. But in Judges 8, Gideon makes an ephod that becomes a 'snare', and in Judges 18–19 an ephod is made by a knavish priest. In this present context, the mention of an ephod has a foreshadowing function, both in this chapter and beyond. Later in 1 Samuel 14 Saul will 'ask' of God, yet not be answered—and still later the ephod will end up in the hands of David. Consequently, this tableau is not favorable for the son of Kish: the rejected king is standing with the rejected priest holding an ephod that will be dysfunctional.

14.4-7

The opening lines of the chapter confirm that Saul is unaware that Jonathan and his armor bearer have slipped out of the camp, and the last part of 14.3 also informs us that 'the troops did not know that Jonathan had gone'. The narrative focus now returns to Jonathan and his armor bearer with a lengthy description of the terrain: between them and the Philistine outpost are rock pillars named Bozez and Seneh, names that apparently mean 'thorn' and 'tooth' respectively. The purpose of this fairly elaborate description is so the reader can visually appreciate the difficult crossing, and this description of the fierce terrain is augmented by the direct speech between Jonathan and his armor bearer. Jonathan's first words in 14.6 are identical to his opening words in 14.1 ('Come, let us pass over'). The only reason I can see for the repetition of Jonathan's words 'Come, let us pass over' (לכה ונעברה) is the connection with Saul's first recorded words in the narrative back in 9.5 when he instructs his accompanying servant lad, 'Come, let us go back' (לכה ונשובה). The similar (yet contrasting) speech accents thus draw an instant comparison between father and son, and this idea of comparison will be developed as chap. 14 progresses.

Furthermore, Jonathan's words—'Come, let us pass over to the outpost of these foreskinned ones'—is a subtle reminder of Judges 14.3, when Samson's parents say to him: 'Is there not a woman among the daughters of your brothers, or among all my people, that you must go to take a wife from the foreskinned Philistines?' Both narratives feature parental conflict as a leading motif, and before 1 Samuel 14 is finished there will be more allusions to the book of Judges. In fact, before this speech of Jonathan is finished there is another allusion, since his utterance, 'Perhaps the LORD will act for us, for there is no restraint for the LORD to save by many or by few', evokes memories of Gideon, confirming that any unlikely victory will be due to God's intervention. Bruce Birch (1998: 1078) comments: 'Jonathan does not presume on God's freedom, but he is certain that if victory is possible it will come from the Lord. He then acts in confidence that God will save when God wills it.'

The language of Jonathan's speech is not only confined to Judges, but also intersects with earlier moments in 1 Samuel. As Diana Edelman (1991: 84) has noticed, the verb 'pass through' (עבר) occurring in the 'hill country of Ephraim' reminds us of Saul's previous passing through this realm in chap. 9, and Jonathan's use of the term 'restraint' (מעצור) echoes the divine words of 9.17, 'And when Samuel saw Saul, the LORD answered him, "Behold, the man whom I said to you, 'This one will restrain (עצר) my people'"'. These intersections of language are striking, since Jonathan is not a son who will reign over Israel, a reality that is further reinforced by the meaning of his name ('the LORD gives'), since the LORD has already given the kingdom into the hands of another. Nevertheless, in view of the Philistine outpost, Jonathan's words are theologically bold, and indicate what he is willing to undertake for Israel on behalf of his father. So far in 1 Samuel, it is only 'Benjamin' who has provided useful sons.

The rejoinder from Jonathan's armor bearer is instructive on several levels: 'Do all that is in your heart. Incline yourself, behold I am with you, according to your heart.' The slightly awkward syntax has usually resulted in paraphrase by recent translators, but a hint of discomfiture in the words actually serves to highlight the lad's own faithfulness to his master, even in this seemingly ill-advised undertaking. But, like Saul's servant lad in chap. 9, Jonathan's armor bearer is also a conduit for other thematic purposes in the narrative. Barbara Green (2003: 242) asks:

> Who is this (masked) armor bearer, speaking about God's options and hearts beating as one? This single sentence is all he says, but the hearts aligned suggest that the boy is a marker for the young David (of one heart with Jonathan, and with God). This is a narrative move, all but subliminal, similar to the slight trace of Saul we may glimpsed in 1 Sam. 4.12.

In the larger storyline, the phrase 'according to your heart' sheds light on the earlier use in 13.14 ('the LORD sought for himself a man according to his heart'), and thus it is now clear that the phrase means *according to God's choice*. The house of Saul is not chosen according to God's heart; ironically, that man will be another 'armor bearer' who will soon enter the house of Saul.

14.8-15

Jonathan's strategic initiative involves a lengthy discussion of a 'sign' that he proposes to his armor bearer: after revealing their position to the garrison, if the Philistines invite them to 'go up', then this should be understood as a sign that the LORD has 'given' (again, the meaning of Jonathan's name) them into their hands. At the outset of the story, the reader may have thought that Jonathan was mounting a surprise attack, not dissimilar to that of his father Saul against Nahash the Ammonite in chap. 11. Any such notion, however, is here dispelled as Jonathan communicates his presence to the Philistine garrison, in accordance with the sign he is seeking. Jonathan's sign, one would admit, is much simpler than the elaborate and stratified 'sign language' of Samuel to Saul in chap. 9. The Philistines show their wit: 'Behold! Hebrews! Marching out from the holes where they hid themselves!' This disdainful remark is followed by a self-assured invitation: 'Come up to us, and we will cause you to know a thing!' Unlike Gideon, Jonathan does not need to have the sign repeated: he interprets the Philistine response as confirmation of the sign and off he goes. 'Come up after me',

Jonathan bids his armor bearer, 'for the LORD has given them into the hand of Israel'.

The Philistines' confidence—not for the first time—proves to be misplaced. In chap. 5, the Philistines underestimate both the ark of the covenant and the potency of their god, Dagon, and end up with deeply disturbing hemorrhoids. Similarly, the Philistines are guilty of overconfidence when it comes to Jonathan here in chap. 14. Accepting their invitation, Jonathan navigates through the previously described terrain of Bozez and Seneh by using his 'hands and feet'. In dramatic fashion, the Philistine's fall before Jonathan, while his trusty armor bearer follows along behind and finishes them off. The tally of casualties is reported as 'about twenty men within an area about half a furrow long in an acre of land' (NRSV). Consequently, there is a great panic among the Philistine troops in the camp and the field. Hardened soldiers—no doubt used to mastery over their Israelite neighbors—are now quaking along with the very ground itself.

The reader can be forgiven for thinking that the Deuteronomist is presenting Jonathan as an impressive chap, and one who would perhaps make a good king for Israel. Yet Jonathan will never reign, although on this occasion God is with the house of Saul and uses this rejected line to deliver his people from the hand of the Philistines.

14.16-19

There is yet another shift in focus, and in this next scene the narrative events are filtered through the perspective of Saul's lookouts: 'behold, the multitude was surging hither and thither' (RSV). Because the event is relayed from the point of view of Saul's watchmen, the sense of surprise is further enhanced: they were not expecting this kind of occurrence. Also, the reader is prepared for Saul's own reaction. So far in the chapter Saul is not afforded any direct speech; indeed, since Samuel's long rejection speech Saul has not spoken a word, as it were. Now, in response to the confusion, Saul says: 'Inspect, and see who went from us!' In terms of narrative chronology, Saul has been sitting under a tree while simultaneously his son is launching the strike against the garrison. Yet the king would have reason to suspect Jonathan is the one who has left the camp; after all, it is Jonathan who commences hostilities—perhaps to Saul's strategic detriment—in chap. 13. Once the roll is called and it is discovered that Jonathan and his armor bearer are missing, Saul's imperatives in 14.18-19 are baffling:

> Saul said to Ahijah, 'Bring near the ark of God!' (For on that day was the ark of God and the sons of Israel.) Saul was yet speaking to the priest, but the confusion in the Philistine camp kept on increasing. And Saul said to the priest, 'Remove your hand!'

If there is confusion in the Philistine camp, then this speech reveals confusion in Saul's own mind as well. Diana Edelman (1991: 86) remarks, 'In vv. 16-19 the narrator reveals to his audience the first ramification of Saul's announced rejection at Gilgal: Saul can no longer act with confidence and is uncertain of his divine backing'. Furthermore, the uncertainty extends even to the textual tradition. As rendered above, the Hebrew text reads 'ark of God', whereas the Greek LXX reads 'ephod'. A number of commentators inquire of this variant, and opt for 'ephod'. Bravely, the NRSV sticks with the more difficult text, which in this case is surely 'ark'. In view of 1 Sam. 7.2, one may have expected the ark to remain dormant in Kiriath-jearim until it is reclaimed in 2 Samuel 6, so its appearance here is something of a puzzle. The peculiarity is intensified by the narrator's aside, 'For on that day was the ark of God and the sons of Israel'.

An equally difficult problem is: What is Saul doing with the ark? There are two options. First, Saul could be 'making inquiry', that is, trying to ascertain the divine will. This is usually done with the ephod, but some scholars point to Judg. 20.27 as a precedent: 'The sons of Israel inquired of the LORD, for the ark of the covenant of God was there in those days'. Thus, in 14.19 when Saul says to the priest 'Remove your hand' he must be terminating the inquiry, for whatever reason. A second option is that Saul could be preparing for combat, and thus he summons the ark to the battlefield much like the elders of Israel do in 1 Samuel 4. In this case, his imperative to the priest ('Withdraw your hand') would abort the attempt, for whatever reason. Perhaps Saul is coming to his better senses; given the fate of the ark the last time it was summoned to the battlefield in 1 Samuel 4—when, incidentally, a son of Benjamin brings the news of 'tumult' to blind Eli (of the rejected house) who falls off his throne—it is better to keep the ark away from the epicenter of battle.

In the end, it may be more likely that Saul is intending to seek the divine will, but either way, having a member of the house of Eli handle the ark is not a good omen for the rest of the chapter. What emerges here is that the house of Eli—though not necessarily with intention—is undermining Saul. This foreshadows the events of 1 Samuel 21–22, where Saul unconsciously fulfills the prophetic word spoken against the house of Eli in chap. 2. As David Jobling (1976: 368-69) explains,

> The axes which here intersect, the rejection of Saul and the rejection of the Elide priesthood, will do so again in 22.11-19, when Saul will bloodily fulfill the prophecy of 2.31-33, wreaking Yhwh's will on the Elides. Even here, in chap. 14, Saul has no joy of his priest. Both of Ahijah's further appearances (vv. 18-19, 36) have to do with needless and unsuccessful attempts to consult the sacred lot.

In the future, Saul's lack of success with seeking a divine oracle will only increase.

14.20-23

Given Saul's recent run of form, it would not be astonishing if he suffered defeat in this battle. However, in 14.20 he rallies the troops and things go better than anyone could have expected. As we recall, the soldiers of Israel have no swords—only the Philistines have them. Such a deprivation now appears in a rather different light, as suddenly the Philistines are monopolizing *each other* with their metallurgical products: 'Then Saul and all the troops with him were assembled, and came as far as the battle, but behold, the sword of each man was against his friend!' The 'behold' particle refracts Saul's point of view, as the incredulity of the situation (the sword of each Philistine against 'his friend') is filtered through Saul's visual perspective.

There are even more reversals to come, since 14.21 reads: 'Now the Hebrews who had been with the Philistines in times past, and had even gone up with them into the camp round about, *even they* turned to the Israelites who were with Saul and Jonathan'. Previously, soldiers have deserted Saul and aligned themselves with the Philistine cause, perhaps in search of a better deal, since the Philistines are the ones with the weapons and sharpening facilities. Since this traitorous situation has not be revealed by the narrator until this point, the reader is compelled to agree with Kyle McCarter's (1981: 241) assessment of the deserters: '...they were loyal Israelites who defected to the enemy in times of distress and who now return as the fortunes of war change again'. Of course, Western democracies know little about the bandwagon mentality of the electorate, but one still has to sympathize with Saul in this instance: hard-pressed on every side, we now discover that some of his troops had actually bolted to the Philistine side.

These 'Hebrews' are not the only ones passing over and back to the Israelite cause. The reader is further informed in 14.22 that those Israelites who previously had 'caused themselves to be hidden' in holes and tombs are now eagerly rejoining their former comrades-in-arms. A generous interpreter might suggest that they are driven by sentiment to recommit themselves to Israel, but the more likely reason is that they—like their defection counterparts in 14.22—are more motivated by the mammon of plunder than loyalty to king and country.

Given this situation of returning Israelites, one might ask: How *many* soldiers returned to Saul in light of the victory? When one compares 14.23 in the RSV and NRSV, a key difference emerges. Both translations essentially render 'So the LORD delivered Israel that day; and the battle passed beyond Bethaven', as reflected in the Hebrew text, but the NRSV includes some additional information supplied by the Greek text: 'the troops with Saul numbered altogether about ten thousand men. The battle spread out over the hill country of Ephraim.' An advantage of the Greek text, I suppose, is that it specifies exactly how many (and, indeed, it is a large number) of turncoats and hiders that Saul has to deal with both when they leave, and then upon their return. Moreover, since we find out that there is a 'sin' with regard to eating of blood and swooping on the plunder below, then we know that there are about ten thousand guilty soldiers.

14.24-26

Despite the victory for Israel over the Philistines, there are still more conflicts and challenges to come in this chapter for Saul: 'Now the men of Israel were hard pressed on that day, and Saul had put the people under an oath, saying, "Cursed is the man who eats food until evening, and I am avenged from my enemies". So none of the people tasted food.' Although my translation of 14.24 follows the Hebrew text, it should be noted that the NRSV opts for the Greek text for the first part of the verse: 'Now Saul committed a very rash act on that day. He had laid an oath on the troops, saying...' While the Greek is helpful if Saul deserves outright condemnation for the oath, in light of the narrator's silences elsewhere, there are a number of reasons for resisting this variant. Building on S.R. Driver's classic summation, Robert Alter (1999: 80) argues, 'the Septuagint's version of the first clause of this verse might be regarded as an interpretive gloss on the lapidary formulation of the received text'. At the same time, if the Greek text is followed, then the 'hard pressed' factor is missing, which leaves no motive for Saul's oath (see A.F. Campbell 2003: 147). The situation of the hard-pressed troops here in chap. 14 mirrors the condition of the troops in 13.6, 'When the men of Israel saw that they were in straits (for the people were hard pressed), the people hid themselves in caves and in holes and in rocks and in tombs and in cisterns'. Just the like the troops in chap. 13 are driven into the ground (literally), the situation in chap. 14 has its own austerity: the people are hard pressed because of a long day of warfare, but also are in a classic double bind because of the restrictions of king's oath.

However, it is not clear *when* exactly Saul makes this oath (אלה). Verse 24 reports an antecedent action, and within the context, one could infer that at some point the troops were 'hard pressed', and Saul swears. Agreeing that this oath represents a flashback in the narrative, Robert Gordon (1986: 138) reflects on Saul's rationale for the oath: 'The point of the fast was, we may assume, to secure Yahweh's continued help. Saul was late in joining the fray, but now that he is involved he will make a proper job of it, though, as events turn out, his contribution has the opposite effect'. This is not the last time Saul will fast. The situation is repeated in chap. 28, when Saul does not eat 'all that day and all that night', before his fast is broken by his last supper served by the witch of Endor.

Furthermore, this is not the first time in the Deuteronomistic History that there has been an 'oath' (or 'curse') involving a parent: in Judg. 17.2, Micah's mother swears an oath (אלה) that implicates her own son. As we will see, there are further similarities with Judges that are evident as the narrative continues.

In terms of content, the language of Saul's oath has aroused discussion among commentators, especially the words 'until I have been avenged on my enemies'. Among those who view Saul's actions in a positive light, Josh. 10.13 is often cited: 'And the sun stood still, and the moon stayed, until the nation took vengeance on their enemies'. But others take a more critical view of Saul's ritual activity here. For example, Robert Polzin (1993: 135) notes, 'This oath fills Saul's character zone with that excessive concern over ensuring the success of one's efforts already dealt with in detail by the Deuteronomist in the negative depictions of judges like Gideon and Jephthah; it reminds us as well of Samson's abiding concerns about personal vengeance upon his enemies'. Indeed, for Saul to have his character zone intersect with Gideon, Jephthah, and Samson is not an affirmation, since Gideon is involved with a ephod controversy, Jephthah makes a vow that is disastrous for his child, and Samson's vengeance against the Philistines has grave consequences. Barbara Green (2003: 244) observes that Saul's vengeance sets in motion a pattern that will recur later in the narrative: 'In fact, when we hear Saul talk like that again (ch. 18), he will be clearly putting his own obsessions above other considerations. Saul's words here begin to develop a pattern in which he will unwittingly snare himself; that is, the personage he most thwarts here is himself.'

The immediate result is that Saul's oath is certainly taken seriously by the Israelite army: 'So none of the troops tasted food'. However, the collective resolve of Saul's troops is put to a rather severe taste test in 14.24-25: 'Then the entire country entered into the forest, and there was honey on the ground. The troops entered the forest, and behold, honey was flowing! But there was none who reached his hand to his mouth, because the troops feared the oath.' There are a couple of textual problems with these two lines, and some scholars emend the text because they feel that the same event is needlessly repeated, concluding that the duplication must be a scribal error. However, I would submit that in these two lines the same event is reported from two different points of view. The first report (14.24) is the narrator's perspective, whereas the 'repetition' in the next line (14.25) is the angle of perception of the famished troops. Indeed, the 'flowing' honey looks even better from the troops' vantage point, yet they do not eat. The narrative purpose of the *double report* is visually to illustrate that the people must have been sorely tempted to eat, but despite the vivid and inviting description that even the reader can virtually taste, no soldier partakes because of fear of the oath.

One is not sure if the army fears the 'oath' as such (and the divine consequences for breaking it) or whether they fear the royal wrath if they get caught, but the king's word is clear, and it is obeyed.

14.27-30

The honey is looking good and there is plenty of it, but the oath is prohibitive. However, there is at least one person who does not hear it. Jonathan—presumably occupied with trouncing 20 men in the area of about half an acre—does not 'hear' his father's oath. At some point Jonathan has rejoined the troops, and now dips the tip of his staff into the honeycomb. Barbara Green (2003: 244) raises a provocative question on the semantic range of 'hear' (שמע), a verb that can also mean 'obey': 'Suppose the verb used for Jonathan, universally translated as "had not heard" is translated as 'did not heed'? The choices are open.' Even if the reader opts for the traditional rendering of 'heard', considering the 'hear/obey' option does raise awareness of an issue that is absolutely central in the next chapter, where Samuel the prophet announces to Saul: 'hearing/obeying (שמע) is better than sacrifice'. But for now, Jonathan's hand extends to his mouth, his eyes 'brighten', and he is under Saul's curse.

Any brightness in this situation is dimmed as a soldier reports the ravenous news about Saul's oath to Jonathan. Notably, the soldier's words do not have a positive spin: 'Your father certainly swore an oath with respect to the troops, saying, "Cursed (ארור) is the man who eats food today", and the troops are faint!' Perhaps the soldier is annoyed that *he* cannot eat like Jonathan. Regardless, from his perspective, the soldier explicitly connects the fast with the faintness, and subtly passes judgment on the oath. In response, Jonathan speaks some serious words, beginning with the assessment, 'My father has troubled (עכר) the country'. Elsewhere in the Deuteronomistic History, this term is used when Achan brings 'trouble' (עכר) on Israel for an infraction in the context of *holy war* in Josh. 7.25. Hence the recurrence of the term is ironic here: Achan 'troubles' the land in Joshua, and is about to be the subject of a lot-casting ceremony, and Jonathan says his father 'troubles' the land, and *he* is about to be the subject of a lot-casting ceremony! The term also occurs in Judg. 11.35 when Jephthah laments, 'Alas, my daughter! You have brought me very low; you have become the cause of great trouble to me (בעכרי). For I have opened my mouth to the LORD, and I cannot take back my vow' (NRSV). Again, the invocation of Jephthah's vow—in which he implicates his own child—is a compelling intertext, since the son of Saul is imperiled in a manner similar to the ill-fated daughter of Jephthah.

As if to embellish his own rhetorical point, Jonathan offers some visual testimony: 'See (ראו) how my eyes brightened (ארו) when I tasted (טעמתי) a little (מעט) of this honey'. Since Jonathan's eyes brightened, it is possible that his hearer might infer that his father's oath was not particularly bright. There is a wordplay between the terms 'see', 'bright', and 'curse' (ארור). According to Robert Gordon (1986: 139), the purpose of the wordplay is to underline the 'antithesis' between what was and 'what might have been'. On the latter note, Jonathan concludes his speech with the point that if the people had 'eaten freely', then the slaughter would have been greater. In Jonathan's view, Saul's oath therefore is not efficacious.

One assumes that the intended audience for Jonathan's speech is the troops of Israel, a beleaguered group who have had a long day that is far from over. If Saul has been well-intentioned and is seriously trying to seek God's favor, then Jonathan rejects this attempt as misguided. Of course, it is possible Jonathan is simply being dramatic, but the son does (whether consciously or not) raise a point about a pattern the father has fallen into during this chapter. Since the events leading up to his rejection by Samuel, Saul has had a hard time doing anything right. David Jobling (1976: 368) suggests: 'Saul in this story is not so much wicked as foolish and frustrated. His intentions are good, indeed thoroughly pious, but he pursues them in self-defeating ways.' Whether Saul has been paralyzed by the trauma of rejection, or whether he has been flawed all along is not stated in the text, but now Saul is losing Jonathan's favor because of an ostensible ritual offence just as he lost Samuel's favor in the previous chapter for a similar reason. In this chapter, the wedge between father and son is growing larger with each successive scene.

14.31-35

Jonathan's remarks about 'slaughter' and 'eating freely' receive no answer. Instead, the narrator suspends this conversation and the reader is confronted with the odd lines of 14.31-32, introducing a scene that is all about 'slaughter' and 'eating freely', yet not in the way Jonathan was suggesting: 'After they had struck down the Philistines that day from Michmash to Aijalon, the troops were very faint; so the troops flew upon the spoil, and took sheep and oxen and calves, and slaughtered them on the ground; and the troops ate them with the blood' (NRSV). This report apparently gives a summary of the day's events and the *reason* why the people are faint, and how they combat their faintness by swooping upon the spoil. Kyle McCarter (1981: 249) wonders if the troops are encouraged by Jonathan's actions (eating) and his words (the oath is folly), and hence are willing to partake of the plunder. Now that the day is seemingly over, perhaps Saul's oath is no longer binding.

Despite some textual uncertainty, the verb for 'swoop down', is, as Robert Alter (1999: 82) notes, used elsewhere for birds of prey. The use of this verb is a graphic way to illustrate that, by association, the soldiers have become like unclean animals such as ravens and vultures. The term 'unclean' is not an understatement, since the narrator immediately reports that the army was 'eating with the blood'. Commentators point to other biblical texts (such as Lev. 17 and Deut. 12) for prohibitions on this kind of consumption. The situation is only described by the narrator, but the action is reported to Saul by an unnamed speaker who specifically labels the action as sinful: 'Behold, the troops are sinning against the LORD by eating with the blood'. Most readers would agree that there is a problem, but, like the soldier in 14.28, the report here has a negative spin, and this might influence Saul's reaction.

In response to the 'sinning' report, Saul utters a strange invective: 'You've acted deceitfully!' While no party is specifically addressed, on the basis of the plural verb one can assume that Saul's comment is directed to the army who are eating blood, a ritual misdemeanor he categorizes as 'deception' or 'treachery'. After this outburst, Saul moves to address the problem itself by issuing a couple more imperatives. First, Saul commands that a large rock be 'rolled' before him. This seems straightforward enough, but the second command is harder to interpret: 'Disperse among the troops, and say to them, "Everyone bring to me his bull or sheep and slaughter them on this, then eat. Do not sin against the LORD by eating the blood".' The difficulty here is that one is not sure *who* is directed here. It is possible that this imperative includes Ahijah, the priest from the doomed line of Eli. If so, it is mildly ironic because sacrificial incompetence and raw meat are some of the principal reasons why Eli's house is rejected (see 1 Sam. 2.12-17). For the present moment, though, the Elides' vast experience with uncooked meat comes in handy, and the troops are compliant.

In 14.35 the last event of this section is recorded, and it is translated by the NRSV as follows: 'And Saul built an altar to the LORD; it was the first altar that he built to the LORD'. The construction of an altar is not without precedent in 1 Samuel. The prophet Samuel builds an altar in 7.17, and in 2 Samuel 24 David will also build one. However, the second clause is more problematic. According to Daniel Hawk (2005: 9), rather than the NRSV's 'it was the first altar he built', another translation option is: 'he began to build an altar to the LORD'. If this is possible, then the implication is that Saul certainly begins to build the altar, but does not quite finish. Such an aborted project would be sadly appropriate for this chapter, given the other projects that are abandoned (such as the episode with the ark in 14.18-19). Construction of the altar may be underway, but the ritual activity of this chapter is far from finished.

14.36-39

This has been a very long day for Saul. The altar could be the end, but this building project only marks a new beginning, and the night is still young. With admirable energy, Saul rallies his troops for a nocturnal pursuit of the Philistines. Whether the altar has boosted Saul's resolve is not certain, but with his opponent on the ropes, Saul is suggesting going for the knockout. In fact, the king wants to pursue the Philistines 'until not a man remains', and this would be a decisive victory indeed. The king's imperative is favorably received by his subjects: 'All that is good in your eyes, do!' There is another voice, though, that the reader hears for the first time in the chapter: 'And the priest said, "Let us draw near to God here"'. In all probability 'the priest' is Ahijah, who is introduced at the beginning of the chapter, and the one whom Saul addresses about the ark in 14.19. It is hard to determine exactly *why* he speaks at this particular moment in the story. Parallel scenes are hard to find, but there are some rough analogies with Jehoshaphat asking Ahab to 'First seek the word of the LORD' in 1 Kings 22. In both cases, a king is invited to seek divine counsel before undertaking a military expedition, and in both cases the king is undermined by such counsel.

Whether the priest's words are in opposition to Saul, or whether he is trying to enhance the legitimacy of the king's proposal and the morale of the troops with this spiritual inquiry cannot be determined. Yet when he says 'Let us draw near to God here', one assumes that the ephod is involved; only mentioned in 14.3 at the time of Ahijah's introduction, the ephod is now activated in the narrative. While the actual operation of the ephod remains elusive, it is oft-noted by scholars that the ephod is wielded by the priest and works on the binary system: a question is posed and a yes/no answer is given. This, at any rate, seems to be Saul's understanding, and in good binary fashion he 'asks' (וישאל שאול) a pair of questions: 'Should I go down after the Philistines? Will you give them into the hand of Israel?'

On a technical level, Saul's manner of asking is faultless, and most computer programmers would agree that his questions are very 'binary'. So it is something of a surprise when the system crashes: 'And he did not answer him on that day'. This lack of an answer presents is yet another setback for Saul in a chapter fraught with ritual problems. Whether the fault lies with the Elide priest or the rejected king is probably a moot point, but nonetheless it is hard to see how this kind of inquiry can go wrong. With the ephod, a question is posed, and an answer is expected. In view of the wider narrative, this lack of an answer sets in motion the motif of Saul getting the 'silent treatment' from God (see Craig 1994: 221-39). But in the short term, this silence is a problem that Saul has to attempt to solve.

Saul's response is to call the 'leaders' (or 'cornerstones') of the people together, to 'find out how this sin has arisen today' (NRSV). Although this matter of the silent ephod is without precedence, Saul equates the silence with an unknown 'sin' in the camp, and now he has to discover wherein the guilt lies. Saul's speech to the leaders occasions yet another oath: 'For as the LORD lives, the one who saves Israel, even if it is in Jonathan my son, he will surely die!' So far, Saul's oaths have not been overly productive, but this one is laced with a certain incongruity: Saul swears by the LORD, who has not answered, and that is why Saul has had to assemble the leaders and swear the oath. Furthermore, there is some dramatic irony in Saul's mention of Jonathan, since the reader knows that Jonathan has undertaken a fair bit of covert activity in this chapter. Does Saul immediately suspect Jonathan is guilty of a ritual breach? My guess is that Saul is only being rhetorical by mentioning Jonathan. But if so, then Saul's rhetoric is one more thing that goes wrong for him in this chapter: even his speeches have blunders. Further, the mention of 'death' is rather foreboding, given the direction of the narrative. Saul's verbal effort, however, evinces no response from the people: there is no one who 'answers' him, and just like the ephod, the people are silent.

14.40-44

At the beginning of this chapter, Israel is on one side and the Philistines are on the other. Once more 'sides are taken', but this time there is a different level of conflict. Saul's plan, on the one hand, is straightforward enough: he and Jonathan are to be on one side, and the rest of the people on the other side. But Saul's *rationale*, on the other hand, is harder to gauge. Peter Miscall (1986: 96) suggests that the ritual activity here is an attempt to offset his previous ritual gaffes: 'the procedure can be an overreaction of Saul, melodrama, or, in a related vein, a dramatic act to cover up his earlier blunders, notably his oath'. In response to Saul's plan, the silence of the people is broken as they reiterate their earlier line: 'What seems good to you, do'. If Saul is in need of some practical advice at this point, the people do not provide it.

Everything Saul has said thus far in 1 Samuel 14 has been controversial. Saul's utterance of 14.41 is no exception; in fact, its controversial profile is enhanced by some textual uncertainty. A literal rendering of Saul's words in the Hebrew text would read: 'Give wholeness'. The NRSV, following the Greek text, translates the utterance as follows: 'O LORD God of Israel, why have you not answered your servant today? If this guilt is in me or in my son Jonathan, O LORD God of Israel, give Urim; but if this guilt is in your people Israel, give Thummim.' The NRSV would make good sense *if* Saul is still trying to procure an answer from the ephod. However, in my view there is something else going on here: having been given the silent treatment from the ephod, Saul now turns to a lot-casting ceremony to reveal the guilty party. Saul's declaration ('Give wholeness') is comprehensible enough in the context of such a ceremony, and it almost sounds like he is nervous. It would be difficult—even with a rejected Elide priest around—for a lot-casting ceremony to go wrong.

For the second time in his life, Saul is chosen by lot. The first time Saul is chosen, one recalls, is in chap. 10, when Samuel orchestrates the proceedings and it is not the most pleasant atmosphere for the son of Kish. In chap. 14, however, Saul himself is in charge, and things are arguably worse: not only is Saul chosen, but his son Jonathan is included. In order to chose between the two of them, Saul calls for a further lot-casting. When Jonathan is 'taken', Saul asks for a confession. Jonathan's reply is noteworthy: 'I really did taste (טעם טעמתי)—with the tip of the staff in my hand—a little (מעט) honey. Here I am, I will die.' There is a grim parallel between Jonathan and Jephthah's unnamed daughter in Judges 11, as both children seemingly acquiesce to their father's oath. Even the most ardent defender of Jephthah would have to concede that his parenting techniques are, at best, dubious, and so it is not positive for Saul's character zone to intersect with Jephthah at this point.

Some commentators, though, argue that Jonathan is speaking sarcastically, a mode of discourse that is surely unprecedented in the history of lot-casting ceremonies. This appears to be the sense conveyed in the NIV, where Jonathan's last clause is transformed into a question, 'And now must I die?' Yet another contrast emerges between father and son. Saul says many things that are unclear, whereas Jonathan is a compelling orator. Jonathan uses inspiring language, clever wordplays, and common sense; none of these are hallmarks of Saul's conversation style. To be sure, Saul may have less wit, but his words are far more deadly. In 14.44, Jonathan is put under a death sentence, as once again Saul swears an oath: 'God do so to me and more also, you will indeed die, Jonathan!' Robert Polzin (1993: 139) notes a contrast here: earlier in his (short) career, Saul was concerned with *saving* lives, as evidenced in his sparing of the 'sons of Belial' who spoke against him in chap. 11. This willingness to sacrifice Jonathan represents a stunning reversal.

14.45-46

The silence of the ephod has put Saul in a difficult position, but now Jonathan is in worse straits because of his father's (most recent) oath. Fortunately, this horrendous situation has some timely intervention from an unexpected source: the people themselves. To this point in the chapter the people have been verbally docile, but in 14.45 they speak with uncommon passion and creativity: 'Does Jonathan have to die, the one who has done this great salvation in Israel? By no means! As the LORD lives, not a single hair of his head will fall to the ground, because he has acted with God today!' Several commentators observe that the people combat Saul's deadly oath with another oath, one designed to save Jonathan's life. Their efforts are successful, since the narrator then reports: 'And the people ransomed Jonathan, and he did not die'. The term 'ransom' is usually deployed in a cultic or ritual context; hence, its use in this context must be somewhat ironic, since the people counteract the oath with some simple common sense, a commodity—like Israelite weapons—that is conspicuously lacking in this stretch of narrative.

Jonathan is ransomed by the people, and he will live to fight another day. And yet, as McCarter (1980: 252) notes, this whole chapter has done little to enhance Saul's image in the reader's eyes: after these recent events, a 'gloomy uncertainty' clouds Saul. If the future looks gloomy for Saul, then bright sunshine is not exactly forecast for Jonathan. While he comes away from this chapter looking better than his father, Saul's oath nonetheless hovers around Jonathan. As Barbara Green (2003: 247) comments, 'Jonathan lives the rest of his life under this proleptic death sentence'. For now, this long day finally comes to an end in 14.46: 'Then Saul withdrew from pursuing the Philistines; and the Philistines went to their own place' (NRSV). Jonathan is saved, but Saul aborts the Philistine project even though this would be a prime moment to strike. Thus the Philistines are not decisively defeated, and their sharpening monopoly continues.

14.47-48

> After Saul had taken the kingship over Israel, he battled against all his surrounding enemies: against Moab, the Ammonites, Edom, the kings of Zoba, and the Philistines. Everywhere he turned, he inflicted punishment. He performed heroically, and struck the Amalekites, and rescued Israel from the hand of their plunderers.

The interminable day that is the subject of 1 Samuel 14 is finally over, and so, for all intents and purposes, is Saul's kingship. Yet Saul does have better moments than those described in the preceding scenes. After a glance at the above paragraph, even the most vociferous anti-Saul reader should concede that Saul *must* have had a few good days during his reign. 1 Samuel 14, though, is not one of those good days, causing to the reader to wonder why the Deuteronomist devotes such a vast amount of space to this disastrous 24-hour period. The brief summary of 14.47-48 gives the impression that Saul is almost successful as a king, in stark contrast to the preceding narratives of 13.1–14.46. In my view, the purpose of this summary is to illustrate that Saul is capable of great deeds, and not just irrationality. But the pall of rejection hovers over everything Saul does in chap. 14, and the denunciation of 13.13-14 ('You have been foolish… For now the LORD would have established your kingdom over Israel forever') is a bitter blow from which he never recovers. On numerous fronts Saul battles valiantly, and this summary is intended to evoke a measure of sympathy for what must be a desperately difficult situation. Of course, Saul has his measure of flaws, and neither Samuel's mentorship nor Ahijah's chaplaincy have proven overly helpful. One wonders what Saul could have accomplished had he not been rejected in the earliest days of his reign as Israel's inaugural monarch. By means of this summary in 14.47-48, the reader is reminded that just like Esau and Ishmael have impressive genealogies in Genesis, Saul does have a career with some high points.

14.49-52
Speaking of genealogies, 1 Samuel 14 ends with some notes on Saul's family tree. After the brief summary of Saul's foreign affairs in 14.47-48, the last lines of the chapter give a précis of internal matters within the house of Saul. Three sons are listed (Jonathan, Ishvi, and Malchishua); of these, Jonathan is the most prominent in the story, while Ishvi is never heard from again. Two daughters are listed (Merab and Michal); of these, the younger will garner a considerable amount of attention in the forthcoming narrative. One wife is mentioned (Ahinoam), and in contrast to later kings, Saul is not guilty of multiple wives (Deut. 17.17). Further, we are told, 'Now the name of the captain of his army was Abner son of Ner, Saul's uncle'. This introduction to the major power broker in Saul's entourage stresses the familial ties between the two. The mention of 'uncle' reminds us of the appearance of Saul's uncle in chap. 10, where the uncle—perhaps with his son's interests in mind—wants to know exactly what Samuel tells Saul. While Saul does not tell his uncle about 'the matter of the kingship' in chap. 10, Abner may have designs on kingship himself later in the story (2 Sam. 3).

There are several reasons why this family tree is an appropriate ending for the chapter. On the one hand, David Jobling (1998: 88) suggests that the conclusion to this chapter 'shows an unexpected resilience in Saul. He is doing quite well for a rejected king. 1 Samuel 14.47-52 demonstrates Saul's ability, after all, to grasp kingship—at least in the absence of Samuel. These verses counteract the expectation that the rejection accounts create, that Saul's reign is virtually over, and prepare us for the long reign he has still ahead of him.' On the other hand, Saul's long reign will have its share of setbacks, many of which are hinted at in this list. That the list begins with Saul's 'sons' remind the reader that Saul will not sire a dynasty. Furthermore, Saul's daughter Michal will prove to be a snare (of sorts) in the later story, and the mention of Abner anticipates a measure of division within the house of Saul and the power struggles to come. But the last line of the chapter is the most intriguing: 'There were hard battles against the Philistines all the days of Saul. So whenever Saul saw a warrior or a man of courage, he gathered him to himself.' This last line, in retrospect, underscores the rejection of Saul *and provides a hint of his successor*, since it anticipates a certain 'warrior' who will enter Saul's rejected household and become his armor bearer. I would submit that this final line actually provides an ironic conclusion to a long chapter that has not gone so well for Saul.

1 SAMUEL 15

Because Samuel does not feature in chap. 14, the reader may be tempted to think that, after his stunning rejection speech of chap. 13 and his subsequent journey to his hometown of Ramah, Samuel is going out to pasture. But, like the odd *professor emeritus*, Samuel has no immediate plans to retire. In fact, his career moves to another level, in this chapter (the main subject of which is, again, Saul's rejection), as Samuel proves to be even better at delivering rejection speeches than Saul could ever have imagined. The chapter is divided into a number of interconnecting scenes. The first words belong to Samuel, who issues a series of imperative to Saul to 'destroy utterly' (חרם) the Amalekites. At first glance, Saul seems to execute the prophet's command, but there is an ambivalence in the narrator's report as to the destruction of the plunder. Saul's actions precipitate both a divine response and a prophetic reaction, leading to a confrontation and extended dialogue between king and prophet. Moving toward the climax of the chapter, Samuel's ripped robe becomes emblematic of Saul's shredded kingship, and chapter concludes as Agag—the spared king of the Amalekites—is hewed into pieces by the prophet, who never sees Saul again until the day of his death.

15.1-3

Ever since Samuel kissed Saul at the beginning of chap. 10, the two have not shared many happy moments. Indeed, Samuel's general disposition toward Saul has not been especially joyful. At the beginning of chap. 15 the situation is not poised to change; in fact, it will be worse. Samuel's first word indicates a stern mood: 'Me the LORD sent to anoint you to be king over his people, over Israel. So now, listen to the sound of the words of the LORD.' By frontloading the pronoun 'me', the prophet sends a message to the king that Robert Alter (1999: 87) summarizes as follows: 'Samuel, by placing the accusative first-person pronoun at the beginning of his speech (normal Hebrew usage would simply attach an accusative suffix to the verb), once again highlights his own centrality to this whole process'. Such words provide a fitting start to a chapter where Samuel is undeniably in charge. 'In this way', Alter continues, 'Samuel sets the stage rhetorically for the prerogative of canceling Saul's kingship that he will exercise later in this episode'. Moreover, since the terms 'hear' (שמע) and 'sound' (קול) are keywords in this chapter, Saul would do well to listen carefully to Samuel's voice.

The solemnity of this occasion is emphasized in Samuel's next utterance: 'Thus says the LORD of hosts: "I am taking account of what Amalek did to Israel, what he set against him when he was going up from Egypt"'. Samuel has never used this kind of language when issuing directives to Saul before. For instance, in chap. 10 the instructions such as 'do whatever your hand finds to do' or 'wait seven days' are serious enough, but do not carry the weight of 'Thus says the LORD of hosts'. Here in chap. 15, though, the subject is an ancient vengeance, so such gravity suits the moment. In terms of background for the Amalekite crimes, commentators routinely point to Exodus 17 and Deuteronomy 25. Some years ago, C.F. Keil remarked that the Amalekites were the first 'heathen nation' to attack the people of Israel after the exodus from Egypt. Their day of reckoning, Samuel says, is now at hand.

To that end, the prophet issues a specific command to Saul (and since the main verb is plural, the army is included): 'Now go and attack Amalek, and utterly destroy (חרם) all that they have; do not spare them, but kill both man and woman, child and infant, ox and sheep, camel and donkey' (NRSV). The idea of 'utter destruction' (or *holy war* as it is often called) is controversial in our contemporary era. However unpleasant, the point to Saul here in 1 Samuel 15 is clear enough: strike, destroy, eliminate. Several scholars observe that the list of animals corresponds to what Amalek takes from Israel in Judges 6, so there is a measure of more recent retribution here as well. Another key part of the instruction is 'do not spare' (חמל), a term that will recur as the narrative continues.

Like an undergraduate student near the end of a semester, one gets the impression that this Amalekite *holy war* is a 'final exam' for Saul. While neither Saul nor the Amalekites initiate this particular battle, it will prove decisive for Saul's reign. The content of the exam is difficult, not least because other instances of *holy war* suggest that it can be a perilous undertaking. Consider Joshua 7 and the case of Achan son of Carmi, whose fate reveals that *holy war* is serious business that demands careful obedience. So far in 1 Samuel, Saul has actually done well in battle, but chap. 15 is no ordinary battle. The *holy war* is a test that failed even under the leadership of Joshua; by extension, if *holy war* is a stumbling block for an undisputed leader like Joshua, how much more for the already rejected Saul? It also should be noted that in chap. 13, Saul's principal fault was to deviate from Samuel's instructions, however well-intentioned. If chap. 15 is a test, then the ground rules of *holy war*—as illustrated in the case of Achan son of

Carmi—permit no deviation, and this does not augur well for Saul's chances of achieving a passing grade from the proph(et).

15.4-6

By 'summoning' (or 'causing to hear', שמע) the people, Saul actually gets off to a pretty good start in this Amalekite *holy war*. His positive start is emphasized by the big numbers; in fact, 210,000 is the largest muster of Saul to this point in the story. Furthermore, setting an ambush is surely a good thing, since it reminds the reader of Saul's finest hour during the Ammonite crisis of chap. 11. The 'city of Amalek' is otherwise unattested, and as Kyle McCarter (1980: 266) comments, 'it is surprising to find the desert-dwelling Amalekites associated with a city at all'. Perhaps the 'city of Amalek' represents the symbolic epicenter of the Amalekite nation, and as such it is an appropriate place for Saul to lay in wait. But before the battle, so vv. 4-6 tell us, something else happens:

> And Saul said to the Kenites, 'Go! Turn aside! Go down from the midst of the Amalekites lest I remove you with him. For you acted loyally with all the sons of Israel when they were coming up from Egypt'. And the Kenites turned aside from the midst of Amalek.

There are several reasons for this Kenite interlude in terms of the narrative architecture of this chapter. On the one hand, Saul's sparing of the Kenites seems positive at first blush. The reader is not sure which act of 'loyalty' (חסד) Saul has in mind, since no incident is specifically mentioned. Even so, there are favorable portrayals of the Kenites elsewhere in the Deuteronomistic History. In Judg. 1.16, the Kenites are aligned with the tribe of Judah, and from this passage the reader learns that the Kenites 'are distant relations to the Israelites by virtue of their descent from Hobab, the father-in-law of Moses' (Knoppers 2003: 316). One also recalls the cerebral achievement of Jael the wife of Heber the Kenite in Judges 4, when she drives a tent peg into the head of Sisera, the former Canaanite military leader. So, the Kenites are worthy of compassion, and presumably out of zeal for Israel's tradition, Saul extends mercy to them. If the Amalekites should be punished for historical antipathy, then the Kenites should be granted amnesty for past kindness.

On the other hand, the Kenite interlude also portrays Saul as acting on his own initiative and going beyond Samuel's instructions. No doubt saving the Kenites is a worthy cause, but Samuel makes no mention of this 'sparing'. In my view, 15.6 is an important narrative event because Saul's activity in this little scene foreshadows later moments in the chapter: he is given orders, and well-intentioned as he may be, he will go beyond the instructions. The Kenites show Saul on the horns of a dilemma, and how difficult it is to pass the *holy war* exam.

152 *1 Samuel: A Narrative Commentary*

In sum, the Kenite scene of 15.6 is necessary for interpreting this chapter. Not only does the scene reinforce the theme of historical memory, but it also sets the stage for the forthcoming dialogue between king and prophet. When confronted by Samuel, Saul will talk about *his* intentions in the *holy war* with the Amalekites. In response, Samuel will talk about *his* instructions. Because Saul goes beyond his instructions, the Kenites will survive the Amalekite battle. For the same reason, however, Saul's kingship will not survive the Amalekite battle.

15.7-9

As is often the Deuteronomist's custom, very little time is spent discussing the details of the battle itself. Saul is successful, insofar as the Amalekites are defeated 'from Havilah as far as Shur, which is east of Egypt'. One assumes that the 'city of Amalek' is included in this campaign that covers a considerable geographical distance. The victory as recorded in 15.7 looks quite impressive, and if this was the end of the story, it would be a good day for Saul. But this is not the end of the story, and like the previous chapter, this will not be a good day for Saul.

Some new information pertaining to Saul's conduct surfaces in 15.8: 'And he captured Agag king of Amalek alive, but all the people he utterly destroyed (חרם) with the mouth of the sword'. As far as the 'utter destruction' (חרם) is concerned, Saul's actions accord with Samuel's word. But the reader is not altogether sure what to do with Agag, and all of a sudden, this is a story about *two kings*, both of whom are now living under a virtual death sentence. What would be Saul's motive for taking Agag alive? For an already rejected king with a fragile confidence, it is possible that a captured king would provide quite a spectacle and give a needed boost. Peter Miscall (1986: 101) suggests an analogy with the king of Ai in Joshua 8, as that king is captured alive, brought before Joshua, and later hanged on a tree. Curiously, Agag's reputation precedes him, since he makes a cameo appearance in Balaam's oracle of Num. 24.7: 'his king will be greater than Agag, and his kingdom will be exalted'. On this basis, one could infer that Saul would have quite a trophy. However, unlike Balaam, Samuel has not mentioned anything about Agag, and presumably has no interest in *any* earthy sovereign at this point in his career.

'Has [Saul's] sparing of Agag resulted from his desire to follow divine commands to the letter or has he done so out of other motivations?' (Edelman 1991: 101). While this is a provocative question, Agag, is not Saul's biggest issue. The heart of the problem is presented in 15.9 by means of another flashback: 'Saul and the people spared Agag, and the best of the sheep and of the cattle and of the fatlings, and the lambs, and all that was valuable, and would not utterly destroy them; all that was despised and worthless they utterly destroyed' (NRSV). One obviously wonders why they are 'unwilling' to 'destroy utterly' the best of the Amalekite possessions, but for the moment, the principal difficulty lies in the verb 'spare' (חמל), since Samuel is very clear when he says 'do not spare'. Consequently, as Walter Brueggemann (1990: 111) intones, 'We are left to observe the incongruity between Samuel's charge and Saul's implementation'. If there was no room for 'incongruity' in chap. 13, the reader suspects it will be the same here.

15.10-11

For the first time in quite a while—at least from the reader's viewpoint—the word of the LORD comes directly to Samuel. In chap. 3, we recall, it is the word of the LORD that comes to Samuel with bad news for the house of Eli. On this occasion in chap. 15, the news is not good for the reign of Saul. The divine utterance of 15.11 merits careful attention, not least because English translations struggle with the content. The RSV renders the line as follows: 'I repent (נחם) that I have made Saul king; for he has turned back from following me, and has not performed my commandments'. The NRSV is similar except that the crucial verb 'repent' (נחם) is instead rendered 'regret'. Since this verb (נחם) recurs later in the chapter, I would suggest from the outset that it ought to be rendered the same throughout, and so I will take a risk and stick with 'repent'.

Of course, when connected with God, 'repent' is a controversial translation. As Barbara Green (2003: 250) summarizes, 'The notion is metaphorical and analogical, and some readers accept it more than others—which is to say that we tend to go along more easily with metaphors for God that do not trouble us than with those that do, which for many includes the notion of God changing the divine mind'. Elsewhere in the Hebrew Bible there are times and places where the LORD 'repents'. First and famously, the text of Gen. 6.6 is instructive: 'And the LORD repented (נחם) that he had made man on the earth, and he was grieved to his heart'. In the Genesis context, the verb 'repent' signals a shift in direction, and steers the course of the narrative toward Noah's ark. By extension, here in 1 Samuel 15 God's 'repentance' alters the direction of the story. Considering the game rules of *holy war* laid down by Samuel, it is hard to deny that Saul has missed the mark. Personally, I was never expecting Saul to 'raise up God's word; he was always going to fall short, because that is generally what happens with the first born. Hence, when God repents, I am now anticipating a different set of rules whereby Saul's successor will be a king who is not subject to the same kind of test(s) as Saul, because *kingship as an institution has been weighed and found wanting*. What I am now expecting as a reader is a situation where the king's status is akin to lifetime tenure, or, to invoke the undergraduate metaphor again, a king who will not be subject to a final exam that he is bound to fail.

Given his recent hostility toward Saul, Samuel's reaction in 15.11b is notable: 'Samuel was angry, and he cried to the LORD all night'. Commentators have proffered a number of suggestions as to why Samuel is hotter than liquid magma after being privy to this divine word. Graeme Auld (2003: 221) balances two different ideas: 'Now that his God tells Samuel what Samuel himself has already told Saul, Samuel appears to show sympathy with Saul—or is he simply concerned with his own reputation since he was intimately concerned with the choice of Saul?' Similarly, Robert Alter (1999: 89) reflects, 'The reasons for his rage are wonderfully unspecified, or perhaps overdetermined. He may well be incensed with Saul, or with the people who coerced him into this whole distasteful monarchic business in the first place, or even with God for making him heed the people.' In my view, Samuel is angry because God repents. An analogous situation takes place in the book of Jonah. At key points there is shared language between 1 Samuel 15 and Jonah 4, especially with the key words 'anger' and 'repent'. The prophet Jonah is angry with God for the same reason as Samuel, because God repents: 'O LORD, is this not what I said while I was yet in my country? This is why I was so quick to flee to Tarshish: because I know that you are a God of grace and compassion, slow to anger and abounding in steadfast loyalty, and repent (נחם) concerning evil!' Thus, in both cases, there is prophetic wrath *directed at God himself because of his character*. In both cases, the LORD is doing something that the prophet does not entirely approve of.

Samuel's anger at God's repentance makes an important contribution to his ongoing characterization. The Deuteronomist chooses Samuel to be the filter through whom the difficult institution of kingship is strained. Consequently, many of the tensions inherent to the monarchic experiment are conveyed through this deeply involved character. While the reader sympathizes with both Samuel and Jonah—after all, kingship is flawed and Nineveh is an evil place—one can still discern a thread of God's grace. The narrative suggests a benevolent guiding hand is at work, even though the circumstances are extreme. Just like Nineveh, God sees a situation with a different view than his prophet. And thus Samuel becomes an ironic means of grace, much like Jonah. In spite of opposition from his own servants, God's beneficent plan moves forward.

15.12

There is no scholarly consensus on how much sleep Samuel gets during the night, but 15.12 dutifully reports that with admirable energy the prophet rises early to meet Saul. At some point in the ensuing morning, new information is relayed to Samuel: 'Saul came to Carmel, and behold, he is erecting a monument for himself, and turned around, and passed over, and went down to Gilgal!' No name or identity is attached to the reporter, and one wonders why this statement is expressed through direct speech from an unidentified character rather than the narrator. Perhaps the reason is to convey a hint of bias in the testimony, as Samuel is told that Saul is building a monument *for himself* (paraphrased in the NIV as 'in his own honor'). There is no evidence one way or the other in the narrative, but one gains the impression that Saul has already lost the *public relations* battle with Samuel.

In this breathless report there is an interesting verbal aspect: 'and behold, *he is erecting* a monument'. Without putting undue weight on the Hebrew participle, the testimony implies that the project is incomplete! Just like the unfinished altar in the previous chapter, the monument is a work in progress, and appears to be yet another aborted project on the Saulide résumé. Even worse, because of this report, Samuel proceeds to Gilgal to meet with Saul *yet again*. The spatial setting of Gilgal produces a reflex to chap. 13, the site of Saul's dynastic rejection. In chap. 13 Saul is chastised for a sacrificial error; the same thing is about to happen once more at Gilgal.

I do not know if Saul is motivated by pride or piety in this building project, but it is worth mentioning that there is only one other construction worker in the Deuteronomistic History who builds a monument for himself. In 2 Sam. 18.18 we discover the following: 'Now Absalom had taken and erected (while he was alive) a monument, located in the King's Valley, for he said, 'There is not a son to me by whom my name is remembered'. He called the pillar by his name, and it is called 'The Monument of Absalom' until this day'. In terms of the narrative design, it is surely no accident that moments before Saul's kingship is effectively terminated, there is a symbolic comparison with the ill-fated Absalom. Neither Saul nor Absalom sire a dynasty; all they end up with are self-erected monuments of sterility.

15.13-15

In the book of Ruth, Boaz greets his servants with a blessing, and they respond in kind with a reciprocal blessing. In a similar vein as Boaz, Saul greets Samuel with enthusiastic words: 'Blessed be you by the LORD, I have raised up the word of the LORD!' Whether Saul is speaking these words in complete innocence or whether he is obfuscating cannot be determined. Nonetheless, his second utterance provides some tension with the previous scene. In 15.11 God says that Saul has not raised up his words, whereas here Saul claims to have raised up the word of the LORD. Even the most sympathetic reader has to agree that there is some ambivalence invading Saul's character zone, and further tensions are imminent.

Unlike the servants of Boaz in Ruth 2.4, Samuel does not reciprocate Saul's blessing. Instead, Saul is presented with a rhetorical question that must be laced with some sarcasm: 'What is the sound of this flock in my ears, and the sound of the cattle I hear?' It is surely not merely for decoration that Samuel uses the keywords 'hear' and 'sound/voice', the same terms as used in his imperatives at the beginning of the chapter.

Samuel's question raises the hearing/obedience issue that will be central to his indictment in a moment. If Saul had heard/obeyed, then Samuel should not be hearing anything: What then is the voice of the cattle in his ears? This transaction of dialogue is reminiscent of chap. 13, when Samuel approaches Saul *at Gilgal* in the context of a sacrifice that goes beyond his instructions. In both cases Samuel asks a question, and in both cases one has the strong suspicion that he already knows the answer. In chap. 13, Saul proffers an excuse that is rejected, just like his dynastic hopes. In chap. 13, Saul is unsuccessful with his reply. So here in chap. 15, Saul has a mountain to climb—roughly the size of Mt Gilboa—if he hopes to persuade the prophet with his rejoinder.

> And Saul said, 'From Amalek they brought them, what the people spared, concerning the best of the flock and herd in order to sacrifice to the LORD your God, but the rest we have utterly destroyed'.

There are a host of commentators, it must be said, who do not believe Saul when he tells Samuel that the best of the Amalekite herds are for sacrifice. A sinning king in the hands of an angry prophet—so these commentators reason—Saul extemporaneously comes up with this sacrificial rationale. The issue, everyone agrees, is plausibility. James Ackerman (1991: 18) frames the question well: 'Has Saul improvised this excuse on the spot, or has this been his true intention all along—an intention deliberately obscured by the narrator?' Despite the awkward syntax of Saul's reply, a smaller group of commentators—roughly the size of the Kenites—takes the words of Israel's first king on trust, and believes that indeed the Amalekite herds that are lowing in Samuel's ears are for sacrifice. To be sure, the spatial setting of Gilgal must enhance the plausibility of Saul's statement. If the herds were in Gibeah, then one guesses that they were intended for Saul's corral all along. But since they are bleating in Gilgal—the place of Saul's sacrificial blunder in chap. 13—it is conceivable that he spares the best of the flocks in order to make up for his earlier error with an utter destruction of the Amalekites at the same spot. In other words, Saul compensates for his earlier disobedience with a sacrifice.

I would be inclined to give Saul the benefit of the doubt, although it is a difficult interpretive decision because of words like 'spare' and the divine speech that announces 'Saul... has turned back from after me'. So far in

1 Samuel, Saul has not been guilty of self-aggrandizing behavior as much as misplaced piety, and already in this episode he has interpreted the *holy war* instructions to save the Kenites. A further difficulty, as some commentators have noted, is Saul's distancing himself from 'the people'. We have previously seen the people acting of their own accord in chap. 14, so it is possible that this is a similar situation. Walter Brueggemann (1990: 113) concludes that Saul seems to say that he is innocent, but it is the people who are guilty. For Bruce Birch (1998: 1088), the problem is that 'Saul excludes himself from the sparing, but includes himself in utterly destroying'. Likewise, Peter Miscall (1986: 104) asks, 'Is Saul here trying to shift blame to the army, i.e., I have been obedient, but they have not, or is he legitimately giving them credit for the sacrifice?' It is possible that Saul brings the Amalekite herds to Gilgal to make atonement for his error in chap. 13, but also to make amends for the 'bad booty' episode in chap. 14, when the troops swoop down on the plunder and eat the blood. Either way, in the context of *holy war* the lesson of Achan suggests that there is not a whole lot of room for flexibility. Saul's explanation of the bleating sheep is already sounding strained.

15.16-19
Samuel plainly is not convinced by Saul's preliminary explanation. After issuing an imperative ('Stop!'), he declares to Saul that he is about to hear what the LORD said to him on the previous evening. However, instead of announcing that God has 'repented', Samuel asks another rhetorical question. Whenever Samuel starts with a question it is not a good portent for Saul: 'Even if you are small in your own eyes, are you not head of the tribes of Israel?' As all Israel knows, Saul is a tall man, so the 'small' reference is a slight. It might also reflect his Benjaminite status, as Saul himself demurs during their very first conversation in 9.21.

After the rhetorical question, Samuel makes several direct statements that reiterate three things: Saul's anointed status, the fact that he was sent on a mission, and the instructions he was given.. For the most part the instructions are the same, but there is an additional description of the Amalekites as 'sinners'. As Victor Hamilton (2001: 250) notes, this is loaded element: 'Samuel's addition of "the sinners" is his way of making his case against Saul as tight and condemnatory as possible'. There is another minor change in 15.18, as the prophet says that the instructions were to 'battle against them until they are consumed'. This statement could imply—though it is difficult to be sure—that the animals should not have been transported for sacrifice, but rather destroyed on the spot. As far as I can tell, Samuel has a degree of hermeneutical latitude that Saul is not afforded.

Samuel's speech concludes with another question and his evaluation: 'Why did you not hear/obey the voice of the LORD? And you swooped down on the plunder, and you did evil in the eyes of the LORD.' One wonders why Samuel does not use the verb 'spare', but instead accuses Saul of 'swooping down' on the plunder, the same verb that occurs in 14.32, when *the people* are the ones who swoop down and eat the blood. Furthermore, the verb 'repent' is not used in Samuel's speech, creating several interpretive difficulties, especially with respect to God's words in 15.11. As Barbara Green (2003: 255) reflects, 'The prophet, we need to observe, is the one who has moved the deity's words from an expression of feeling to an action step, unprompted in any way we can witness'. It is entirely possible that Samuel—by virtue of his office as prophet—is permitted to take liberties based on his own feelings, but at this very early point in Israel's monarchic history, such details have not been clarified. Still, there are difficulties with Samuel's speech. Diana Edelman (1991: 105) outlines the problematic elements of the speech as follows:

> The temporal reference seem to point back to v. 11, which had taken place the previous night. Yet the expanded argument that ensues contrasts dramatically with Yahweh's directly quoted statement in v. 11, leaving the audience to question whether Samuel's comments in v. 17 are his own elaboration and interpretation of Yahweh's message or part of an additional, unreported message that accompanied the quoted statement. Once again, the issue of the reliability of a prophet's words is raised, and more specifically, Samuel's motivations.

15.20-23

On the last occasion when Samuel denounced Saul in 13.14-14, he abruptly departed from Gilgal while Saul remained to fight the Philistines with 600 soldiers. Perhaps Saul learned something from that occasion, because here in chap. 15, despite Samuel's scathing words, Saul utters a rejoinder on his own behalf. His long speech is divided into two parts. Part one is a declaration of his own innocence: Saul affirms that he has obeyed, brought Agag, and utterly destroyed (חרם) the Amalekites. No rationale is provided for bringing Agag, but Saul does not, wisely, use the verb 'spare' again. Part two of Saul's defense turns to the action of the people: *they* took the best of the flocks and herd that were devoted to destruction in order to sacrifice 'to the LORD your God at Gilgal'. It is quite possible that Saul has dug himself into a cistern from which there is no Ebed-melech ('servant of the king') to send down a rope and lift him out (Jer. 38).

As far as Saul's speeches have gone to this point in the narrative, his defense in 15.20-21 is probably his best ever oration to Samuel. However, the experienced Samuel is equal to the task, and in a relatively long poetic articulation, rejects Saul's defense. Once more, Samuel begins with a question, but this time he proceeds to answer it himself: What is better, impressive sacrifices or obedience? The answer: 'Behold, obeying is better than sacrifice, to pay attention is better than the fat of rams'. The genius of Samuel's indictment here is that *it does not matter* whether Saul is bluffing (and the plunder was spared for economic gain) or whether Saul is sincere (and indeed, the best is saved for sacrifice) because paying attention is superior to sacrifice. Samuel's poetic impeachment moves to crescendo by telling Saul that rebellion and stubbornness are equivalent to divination and idolatry, and because he has rejected the divine word, he has been rejected as king. Some commentators assert that the king gets exactly what he deserves: rejection. Other commentators argue that there is an imbalance between Saul's sin and the harsh consequences. However, there is still more to come, and this chapter has several more scenes before such judgments can be evaluated.

15.24-26

The Amalekites are not the only sinners (החטאים) in this chapter, as now Saul confesses to Samuel that he is in the same category: 'I have sinned (חטאתי), for I have passed over the mouth of the LORD, and your words, for I feared the people, and I obeyed their voice'. To begin with, Saul says that he is guilty of a double transgression: not only has he contravened the divine order, but he also tells Samuel that he has transgressed '*your words*'. It is hard to be sure if Saul is pointing out that there *can* be a difference between God's word and the prophet's, but it is a subtle reminder that there have been times when God's design has not been aligned with the prophet's opinion. The keywords 'hear/obey' and 'voice' also occur in Saul's confession. But, as with dynamite, location is important, and the keywords are not detonated in the right area. Saul discloses that he has not obeyed God, but that he has obeyed the people *out of fear*. This fear factor is new information. There has been no evidence so far in the narrative that Saul has feared the people; quite the opposite, Saul has usually seemed firmly in charge. Of course, Saul does listen to the people about Jonathan in chap. 14, when his son is ransomed. Still, it is hard to be sure if this is a genuine confession, or an improvised excuse as part of his desperate plea for forgiveness: 'So now, please forgive my sin, and return with me so I may pay homage to the LORD'.

It should be emphasized that Saul asks for *forgiveness* from Samuel. He does not ask for a restoration as king, but rather for the prophet to accompany him to worship God. But Samuel refuses, and his negative response seems harsh. In fact, Samuel prosaically repeats, essentially, his earlier line: 'I will not return with you, because you have rejected the word of the LORD, and the LORD has rejected you from being king over Israel'. To be sure, royal sin is serious business, and one malaise of our postmodern condition is to downplay such seriousness. Genesis 4.7 sounds the primordial warning: 'Behold, sin is laying in wait at your door. Its desire is for you, but you must have dominion over it.' Still, Samuel could have been more pastoral, and as the mentor for the first king of Israel, he may have offered some counseling. The austerity of Samuel's reaction has caused Peter Miscall (1986: 111) to inquire: 'Is this the stern, true prophet of the Lord declaring the Lord's word versus a sinner, or is this a stern, unrelenting prophet denouncing a rival?' It is hard to deny that Samuel has had a lingering animosity toward Saul ever since the Benjaminite king first appeared on the scene. One is reminded of an earlier rejection, when God says to Samuel, 'It is not *you* they have rejected, but *me* they have rejected as king over them'. When Samuel uses the same term 'reject' here, the personal dimension cannot be entirely discounted.

In the end, it is hard to determine the precise reasons for Samuel's refusal to forgive Saul here. As Diana Edelman (1991: 109) reflects,

> Samuel's failure to include God's reasons for rejecting Saul in his reiteration of Yahweh's pronouncement raises again the specter of Samuel's self-serving interests. Has Samuel refused because all mediation is useless in light of Yahweh's final decision, or has he refused because he does not want to allow Saul a rapprochement with the Lord? The ambiguity is not quickly resolved.

Glancing ahead in the story, Saul's pleading for Samuel to return with him anticipates his pleading in chap. 28. Saul is desperate for direction in both cases, though in chap. 28 he will walk the path of 'divination', a form of rebellion that Samuel raises in this very denunciation. Looking even further ahead, another king in 2 Samuel 12 will utter the same words, 'I have sinned', but immediately a prophet will respond 'your sin has been passed over'. Most readers would agree there is a world of difference between these two responses to royal sin.

15.27-29

Without granting forgiveness, Samuel turns to exit the stage. His departure, though, is physically interrupted by Saul taking hold of the wing of his robe. The robe rips, and 'Samuel, who never misses a cue to express his implacability toward Saul, immediately converts the tearing of the cloak into a dramatic symbol of Saul's lost kingdom' (Alter 1999: 92). Indeed, the accidental tearing is transformed into an illustration of Saul's fate: 'The LORD has ripped the kingdom of Israel from you today, and given it to your friend, one who is better than you!' Not only is the kingdom torn away, but ironically, it is give to someone who himself will damage *Saul's own robe* in the future (see 1 Sam. 24). In chap. 13, Saul received news that he will not choose his successor. Now, we discover that not only has the successor already been chosen, but, with heightened specificity, the successor is Saul's own friend and neighbor. Furthermore, Saul is told that his successor is 'better' than him. When Saul is first introduced, the reader is told that there is no Israelite 'better' than him; now, things have changed, and Saul is told that one 'better' than him has been chosen.

The robe may be torn, but Samuel is not finished ripping into Saul: 'Also, the Unchanging One of Israel does not deceive, and does not repent, for he is not a man to repent'. It should be noted that Samuel here uses a unique title for God (נצח ישראל), or at least, this is the only place in the Hebrew Bible that such a title is used. I opt for the rendering 'Unchanging One' (compare the NRSV 'Glory of Israel') in order to capture the 'everlasting' dimension within the semantic range of the root. It is possible that this unique nomenclature functions as a signal that what follows is the prophet's own theological opinion or advice. As one would expect, the 'Unchanging One' of Israel does not 'deceive'. While there is a slight tension here with an episode such as 1 Kgs 22.22-23 (where God sends a deceiving spirit to offer unsound counsel to Ahab), most readers would agree the God does not deceive. The real problem lies with Samuel's next term, as he says that God does not 'repent' (נחם). Just in case the reader breezes by this problem, Samuel repeats it, using the controversial verb 'repent' *twice*.

The trouble here is that God performs an action (נחם) earlier in the story, and now Samuel says that God *does not* perform this action (נחם). As a reader, who do I believe: God or Samuel? Of course, a host of commentators and translators simply change the nuance of the verb, and deftly avoid dismemberment on this narrative minefield (e.g. NRSV, 'regret' in 15.11, and 'change his mind' in 15.29). However, the Deuteronomist obviously could have used different (and less controversial terms), so my guess is that this is an intentional quandary. Some have argued that Balaam makes the same statement in Num. 23.19, but as Victor Hamilton (2001: 252) counters, 'Balaam may not be the best theological ally to have in one's corner'. Even so, Balaam's utterance hardly resolves the tension in this chapter.

Elsewhere in the Hebrew Bible, there are examples of a tension between the words of the narrator (or God) and the words of human characters. Take the example of Exodus 32, the infamous episode of the golden calf. In 32.4, the narrator states: 'And all the people took off the gold rings from their ears, and brought them to Aaron. He took them from their hand, and fashioned it with a tool, and made it a golden calf'. Since a statement from the narrator is highest on the index of reliability, the reader takes Aaron's metallurgical action as 'the facts'. However, when Aaron gives his testimony to Moses a little while later, he makes the following claim: 'I said to them, 'Whoever has gold, take it off', and they gave it to me, and I threw it into the fire, and out came this calf"' (Exod. 32.24; note also, coincidentally, the verb נחם in v. 14). It is apparent that Aaron contradicts the narrator. I have yet to meet anyone who believes Aaron, which illustrates the general principle: if there is a tension between the words of a human character on the one hand, and the words of God or the narrator on the other hand, always opt for the latter (see Alter 1981: 183). Yet commentators are loathe to apply this principle to Samuel, for fear, I imagine, of opening up an ideological can of worms. It is far easier simply to change the translation than accuse Samuel of occasionally inserting his own opinion.

When Samuel speaks these words in a moment of profound disappointment with Saul, he says that God does *not* do something that God says he does do. Thus, in his anger he contradicts the earlier statement from God himself. After reading Walter Moberly's provocative essay (1998: 120) on the subject of divine repentance, I would argue that there is an unconscious irony at work here. In view of the larger Deuteronomistic History, it is intentional that the assertion 'God does not repent' comes in a moment of disobedience *immediately* after a declaration about election of Saul's successor. The narrative purpose, therefore, of this 'contradiction' is to emphasize that even if Saul's successor has moments of disobedience that transcend Saul, his election is non-negotiable. But of course for the prophet in the context of 1 Samuel 15, it is an unconscious irony. As Yairah Amit (1992: 209) argues, 'It is not surprising that Samuel's statement in v. 29 is unreliable. The statement embodies the anger, the personal experience and Samuel's hidden desire for a God who never changes His mind, a desire shared by other prophets as well.'

In spite of Samuel's statement, the verb 'repent' (נחם) marks a turning point in this story, just as it does in other biblical narratives. As Gordon McConville (1984: 73) summarizes,

> The idea of God repenting can constitute an intellectual difficulty for some people, because of the apparent implications (i) that he has somehow mismanaged things and (ii) that he is morally blameworthy. In fact both of these are illusory. When it is said that God 'repents' the meaning is that from now on he intends to proceed in a different way.

In my view, the verb 'repent' (נחם) functions as a thread of grace in the narrative, despite the folly of the people's request for a king. Just as God condescends to this request for a king, the suggestion now is that an alternative vision of kingship is beginning to unfold. For an audience who understand the trauma of exile and the crisis of Jerusalem's collapse, there is a positive message here. Even though both prophet and king are not successful in 1 Samuel 15, from this point onward a *new character* and a *new dynastic possibility* will be the central focus for the remainder of the Deuteronomistic History. Saul has been judged, and Samuel's career as a judge is drawing to a close. Samuel will only have one more major task in his career, and that task concerns the anointing of *Saul's neighbor!*

15.30-31

For Saul of Benjamin this has been another difficult inning. It might be the pressures of *holy war*, but so far in the chapter, there is a vacillation in Saul's portrayal. Some aspects of his actions are presented sympathetically (such as the Kenites), while other aspects are not presented so (such as his blaming of the people). The robe-ripping tableau with Samuel is similar. Saul's desperate grasping of the robe looks almost pathetic, but Samuel's dramatic pronouncement seems overly vindictive. Such contrasts are part of the reason why Saul's characterization is complex in this chapter. Consider his reaction to Samuel's speech: 'I have sinned. Now, please honor me before the elders of the people, and before Israel, and return with me, that I might worship the LORD your God'. The term 'honor' hearkens back to Eli, and reminds the reader that Eli is guilty of honoring his sons more than God, who says 'those who honor me, I will honor'. It is difficult to gauge the reasons why Saul wants to be honored before the elders. The elders, we recall, are the ones who ask for the king in the first place, so perhaps this is a political move on Saul's part to keep his kingship alive. One would think that Samuel would refuse such a request, but if Saul's characterization in this episode is complex, Samuel's is even more so. His reaction to Saul's words is baffling: 'And Samuel returned after Saul, and Saul worshipped the LORD'. After all his refusal and opposition, it is not clear why Samuel is willing to return with Saul now. While it is remotely possible that Samuel is 'repenting', my guess is that Agag—the still-breathing Amalekite king—has something to do with his decision.

15.32-33

> Then Samuel said, 'Bring me Agag, king of Amalek'. And Agag walked toward him confidently, and Agag said, 'Surely the bitterness of death has turned aside'. Samuel said, 'Just like your sword has bereaved women, so your mother is about to be a bereaved woman!' Then Samuel hacked Agag into pieces before the LORD in Gilgal.

While Saul is worshipping, Samuel has a further item of business on his agenda. When Samuel demands that Agag be brought to him, there is a compelling narrative analogy: just as Saul approaches Samuel in v. 13 in complete naiveté of Samuel's forthcoming wrath, now Agag approaches Samuel with a similar naiveté in v. 32. Saul approaches Samuel in v. 13 little knowing that his kingship is about to be hewed into pieces; Agag does the same thing! Of course, I am assuming here that Agag approaches 'confidently', and this is a big assumption since the Hebrew word מעדנת has given rise to a number of different English translations. Still, I am prepared to follow the RSV ('cheerfully') and argue that Agag's disposition and discourse testify to a woefully misplaced confidence. Saul is not the only king in this chapter who is on the wrong end of Samuel's poetic thundering. Agag hears poetic words that terminate his reign over Amalek, and this is probably why Meir Sternberg (1985: 514) refers to Agag as Saul's 'veiled analogue' (see also Polzin 1993: 139). Consequently, neither Saul nor Agag will have fond memories of Gilgal, as both come cheerfully toward Samuel only to be theologically (Saul) and literally (Agag) hacked to pieces.

15.34-35

With Agag safely dissected, Samuel goes home to Ramah (with all the pleasant memories of Hannah and Elkanah). Saul—having destroyed not quite enough of Amalek—goes home to Gibeah (with all the unpleasant memories of tribal rage and civil war). While the reader is told that Samuel does not see Saul again 'until the day of his death', there is a brief moment when they are in the same vicinity in chap. 19. However, since Saul is barely clothed and madly prophesying in that scene, I assume it does not really count as a 'meeting' in the normal sense. The real irony is that the two *will* meet again, when Samuel is larger than life after death in chap. 28. Further, the reader is told that Samuel 'mourned' for Saul, and this verb usually occurs in the context of lament or funeral grief. Commentators have proffered a number of reasons as to why Samuel mourns for Saul here. I think it is because, having rejected Saul, he has no alternative. Without Saul, Samuel has no future. Indeed, the narrative bears this out: after one more climactic appearance in chap. 16 where he anoints Saul's successor, Samuel finally recedes from the center of the narrative action.

The final line of the chapter returns us to the 'repent' issue: 'The LORD repented (נחם) that he caused Saul to reign over Israel'. I have maintained throughout my analysis that 'repent' (נחם) needs to be translated the same way in all four of its occurrences in this chapter. This final sentence in the chapter is vital because it leads us to the next chapter in Israel's story of kingship, where Saul's successor enters the scene. We already know this new king will have a better destiny *before this new king is even formally introduced!* Saul does not raise up the word of the LORD. In fact, many more kings will have the same struggle, and this is why נחם marks a new beginning in the narrative: from this point onward, things will be different in several respects. First, Saul's successor will have a virtual dynastic promise before he is even introduced in the story. This is why David Jobling (1998: 84) asserts, 'It is not possible to make a sensible comparison between the monarchies of Saul and David, for different rules apply to them from the outset. Davidic monarchy represents a *new* divine dispensation in Israel, not a continuation of the dispensation under which Saul reigned.'

Second, things will be different even with non-Davidic kings. In my reading of chap. 12, I argued that Saul's kingship is emblematic of the northern monarchic experience. Yet even Jeroboam at least has a *conditional* kingship from the outset ('If you will listen to all that I command you, walk in my ways, and do what is right in my sight by keeping my statutes and my commandments, as David my servant did, I will be with you, and will build you an enduring house, as I built for David, and I will give Israel to you', 1 Kgs 11.38). While conditional kingship may be assumed in Saul's case (see the warning of 1 Sam. 12.24-25), the conditions are stated unambiguously to Jeroboam before he even accedes the northern throne. It is not by accident that Jeroboam's conditional kingship is clearly articulated by another Shiloh prophet with a ripped robe. At the end of chap. 15, the verb נחם signals a new dawn for Israel's royal experiment.

1 SAMUEL 16

The threefold repetition of the verb 'repent' (נחם) in chap. 15 suggested that a fresh start in the narrative was imminent. Indeed, chap. 16 is a narrative of new beginnings, and Samuel is given one final task in his prophetic ministry. In many ways the career of Samuel has led to this point in the story. Years earlier Samuel's mother sang, 'He will give strength to his king, and exalt the horn of his anointed'; in this chapter God carefully instructs Samuel to pick up his horn and anoint a king among the sons of Jesse. With the advent of 1 Samuel 16 we have reached the half-way point in the book, and there are two major parts in this chapter. In the first part, Samuel is given a specific directive to travel to Bethlehem for a sacrifice, and anoint the one whom God points out. Samuel—impressed by the stature and appearance of Jesse's first born—makes a hasty judgment, and is rewarded with a divine rebuke for his lack of insight. After a long procession of Jesse's sons in which Samuel has no success, the youngest and seemingly least likely son is chosen, one who was not even invited to the sacrifice! The second part of the chapter takes place in Saul's court. Indeed, though Saul's successor has been anointed, Saul himself will continue to occupy the narrative stage for an awfully long time, and the purpose of this next part of the chapter is to bring together the two major characters who dominate the rest of the book. Tormented by an evil spirit from God, Saul's servants advise music therapy as relief for the troubled king. Based on the testimony of one of his servants, Saul invites Jesse's son to the royal court, with the serendipitous result that when David plays, the evil spirit turns aside from Saul. To paraphrase Barbara Green, the ending of this chapter tells the remarkable story of how the rejected and the selected come to live under the same roof.

16.1

When God speaks in biblical narrative, it is a usually a big event. Chapter 15 ends on a note of stalemate—with Samuel mourning for Saul—but now the plot resumes with a divine speech to the prophet: 'How long will you be mourning for Saul, and I have rejected him from reigning over Israel?' Back in 15.11, God's word to Samuel is a general statement, and Samuel has an angry reaction. By contrast, here in 16.1 God seems to be slightly annoyed with Samuel, and asks a rhetorical question. Such annoyance is confirmed though the interrogative 'How long' (עַד־מָתַי), the same utterance that Eli uses to Samuel's mother Hannah when he asks how long (עַד־מָתַי) she will be drunk. Evidently, Samuel has spent enough time lamenting at Saul's (virtual) funeral, and now God is ready to move on.

Following the mild chastisement of the prophet's immobility, the LORD's specific instructions commence: 'Fill up your horn with oil and go! I am sending you to Jesse of Bethlehem, because I have seen among his sons a king for me.' It is notable that God commands Samuel to fill his *horn*. Earlier in chap. 9, Samuel is simply told to anoint Saul, with the instrument of anointing left unspecified. When anointing Saul in 10.1, we recall that Samuel does not use the *horn* but rather a *vial* of oil, raising the possibility a deficient anointing. Here in chap. 16, one gets the sense that things are going to be different from the outset: this new king will not get the vial treatment from Samuel. Peter Miscall (1986: 115) notices a further contrast with chap. 9: 'The Lord sends Samuel to the one to be anointed, rather than sending the one to be anointed to Samuel'. Whether this implies that Samuel was given too much latitude with Saul and now he has to do it *God's way* with the new king, I will not hazard an opinion. The focus of the instructions is squarely on God's initiative, with little room for prophetic creativity.

After the modest rebuke and the anointing instructions, God's opening speech to Samuel also includes the rationale for sending the prophet: he has 'seen' a king for himself. The verb 'see' (ראה) is a keyword in this chapter, and one senses that it has to do with spiritual perception and discernment. Just as the verb 'hear' is a keyword in chap. 3 (when Samuel is initially called), so now 'see' is the focus (where Samuel must anoint God's chosen one). In chap. 3, the accent is on Samuel's deficient hearing. Here in chap. 16 the stress will be on Samuel's faulty vision.

16.2-3

A brief glance across the range of biblical literature yields the following principle: when God gives a direct command, it is best to listen. After all, 'obedience is better than sacrifice', as we have recently had occasion to hear. In fact, since it is Samuel himself who utters those words, it is rather ironic when—in response to God's direct command to go to Bethlehem—the prophet raises objections: 'How can I go? Saul will hear, and he will kill me!' Given the recent emphasis on absolute compliance with the word of God in this narrative, Samuel's non-compliance here raises an eyebrow.

Samuel has been mourning—as at a funeral—and claims Saul will kill him, and he will have his *own* funeral! To this point in the story, however, Saul has not seemed to have murderous designs on Samuel; if anything, it is the other way around. Some commentators look ahead in the narrative and find evidence of later Saulide homicide, and thus deduce that there must be a palpable threat to Samuel's person here. Yet such a reading seems strained in the present context. Therefore the question remains: Why is Samuel obfuscating? Is he bluffing? God has given the prophet a direct order, but the prophet is hesitant to obey.

On the one hand, Samuel's unwillingness to obey God can be viewed as reasonable, especially since some scholars have suggested that to anoint *another* king while the present incumbent still occupies the throne is treasonous. (If a parallel is needed, one might compare the clandestine anointing of Jehu in 2 Kgs 9.) Traveling to southern Judah—Saul's neighboring tribe—does constitute a risk, I suppose. On the other hand, surely there are bigger risks in defying God than any human monarch. Besides, a prophet of the LORD is obligated to no breathing mortal, and should be beyond such temporal fears. Such disobedience proves fatal for Saul and his kingdom, but I have no interest in raising these matters again.

Still, this chapter represents the final prophetic acts in Samuel's earthly career, so we wonder why there is so much ambivalence here. Why does the Deuteronomist not have Samuel go out in a blaze of glory? Why not end Samuel's story with the stirring words of chap. 12? As Bruce Birch (1998: 1098) observes, the portrait of Samuel in this capstone episode is not flattering. No doubt this is intentional, and, in the end, a more complicated portrait of Samuel emerges than is often acknowledged. In this episode it is clear that Samuel's agenda is getting in the way of God's plan.

To counter Samuel's lack of obedience, the LORD issues another command: 'Take a heifer in your hand, and say, "For a sacrifice to the LORD I have come"'. So, in order to deceive Saul, a 'sacrifice' is designed. For Saul himself, this event is unfortunately fitting: first his downfall is precipitated by a faulty *sacrifice*, and now his replacement is covertly anointed by means of a *sacrifice*. While this is probably not a subtle judgment on some of Samuel's conduct in chap. 13 with the sacrifice affair of Saul, in light of the overall storyline deception through sacrifice represents an irony. Of course, Samuel has to be correct in chap. 15 when he says that God does not 'deceive', but this is nonetheless a rather clever ruse.

Samuel is then given further instructions: 'And you will call to Jesse at the sacrifice, and I will cause you to know what you will do, and you will anoint for me the one whom I say to you'. The second component of the command in 16.3 should be underlined, as there is *no* latitude here for prophetic creativity, and Samuel is seemingly not allowed to exercise his own discernment. Robert Polzin (1993: 153) observes a contrast with the Saul era—when Samuel's opinions were front and center—and the intersection with the language of 10.8, when Samuel says to Saul 'I will show

1 Samuel 16

you what you are to do'. In this case, it is God who will show the prophet exactly what to do.

16.4-7

There are times in the Deuteronomistic History when a visit from the prophet is not a time for rejoicing. One recalls the visit of the itinerant man of God in 1 Samuel 2, as his visit to Shiloh spells doom for the house of Eli. The elders of the city of Bethlehem seem alarmed when Samuel shows up. Their trepidation is evident as they 'tremble' and ask Samuel 'Are you coming in peace?' There is funny twist here: Samuel *says* he is afraid of Saul, whereas the elders of Bethlehem *really are* afraid of Samuel. But then, since the last public act of Samuel was to hack Agag to pieces, such an inquiry is justifiable. Samuel assures the elders that he has come in peace, and shows his obedience to the divine command by mentioning the sacrifice and inviting Jesse and his sons, just as God has directed. Now the reader is poised for God to speak; after all, he has told Samuel to do exactly as he tells him. Verses 4-7 read:

> It happened when they came that he saw Eliab, and he said, 'Surely in the presence of the LORD is his anointed one!' And the LORD said to Samuel, 'Do not gaze at his appearance nor at the height of his stature, for I have rejected him. But not as a human would see: for humans see according to the eyes, but the LORD sees according to the heart'.

If the reader was waiting for a divine word, such an utterance will be slightly delayed, as it is Samuel who gets the first word in. Samuel sees Eliab, and makes a quick assessment—based on outward appearance—that Jesse's firstborn must be the LORD's anointed. Some translations render Samuel's words as *inner speech* (such as the NRSV: 'When they came, he looked on Eliab and thought…'), but a usual marker for interior discourse (such as 'and he said *in his heart*') is missing. Whether Samuel's words are internal or external, there is a certain drama: it is quite possible that Samuel has the horn of anointing poised and ready for action when God interrupts with a speech of his own. God's words constitute a (second) rebuke of Samuel's conduct, since the prophet was given specific instructions to anoint the one whom *God* pointed out. After spending too much time mourning, now Samuel jumps the gun on the anointing ceremony, and in both cases God decisively intervenes.

Samuel is given a further command: 'Do not gaze'. Here the keyword 'see' (ראה) is not used, but a synonym (נבט, 'gaze' or 'stare') is deployed to underscore that Samuel is impressed with Eliab's external person. Evidently Eliab is tall and handsome, just like Saul, whom Samuel has denounced on numerous occasions. Is it possible that Samuel is reverting to the Saul paradigm? The comparison with Saul is heightened through the verb 'reject', as the same verb that begins the chapter (God has 'rejected' Saul) is now used for Jesse's firstborn. Perhaps the rebuke of Samuel here is not just local, but pertains to other facets of his long career: has Samuel been guilty of hasty judgment on the basis of external criteria before? If so, then God sets the record straight, and these words are an important component of the narrative. To adapt the insight of Bruce Birch (1998: 1097), God sees differently and far better than Samuel in this anointing episode: 'The reality of God's future for Israel does not always appear clear to human eyes, even to those of a prophet'.

Samuel is led astray by outward appearance, but God looks at matters of the heart. In the context of 1 Samuel, my guess is that *heart* refers to chosenness, and sometimes, God's choice is hard to see. In his old age, Samuel's eyesight may be better than Eli's, but his perception leaves something to be desired. Over the course of his career, one hopes that Samuel's error with Eliab is the exception, rather than the rule. Incidentally, we will 'see' Eliab again in chap. 17, when matters of the heart are again at issue. I have remarked elsewhere that Eliab is used by the Deuteronomist to make a thematic point: just as Eliab is involved in a rebuke of Samuel here, so another rebuke will feature in Eliab's only other formal appearance in the Deuteronomistic History (17.28).

16.8-11

Despite Samuel's first impressions, Eliab is rejected by God. But Jesse has plenty of more sons, and almost all of them are individually paraded past the prophet. Samuel has to supply a verdict for each one, but rather than the harsher verb 'reject' Samuel uses a more positive locution 'not chosen' *three times*. Neither are any of the remaining sons chosen, and it must be a rather exasperated Samuel who interrogates Jesse: 'Is this the end of the lads?' With Flannery O'Connor, one might conclude that God's man is hard to find, but fortunately Jesse has been very fruitful and multiplied to the point where he can inform Samuel that he has *yet one more son*. Jesse's words, though, sound almost incredulous: 'There yet remains the youngest one, but behold, he is shepherding the flock!'

It is conceivable that Jesse—like Samuel—is swayed by the outward appearance, and feels that physical stature and the firstborn status are the ultimate measures of worth. If so, such assumptions are poised to be undermined. Otherwise, why would the 'youngest' not be invited to the sacrifice? Fortunately, there is a light moment of humor to alleviate the stress: for the second time in the story, the chosen one cannot be found! One recalls that Saul was chosen in chap. 9, but he was hiding among the baggage. Here in chap. 16, Samuel cannot find Jesse's youngest *not because* he is hiding, but rather because he is busy acting as a 'shepherd'. Whether Samuel is cognizant of the metaphor of Israel's king as 'shepherd' is not my interest here.

Instead, Samuel says 'Send and take him, for we will not turn around until he comes here', and thus one of the first things we learn is that we are not dealing with a *firstborn*.

16.12-13

One of the great paradoxes of the Deuteronomistic History is apparent in these next lines, which must be refracted from Samuel's visual point of view: Jesse's youngest is brought in, and we are told, 'He was ruddy, with beautiful eyes, and good looking, and the LORD said, "Arise, anoint him, for this is he"'. For the first time in this chapter I have some genuine sympathy with the prophet. Samuel has just been on the wrong end of a divine rebuke for gazing at the outward appearance, and now God's choice is brought forward, and he is handsome, and ruddy like Esau! When God commands Samuel to 'rise and anoint him', a certain inscrutability of the divine ways is apparent, and here is the paradox: God has just rebuked his prophet for being misled by outward appearance, yet here is *his* choice, a 'new kid on the block' who is pleasant of outward appearance.

'Anoint for me', God ordered Samuel in 16.3, 'the one whom I say to you'. In the end, Samuel finally carries out this command, and the reader observes that the prophet uses the 'horn' of oil (rather than the 'vial', as with Saul). While Saul is anointed privately by Samuel, Jesse's youngest is anointed 'in the midst of his brothers', presumably at the sacrifice. Whether anyone outside the family circle knows about the anointing is not stated, but one guesses that there is an air of secrecy around this ceremony. Immediately after the anointing by the prophet, there is a pneumatic moment: 'and the spirit of the LORD rushed upon David, from that day and onward'. After the spirit alights upon the chosen one, the proper name 'David' is finally disclosed by the narrator. Unlike Samuel, David gets no type-scene for his birth narrative. His rather humble beginnings as an eighth son who is exiled with the sheep suggests that God, as Samuel's mother (2.8) sang those many years ago, intends to 'raise up the poor from the dust, and lift the needy from the ash heap, to seat them with princes'.

The first part of the chapter draws to an end as, once more, Samuel arises and walks home to Ramah. David is not told he will 'prophesy', nor is he told to wait seven days until Samuel shows him what to do. This time the prophet's retirement is a more realistic possibility. In fact, never again will Samuel be afforded any direct discourse as an inhabitant of the land of living. He will of course speak once more in his post-mortem cameo of chap. 28, but he will not have any new material, only recycled words of doom long since pronounced on David's tall and handsome predecessor. 'The LORD brings death and gives life, sends down to Sheol and raises up' (2.6).

16.14

The pneumatic activity of this chapter is far from finished, since the reader is told that the spirit of the LORD has turned aside from Saul, 'and an evil spirit from the LORD tormented him'. Over the years this line has proved to be disturbing for commentators, though, I venture to submit, more so for Saul. The syntax of 16.14 can be construed as the Hebrew equivalent of a pluperfect verb. Thus, one gets a sense that *at the same time* the divine spirit comes upon David, the divine spirit departs from Saul himself. The verb 'torment' (בעת) has never been used so far in the Bible, suggesting a new and terrifying experience. Statistically, the highest concentration of this verb (בעת) is in the book of Job, so we gain the impression that this is a highly unpleasant situation. Samuel may have retired, but for Saul there are new sources of torment.

I am hesitant to embrace a psychoanalytic reading here, since there are other ways to express despair or depression in the Hebrew Bible. As expressed in chap. 16, Saul is on the wrong end of a spiritual affliction that transcends a bad mood. No doubt he is upset about it, but the torment here originates from an *external* source. This episode presents an arresting view of divine power, and for a reader who is acquainted with the trauma of exile, it is evident that even the 'evil spirit' is under the aegis of God's sovereignty. The last time an 'evil spirit' has surfaced in the Deuteronomistic History is in Judges 9, when God sends an evil spirit between Abimelech (a king who eventually asks his servant lad to draw his sword and kill him) and the leaders of Shechem. In both cases, the evil spirit will (eventually) induce hostility between two parties, and as the David–Saul relationship continues, this certainly will be the case, just as there is hostility between Abimelech and the Shechemites in Judges 9.

16.15-19

The formal action of the second part of this chapter begins with dialogue, as Saul's servants illustrate their discernment: 'Behold, please, an evil spirit from God torments you!' On one level, the servants merely point out the obvious to the reader. Yet, on another level, we wonder how they know this, and is this how Saul discovers that the source of his affliction is an evil spirit from God? Other than the generic label 'servants', there is no further identity disclosed as to these speakers. We recall Samuel's stinging words in chap. 8 that the king will seize the best of the fields and vineyards and give them to his 'servants'. That day may come, but there are other items on the present agenda. The servants also move beyond diagnosis toward therapy: 'Let our lord now command the servants who attend you to look for someone who is skillful in playing the lyre; and when the evil spirit from God is upon you, he will play it, and you will feel better' (NRSV). The servants concede that their solution is provisional: the evil spirit will continue to torment Saul, and although he will feel 'better' (טוב) with the music, there is no end in sight. There is a further irony: in the previous chapter, Samuel informs Saul that his kingdom has been given to a neighbor who is 'better' (טוב) than him, and this is *exactly* where the narrative is leading, especially since Saul agrees to his servants' proposal:

> And Saul said to his servants, 'See for me, please, a man who is a good on the strings, and bring him to me'. One of the servant lads answered, and said, 'Behold, I have seen a son of Jesse the Bethlehemite. He knows the strings, and is a mighty warrior, a man of war, a prudent speaker, a handsome man, and the LORD is with him'. Then Saul sent messengers to Jesse, and he said, 'Send your son David to me, who is with the flock'.

The reader should observe that Saul uses the keyword 'see' (ראה) in his directive to the servants. A preferable translation is probably 'provide' (as NRSV), but I have tried to capture the keyword even if it is awkward in English. Saul's use of this verb is surely unintentional, but it is the first in a whole series of unintentional actions in this chapter that will undermine Saul's own authority. Furthermore, the king is not the only one to use the keyword. Immediately after uttering his directive, one of the lads pipes up, 'I have seen (ראה)...' As it turns out, this young lad has seen a great deal, and his voluble outpouring about an unnamed son of Jesse outlines a very impressive résumé. Beyond the requisite musical skills, this Bethlehemite possesses (according to the servant lad) martial prowess, good looks, and is armed with a divine presence that, unlike Saul's recent experience, does not sound hostile. With Walter Brueggemann (1990: 126), I would like to know the identity of this servant lad in Saul's court and *how* he knows so much: 'The narrative invites us to wonder how it is that a member of Saul's company should have ready a nominee from an obscure Judean village'. Jesse certainly is not reported to have shared any of these details with Samuel.

In my analysis of 1 Samuel 9 above, I mentioned that there are notable comparisons between Saul's unnamed servant lad there, and the servant lad here in chap. 16. In the first instance, the same phrase is used to introduce them both ('one from the lads', אחד מהנערים). Further, both servant lads are knowledgeable about people who live out of town (Samuel and David), and both servant lads speak *way too much*. Both servant lads are cognizant of things that Saul is not, and in both cases the servant lad takes initiative. In chap. 9, it is the servant lad's bright idea to go to Samuel (a decision that, arguably, does not accrue to Saul's benefit), just like in chap. 16, where it is servant lad's idea to mention the son of Jesse. There is one slight difference: the lad of chap. 9 speaks *about* a prophet, whereas the lad of chap. 16 speaks *like* a prophet.

The servant lad of chap. 16 says many things about the son of Jesse, but there are two rather important items that he omits: namely, he does not mention the name 'David', nor does he mention David's known vocation at this point in the story, that is, shepherding. This is worth mentioning, because when Saul sends word to Jesse, he asks for *David who is with the sheep* to be sent! Of all things, Saul only mentions details that his servant *does not* tell him. How does Saul know that the 'son' is named David, and that he with the sheep? Saul is the first character to use the name 'David' in the story, and, in his desperation to be comforted from the torment of the evil spirit, Saul unwittingly invites his successor to the court.

16.20-22

There is no recorded response from Jesse when Saul's messengers arrive to fetch David. Yet it is not impertinent to ask: From Jesse's point of view, why on earth would Saul want David? He was peripheral enough not even to be invited to the sacrifice with the prophet in Bethlehem, so why is he now summoned by the king? However, Jesse's actions are deferential enough: he obeys the royal word, and sends David along with some gifts that are fit for a king. For some commentators, the mention of a donkey and gifts such as 'bread, and a skin of wine' are reminiscent of Samuel's sign language to Saul in chap. 10. But there is no further action on Jesse's part, and he will only speak again in the next chapter.

David is obedient to his father's bidding, and duly arrives at Saul's court 'and stood before him'. The next sequence is translated by the NRSV as 'Saul loved him greatly', but the Hebrew text does not name the subject. Of course, it certainly could be inferred that Saul loves David, but exploiting the ambiguity, some scholars opt for David as the one who loves Saul. In my view, it is most likely Saul who is the subject here, a notion that is enhanced when we see that a larger pattern is set in motion here: *everybody* loves David. This is the first of numerous occasions where someone will be said to 'love David'. By contrast, David will hold his cards close to his chest, and act in a very circumspect manner in the court of Saul even while he grows in popularity. But Saul is the first to love him, although as time goes on, an inverse proportion will be noticeable: in the ensuing chapters, the more that people love David, the more manic Saul becomes.

Bruce Birch (1998: 1103) gives a thoughtful summary:

> Alongside the public story of emerging kingship in Israel there begins here a personal story of relationships between David and the household of Saul. The tragedy of Saul's insane jealousy toward David at a later point in the story is compounded by this simple statement of Saul's great love for David. It is not only Saul's kingdom that is torn (chap. 15) but his heart as well.

An immediate sign of Saul's favor—so it would seem—is David's rapid promotion to the position of 'armor bearer'. Before long, David is retained for more reasons that music. The servant lad claimed that David was 'a man of battle', and one recalls at the end of chap. 14 that Saul was always on the lookout for such individuals: 'whenever Saul saw a warrior or a man of courage, he gathered him to himself' (14.52). Once more Saul sends to Jesse, asking that David continue to 'stand' before him, as he has 'found grace' in the king's eyes. By bestowing favor on David, Saul (inadvertently) furthers the divine plans for one who has been anointed with a horn (rather than a vial) of oil.

16.23

> And so it would be: whenever the spirit of God was on Saul, David would take the lyre and play the strings with his hand. It was soothing for Saul, and good for him, and the evil spirit would turn aside from him.

As the servants of Saul predict, the skilled musician is able to provide (temporary) relief for the tormented king. The Hebrew text of the first part of 16.23 does not include the word 'evil', but based on the latter portion of the verse, the malevolent spirit can be assumed. In fact, the evil spirit will be with us for some time. Unquestionably, Saul appreciates David's musical gifts, and it should be noted that David's lyrical abilities will leave a long scriptural legacy. David's music soothes the king and he 'feels better', and the Hebrew verb 'soothe' (רָוַח) forms a pun with 'spirit' (רוּחַ). Music brings David and Saul together in the short term, but in the long term it will bring division (that is, the animosity caused by the singing of the ladies in chap. 18, will culminate with Saul hurling his spear while David is playing). To my mind, the end of chap. 16 unfolds one of the great ironies in world literature: a rejected king is tormented by an evil spirit from the LORD, and the only one who can minister to him is the one secretly anointed to replace him.

1 Samuel 17

David's primary actions in chap. 16—shepherding and music—are appropriate, since they eventually fund a host of metaphors within his biblical legacy. But based on the servant lad's testimony, David has other talents as well, such as prudent speech, martial prowess, and an accompanying divine presence. It is these and other qualities that come to light in chap. 17, the highlight of which is surely the face-to-face combat with the huge Philistine. Indeed, the showdown between David and Goliath is probably one of the best known episodes in the Hebrew Bible. Yet there are a host of lesser known details in this long chapter that are important for characterization and plot, such as the description of Goliath's armor, David's first words, and the fate of Goliath's (severed) head. My analysis will pay attention to such features, since they will play a role in the later narrative. This long chapter is divided into several parts. As Israel and the Philistines take up their battle formations, the reader is introduced to the principal adversary from Gath and his impressive physical attributes and weaponry. As if to offset this formidable introduction, an alternative hero (David) is leisurely—in an almost pastoral manner—*re-introduced* into the narrative, along with the reasons why he ends up on the battlefield. As the action unfolds, David has several dialogues with both the king and the giant, culminating in the confrontation between the Philistine war machine and the Israelite shepherd. The aftermath of battle produces several important details for the story, and the chapter concludes with an enigmatic dialogue between Saul, Abner, and David.

17.1-3

After a brief hiatus while Saul is being rejected by means of the Amalekites, the Philistines return to the narrative with a vengeance. No particular reason is stated for this gathering in Ephes-dammim, but since the Philistines are camped in Israelite territory, we assume (as with 1 Sam. 4) there is hostile intent, and a significant battle will ensue. More specifically, the Philistines have gathered in Judah. There was considerable interest in Judah in the last chapter. Samuel the prophet has recently visited the same area and anointed a new king in Bethlehem, even though the old king still lives and breathes.

The Israelites also assemble in the valley of Elah, and as titular leader, Saul is mentioned by name. Evidently there is a brief respite from the torment of Saul by the evil spirit. This must be something of a relief, although Goliath will prove to be a capable surrogate over the next forty days or so. The depiction of places and terrain in 17.3 is slightly reminiscent of the kind of descriptions in chap. 14, a day that did not go so well for Saul. In this instance, the narrator presents a tableau: Israel on one side, the Philistines on the other, with a 'valley between them'. This valley, as J.P. Fokkelman (1986: 147) intones, will prove to be 'the arena of decision'. The Israelites, we recall, want a king to lead them forth into battle, and further, a key 'purpose' of Saul's anointing as leader is to deliver Israel from the Philistine threat (9.16). So far this deliverance has not decisively occurred, and so the reader wonders if this is the moment.

17.4-7
In 1 Samuel as a whole, the Philistines enjoy a number of military advantages over the beleaguered Israelites. In chap. 13, the Philistine are said to enjoy a monopoly on chariots and weapons; now in 17.4 there is an even better card up their sleeve: a 'champion' (NRSV). The term 'champion' (איש־הבנים) can be translated literally as 'a man of the [space] in-between'. As one imagines two armies lined up opposite each other, the last man standing at the end of a battle is still alive, and thus a 'champion'. Goliath here stands as the representative of the Philistine army, a quintessential 'middle-man' as C.F. Keil presciently remarked many years ago.

The elders of Israel also want a king 'just like all the other nations'. To this point in the biblical narrative, a number of Philistine kings have been mentioned, but the person who steps forward here is not a king but a champion, and one who looks far more formidable than any earthly sovereign in the story so far. One recalls that Saul's outstanding physical characteristic is that he is a 'head taller' than any other Israelite. Next to this description of the Philistine, however, Saul shrinks, since Goliath is listed in the Hebrew text as measuring 'six cubits and a span'. There is a slight controversy over the precise height of the Philistines in the textual witnesses since the Greek text reads 'four cubits and a span'. So, the Greek Goliath is 6 feet nine inches, while the Hebrew Goliath is 9 feet nine inches (perhaps the Greek text measures Goliath *without* his head?). Either way, of course, we are dealing with a large biped, and since Goliath is from Gath, such height is not entirely unexpected. Numerous commentators point out that according to Josh. 11.22, Gath is a place of residence for the 'Anakites', the Canaanite race of giants. The Philistines are sea peoples and recent arrivals to the shores of Canaan, whereas the Anakites are figures of renown; with Goliath we have a marriage, as it were, of both traditions. He is from a town known for its legendary heights, and he is armed with the latest high-tech weaponry from the Greek islands, making him a considerable adversary indeed.

The lengthy description of Goliath's military hardware begins at the highest point—the bronze helmet on the giant's head—and proceeds downward from the coat of mail to the 'greaves' on his legs. Even the weights of several pieces are provided, and the weight is substantial. As is fitting for a man of his stature and pedigree, Goliath's weaponry is vast and varied—the Deuteronomist here uses rare (for the Hebrew Bible) and cosmopolitan terms. Robert Gordon (1986: 154) comments on one unique piece of equipment in this arsenal: '*greaves* are mentioned only here in the Old Testament, though they were commonplace in Aegean world, and figure in the panoplies of the Trojan heroes of the *Iliad*'. This reference to the *Iliad* is worth noting, since Azzan Yadin (2004: 373-95) has recently argued for a host of Greek connections in 1 Samuel 17; specifically, that Goliath is clothed as a Homeric hero and represents the best of the Hellenistic martial culture. If this is plausible argument, then it buttresses the above argument that 'Goliath' is presented as a composite portrait that showcases the best of the old (Anakites) and new (Achilles). Goliath thus embodies a host of threats to Israelite faith and identity.

Goliath's heavy metal is appropriate, I suppose, in light of the Philistine's cornering of the metallurgical market—a monopoly sufficient enough to cover *almost all* of Goliath's person. The reader has been cautioned in the previous chapter not be misled by outward appearances (this is Samuel's mistake with the height of Jesse's firstborn, Eliab). So, despite the apparent inviolability of the Goliath fortress, there may be a 'water shaft' in this description (see 2 Sam. 5.8); that is, there might be *one* defenseless place—an Achilles' heel as it were—that a clever opponent could exploit. As Kyle McCarter (1980: 292) notes: 'The description of the giant's armor serves not only to emphasize further the inequality of the coming contest but to divulge to the alert reader the one vulnerable spot on the giant's body, viz. his forehead. His head, body, and legs are well-shielded; only his face is exposed.' Furthermore, if the NRSV is correct in rendering כידון as 'javelin' (slung between his shoulders), then—despite this seemingly comprehensive description—Goliath actually has one more weapon that is not mentioned, but it will later have grave consequences for its owner: *his sword*.

17.8-11

> He stood, and called aloud to the battle-lines of Israel, and said to them, 'Why have you marched out to arrange yourselves for battle? Am I not the Philistine? But you are the servants of Saul! Choose a man for yourselves, that he might come down to me. If he is able to fight with me and strike me down, then we will be your slaves. But if I overcome him and strike him down, then

you will be our slaves and serve us.' And the Philistine said, 'I insult—this day—the battle-lines of Israel! Give me a man, and let us fight together!' Saul and all Israel heard these words of the Philistine, and they were shattered, and greatly afraid.

Equally imposing as Goliath's armor is his discourse, and in this long speech he is proposing a one-to-one combat. There is a good deal on offer here: according to the terms set by Goliath, the winner takes it all, while the loser is reduced to subservient status. There is no way of determining whether Goliath *intends* for his Philistine colleagues meekly to surrender in the event that he loses the fight; rather, I doubt he even entertains the notion of losing. For my analysis, the key point that emerges in this speech is that Goliath is pictured not only as a champion with weapons, but also as a champion with words.

Such a notion appears confirmed on two fronts. First, in 17.10, Goliath 'resumes' his speech, meaning that there is no response whatsoever to his words in vv. 8 and 9. Such silence implies terror on the part of his audience. Second, when all Israel *hears* the words of Goliath, they are dismayed and filled with fear. In 1 Sam. 13.6, Israel 'see' their desperate situation, and hide in tombs, etc. Here in chap. 17, they 'hear' and are full of fear, exposing the reader to the power of Goliath's speech. One suspects that Goliath's communication skills are just as intimidating as his weaponry.

17.12-19

As Saul and the troops of Israel are quaking with fear, the narrator shifts direction: 'But David was the son of this Ephrathite from Bethlehem of Judah, and his name was Jesse. He had eight sons, and the man was old in the days of Saul...' By any measure this is a startling change of pace after the dramatic description and words of the Philistine champion. Here—in what must be a deliberate contrast with Goliath—there is no emphasis on physical stature or armament, but rather on the tribe of Judah, and the fact that David has three older brothers who have followed Saul to battle. Scholars have puzzled over this narrative shift, since some of this information has already been imparted in the previous chapter. So why is there a repetition? The Deuteronomist re-introduces David at this point as a virtual anti-hero, a foil to the Philistine champion.

As the youngest son, David's limited worldly prospects are also highlighted. Even though anointed by the prophet, he appears to be no more than an errand boy: 'but David was going back and forth from Saul, to tend his father's flock at Bethlehem'. David's back and forth movements presumably are in synch with the comings and goings of the evil spirit; when Saul is having a good day, so are Jesse's sheep. The brief note at 17.16 ('The Philistine drew near, morning and evening, and took his stand for forty days') serves to contrast the movements between David and Goliath, and remind the reader of the palpable threat to the flock of Israel. The notice of 'forty days' is interesting, since remarkable things tend to happen in the Bible after such a length of time. After forty days a window of opportunity is opened for Noah's ark, and Moses dwells on the mountain of God for the same length of time.

> Jesse said to his son David, 'Take for your brothers an ephah of this parched grain and these ten loaves, and carry them quickly to the camp to your brothers; also take these ten cheeses to the commander of their thousand. See how your brothers fare, and bring some token from them.' Now Saul, and they, and all the men of Israel, were in the valley of Elah, fighting with the Philistines. (NRSV)

One recalls that at a 'turning-point' moment in Saul's life, he is sent on an errand by his father. A similar experience is now befalling David, as Diana Edelman (1991: 127) explains: 'After a forty-day span with the older sons absent (v. 16), Jesse begins to worry about their welfare, just as Kish did about Saul in 10.2, and sends David, another son, with provisions and orders to return with a token indicating their safety'. Jesse seems more concerned about the fate of his three eldest sons than with that of his youngest. I have included the NRSV translation of 17.17-19 above because there is an issue of who 'speaks' the words of v. 19: it is either the narrator (as NRSV), or Jesse (e.g. NIV). My reading of the Hebrew syntax suggests that these are Jesse's words, and this line reveals a rather positive spin on the matter: Jesse says that his sons are 'fighting' with the Philistines, but really they are paralyzed with fear on the battlefield. Again, Jesse seems more interested in the fate of his older sons, whereas David is simply used as a go-between. First impressions—to continue a theme set in motion in the previous chapter—can be misleading, a lesson that Goliath will have imprinted in his mind shortly.

17.20-25

As Saul's armor bearer, one may have expected David to be present on the battlefield. The preceding section helps explain why David is not there, but also how circumstances unfold in such a way that he eventually does join up with his brothers in the valley of Elah. In accordance with Jesse's instructions, David arises early and proceeds on his journey. Before leaving, he 'abandons' the flock under the care of a watchman, and several commentators note the symbolic dimension here: David will not be returning again to his shepherding career after this errand is over.

David's arrival at the frontline approximately coincides with the 'daily double' of Goliath's taunt, and 17.21 is presented from David's visual perspective: 'Israel and the Philistines were arrayed for battle, army to meet army'. For the second time, David 'abandons' something under the care of a watchman; previously he entrusts the flock to a keeper, and this time he deposits the 'equipment' (most likely the cheeses and supplies) with the keeper of the 'baggage'. One is reminded of Saul hiding among the 'baggage' during a national assembly, but by contrast, David 'runs' from the baggage area to the battle lines. It is here that David 'asks his brothers about *shalom*', and if he is about to get a token of their safety for Jesse, such matters are interrupted by the entrance of Goliath.

The re-introductions of 1 Samuel 17 continue, as the Philistine giant is again labeled a 'champion' (man of the in-between), and referred to as 'Goliath by name'. While Goliath speaks his customary words of derision, a crucial difference is that this time David 'hears'. The reaction of the soldiers is to flee, but as they are busy running away, both David and the reader can overhear their conversation: 'Do you see this man who is coming up? Indeed, he comes up to insult Israel! But the man who strikes him the king will make very rich, and his daughter he will give to him, and his father's house will be granted exemption in Israel.' This substantial matter of reward has not been previously reported, and surely the timing is not coincidental: just as David arrives on the battlefield, the information about a generous reward surfaces.

Notably, Saul himself is not reported as saying these words or dispensing these promises. The reward issue is raised by the (fleeing) troops, and hence this is a general utterance from Israel's soldiers. Either Saul has made such an offer, or this is an example of military hyperbole from the soldiers. I suspect the former, since 18.17-27 will be all about brides and riches. In the event, securing the payment from Saul will prove harder than slaying the giant. As Barbara Green (2003: 287) mentions in passing, Goliath engages in a similar rhetorical strategy as Saul: he presents offers that will not really materialize in the way they were asserted on the battlefield. Still, David hears the report of Saul's offer, and for number eight of eight sons, the prospects of worldly wealth, a princess bride, and tax-free status in Israel must be a rather attractive opportunity.

17.26

It may come as a mild surprise that so far in the narrative David has not been afforded any direct speech. He has performed a number of actions, been introduced twice in the story, and been discussed by others, but David himself has not uttered a word to this point. As mentioned in the above discussion of 1 Samuel 9, a major character's first words can be an important moment for characterization, and with David this is certainly the case, as he speaks to the men standing with him, saying: 'What will be done for the man who strikes this Philistine and turns aside the insult from upon Israel? For who is this foreskinned Philistine that he should insult the battle-ranks of the living God?'

David's first words unfurl a pair of rhetorical questions that address two rather different spheres. In the first instance, David asks for the matter of reward to be reiterated. Of course, he knows full well what is on offer, but by asking a question, he is actually making a statement. I would argue that David's *political* consciousness is here unveiled: he asks for the reward to be repeated because he has every intention of seizing this occasion. Such timing and opportunity will be a hallmark of David's career. With the second question, David reveals an alternative theological imagination. While the rest of the troops are paralyzed before Goliath, David puts a radically different construal on the situation. Not only does he bring God into the equation, but his second rhetorical question belittles the giant and turns the insult on its head.

The first words of David reveal two sides of this most complex of biblical figures: the earthly and the spiritual, the private and the public. On the one hand, David is interested in reward and accomplishment; on the other hand, he has the uncanny theological insight that is lacking among Israel's troops. In the words of A.F. Campbell (2003: 173), 'David is portrayed in a double light, both as ambitious and as faith-filled'. For Campbell, these qualities will remain in tension, as 'the full range of [textual] signals seems to be set against reconciling them'. In the immediate context, David intuits that the struggle with Goliath initially is a *war of words*! As this scene continues, David begins his battle with rhetorical success. Through the strategy of asking questions, David begins the long work of planting seeds of doubt as to the Philistine's words and weapons.

17.27-29

On the surface, David gets the first answer he is looking for from the people. Without actually delineating the rewards, 17.27 gives their response: 'And the troops said to him according to this word, saying, "Thus will it be done for the man who strikes him!"' I doubt the troops are being evasive, but their answer is slightly vague. However, there is another response that no one may have anticipated: David's older brother hears the younger one speaking with the men, and 'Eliab's wrath was kindled against David'.

We recall, according to vv. 22-23, that David has already spoken with his brothers, so Eliab's anger is evidently not kindled in their initial conversation. But it is *after* David utters his fighting words that Eliab's wrath is kindled, and therefore some element of David's speech ignites this controversy between them. Like David, Eliab can ask rhetorical questions as well: 'Why is this you have come down? With whom have you left those few sheep in the desert? *I* know your insolence and your evil heart, for just to see the battle you have come down.' The particular reason (or reasons) for Eliab's anger is not stated. Like Samuel, Eliab may only be staring at the outward appearance. Eliab could be a jealous older brother in the same vein as the 'sibling rivalry' issue that we see in the Joseph narrative (Gen. 37–50), but my guess is that there is more.

I have argued elsewhere that in Eliab's only other appearance in the story, he is used by the Deuteronomist to rebuke a main character: in chap. 16, Eliab is used to rebuke Samuel, who judges by *outward* appearance. It is noteworthy that now Eliab is used as a voice of rebuke for David, stating that David ought to be cautious about *inward* matters. While in the present context Eliab could be seen as guilty of raining on his younger brother's parade, it should be mentioned that a host of Eliab's speech clusters (terms such as sheep, few, battle, see, wrath, evil, anger, and kindle) recur at a crucial point later in the story: 2 Samuel 11–12, the disastrous affair of David and Bathsheba and the parabolic judgment of Nathan the prophet. Even at this triumphal moment in the Davidic career, Eliab is used to sound a note of warning: David should always attend to matters of heart, lest another man's wife ends up murdered. When Eliab accuses David of neglecting 'those few sheep', in this context it sounds like a rant. Later in the story, David will neglect his role as a 'shepherd' of God's people. There is 'one little ewe lamb' mentioned in 2 Samuel 12 that becomes an occasion of great stumbling and national disaster.

David responds to his brother's chastisement with two more rhetorical questions: 'Now what I have done? Was it not a word?' As it turns out, 'What I have done?' will become an oft-used Davidic refrain (as we will see, in chaps. 20, 26, 29). In the present context, though, the response to Eliab is either a protest of innocence or a dismissal of Eliab's harsh opinion about his 'evil heart'. Peter Miscall (1983: 63) wonders if these are rhetorical questions, or whether David is actually looking for an answer from Eliab. Miscall argues that 'it is impossible to decide which interpretation should be accepted, and this entails unsettling consequences for the entire reading. Many of David's future "questions" will be marked by the same problematic, and will similarly destabilize the reading.' Other commentators have noted that this interlude with Eliab is a diversion from the main storyline, which it certainly is. But there are questions raised here—at an early and euphoric moment in David's career—that will be revisited at later points in the narrative.

17.30-37

The caution of Eliab will have to wait for another day because David 'turned around from beside him toward the front of another, and spoke the same way'. The Hebrew syntax here is deliberately a bit awkward, but the point is clear: instead of further dialogue with his brother, David turns to more favorable interlocutors. Not only do the people speak the same words as before, but now Saul is informed. For the second time in as many chapters, Saul hears a report about David, and for the second time he sends for him. Regardless of the exact contours of the report Saul has heard, David gets the first word in, and signals his intention to the king: 'Let the heart of no man fall—your servant will go and fight with this Philistine!'

Despite the confident ring of this speech, Saul is not immediately persuaded. Saul's principal reason for refusal is on the grounds of experience: David is just a lad, whereas the Philistine has been a fighting machine *since* he was a lad. The problem is that Saul only knows David as a harp player. While David has been promoted to the rank of 'armor bearer' along the way, Saul would still argue that David is principally a musician, not a combatant. So it would be a tough sell to allow him to face the Philistine giant. However, in 16.18 the 'servant lad' testifies that this son of Jesse is 'prudent in speech'. There is ample evidence for this claim when David's rejoinder in 17.34-37 is considered:

> David said to Saul, 'When your servant was a shepherd for my father among the flock, the lion and the bear would come and lift up a sheep from the herd. Then I would march out after it, and strike it, and rescue from its mouth. It would rise up against me, but I would seize it by the beard, and strike it, and kill it. Even the lion, and even the bear your servant has struck—this foreskinned Philistine will be just like one of them, for he has insulted the battle-ranks of the living God!' And David said, 'The LORD—who rescued me from the power of the lion and the power of the bear—he will rescue me from the hand of this Philistine'. And Saul said to David, 'Go, and may the LORD be with you'.

Saul's primary objection is that David is a youth, and hence inexperienced. The cornerstone of David's counter-argument stresses the opposite: God already has rescued him in similar experiences. David claims to have had ample experience in hand-to-hand combat, and has grabbed the 'beard' of many an unpleasant creature, who probably object to the inconvenience. One should note that RSV is happy with the plain sense 'beard', whereas the NRSV prefers to render the noun as 'jaw', evidently unable to imagine the notion of the bearded bear. I also doubt that bears have beards, but Goliath in all probability does, and this is part of David's strategy: to convince Saul that although he is a youth, he has lots of experience in fighting formidable bearded creatures. In 16.18 the servant lad has also said that the LORD is with the son of Jesse; David himself now makes the same declaration.

The overall effect of David's speech is such that Saul buys it. Somehow his previous doubts are assuaged, and Israel's king has been convinced. In commercial terms, David's presentation could be labeled as marketing genius: David makes it sound as though it is worse to come in contact with a lion or bear than with a foreskinned Philistine. This was a difficult sell, but the 'prudent in speech' David triumphs over Saul's objections with his startling words. In reality, David has no intention of grabbing Goliath by the beard or even fighting him at close proximity, but Saul is not informed of such contingencies.

17.38-40
Not only does Saul send David off with words of benediction ('Go, and may the LORD be with you!'), but he also tries to outfit David properly for hand to hand combat. Commentators have various responses to Saul's outfitting his own armor bearer here. Most athletes and warriors would agree that one's helmet is the last piece of equipment to be donned, but in a 1999 article Gary Rendsburg argues that Saul puts the helmet on David far too early. Hence, David tries in vain to walk around; because he cannot see very well, he has to concede: 'I am not able to walk around with these, for I have not tested'. So, there is a practical value in David's rejection of Saul's armor. 'I cannot walk with these' is a sensible utterance, since in a moment David will be 'running' (unencumbered) toward Goliath, who is weighed down by a lot of heavy metal. Yet there is also a symbolic dimension when David turns aside Saul's armor. For Walter Brueggemann (1990: 131), Saul is sufficiently emboldened by David to utter the name of 'Yahweh', but Saul has 'not yet grasped the radicalness of David's faith', and hence 'Saul tries to accommodate David's faith to the conventions of war'. In terms of the wider narrative, Ora Horn Prouser makes a compelling argument for the symbolic use of clothing in 1 and 2 Samuel. According to Prouser, 'clothes make the man' in this narrative, in that clothing is often used to highlight the rise of David coinciding with the fall of Saul. My analysis will be alert to this symbolic device as the story continues.

At the same time, David does not wholly reject the weaponry of Saul of Benjamin, for we discover in 17.40 that David has a *sling* in his hand. David's sling is somewhat unexpected, since he (as we are carefully reminded in v. 12) is from Judah, and the sling is usually associated with tribe of Benjamin. For example, Judg. 20.16 reports about the Benjaminite troops, among whom were 'seven hundred chosen men, left-handed, all of whom could sling a stone at a single hair, and not miss the mark'. David is thus taking a page out of the Benjaminite playbook. He wants the wealth allegedly on offer, so—to re-coin an American phrase—his strategy is all about the Benjamins! (The face of Benjamin Franklin, I am told, graces the American $100 bill. In God David trusts.) After rejecting Saul's weaponry, David does choose a series of implements with which to confront his well-armed adversary, but they are rather unlikely ones. The 'stick' in his other hand, I will suggest below, is a mere distraction. Still, readers have often

186   *1 Samuel: A Narrative Commentary*

wondered why David chooses *five* stones from the stream. Some have suggested that there is one stone for each book of the Torah, while others suggest that Goliath has four brothers. Still others surmise that five stones are chosen just in case David, as a non-Benjaminite, by chance should miss the mark.

17.41-47
Goliath's first impression of David—as with Samuel's view of Eliab in the previous chapter—is misleading. The problem, in the diagnosis of Diana Edelman (1991: 131), is that 'Goliath, like the Israelites, focuses on outward appearances'. Preceded by his (otherwise action-less) shield-bearer, Goliath 'stares' at David. J.P. Fokkelman has noticed the same verb (נבט) is used in 16.7, where Samuel is told not to 'stare' at Eliab. Just as Samuel arrives at an incorrect conclusion ('Surely in the presence of the LORD is his anointed!'), so Goliath stares at David and all he sees is the equivalent of a teenage pop idol: 'The Philistine stared, and he saw David, and he despised him, because he was a lad, and ruddy and good of appearance'. Note that David's appearance is refracted through *Goliath's perspective*, and further, Goliath 'despises' him, the same verb used in 10.27 when the sons of Belial 'despise' the newly selected Saul.

Goliath's quick wit and penchant for insult has by no means abated over the past forty days: 'What, am I a dog, that you are coming to me with sticks?' No doubt the Philistine galleries would be amused at this repartee, but several commentators remark that the 'stick' is merely a ruse on David's part: he is using it as a distraction so the big man does not notice what is in the *other* hand! Goliath's confidence is reminiscent of the Philistine garrison in chap. 14, where they taunt their foe, 'Come up to us, and we'll teach you something!' Similarly, Goliath has a low estimation of his opponent: 'Come to me, so I can give your flesh to the birds of the sky and to the wild creatures of the field!' Goliath also curses David 'by his gods'; out of decency, the Deuteronomist does not share the specificities of either the gods or the curses. David himself will use plenty of religious language in this war of the words, and in 17.45-47 David proves more than rhetorically equal to the giant:

> David said to the Philistine, 'You are coming against me with spear, sword, and javelin, but I am coming against you with the name of the LORD of hosts, God of the battle-lines of Israel, whom you have insulted. This day the LORD will close you in my hand, and I will strike you, and I will turn aside your head from upon you, and I will give the corpse of the Philistine army this day to the birds of the sky and the wild creatures of the land, and all the land will know that there is a God for Israel. All this assembly will know that it is not by sword or spear that the LORD saves—for the battle belongs to the LORD, and he will give you into my hand.'

In the face of demoralizing odds, David is not shaken and his words are stirring. Goliath invokes religious language by 'cursing' David by his gods. David also invokes religious language, but instead of cursing, he outlines the character of Israel's God specific to this situation. David's uncommon valor is underwritten by a conviction of God's capacity to save in this particular moment. If David's speech to Saul in 17.34-37 is impressive, then this speech trumps it. So now, after an extensive build-up, we are about to witness the long-awaited confrontation.

17.48-53

The Philistine, we recall, is carrying a good deal of weight, and limited mobility might be a factor. David, having turned aside the armor of Saul, is comparatively unencumbered, and is thus able to 'run' to meet Goliath. At the crucial moment, the narrative slows down as David reaches into his shepherd's pouch to load a stone, which he slings toward the giant and lands a direct hit right in the 'brow' (מצח). I mentioned above that Goliath's wit is evidence that he has a good mind; now he has something else in his mind, namely, one of David's five stones. In the end, David does not need the other four stones from the stream, since he is able to sling at the hairs of Goliath's eyebrow and not miss (similar to the left-handed Benjaminites). Goliath's first impression—unlike the stone from David's sling—proves to be misguided.

Evidently, the bronze helmet did not quite cover enough of the giant's head. It may have been advisable for Goliath—like many European ice hockey players—to wear a helmet with a visor. David has made the claim that he will cut off Goliath's head—and with no sword in his hand, this is quite a boast. With no stated resistance from the shield-bearer, David unsheathes Goliath's own sword, and removes his head. Speaking of being prostrate and headless, Goliath is not the only Philistine subjected to such a posture and predicament. As several commentators have observed, the Philistine god Dagon also falls forward before the ark of the covenant in 1 Samuel 5, and eventually loses his head. One wonders if Dagon is invoked when Goliath curses David. Dagon the deity is headless, and now the giant experiences a similar discomfiture. The end result is that the Philistines flee, and Israel raises a jubilant war shout. Israel's pursuit covers a good deal of ground, and while the Philistines do not surrender as slaves (according to Goliath's terms), the Israelites do at least plunder their camp.

17.54

It would appear that David does not join the pursuit of the Philistines, as there are a couple of items on his post-Goliath agenda. I find 17.54 to be one of the most intriguing lines of this chapter: 'And David took the head of the

Philistine and brought it to Jerusalem, but his weapons he placed in his tent'. This sentence foreshadows two important events in David's career and, for that matter, the larger narrative. As for the weapons, the sword of Goliath will surface again in due course. In 1 Samuel 21 the sword of Goliath for some reason ends up under the care of Ahimelech the priest. In the event that will be referred to as the 'collusion at Nob', the sword of Goliath has a further role to play. 1 Samuel 21–22 are a vital component of the prophetic word spoken against the house of Eli finding its fulfillment in the narrative. But why does David take the head of Goliath to Jerusalem? Bethlehem (or even Hebron in Judah) might be understandable, but at this point in the story Jerusalem is a Canaanite stronghold in the midst of the promised land. Despite several attempts at conquest in Joshua in Judges, it is still inhabited by the Jebusites. Perhaps—even at this early point—David is already thinking of a neutral capital city for his kingdom. If this is an early example of David's *venture capital*, then walking into town with the head of Goliath would certainly make a statement. At any rate, Jerusalem will eventually be renamed the 'city of David', and will feature prominently in the story.

17.55-58

> Now when Saul saw David marching out to meet the Philistine, he said to Abner, commander of his army, 'Whose son is this lad, Abner?' Abner said, 'As your soul lives, O king, I do not know'. The king said, 'You ask whose son the youth is'.
>
> Now when David returned from striking the Philistine, Abner took him and brought him before Saul, and the head of the Philistine was in his hand. Saul said to him, 'Whose son are you, lad?' David said, 'The son of your servant Jesse, the Bethlehemite'.

The final paragraph of this long chapter has been a source of problems for many a reader. Either a variant tradition is here preserved—out of some sort of scribal obligation—despite the apparent disharmonies, or else there is more symbolic dimension to this transaction of dialogue. On the surface, there are palpable difficulties: How do we reconcile these questions with Saul who 'loves' David? Why on earth would Saul be asking questions about the identity of his own music therapist and armor bearer? Why would he ask whose 'son' when the first thing he learns about David in chap. 16 is that he is a 'son of Jesse'. Rejecting the suggestion that Saul is suffering from temporary amnesia or madness, some innovative analysis has been provided by Robert Polzin (1993: 172):

> That Saul's question about David is expressed not just once but three times in these four verses should at least alert the reader that Saul's questioning is being emphasized here with a vengeance. It simply will not do to dismiss these verses with a redactional shrug; such an attitude robs the story of its

esthetic brilliance and ideological complexity, even as it severely weakens the drama of reading.

I certainly agree that this episode is deeper than it seems. First of all, this episode is presented as a *flashback*, an obvious point, but one overlooked by many interpreters. There are two scenes in this final episode: one while Saul 'sees' David, and the other as David 'returns' successful. The first scene takes place *before* the result has yet to be determined; the second scene takes place *after* David has triumphed. The episode begins immediately after David takes the head of Goliath to Jerusalem, and the first scene opens with the flashback refracted from Saul's point of view: *while Goliath is still very much alive, Saul perceives that David might be a threat.* This final episode in the chapter episode reveals—after the fact—that Saul has second thoughts, unsure what to make of David, maybe even seeing him as a potential danger. The calculating side of Saul is very much evident here, and this pattern foreshadows how Saul will view David throughout the rest of the narrative. Saul is often exposed through inner thought, and the pattern begins here.

After re-stating the problem, Graeme Auld (2003: 223) points to a helpful intertext:

> Why does Saul no longer recognize David? Yet several of the added elements serve to compare and contrast David with the figure of Saul as described in chs. 9–10. The answer may be that David after his great exploit, like Saul after his encounter with the prophets, has 'turned into another man' (10.6), and onlookers have to inquire after the parentage of both.

Auld's comment raises two issues. First, we should note that Saul is not asking *who*, he is asking *'whose son'*. The distinction, I will suggest in a moment, is crucial. Second, Saul is not vaguely inquiring, he is specifically asking the captain of his troops, Abner. According to 14.50, we assume that Abner is the son of Saul's uncle (דוד), the same uncle who questions Saul in chap. 10. Both episodes, we recall, feature strange questions, and evasive answers are hallmarks of both scenes. In both episodes, questions about the kingdom are lurking below the surface.

Here in chap. 17 Saul has to address Abner because, after Saul himself, Abner's interests are most threatened by the rise of a rival. Abner swears by the king's own life that he does not know the answer to the king's question, but this is missing Saul's drift. Saul is warning Abner about this rival, but Abner misses the signal. This is the first of several miscalculations on Abner's part. He underestimates David now, and it will cost him his life in 2 Samuel 3. Saul knows David, but is intentionally avoiding the proper name. As Diana Edelman (1991: 133) explains, 'His reference to David as *the youth* instead of by name could also derive from an attempt to denigrate him by refusing to call him by name, implying he is a nobody. In this case, it would not indicate his ignorance of David's identity, as is commonly presumed.' Saul has been told on a couple of occasions that his 'friend/neighbor' will succeed him, and now he is wondering if this 'son' could be the one. The central issue in this episode of 17.55-58 is sonship (i.e. succession).

That David is standing with Goliath's head during the final interrogation by Saul also implies that 'headship' is a subtext for this enigmatic conversation. Saul does not congratulate nor thank David; this certainly foreshadows Saul's 'ignoring' of David's triumph over the Philistine and his future deeds—indeed, Saul never mentions this victory again. Again, the scene begins with Saul seeing David marching out, and as Barbara Green (2003: 291) reflects, 'The whole urgency of the erstwhile Philistine threat—now suddenly removed—melts away before the question of Saul's survival'. The scene ends with a circumspect David standing before Saul—watching his words, certainly not communicating any overt political ambition. But still, in his hand is a trophy, and it serves to symbolize the different paths that the two men will take: David is *en route* to Jerusalem with the Philistine's head, while Saul's head will be removed by the Philistines. Peter Miscall (1983: 72) comments, 'At the close of 1 Samuel 17, Saul is already exhibiting his jealousy and fear of David that will dominate him from 1 Samuel 18 on. He is attempting to 'put David in his place' by ignoring his feat of arms and his own person, the latter by referring to him as someone's son and as "a youth".' From the standpoint of the larger narrative, it is appropriate that this episode does not end with v. 58, but continues well into chap. 18.

1 Samuel 18

In terms of individual heroics and discourse, David's actions are somewhat unprecedented in the Hebrew Bible so far. To be sure, there have been heroic acts and brave speeches by leading figures, but the very construction of 1 Samuel 17 is unique to this point in the story. It is strange, then, that such a triumphant chapter should conclude with the dialogue between Saul, Abner, and David. However, the conclusion does serve as an effective introduction to chap. 18, which itself is fraught with evasive discourse and hidden motives. While there is something of a spatial movement from the fields of war to the court of Saul, the 'battle' continues, and Saul's own children are deeply involved with both the rise of David and the fall of Saul. There are a number of interlocking scenes and summaries in this chapter. The first event continues the last episode from the previous chapter. Taking place on the same day, this opening scene introduces the relationship between David and Jonathan, and then outlines David's promotions within Israel's army. This is followed by another interior glimpse of Saul's mind, this time as he reacts to the women's song that attributes deeds to both him and David. After a brief withdrawal, the evil spirit resurfaces and, with spear in hand, Saul makes an attempt on David's life. The chapter moves toward a conclusion with some matrimonial issues, as David eventually marries Saul's daughter Michal and enjoys high standing in the nation.

18.1-2

For the most part, 1 Samuel 17 highlights the action of a single day. An eventful day already, more is yet to come. The temporal indicator at the beginning of chap. 18 reveals another event on that day, and implies that Saul's son Jonathan somehow is present during the conversation between David and his father: 'When he finished speaking to Saul, then the soul of Jonathan was bonded to the soul of David, and Jonathan loved him as his own soul'. Jonathan has not made a narrative appearance for a while now. He is last heard from in chap. 14, where he is mentioned in a genealogical notice of Saul's sons, right after he is ransomed from death by the people. When Jonathan resurfaces here, it is in the context of loving David as himself. No reason is stated for this love. Presumably David still has the head of Goliath in his hand, so maybe Jonathan loves David because of David's courage on the battlefield earlier in the day. David and Jonathan thus have something in common: taking big risks against Philistine opponents. Saul is the first person said to love David, and his son quickly follows in his footsteps. But the matter is trickier for the son, since, as A.F. Campbell (2003: 183) reminds us, 'Jonathan is Saul's heir presumptive'.

Numerous commentators define Jonathan's love for David in terms of political fealty, and clearly this nuance is plausible. However, in light of Saul's love for David (16.21), perhaps it is both political and personal. Jonathan and Saul will not love David in the same way as the narrative continues: Saul will see David as an enemy, while Jonathan is an ally. But why does this declaration of Jonathan's love come at this particular point in the story? On the wider level, one purpose of emphasizing Jonathan's here is that—for the rest of the Deuteronomistic History and beyond—hope lies with Judah in general and the house of David in particular. Jonathan wisely hitches his wagon to the 'house' of David. On a more local level, another purpose of Jonathan's love in the immediate context of the story is to contrast father and son. While Saul is wary of David, Jonathan is self-emptying. Saul will spend the remainder of his days trying to move away from David; Jonathan will do the opposite. This scene begins 'when David finishes speaking to Saul', and indeed, Saul and David will never speak 'openly' (that is, without posturing, dissimulation, hidden agendas, or *double entendre*). Yet with Jonathan there will be a rather different pattern of communication, hinted at even in this scene.

After David finishes speaking with Saul, in 18.2 the reader is told that Saul makes a decision: 'And Saul took him on *that day*, and did not give him leave to return to his father's house'. As with Jonathan in the previous line, there is no stated reason as to why Saul wants David to remain (in the royal court). Is it to keep an eye on David, or does he know about Jonathan's 'binding' of soul? In 16.22, Saul politely requests *to Jesse* that David stand before him. But in 18.2 the language is different, and Jesse is not involved here. There is no direct speech recorded; the narrator simply reports that Saul does not 'permit him to return', suggesting it is a personal order to David himself. Is there a danger posed by David's 'father's house'? At any rate, David will no longer go 'back and forth' between Jesse's flock and Saul's court. When David leaves his father's flock under the care of a watcher in 17.20, it turns out to be proleptic after all.

18.3-4

While Saul is not allowing David to return to his father's house, Jonathan is the subject of two more actions. First, Jonathan cuts a covenant with David. The last time we have see any trace of a covenant is at the beginning of chap. 11, when the besieged residents of Jabesh-gilead ask to cut a covenant with Nahash the Ammonite. There, the covenant offer revolves around servitude, whereas here it involves sacrifice, since Jonathan makes the covenant out of love for David. If there is some vague uncertainty in the present moment, these actions become more clear later in the story. Second, Jonathan gives David his royal robe and weapons. 'The robe', says Bruce Birch (1998: 1120), 'symbolizes the kingdom'. The same word for robe (מְעִיל) is used in 15.27, when Samuel's robe is ripped, and betokens the kingdom having been ripped away from Saul. The robe that Jonathan gives to David is not ripped, however, and it would appear as though Jonathan is voluntarily renouncing any claim on the throne in favor of David, with whom he has cut a covenant.

Jonathan also gives David his armor and weapons, much like Saul attempted to do in the previous chapter. Jonathan's robe and the armor, as Ora Horn Prouser (1996: 31-32) is careful to emphasize, is a gift, and the gift of Jonathan fits far better than the similar offers of Saul. Commentators note that David rejects Saul's armor, but accepts the gift of Jonathan. No doubt there are practical and symbolic reasons behind these actions, but at the very least they indicate that David's relationship with Jonathan will be considerably different from that of Saul. Yet it is curious, then, that there is no stated response from David after receiving these generous gifts. Notably, this pattern will continue: everyone will love David, but David consistently holds his own cards close to his chest. I am not saying that the love is unrequited, but only that David has an air of the senior partner in these transactions. He certainly does not wear his (elected) heart on his sleeve at this point in the story.

18.5

As the long day of chap. 17 seems finally to be over, there is a narrative fast-forward that reports on David's success 'in every place where Saul sent him', and the accompanying promotion and position of responsibility over the men of war. The chronology is so puzzling that Robert Polzin (1993: 176) is driven to remark: 'In chapter 18 we find a ragged shifting between exposition and narrative event combined with temporal discontinuities between the events themselves'. After this generic description of 18.5, there will be another flashback. Consequently, we read about David's success and promotion *before* hearing Saul's inner thoughts about David and the kingdom (prompted by the song lyrics in the next episode of 18.6-9). In my view there are at least four reasons why the Deuteronomist tells the story this way. First, to illustrate that the rise of David has a certain inevitability despite the actions or reactions of the incumbent king, Saul. Second, the sequencing of this chapter emphasizes the different destinies of these two major characters: David is ascending to increasing public acclaim, while Saul is descending into private brooding. Third, David's meteoric rise and success is good in the eyes of all the people, and also in the eyes of 'Saul's servants', whose interests are threatened by the upward mobility of this southerner. Fourth, the various temporal discontinuities prepare the reader for a change in David's relationships. In chaps. 16–17, David only interacts with Saul and his own family in Bethlehem; now there is a wider network of connections being established, and, by the end of the chapter, David will be legally engrafted into Saul's house.

18.6-9

The general timeframe of this episode is *prior* to David's success and approval ratings in 18.5, and a return to the narrative present after the battle of chap. 17. A literal rendering of the Hebrew text would read: 'When they were coming, when David returned from striking the Philistine, the women marched out from all the cities of Israel...' The NRSV paraphrases the temporal clause at the beginning: 'As they were coming home...' The very fact that women come forth from all the cities of Israel signifies that his deed—and we assume the larger victory of Israel and the plunder of the enemy camp—is well known throughout the land. There is all manner of melodious instruments and merry-making in this celebration, such that the lyrics are even preserved: 'Saul has killed his thousands // David his ten thousands'. On the surface, the song lyrics sound like a celebratory parallelism, yet Saul is greatly angered, 'and this matter was evil in his eyes'. The interpretive issue is as follows: do these song lyrics elevate David and belittle Saul? Or do the lyrics conform with the normal conventions of biblical poetry?

Commentators have a myriad of views on the substance of the song lyrics. In a fine discussion of this passage, Kyle McCarter (1980: 311-12) poses the question of whether an 'invidious comparison' could be intended. The coupling of the names 'Saul and David' suggests an elevation of the latter to royal status, so Saul may well have grounds for profound discontent, if not a suspicion of conspiracy theories. Yet for my analysis, the context encourages—such as the lengthy description of pure joy—a happy reading of the song, a celebration of Saul and his armor bearer against the odds. Micah 6.7 is a helpful poetic comparison: 'Does the LORD delight in thousands of rams / ten thousand streams of oil? // Should I give my first-born for my transgression / the fruit of my body for the sin of my soul?' Between them, Saul and David have killed but one enemy soldier, so the women's song is just popular music enshrining a happy moment. Furthermore, the women are 'answering' each other, which suggests a simple choral celebration and corresponding dance. Even today, this kind of dynamic will surely keep happening in popular songwriting until the day the music dies.

So, in my view, there is no hostile intent in these lyrics. But my view is not the most important one: for Saul, this song is decidedly off-key. Actually, the matter is evil in his eyes: 'They have given ten thousands to David', he said, "but to me they have given thousands. There only remains for him the kingdom!"' One should pay close attention to Saul's manner of interpretation here, since it will surface again. Unlike modern biblical scholars, Saul's exegesis is speculative, and he interprets the 'text' according to his own (sub)conscious agenda. There is a psychological complexity here: Saul knows all too well that he has been rejected, but he will fight against this rejection until his last supper in chap. 28. As Barbara Green (2003: 296-97) remarks, Saul's interpretation shapes his reality, and he has now 'voiced, if only to himself, the matter that will absorb him for the rest of the story'.

If Saul is subliminally worried about David in 17.55 when he sees him going forth against the Philistine, he is *very* angry when he hears the words of the song. Music is what first brings Saul and David together—now it begins to tear them asunder. Music will no long be the food of love for the Saul–David relationship. In several ways this scene will become typical of Saul: in the midst of a collective ambiance of celebration, he withdraws. Notably, his worst fear ('there only remains for him the kingdom!') is in reality a correct forecast of the future; in terms of this prediction, Saul is certainly among the prophets. From this point onward, Saul 'eyes' David. The Hebrew term is a hybrid of 'evil' and 'eye' (עָוֹן is written, and עוֹיֵן is to be read) and signals Saul's increasing apprehensiveness before David. It is curious that the reader will tune into these song lyrics on several more occasions before the story is over; this 'hit' song will not only get plenty of international air time, but will be interpreted by Philistine listeners in due course.

18.10-11

Chronologically sensitive readers have noted the timing of this scene: *the next day* after Saul's brooding thoughts on David and the kingdom, he is then plagued by the evil spirit, and he reacts to his harpist with hostile intent. For the second time in as many scenes, a certain rhythm gives Saul the blues. The women's music put Saul in a bad state earlier, and now David's music is without its usual efficacy. There is a difference this time: Saul is 'prophesying' (or as the NRSV prefers, 'raving'). This is the second time Saul has been the subject of this verb. In 10.10 Saul publicly prophesies 'in the midst' of the group of prophets; here Saul privately prophesies 'in the midst' of his house, with his spear in hand. As if to offset the spear in Saul's hand, David has his strings in his hand. As is his custom, David plays 'day by day'. However, on this 'next day' after the musical celebration there is a sharp difference. When Saul offers David his armor in chap. 17, David quite rightly refuses it, but it may have been a useful idea to take the spear, since whenever Saul is mentioned with 'spear in hand' it will usually be aimed with malevolence at the Davidic head. The striking of a king will also recur later in the story, as Robert Polzin (1993: 180) notes:

> This image of Saul with the upraised spear, upon whom David turns his unsuspecting back not once but twice yet still escapes, also foreshadows and contextualizes the double opportunity of David to kill a defenseless Saul in chaps. 24 and 26. Here Saul refrains from action out of a profound fear of David; there David will refrain out of respect for the LORD's anointed (24.10; 26.23).

Just as Saul is hurling his spear at the harpist, the reader is given another glimpse of his thoughts: 'I will strike through David and into the wall!' Even though Saul is 'prophesying', this utterance will not find fulfillment in the story. Despite future attempts, Saul will never succeed in striking David. Ironically, his previous utterance in 18.8 does turn out to be a prophetic statement, whereas this utterance while he is prophesying will not. The reason this utterance does not find fulfillment here in 18.11 is because David eludes the Saulide spear, literally: 'And David circled around in front of him twice'. Evidently Saul *twice* attempts to pin David to the wall, yet David—without any recorded word of direct speech—adroitly avoids the spear. Unlike his Benjaminite colleagues in Judges 20, Saul takes aim at a head of Davidic hair but misses. While there is no overt mention of *divine protection* from this assault—and it is possible that David eludes Saul out of his own talent and resources—one senses that Saul cannot stretch out his spear against the LORD's (other) anointed. Pointedly, David of Judah says 'I will strike' (נכה) in 17.35 and hits the mark; in this scene, Saul of Benjamin says 'I will strike' (נכה) but does not hit the mark. Consequently, there is damage to the wall of Saul's house, and further indentations will be made before long (19.10).

18.12-16

For quite some time the reader has been aware that the spirit of the LORD has turned aside from Saul (16.14). Whether Saul is aware of this reality, though, is another question, since the last clause of 18.12 could be a parenthetical aside from the narrator, or a refraction of Saul's point of view. The action of 'turning aside' (סור) is emphasized with a double use of this verb: the LORD 'turned aside' (סור) from Saul, 'so Saul caused David to turn aside (סור) from him, and he set him as a captain of a thousand'. This is not the first time Saul has promoted David; in chap. 16 the promotion to 'armor bearer' draws David closer to Saul, but here the elevation to a 'captain of a thousand' drives him away. The particular promotion of 18.13 evidently takes place *prior* to 18.5, where Saul sets him 'over the men of war'. Publicly it may look as though David is promoted for good reasons, but privately the reader knows otherwise: having failed at killing David himself, Saul promotes David out of 'fear'. Nonetheless, David has success in every campaign. Counter to Saul's intent, not only is David victorious, but he is 'loved' by all Israel and Judah.

Saul and Jonathan love David, but there is no explicit motive supplied as to the reason. Here, though, the narrator does supply a motive: all Israel and Judah love David 'because he was marching out and coming in before them'. After all, the people want a king to march out in front of them and fight their battles (8.20). King Saul 'turns aside' David out of fear, but David ends up being loved for a *royal* reason: he leads them in battle. Just as everything David does is triumphant, so every Saulide strategy for Davidic diminution is a failure. Kyle McCarter (1980: 313) comments on how Saul ironically undermines himself: 'every action he takes relative to David—whether motivated by goodwill, as in 16.21-22, or fear and suspicion, as in the present passage, or downright malice, as later in 18.20-27—contributes to David's success'. The specification of 'Israel and Judah' has an interesting political edge. On the one hand, there is a suggestion of unity. As Theodore Mullen (1993: 237) notes, 'The symbolic power of David's victories unified the people of both Israel and Judah under his leadership'. But on the other hand, there is a hint of disunity. Glancing ahead in the wider Deuteronomistic History, 'Israel and Judah' will not always be so unified, and the *very mention* of the two groups implicitly gives an inkling of a disunity to come.

18.17-19
In the previous chapter we recollect that substantial rewards were on offer to the man who strikes the Philistine. Since then, there has been ample interaction between David and the king, yet no record of such rewards being distributed in David's direction. However, the background of reward seems presupposed in this scene, although nobody mentions it outright. Unexpectedly, Saul initiates a dialogue with David and announces that his older daughter will be given as a wife. This is not quite a reward, though, as Saul outlines a further condition in the next clause: 'only (אך) be a son of valor for me, and fight the battles of the LORD'. Of course, Saul is asking David to do exactly what he has been doing since the last chapter. Yet the matter is complicated by another internal angle of Saul's mind: 'Let not my hand be against him, but let the hand of the Philistines be against him'. Having failed himself, Saul hopes the Philistines will eliminate David.

Saul's reasoning is not altogether clear here: David has *already* had immense success fighting 'the LORD's battles', yet Saul hopes he will fall. So, Saul's deceitful strategy is engineered so that David falls by the hand of the Philistines. But a deadly twist will occur later in story, in that Saul himself falls by the hand of the Philistines, while David deceitfully falls in with the Philistines. Further, Peter Miscall (1983: 64) notes that Saul's 'reward' stands in ironic contrast to the original offer: Princess Merab is here offered not because David *has* killed a Philistine, but rather in the hope that he *will be* killed by a Philistine.

David's response to Saul's invitation is framed as yet another question, not unlike his response to his brother Eliab in the previous chapter. Does David expect an answer from his prospective father-in-law, or is his question ('Who am I?') merely rhetorical? Similar to Saul, David's utterance has a certain multivalence. On the surface there is apparent modesty, but at this point the reader does not know whether David is truly in awe of entering the king's household, or whether he (like Saul) is posturing and has other motives. Furthermore, it is hard to know what Saul makes of David's self-deprecation. Saul's action is decisive ('And it was time to give Merab daughter of Saul to David, but she was given to Adriel the Meholathite for a wife'), yet what is it in David's response that causes Saul to pursue an alternate path? Does he see through David? Is he angry, or relieved, or offended? Adriel apparently constitutes far less of a threat than David. Saul is never recorded as thinking: 'What is next for Adriel but the kingdom!' The marriage between Adriel and Merab brings closure to this scene, but the betrothal controversy is far from over.

18.20-21

For the second time in this chapter, one of Saul's progeny is said to 'love' David: his daughter Michal. With Jonathan, there is no expressed motive, nor is there any recorded motive for his sister's love for David. As a handsome, courageous, and successful young man, David has an ample fund of admirers, and perhaps Michal loves him for similar reasons. Robert Alter has noted that this is the only instance in the narratives of the Hebrew Bible where a woman specifically is said to love a man. For my analysis, an equally important component is that other people find out about Michal's love: 'And Michal daughter of Saul loved David. They reported to Saul, and the matter was upright in his eyes.' The precise identity of 'they' (the ones who report to Saul) is not disclosed, nor is the manner in which they find out about Michal's love, or why they in turn report it to Saul. I assume Saul's servants are the ones, but the sense of anonymity is a fitting introduction to the gossip and rumors that flow in the next few lines.

Once more we are given a glimpse of Saul's thinking. This time, his motive is expressed *before* his speech to David. Upon finding out about his daughter's love for David, the matter is upright in Saul's eyes, and he said: 'I will give her to him, and she will be a snare for him, and the hand of the Philistines will be against him'. Ironically, Michal will prove to be more of a snare for Saul himself, but I will defer that discussion until the next chapter. Saul estimates that David will somehow be motivated to participate in this scheme, and Michal's love—like Gideon's ephod in Judg. 8.27—will lead David into disaster. The NRSV translates 18.21b as 'Therefore Saul said to David a second time, "You shall now be my son-in-law"'. Another way of rendering this line would be: 'By the second you will be my son-in-law today'. Either way, it is Saul who now uses the language of 'son-in-law', a key term in David's professed humility in 18.18. Saul does not state any condition yet, and most poignantly, there is no response from David.

18.22-25
There is another variation in the protracted dialogue between David and Saul in this chapter, as Saul opts to address David through his servants. Saul instructs his servants to have a private communiqué with David, and stress that he is the object of affection of the king and his court. The servants, according to Saul's instruction, should then move to the climax: in light of this universal warmth, it is natural that David should be the king's son-in-law. Robert Gordon (1986: 161) makes the point that Saul resorts to a third-party intermediary because his credibility is in question: 'Since Saul had previously reneged on his promise to give Merab to David (v. 19), he forestalls suspicion by making the approach through his servants. Their involvement is evidence of his good faith.'

The servants dutifully speak these words 'into the ears of David', and this time David does respond. He again downplays his own station with another question, but it is categorically different from his earlier deprecation before Saul. I would argue that Saul is only *one* of the intended audiences for this speech, as David is also delivering a political lecture to Saul's servants: 'Is it trivial in your eyes, becoming the king's son-in-law? I am a poor man, of little account!' With Saul, David bewails the status of his family; with the servants he stresses personal unworthiness. The mention of poverty must be a barbed allusion to the 'reward' that has not quite been dispensed by the king—David is a poor man because the great wealth has yet to be lavished on the man who killed Goliath. In terms of the forthcoming narrative, the most important thing to note is that David is speaking to the servants of Saul and already posturing before them. So, even now, he is sending a message to his future subjects: it is *not* a trivial matter to try and enter the king's household. Such political speeches will occur often in the chapters ahead, with the most piquant being 'never stretch forth your hand against the LORD's anointed'.

When the servants of Saul report back to their master in a summary way, the king does not call the 'poverty bluff'. Instead, Saul puts his own spin on David's words and instructs his servants to deliver a further message: 'There is no delight for the king in a bride-price, except for one hundred Philistine foreskins, to take vengeance on the enemies of the king'. Just in case the reader misses the machination, the narrator reminds us that Saul was calculating for David to fall at the hand of the Philistines, who no doubt would vehemently object to this unwarranted surgery. In the annals of biblical history, this is not the first time a father has suggested (free) labor in return for daughter's hand. Laban the Aramean unveils a not dissimilar strategy in Genesis 28. Since the allusion to the Jacob cycle continues in the next chapter, I will further discuss the parallels between Saul and Laban, two fathers who use disingenuous language with their prospective son-in-laws. Meanwhile, David will require all the wily recourses of his ancestor Jacob if he is to escape the snare of Saul.

18.26-27
When Saul is told Michal loves David in 18.20, the matter is 'upright in his eyes'. This reaction is owing to what Bruce Birch refers to as Saul's 'own devious purposes'. Now, in a curious intersection of language in 18.26, the matter is 'upright in the eyes of David to become the king's son-in-law'. The implication here is that David is not necessarily marrying Michal for love, but rather for its political utility. None of this is stated, but the language of the narrator points in this direction. Diana Edelman (1991: 142) asks: 'Why is David so eager to marry royalty? Because of the established analogy, a veil of suspicion is cast over his motivations for joining the royal family.' David seems motivated, because on this occasion the time does not 'expire' (literally, 'the days were not filled').

Along with his men, David strikes the requisite number of the Philistines, although the ancient texts have different accounts of the numbers. The Hebrew text (followed by the RSV) lists *two hundred* Philistine victims, whereas the Greek LXX (preferred by the NRSV) has *one hundred*. Later in the story (2 Sam. 3.14), David will refer to one hundred being the amount required, but of course he could be referring to the legal number that was requested. There is another allusion to the Jacob cycle in the Hebrew text here: like Jacob, David pays *double* the price for a younger sister. Just as David eludes Saul's spear earlier, here he outfoxes the king in the matter of the princess bride. The macabre dowry is presented to the king in dramatic fashion: 'And David brought their foreskins, and they gave them in full to the king, to become the king's son-in-law. Then Saul gave Michal his daughter to him as a wife.' Note that David brings (singular verb) the foreskins, while 'they' (plural verb) count them out before Saul, who is probably not thrilled. The Deuteronomist does not specify what the king does with dowry.

18.28-30

The chapter moves to a conclusion without any dialogue, only a few summary notices from the narrator. Again, the RSV and NRSV have different translations. This time the NRSV opts for the Hebrew text ('But when Saul realized that the LORD was with David, and that Saul's daughter Michal loved him...'), while the RSV follows the Greek ('But when Saul saw and knew that the LORD was with David, and that all Israel loved him...'). I prefer the Hebrew text because Saul is already aware of the national dimension of David's popularity. The force of 18.28 is that Saul now clearly sees the popularity of David *within his own family*. There is a further contrast: David has lots of admirers even in Saul's court, whereas the king is becoming increasingly detached from all around him

Because the LORD is with David and his daughter loves him, Saul's fear of David greatly increases. In Saul's view, David's status is now 'an enemy'. The term 'enemy' reminds us of Saul's statement in 18.25, where he talks about being avenged from his 'enemies'. While the Philistines were the obvious subject, I suspected a double meaning, since he was hoping that David would fall. Now in 18.29 David is officially 'the enemy'. Hence there is an irony in the final verse of this chapter: Saul has tried numerous schemes for David to fall by the hands of the Philistines, but David only has success, which enhances his popularity. Even when the 'captains of the Philistines march forth', David is the one who triumphs more than any of Saul's servants. David's name is becoming 'valuable', whereas Saul is inching toward monomania.

1 SAMUEL 19

In the past two chapters the meteoric rise of David's popularity is set against the plummeting fortunes of Saul's life and reign. David has thus far displayed remarkable resiliency, having withstood a host of internal pressures (i.e. assassination attempts by the hand of Saul) and a number of eternal skirmishes (i.e. against the Philistines). David has also navigated the tricky terrain of a royal betrothal, and now finds himself as the son-in-law of Israel's king. However, David's difficulties will not subside in the days ahead. If anything, such difficulties are intensified in this chapter, which has three interlocking sections. Each of these sections include a palpable threat to David's person, offset by a timely intervention from someone who is close to Saul (his children, and the prophet Samuel). While one might expect these characters to be loyal to Saul, they end up being invaluable allies of David. In the first section of chap. 19, Saul announces lethal intentions with respect to David, but Jonathan intervenes and negotiates a reconciliation. The cease-fire is short-lived, however, as the second section of this chapter features yet another direct attempt on David's life by Saul, followed by a nocturnal escape facilitated by his daughter Michal. In the third section of the chapter the prophet Samuel makes a surprising appearance and harbors the fugitive David, and the chapter ends with a reiteration of the enigmatic line, 'Is Saul among the prophets?' In this entire chapter David is not afforded a single word of direct speech, as key allies speak and act on his behalf.

19.1-3

When Saul speaks to his son Jonathan, the topic is usually something violent. For example, in chap. 14, the staccato dialogue between father and son revolved around Jonathan's potential death. Here in chap. 19, the topic is the potential death of David. In the final lines of chap. 18 David is labeled as Saul's 'enemy', and now this chapter begins with public words of execution. There has been a gradual movement: we first hear Saul's 'private' voice speaking negatively about David, but now we hear his 'public' voice breathing out murderous threats. Nonetheless, there is an element of indirection in the opening line: 'And Saul spoke to Jonathan his son and to all his servants about causing David's death'. Is Saul telling his son and servant about *his own* objective, or is he (in a roundabout way) ordering *them* to make David a target? Perhaps Saul is hoping someone will volunteer, even though is he aware that all his servants 'love' David (18.22). However, in the ensuing conversation with David, Jonathan stresses 'Saul my father is seeking to kill you', and the servants are not mentioned.

The narrator's aside about Jonathan's 'great delight' in David is curious, since Saul *quotes himself* using the same word in 18.22. Consequently, disingenuous dialogue with David in the betrothal controversy above becomes a foil for Jonathan's genuine affection here. Furthermore, Jonathan is twice referred to as Saul's 'son'. For Robert Alter (1999: 118), this repetition is intentional: 'In keeping with the biblical practice of using relational epithets to underscore a thematic point, Jonathan is identified as Saul's son at the very moment when he takes David's part against his father'. For Diana Edelman (1991: 143), the double mention of 'son' highlights Saul's dynastic anxiety: 'Jonathan's status as Saul's son is emphasized through repetition in v. 1, seeming to suggest that Saul has become very concerned for the security of his son's future in the face of David's popularity among the people and with God'. One might add that the contrasting attitudes of Saul and Jonathan in the opening moments of this chapter illustrates the 'house divided', a theme that continues throughout the narrative.

Jonathan implores David to hide in a field, but not necessarily to eavesdrop on the conversation between father and son. This directive is not altogether straightforward, a tension that has led some scholars to detect a conflation of sources. Alternatively, the focus of Jonathan's instructions in vv. 2-3 is not on hearing, but rather on seeing. For Jonathan, it is the visual angle that matters, and he wants David to see father and son together in the neutral spatial setting of 'the field'. As a result, Jonathan's own loyalty to David is underscored. The juxtaposition of Saul and Jonathan in this chapter is such that the son becomes a foil to the father. Jonathan's political interests are threatened just as much (if not more) than Saul's by the rise of David, yet he gives David his sword, whereas Saul hurls his weapon at David. Perhaps Jonathan's acquiescence before the election of another would have currency for the Deuteronomist's immediate readership.

19.4-7

In light of Saul's discourse about killing, it must be a considerable risk for Jonathan to speak 'good' of David to his frenzied father. Jonathan's unmitigated defense of David has three movements. First, Jonathan begins by imploring 'the king' not to sin against David. The rationale for this is simple: David has not 'sinned' against him, in fact the opposite is the case, as Jonathan argues that every deed of David has been 'good'. Second, Jonathan concretely alludes to the Goliath episode, referring to the giant as 'the Philistine'. Not only did David take an immense personal risk, but he was also the LORD's instrument for working salvation in Israel. Further, according to Jonathan's assertion, Saul 'saw' David's actions, and rejoiced. We certainly recall Saul 'seeing' in 17.55, but one struggles to remember any rejoicing on Saul's part. If anything, Saul was eyeing David with suspicion. Whether Jonathan really believes Saul's rejoicing to be true, or whether it is a joyful embellishment is indeterminate. The point is that Jonathan's words are at odds with what the reader knows to be the case. Third, Jonathan concludes with a rhetorical question that cautions the king about incurring needless bloodguilt. Other things being equal, this is an impressive piece of oratory, presumably in the field where David is hiding.

Jonathan's discourse produces the intended effect, and Saul is amenable to Jonathan's voice of reason. Not only does he 'hear the voice' of Jonathan, but Saul also swears an oath: 'As the LORD lives, he will not be put to death'. As the chapter unfolds, this oath will become a virtual prophetic utterance because, despite a number of further attempts, David will not be put to death regardless of Saul's best efforts. I assume that David does not actually hear this oath, since in v. 7 Jonathan recounts 'all these things' to him, and then brings David to Saul for a reuniting. So, the purpose of the hiding in the field was not to eavesdrop on the actual conversation, but rather to read the body-language and to see Jonathan's good faith in the transaction. As the dialogue draws to a close, the picture is one of modest intimacy, as father and son can still have a civil conversation at this point in the story. This modest intimacy will be brutally shattered in the next chapter with abusive language and hurled spear. Meanwhile, Saul has sworn that David will not be put to death. Yet as we recall from chap. 14, whenever Saul swears an oath, complications quickly follow.

19.8-10

What might look like a fairly routine summary of a battle actually provides motivation for the next scenes in the chapter. Conflict against the Philistines continues, and David marches out for attack. Having been 'brought before' Saul by Jonathan, David takes his leave to fight. He is victorious—courtesy of a 'great striking'—and the Philistine's flee before him. But extenuating circumstances make it necessary for David to return to court; namely, the return of the evil spirit of the LORD. Saul's place and posture are familiar: he is 'sitting in his house', and he is not empty-handed either. In fact, both main characters are handling their usual instruments: David plays the strings while Saul holds his javelin. Given this tableau, even the most conservative gambler would find it hard to resist a wager: Saul's javelin will not long remain in his hand. To be sure, David's recent success coupled with the evil spirit are a hard combination for the manic Saul: twinned with the evil spirit and Philistines' fleeing before David, Saul takes aim at his usual target.

Even today, young men occasionally encounter conflicts with a father-in-law. But by any measure, David has grave issues with his father-in-law. Nevertheless, David is able successfully to 'remove' (פטר) himself from Saul's presence. Verse 10 records no inner speech from Saul, only a wordless launch of the deadly projectile; once more, the wall of Saul's house has little choice but to absorb further collateral damage. Saul's ballistic effort seems to trigger a new reaction in David: he flees. Just as the Philistines 'flee' (נוס) before David in 19.8, he now 'flees' (נוס) from before Saul.

Not only is David able to escape his father-in-law's spear with his head intact, but he will dodge other forms of Saulide skullduggery as well. The next episode of 19.11-17 shows how this is accomplished. There will be a bit of wry humor: just as Saul's spear makes a hole in the wall, so David will escape through a hole in the wall!

19.11-13

> But David fled, and that night he was able to slip away. Saul sent agents to David's house in order to keep watch and kill him in the morning. His wife Michal reported this to him, saying, 'If you don't slip away tonight, then tomorrow you're a dead man'. And Michal lowered David out through a window, and he went out and fled and slipped away. And Michal took *teraphim* and set it on the bed, along with a quilt of goat's hair that she set at its head-place, and covered it with clothing.

David has not been safe in Saul's house, and this scene indicates that he is no longer safe in his own. Despite swearing an oath to the contrary, Saul makes a further attempt on David's life, on the same night that Saul damages the wall and David flees. Earlier, Jonathan warns David 'watch yourself in morning'; now Saul sends agents to 'watch' David's house and kill him 'in the morning'. But just as David is the beneficiary of Jonathan's timely intervention, he is now helped by another member of Saul's family. For the first time in the story Michal speaks, and presumably it is her love for David that motivates this life-saving discourse. We know that Jonathan has insight into his father's intentions because of Saul's speech at the outset of the chapter, but it is not clear how Michal finds out. There are some verbal similarities between brother and sister, as Barbara Green (2003: 315) points out: 'Her speech is a variant of Jonathan's in 19.2, but more succinct. She urges escape instead of hiding, noting that the morning will bring death, not mediation and reconciliation.' On the whole, Michal is far less optimistic than Jonathan, and it is possible that the betrothal fiasco has given her insight into her father that her brother presumably lacks.

Michal does a good imitation of Rahab (Josh. 2) by letting a hunted man out of a window. But there are also several echoes of the Jacob cycle here. Michal covering the bed with 'clothes' is reminiscent of Rebekah covering Jacob with Esau's clothes in Genesis 27 in order to deceive a father. Further, the mention of 'goat's hair' conjures up the image of Jacob's 'stick trick', as Alter (1999: 120) notes: 'Michal puts goat's hair at the head of the bed because, being black or dark brown, it would look like a man's hair, but goats (and the color of their hair) are also prominent in the Jacob story' when Jacob increases his flock at the expense of Laban. But the most striking feature for our present inquiry is the presence of *teraphim*, surely an echo of Genesis 31. There is a network of correspondences between Genesis 31 (when Jacob is fleeing from Laban, and Rachel steals her father's *teraphim*) and this episode in 1 Samuel 19 (when David is fleeing from Saul, and Michal aids his escape by means of some clever work with *teraphim*). Both of these episodes feature *deceptive father-in-laws* (Laban and Saul), *younger daughters* (Rachel and Michal), *fugitive husbands* (Jacob and David), and *hidden idols* (that is, Rachel hides her father's *teraphim* under her camel's saddle to fool her father, and Michal hides the *teraphim* in David's bed to inveigle her father and his agents).

The allusion to Genesis 31 has elements of theological satire. In the Genesis narrative, the *teraphim* are sat on, and in the Samuel narrative, the *teraphim* are used instruments of deception. In light of other prophetic harangues (e.g. Hos. 3.4; Zech. 10.2), it is evident that *teraphim* were stumbling blocks for the people of Israel, but in these texts they are mocked. Moreover, there are two other uses of *teraphim* in the Deuteronomistic History that merit comment. First, in Judges 17 Micah makes for himself an ephod and *teraphim*, and just like Laban, in the very next chapter the *teraphim* are stolen! The first two owners of *teraphim* in the Bible—Laban and Micah—both experience burglary with respect to their idols. Owning *teraphim* is a perilous enterprise.

The next mention of *teraphim*—and indeed the only other occurrence of the term in the books of Samuel—is in Samuel's second denunciation of Saul in 1 Sam. 15.23, where Saul is told: 'For rebellion is like the sin of divination, Defiance, like the iniquity of teraphim'. The recurrence of *teraphim* for Saul—courtesy of his daughter Michal—serves to underscore his rejection in favor of David, and thus *teraphim*, in the words of Robert Polzin (1993: 182) 'comes back to taunt him'.

19.14-17

> Saul sent agents to take David, and she said, 'He's ill'. So Saul sent the agents to see David, saying, 'Bring him up to me on the bed to kill him'. The agents came in, and behold, the *teraphim* on the bed, with a quilt of goat's

hair at its head-place! Then Saul said to Michal, 'Why have you deceived me like this, and let my enemy go, and he has slipped away?' Michal said to Saul, 'He said to me, "Let me go! Why should I kill you?"'

As Saul's henchmen move in for the arrest, Michal delays them with a ruse. She alleges indisposition, but Saul does not give up that easily. Again, despite his oath to the contrary earlier in the chapter, Saul—looking nastier, and there is no evil spirit this time—directs his servants with deadly instructions. Even so, Michal's tactics are successful, and when the messengers enter the house, the narrative switches to their perspective, as they behold the mannequin on the bed. The deception precipitates a heated confrontation between father and daughter, with the former accusing the latter of aiding and abetting his 'enemy'. Saul's use of the term 'enemy' should be noted: previously, David was referred to as his enemy in a private sense, or as an interior reflection. Now, Saul verbalizes David as an enemy, commencing a new phase in the story where David will be relentlessly pursued. After his initial 'love' for David, Saul has veered a long way. Glancing ahead in the story, Michal will share a not dissimilar trait with her father: both love David early in the narrative, but have antithetical feelings later on. Meanwhile, Michal acts on David's behalf in this chapter over and against her father's interests. In this Saul is ironically correct: she is a 'snare', but not for David!

The words and actions of Michal in this chapter continue the allusions to Genesis 31, and a set of resemblances emerge between the house of Saul and the clan of Laban. There are grounds for arguing that the Deuteronomist configures the portrait of Michal on the Rachel model. On the positive side, both stories feature aggressive initiative by a younger daughter against her father in favor of her husband. The plea of ill-health is deceptively used by both daughters. Michal declares that David is 'ill' after putting the *teraphim* on the bed, and Rachel conceals the *teraphim* from her father by stating, 'Let not anger be kindled in the eyes of my lord, for I am not able to rise before you, because the way of women is to me'. In both cases, it is arguable that the female interests are served better through the husband; that is, Rachel has better prospects for wealth through Jacob, and Michal is better off (royal terms) through the house of David rather than the house of Saul.

But on the negative side, Rachel suffers through years of barrenness, and so the reader of 1 Samuel 19 wonders about the future of Michal. Peter Miscall (1986: 127) discusses this comparison, and contends that the literary intention of this allusion is to 'foreshadow a fatality shared by Michal with Rachel' (cf. Alter 1981: 120). Indeed, both wives are involved with 'cursing', so to speak. Rachel is unintentionally cursed by Jacob in Gen. 31.32 ('With whomever you find your gods', Jacob says to Laban, 'he shall not live'). Michal also has a grim confrontation with her husband: in her last scene with David in 2 Samuel 6 she is looking down from a window as David brings the ark to Jerusalem, and the chapter ends with these words: 'As for Michal daughter of Saul, she had no child till the day of her death'. Whether Michal 'curses' David by avoiding his bed, or whether David exiles Michal from his bed and so 'curses' her with barrenness cannot finally be answered. Rachel dies in labor as she gives birth to Benjamin, Saul's eponymous ancestor. Michal will not die in child-birth, and will not continue the royal line of Benjamin. In terms of the wider Deuteronomistic History, one wonders if this portrait of Michal as 'Rachel recycled' will symbolize the barrenness of Saul's house and the sterility of the northern monarchic experience.

As for Saul, he shares many characteristics with Laban the Aramean. I would submit that the reason why these two *deceptive fathers* in Genesis 31 and 1 Samuel 19 have intersecting *character zones* is because Saul is being presented here as a 'new Laban'. By comparing Saul with Laban, the Deuteronomist is able to provide some implicit appraisal of Saul's conduct and even perhaps some unspoken censure. Further, if Saul's portrait is configured on the Laban model, then both of these fathers are having to respond to a son-in-law who is under the promise of election, and in both cases, the father-in-law's schemes are ultimately foiled.

Consequently, David is 'Jacob-like' throughout this stretch, in that he escapes the clutches of an angry father-in-law who chases him with hostile intent. In my view, the Deuteronomist configures this experience of David in 1 Samuel 19 on the earlier experience of Jacob in Genesis 31 to illustrate that just as Jacob is eventually vindicated in his struggle with Laban, so David—at this precipitous moment in his own career—will also be vindicated in his struggle with Saul. Just as Jacob cuts a covenant with Laban after their confrontation, so David will eventually swear an oath of amnesty with the descendants of Saul after their confrontation. After many years of wandering, David will overcome, just like Jacob. So, there is the personal dimension, but there is also the *family* side of the equation. The familial problems of both Jacob and David have a set of uncanny parallels. Indeed, just as the conflict between Jacob and Laban foreshadows that of David and Saul, so the family history of Jacob shares numerous similarities with the house of David, including fraternal strife, and the looming issues of succession, inheritance, and leadership in these two families of promise.

19.18-20
Once more the reader is told that David flees and escapes, but this time the destination is specified: he goes to Samuel at Ramah. To this point in the story David has not had very much fellowship with Samuel, so one pauses to wonder why he seeks the prophet now. It could be desperation, or perhaps

David is trying to intimidate Saul, as it were. Either way, David has not come in contact with the prophet since his anointing of chap. 16. The northern locale of Ramah should also be noted. Bruce Birch (1998: 1127) questions why David would not travel south, to his own tribal territory of Judah. The mention of Ramah, though, takes the reader back to earlier moments of the story, and therefore it is a fitting backdrop: there are a number of echoes of earlier events as this final episode of the chapter unfolds.

When David arrives in Ramah, he reports to Samuel 'all that Saul did to him'. This would be a long and exhausting account, and hence the Deuteronomist does not present the report in direct speech. It is unclear why David and Samuel then proceed to Naioth, a site that does not occur elsewhere in the Bible. Scholars have speculated that Naioth could be a temporary encampment or a group of huts. Naioth is certainly located in the vicinity of Ramah, and must be well-known enough, because Saul receives the report that 'David is at Naioth in Ramah' without any qualification or explanation. Even though David slips out of window by night, his whereabouts quickly become known. In the frayed kingdom of Saul, court gossip is becoming quite a force.

Increasingly, a single agenda is dominating Saul, and the fixation on David cannot be healthy for king and country. As Walter Brueggemann (1990: 142) reflects, 'Saul is so obsessed with David he abandons all good judgment concerning the well-being of his own rule'. Once again in this chapter, messengers are sent to apprehend David. But as Saul's agents draw near to apprehend the suspect, there is a pneumatic event: 'And when they saw the company of the prophets prophesying—with Samuel standing as a pillar over them—the spirit of God was upon Saul's messengers, and they prophesied, even they'. Samuel has not, the reader learns, been idle in retirement; he may have drawn back from public life, but he has an apparently thriving pupillary establishment, and is still exercising power after all these years. The assembly of prophets are evidently under Samuel's tuition, since he is described as standing over them. To say the least, Samuel has had some prickly moments during his prophetic career, so one can only hazard a guess at what he would be like as an academic dean.

19.21-24

Saul is the recipient of a number of reports in this chapter, and from his perspective the reports are usually bad news. This time the fate of his messengers is reported to him, and he responds by sending other agents in their stead. However, this strategy has little efficacy, as the next group also 'prophesy'. In a pattern that will be repeated later in the Deuteronomistic History (see 2 Kgs 1), a third group is sent in vain, such that Saul himself proceeds to Ramah in 19.22. For this journey, I am guessing that Saul is wearing his royal robe.

For the second time in his career, Saul finds himself searching for Samuel. He has been told that David is in Naioth at Ramah, yet at the great cistern of Secu he pauses to ask: 'Where are Samuel and David?' I am understanding this question as a moment of hesitation on Saul's part. He knows where David is, and must know that he is harbored by Samuel, yet he still posits the query. So often Saul asks a question that gets no answer, but here he already knows the answer before he asks. The spatial setting for this otherwise pointless inquiry is a *place of water*, the 'great cistern'. J.P. Fokkelman (1986: 281) makes the shrewd observation that this is the second time Saul has asked for directions to Samuel near a place of water (9.11-13). Consequently, the reader is reminded about Saul's aborted type scene and its grim forecast for his career, the end of which Samuel was not slow to announce.

At the same time, Saul's asking for Samuel stands in tension with the notice of 15.35: 'Samuel did not see Saul again until the day of his death'. However, the potential contradiction is skillfully avoided because the same fate befalls Saul as his messengers before him. As Saul is walking toward Naioth of Ramah, he is seized by the spirit and begins to prophesy, and thus he is in some sort of ecstatic state *before* he reaches Samuel. So it is true, Samuel does not again see Saul *in his right mind* prior to the day of his death. Samuel will of course see Saul again, but he will have been long buried before that day. Moreover, this 'meeting' in chap. 19 is somewhat unique, in that Samuel does not say anything to Saul. This is an atypical moment: for once, Saul's humiliation is not a result of Samuel's words.

The last line of this eventful chapter operates as symbolic commentary on the preceding scenes: 'He put off, even he, his clothes, and prophesied, even he, before Samuel, and he fell naked all that day, and all that night. Therefore they say, "Is even Saul among the prophets?"' Saul is not the first to 'put off' (פשט) his clothing, but in contrast to his son Jonathan in 18.4, Saul's action appears involuntary. For the second time in the chapter, clothes are involved in David's rescue. As Ora Horn Prouser (1996: 32) notes, Michal uses clothes as a delay tactic, but here the *absence* of clothes again works in David's favor, as a disrobed Saul is deflected from his homicidal pursuit. Robert Polzin (1993: 181) also comments on this connection: 'Whereas Michal covers David's bed with his clothes (v. 13), Saul strips off *his* clothes and lies naked all day and night (v. 24)—a graphic picture of how the narrator hides David and bares Saul throughout the last two chapters'. To pick up Polzin's later point, David is able escape from Saul's prophetic delirium earlier in the chapter, but now he escapes *because of* Saul's prophetic delirium in the last part of the chapter. The final repetition of the strange question 'Is even Saul among the prophets?' evokes memories of Saul's first mingling with the prophets in 10.10-13. In the present context of chap. 19, Saul has now fallen down before Samuel, the one who earlier declared that his kingdom would not 'arise' (13.14).

1 Samuel 20

Of the many events that have befallen David since his first introduction to Saul's court, the friendship of Jonathan is of considerable significance. The David–Jonathan relationship receives a vast amount of attention in this chapter, probably because *loyalty* (and the often difficult choices that surround it) emerges as a key theme. Should one's primary loyalty lie with family, clan, or tribe, or does one's primary loyalty lie with God's anointed? Because loyalty is a primary theme, there is a good deal of talk about *the future* in this chapter, and the disproportionate amount of direct speech in 1 Samuel 20 means that it is more important for character than for plot, as such. Saul has not been handling David's success very well. He swears an oath regarding David's life, but three different attempts on the latter's person all fail, culminating with his own disrobed fall before Samuel that leaves the reader with the unsettling question of why Saul is among the prophets. Yet Saul is still king, and, as this chapter reveals, he is frequently plagued by dangerous thoughts and dark brooding. It is the actions and the reactions of Saul that dominate much of the discourse of the chapter. While Jonathan mediates a reunion between David and Saul at the beginning of chap. 19, the short-lived nature of the reconciliation creates a problem for his loyalties to father and friend. Consequently, this chapter is a turning point for Jonathan, in what turns out to be his last major appearance in the story. Once Jonathan realizes (or admits?) David's state of danger with respect to Saul, his words turn toward the future. In the previous chapter, there is not a word of recorded direct speech from David, but the situation is poised to change. In fact, 1 Samuel 20 is framed by dialogues between David and Jonathan, and in between there is a histrionic confrontation between the king and his son. In the first dialogue, David attempts to persuade Jonathan that Saul's intentions toward him are evil, and formulates a plan to hide in the field during a new moon feast. With David hidden, Jonathan attends the three-day feast, and proffers an excuse for David's absence. Upon hearing the news, Saul goes ballistic, with both spear and vicious language aimed not at the absent David but rather at the present Jonathan. The chapter eventually concludes with David and Jonathan's emotional parting in the field, and re-affirmation of their covenant status.

20.1-2

Either during or after Saul's fusion with the prophets, David flees from Naioth in Ramah and comes before Jonathan. It is not immediately clear why David prefers to take refuge with Jonathan rather than Samuel at this point, but it is appropriate that the location of Jonathan is unspecified: not only does it create a sense of secrecy in the first instance, but throughout the first dozen lines of this chapter the location and to some extent the *intentions* of the interlocutors are camouflaged. David begins the dialogue with Jonathan, giving the reader the first recorded words of David in a long time, and as Robert Alter (1999: 123) notes, these are David's first recorded words to Jonathan. To this point, only Jonathan has spoken (19.2-3) and initiated conversation, but now David speaks prior to Jonathan. David also speaks 'before' (לפני) Jonathan, and the Hebrew preposition implies a more official kind of discourse rather than friendly banter.

David unleashes a triple-barreled barrage of rhetorical questions to Jonathan, demanding to know why Saul seeks his life. In rhetoro-spect, the reader has heard David ask 'What have I done?' before. This same question represents David's initial response to the speech of Eliab (17.28-29), and David is less interested in a formal answer, but rather is keen to avow his 'innocence' in the face of his older brother's charges. But here with Jonathan, David's question is meant to shape a reaction from the hearer because a certain impression is created—he *does* want an answer. Further, traces of David's third question ('What is my sin before your father?') have previously appeared, most poignantly in Jonathan's question to Saul in 19.25, 'Why would you sin against innocent blood?' The recycled language indicates that some exasperation on David's part is warranted, and his words are designed to persuade Jonathan that Saul's conduct represents a case of misprision in the highest degree. Given Jonathan's recent efforts on his friend's behalf (e.g. the giving of robe and weapons in chap. 18, and the reconciliation with Saul achieved in chap. 19), David's sounds more legal than grateful. It remains to be seen exactly what David seeks to obtain from this dialogue: is he looking for an 'official' dismissal and a license to flee, or does he merely want some support and defense in Saul's court?

It is conceivable that David starts in a reproachful manner in order to elicit a truthful and immediate response from Jonathan. Jonathan certainly replies in an animated manner, commencing with an interjection ('Far be it', חָלִילָה), then moving to a denial of David's main assertion, and concluding with another exclamation, 'Is it not so!' Jonathan, we should note, does not launch into a defense of Saul's past actions, but instead emphasizes the David is not in present danger because Saul has not intimated any plans to Jonathan himself about killing David. According to Jonathan, Saul never does anything 'big or little' without first acquainting him, an assertion that Jonathan underscores with a rhetorical question of his own: 'Why would my father hide this thing from me?' Ironically, Jonathan says that his father always 'opens his ear' to his plans, yet we have had occasion to see Jonathan do the *opposite*, and not acquaint his father with plans (e.g. 14.1). As Peter Miscall (1983: 107) remarks, 'In 1 Samuel 14 Jonathan himself came close to dying at his father's command; he should have no doubt about that of which Saul is capable'. On the one hand, Saul has informed Jonathan about his intentions toward David in the past (19.1), but on the other hand, one wonders where Jonathan has been during the rest of chap. 19 (where there is a series of attempts on David's life), culminating in his father's naked flailing during the unsuccessful arrest in Naioth of Ramah. In 1 Samuel 20, Jonathan is remarkably far-sighted, but this initial response reveals something of a blind spot. In this opening dialogue David and Jonathan are discussing Saul, but we learn rather more about *them* than about Saul.

20.3-4

Saul has not revealed any malignant plans to him, and therefore Jonathan resists David's concerns. Jonathan's objection, though, is emphatically countered as David 'swears an oath' in 20.3. Although the RSV simply has David 'reply', the NRSV more accurately follows the Hebrew text and renders 'swore'. As a preamble to the oath, David explains why Jonathan is out of the loop: Saul knows that David has found grace in his eyes, and thus the father conceals his plan from the son. To buttress this argument, David then supplies a 'quotation' from Saul. Jonathan claims that Saul does nothing without 'uncovering his ear' first, but David claims to know the inner workings of Saul's mind: 'for he said [thought], "Jonathan must not know this, lest he be pained"'. After this alleged word from Saul's interior consciousness, David's oath is sworn, to the effect that the space between him and death is a short distance: 'about a step'. On the whole, David presents a case whereby Jonathan is uninformed because Saul has been dissembling: the king's public speech and private actions are not in harmony.

For some reason, Jonathan's pattern of denial is broken. Whether he is persuaded by David's argument or simply acquiesces to his friend's speech is not clear, but his response ('What your soul says, that I will do') indicates a change of direction. Several commentators note a resemblance between the words of Jonathan here and the words of Jonathan's armor bearer in chap. 14. As Diana Edelman (1991: 155) explains, 'His words are reminiscent of those spoken to him by his weapons-bearer in 14.7; he now symbolically becomes David's weapon-bearer, having already turned over to him the weapons of the office of king-elect'. I suppose one could argue that Jonathan's armor bearer and his brave willingness to follow his master anticipates Jonathan's conduct toward David here in chap. 20, in another episode where Saul is not fully informed. At any rate, in light of the weapons and arrows that occur later in this chapter, the comparison with an earlier armor bearer is apt.

20.5-8

Jonathan's compliance paves the way for a long articulation of David's strategy to prove Saul's evil intentions. Saul has several times now been the object of deception; Samuel's 'sacrificial' pretext for going to Bethlehem in chap. 16, and Michal's trick with the *teraphim* in chap. 19 immediately come to mind. Both times David is the reason for the deception, but here in chap. 20 David is the author. Tomorrow, David tells Jonathan in 20.5, he will be expected at the new moon gathering, but he is not planning to be there, as he will be hiding. Jonathan earlier tells David that his father 'hides' (סתר) nothing from him, and now David says he will 'hide himself' (סתר) in the field until the third day of the gathering. Should Saul note his absence, Jonathan is to provide an excuse: David asked permission to attend an annual sacrifice in his city of Bethlehem, where all his family will be gathered.

In light of the larger storyline, some of the terms (e.g. Bethlehem, clan, and sacrifice) in David's stratagem are incendiary: Saul knows about a 'neighbor', he knows David is from Bethlehem, and he has been twice rejected in the context of sacrifice. I would venture to guess that the reader is *not* expecting Saul to say 'Good' when he hears this report. But this is the epicenter of David's test: should Saul answer favorably, then all is well. However, if Saul's wrath is kindled, then he has deadly designs on David. Notably, David supplies a 'quotation' for a pacific Saul ('Good'), but he does not supply a quotation for an angry Saul. As events unfold, Saul will prove capable of some rather vulgar language—children's Bibles most likely omit such outbursts (i.e. 20.30).

The complexity of this plan militates against extemporaneity. Indeed, David's concluding utterance is carefully weighed: 'And you will act loyally (חסד) with your servant, for you have brought your servant with you into a covenant of the LORD. But if there is guilt in me, then *you* put me to death. Unto your father, why should you bring me?' First, if Saul's anger is kindled, then Jonathan is to act with loyalty and remember the 'covenant of the LORD' with David. In 18.3, Jonathan cuts a covenant with David out of his love for him. Here in 20.8, presumably that covenant becomes a 'covenant of the LORD' in David's mouth. Some commentators argue that it is the same thing, while others assert that another covenant has been made between David and Jonathan, but not recorded. Still other commentators suggest that David 'expands' the terms of reference, and thereby the stakes are raised (and, by implication, the consequences for violation). Either way, Jonathan's voluntary efforts in chap. 18 are recalled, and become the surety for his loyal conduct toward David over and against Saul. David concludes with a similar phrase that he starts with: if I am guilty, put me to death yourself, and why should you betray me to your father?

20.9-11
Of all David's comments in the long speech of 20.5-8, it is the last clause that evokes the strongest reaction from Jonathan. Once more, Jonathan uses the interjection 'Far be it' (חָלִילָה), and declares in unequivocal terms that he would inform David if he knew that Saul's intentions were evil. Whether this is a tacit agreement to go along with the plan of hiding, David certainly spins Jonathan's response that way, and asks a question that demands a response: 'Who will report to me if what your father answers is fierce?' Without directly answering the question, Jonathan suggests a journey to the field, and thus the reader assumes that he is ready to try the test of David. The last word in the scene (20.11b) goes to the narrator, describing the two of them walking 'to the field'.

In this dialogue, there are some interesting components in the characterizations of David and Jonathan that emerge. As for David, he formulates a plan that evinces knowledge of both Saul and Jonathan—how both of them will respond in given situations. Robert Polzin's (1993: 192) comment is provocative: 'Briefly put, David directs Jonathan to lie, that is, to use duplicitous language. Here we have the first indication in the story that David can dissemble when it is in his best interest to do so. The question remains open, then, whether David is dissembling as he swears the oath that Jonathan makes him swear'. It should be noted that these are the last words of David in this very long chapter. The rest of the dialogue is carried by Jonathan. Consequently, one should not underestimate Jonathan's part, as his words will be the focal point for the next segment of the chapter. It is Jonathan who suggests that he and David go to 'the field', and it will be this spatial setting where Jonathan chooses to express his own longer-term interests. Jonathan will be far less idealistic in the spatial setting of the field, away from any eavesdropper from his father's court. There is a real possibility that Jonathan's forthcoming speech in the field will border on treason.

20.12-17
Jonathan's clandestine location in the field is probably a good idea: there is a gossip network of Saul, as we have seen (18.20; 19.19), and given the subject matter of this conversation, every precaution should be taken. Jonathan's long speech in the field is interrupted only by narrational asides in vv. 16-17. While the Hebrew text of this long speech is difficult in places,

the general sense can be followed. Jonathan begins with an invocation of the divine name, and while some translations provide more of a paraphrase (e.g. RSV), it may be that Jonathan simply uses the divine name to invoke a high degree of solemnity to the occasion. Jonathan pledges to search out his father, and after ascertaining Saul's mind toward David, he promises to communicate the result (whether good or ill) to David. After a benediction from Jonathan ('May the LORD be with you, just as he was with my father'), 20.14 has a different horizon in view. Jonathan is clearly acquainted with the idea that David is moving toward the throne of Israel, while Saul's house is on the way out. Hence Jonathan implores David not to cut off his 'loyalty' (חסד) toward him or his house when the LORD cuts off David's enemies. In light of Saul's reckoning David as an 'enemy' (18.29; 19.17), this is incisive covenant language.

Many a source-critic has no doubt been tempted to wield Jehoiakim's scribal knife and cut all kinds of columns in this stretch of text. Yet there is a certain coherence to this chapter in general and Jonathan's speech in particular, and a useful contribution to the overall storyline. For my analysis, the key issue of this speech is *house*. Jonathan is quite unlike earlier sons from another dynastic house in 1 Samuel, namely, Hophni and Phinehas. At the end of chap. 2, the man of God announces that another (priestly) house will be firmly established, in contrast to the last remnant of the house of Eli who will be reduced to begging (2.35-36). Jonathan too is from a rejected house, but here is where the similarity with Hophni and Phinehas ends, as Jonathan has the necessary discernment and foresight to ally himself with the elected house in advance. As Robert Gordon (1986: 166-67) summarizes,

> It is Jonathan's turn to invoke the covenant between himself and David (*cf.* v. 8), as he contemplates the accession of David and the possible consequences for the disinherited house of Saul. He knew well that usurpers were wont to adopt a root and branch policy toward ousted royal families, lest they became alternative foci of loyalty at a later date (*cf.* 2 Ki. 10.1-11; 11.1). Whether or not David was reckoned as a usurper, he was likely to suffer from the same disadvantages if the family of Saul were left unculled.

Jonathan intuitively recognizes that it is difficult for a king to be loyal to the memory of a rival house, and indeed, this thesis is borne out in the later narrative. One notes a recurring pattern within chaps. 19–22: at Saul's expense, key allies and information accrue to David. But as we will see, some present allies will become liabilities later on, and it is exactly this 'liability' status that Jonathan seeks to avoid. Just as David is in danger from a present king, Jonathan fears his house will be in danger from a future king. To offset such cutting off, Jonathan cuts a deal with the house of David.

20.18-23

In the next phase of Jonathan's speech matters return to the shorter-term and the pressing exigencies of the moment. He reiterates that David will be missed at the feast because—as David, Jonathan, and the reader know—David will be hiding. The precise location of David's hiding place has vexed scholars and translators. The RSV renders the tricky Hebrew phrase (אֵצֶל הָאֶבֶן הָאָזֶל) rather generically as 'beside yonder stone heap', while the NIV ventures greater specificity with 'by the stone Ezel'. Obviously David and Jonathan know where the stone is: in the RSV the stone would be located in the field where they are, but in the NIV Jonathan presumably would be referring to another site. Either way, it is remote from Saul's court, which leads to a problem: David will not know the result of their 'experiment' to test Saul's disposition. In order to communicate the news, Jonathan devises an arrow scheme. Evidently Jonathan has acquired new weapons, because he plans to shoot arrows with the accompanying directions to his servant lad coded to mean good or bad. If Saul is disposed to do evil with David, then David will have to imitate an arrow, and take flight himself. There is an important conclusion to Jonathan's address, one that emphasizes 'the word and the witness' between them. Despite impending exile of indeterminate length, the covenant between them will stand forever.

Thematically, there are some tensions in Jonathan's speech that add some complexity to his character. On the one hand, the elements of 'love' and commitment to David suggest self-denial on Jonathan's part. But on the other hand, there are currents in the speech that suggest self-interest. Peter Miscall (1983: 114) develops this latter point: 'Jonathan is willing to help David against his father, but he also apparently fears that David may betray him, that he may be using him for the moment and will turn against him in the future when he is in a less precarious situation'. On the one hand, spiritual statements that Jonathan makes are not trite. With phrases such as 'The LORD has sent you away', there is a high recognition of divine sovereignty even in the midst of expulsion. On the other hand, Jonathan also uses the divine name as a warning to his friend. His use of 'witness' language in 20.23 is important in the framework of the story, and surely he is issuing a word of caution about being cavalier with this oath.

It would appear that Jonathan's love for David is sacrificial, and there are real emotional currents that connect the two friends. But upon further review, Jonathan makes a well-calculated gamble. If David is destined to reign and replace the house of Saul, Jonathan sacrifices his 'crown-prince' status for a longer-term guarantee of survival. Diana Edelman (1991: 158) summarizes this idea: 'In the narrative flow of events, he has just secured his personal safety and that of his immediate family against the typical bloodbath that accompanied changes of dynasty by appealing to the pact. He has been willing to sacrifice his crown in exchange for the guarantee of the lives of his family, showing himself to be a pragmatist'. Is there a sense—by virtue of the constant repetition and reinforcement—that Jonathan has doubts about David's fulfillment of the oath, and hence the language of covenant is continually enhanced and emphasized? Some commentators argue that throughout the story David manipulates Jonathan, while other recent advocates suggest an erotically charged relationship. The text itself resists both of these readings, and I would submit that Jonathan is a more complex character than is acknowledged by either of these extremes.

20.24-26

The arrival of the new moon feast is greeted by the empty seat of David, who is hiding either beside the rock of Ezel or beyond yonder stone heap. The king is present and seated, and his location is worth noting: 'The king sat upon his seat, as at other times, upon the seat by the wall' (NRSV). The wall, one recalls, has often been punctured; thus, not only are a series of attempts on David's life brought to mind, but another such attempt is anticipated. There is further foreshadowing in the last half of 20.25. The NRSV translates this line as 'Jonathan stood, while Abner sat by Saul's side', but a more literal rendering of the Hebrew text would read, 'And Jonathan arose, and Abner sat down beside Saul'. If one opts for the NRSV reading, then Jonathan is part of the seating arrangement and is included in the triumvirate along with Saul and Abner. Alternatively, if Jonathan 'arises' and makes way for Abner, it is symbolic of an abdication of sorts, as he vacates the seat beside Saul. Later in the story, Abner will strengthen his own position in the house of Saul, after the deaths Saul and Jonathan (2 Sam. 3). But meanwhile, in this present chapter that reflects on the rise of David and the fate of the house of Saul afterward, Jonathan's 'arising' is worth noting.

Whatever Jonathan's position during this new moon feast, the seat of David is empty, and this absence is duly observed by the king. While Saul does not publicly comment on this absence, he does privately speculate as to why David is elsewhere: 'But Saul did not say anything on that day, for he thought, "It is an accident, he is not clean. Surely, he is not clean."' A question emerges here: Why is Saul mystified over David's empty seat? Robert Polzin (1993: 187) is also perplexed:

> In verse 26 Saul raises a royal eyebrow in apparent wonder over David's absence from the king's table—an absence not particularly puzzling, we would think, given Saul's earlier directions to his son and servants to kill David (19.1), his castigation of Michal for helping David escape the murderous clutches of his servants, and his many attempts to take and kill David at Ramah.

Despite a bevy of hostile javelin launches, Saul does not link David's absence with his own conduct, but rather he postulates a different kind of reason, that David must be ceremonially unclean. The precise nuance or reason for the 'uncleanness' is not subject to Saul's speculation, but the double mention sounds a note of apprehension. Further, the reference to 'not clean' reminds the reader of Saul's altar, vow, fast, and accusations of impurity in chap. 14, and continues to reveal Saul's preoccupation with cultic and ritual affairs.

20.27-31

The still empty seat of David prompts a Saulide inquiry on the second day, as he asks his son Jonathan the reason for 'the son of Jesse's' absence. Despite Saul's certainty on the day before that David is unclean, Barbara Green (2003: 342) comments on the doubt that entered Saul's mind: 'His question now, flushed from the underbrush of his selftalk, reveals the inadequacy of his own previous effort to convince himself that it must be temporary uncleanness, since he backs up to the absence of the previous day'. Saul's inquiry is probably a request for information rather than a 'test' of Jonathan. Still, Jonathan's response is striking, since he deviates from the previously rehearsed script. I mentioned above the incendiary nature of the some of the terms that David proposes, but whether conscious or not, Jonathan pours fuel on this prospective fire. Other than terms like 'Bethlehem', 'family', and 'sacrifice', Jonathan's use of 'escape' is surely a *faux pas* given its earlier uses in chap. 19, when Michal aids David's escape from Saul (see 19.12, 17). In general terms, these are words that J.P. Fokkelman (1986: 332) says 'make Saul jump from his chair as if stung by a wasp', but specifically the term *escape* 'must act like a red rag to a bull. Placed in the mouth of the "feigned" David, and addressed to Saul, it is a first class Freudian slip.'

Saul's wrath is targeted not on David, as one might expect, but on his son Jonathan. The angry outburst of the father to the son ironically underscores a key theme to the chapter: Jonathan takes many steps to ensure the survival of his 'house' when David's rise reaches its zenith, and perhaps these efforts will be intensified *because of* Saul's angry tirade here. Saul's eruption begins with a slur on Jonathan that is enveloped in a horribly uncomplimentary set of words involving the mother/wife. That Jonathan would choose David is a shame to his mother's 'nakedness', a rather surprising term given Saul's own dubious state of undress in the previous chapter. The reason why Jonathan's choice of David is so foolish, according to Saul, is because it destroys any prospects for the throne: 'For all the days that the son of Jesse lives on the earth you and your kingdom will not be established. So therefore, send and take him to me, for he is a son of death!' It is hard to fathom how Jonathan's kingdom could be 'established' (כון) in light of Samuel's first rejection speech in chap. 13, where Saul clearly hears that his dynasty will not be 'established' (כון). Equally perplexing is why Saul would then instruct Jonathan to bring David to him, in light of Jonathan's obvious loyalty and 'choice' (to use Saul's word) of David.

20.32-34

Given Saul's fury, he is probably in no mood to negotiate with his son. Consequently, this is not the most prudent moment for Jonathan to launch into a defense of David by means of a pair of rhetorical questions. Jonathan's efforts have little efficacy, and a familiar sight ensues: Saul's spear of chaos—with a consistency that is beginning to rival the annual inundation of the Nile—is unleashed once more. A contradiction of sorts is observable here: Saul speaks of Jonathan's future and his 'kingdom', but then hurls the spear at him. Should Saul's spear finally hit its target, Jonathan's kingdom would certainly not arise.

Fortunately for Jonathan, Saul's accuracy has not improved over the past few chapters. The spear misses the mark, but now Jonathan knows that his father has malevolent designs on David. Having already dealt the son of Jesse a full house of homicidal attempts, Jonathan is now on the wrong end of the Saulide wrath. So, for the second time in this episode Jonathan 'arises'. This time Jonathan does not arise to make way for Abner, but rather to leave the table: 'And Jonathan arose from the table, hot with rage. He did not eat food on the second day of the new moon, because he grieved for David, because his father humiliated him.' When Jonathan departs and does not eat, only Abner remains with Saul at the table. Jonathan's 'not eating' reminds us of chap. 14, when the first division between father and son became apparent. There, Jonathan eats, and incurs Saul's wrath; here he does not eat *because of* Saul's wrath, and he departs grieving for David. David's earlier words in 20.3 turn out to be partially right: there is 'grieving' but it is Jonathan, not Saul, who does the grieving. The last clause of 20.34 has an ambiguity, nicely summarized by Graeme Auld (2003: 224): 'As Jonathan angrily leaves the table, we wonder whether the disgrace mentioned in the last words of v.34 is David's—or in the light of what his father has publicly said and done to him—Jonathan's own'. This deliberate ambiguity provides an effective transition to the final episode of the chapter.

20.35-42

The last moments of the chapter—barring some sort of hyper-symbolic reading—are fairly straightforward to interpret. Jonathan shoots arrows for his (oblivious) servant lad to collect, and Jonathan speaks, more or less, the agreed-upon words to communicate that David should flee. But after the lad departs, there is an unscripted moment where Jonathan and David come together for a moving farewell. In a chapter where many things are carefully constructed, this spontaneous outpouring is telling. This moment of weeping deconstructs the notion of 'love' as a strictly political entity, and betokens a genuine friendship. But at the same time, Jonathan twice mentions the divine name, and accentuates the oath sworn between them, that the LORD will watch over. As David leaves Saul's court, the final words of Jonathan summarize much of the dialogue transactions in this chapter. And thus we enter the beginning of what Julius Wellhausen—in his *Prolegomena to the History of Israel*—ascertained as a new period in the story, 'the freebooter life of David'. In this phase, David is a fugitive, away from home and court, forced to be resourceful in the wilderness, and a long way (literally and figuratively) from Goliath's head, which he once took to Jerusalem.

1 Samuel 21

When Jonathan shoots the arrow and counsels that David should flee, there are no accompanying directions as to where the son of Jesse should go. But then, David is not the first biblical figure to have leave town: thinking back in the biblical story, one recalls another major figure fleeing the wrath of a relative, and being forced to become a fugitive. When Jacob flees the wrath of his brother Esau, he takes refuge among allies of his mother. But it is during this period that new facets of Jacob's character emerge amid new challenges and life circumstances. Likewise, in 1 Samuel 21 David departs from Saul and Jonathan, and in altered circumstances takes refuge with a couple of unlikely allies. Just as different shades of David's character emerge, different techniques of characterization come to the fore in this stretch of narrative. This short chapter is divided into two parts. In part one, David makes a brief visit to Ahimelech, the priest of Nob, but one of Saul's employees is present on that day. In part two, David ventures beyond the boundaries of Israel and takes temporary refuge with a foreign king, Achish of Gath. The various characters presented in this chapter all re-appear as time goes on, so their introductions are important. The reader has just seen Jonathan throw his lot in with David, calculating that David will reign at some point in the future. Other characters will gradually begin to do the same, acknowledging David's ascent and allying themselves with him even at the risk of alienating Saul.

21.1

After David and Jonathan go their separate ways, Jonathan departs for 'the city', while David journeys to Nob, to Ahimelech the priest. Neither Nob nor Ahimelech have been mentioned before in the story, so this expedition of David could not have been predicted. It might also be surprising that 'priests' have not figured in David's life to this point either. But this visit to Nob is not arbitrary, and I will suggest in a moment that the paths of David and Ahimelech have crossed before.

The last time a levitical priest has featured in 1 Samuel is back in chap. 14, when Ahijah—of the doomed house of Eli—is attending Saul and overseeing cultic affairs. There is a careful tracing of Ahijah's lineage in 14.3:

'Ahijah son of Ahitub, Ichabod's brother, son of Phinehas son of Eli, the priest of the LORD in Shiloh, lifting up the ephod'. With Ahimelech of Nob, though, no genealogy is provided, just the generic designation 'priest'. So far, priests in 1 Samuel are from the house of Eli, so one could hazard a guess that Ahimelech is an Elide. To be sure, the reader will discover the ancestry of Ahimelech later on, but for the moment there is a delay in reporting such vital statistics. Furthermore, there is an interesting chronological dimension to this episode in Nob: the story glances backwards and forwards and backwards, and three characters will later comment on the events that transpire in the sanctuary 'on that day'.

David's journey to Nob leads me to suspect that Ahimelech must be an ally of David. Yet when Ahimelech (whose name means 'my brother is king') comes out to meet David, he is 'trembling'. A number of commentators have reflected on Ahimelech's deportment here. Graeme Auld (2003: 224) notices that the same verb 'tremble' occurs in chap. 16, when Samuel makes a covert journey to deceive a king: 'Ahimelech responds to the arrival of the lone David as the elders of Bethlehem did earlier to Samuel (16.4-5); both are afraid and suspect that something is up'. Diana Edelman (1991: 162) notes a further detail: 'Both instances of fear result from the arrival of a public figure who has fallen from favor with the king—a royal "enemy"'. Peter Miscall (1983: 127) points to other connections between the two chapters: 'Both incidents involve deception, trembling at meeting the lone figure, consecration (קדש), and sacrificial food. 1 Samuel 16 is followed by the David and Goliath story, 1 Sam 21…alludes to it.' These commentators agree that Ahimelech is trembling out of fear for Saul and his retribution. In my view, Ahimelech fears because a representative of Saul is present, and as an ally of David, Ahimelech is aiding the fugitive.

Ahimelech does not greet David like the elders of Bethlehem greet Samuel. Ahimelech does not ask if David has come in peace, and though he is trembling, his words sound like a demand for information: 'Why are *you* alone, and no man is with you?' Both Ahimelech and the Bethlehem elders tremble and ask rhetorical questions because of fear of a royal reprisal. Ahimelech, though, has more concrete reasons for worry: Ahimelech is not alone, and this prompts his strange welcome, which actually is a covert warning to David that all is not well in the sanctuary at Nob on that day. So, it is not the *fact* that David comes to Nob (there are reasons to suspect that he has been there before), but rather that he arrives in Nob at a bad time: when one of Saul's henchman is present, as will be disclosed shortly. It is not David who makes the priest tremble, it is the king.

21.2-3

It is fair to say that the vast majority of commentators on this passage have assumed that David bamboozles Ahimelech, and having convinced the priest that he is on a top-secret assignment from the king, entices him to provide bread and a sword. For my analysis, I assume the opposite, and here I am following the creative hypothesis sketched by Pamela Reis (1994: 59-73). I have elsewhere summarized the main lineaments of this interpretation as follows:

> Reis begins her study by observing that there has been a considerable (and somewhat surprising) degree of unanimity in the interpretation surrounding David and his encounter at Nob. As far as the main plot of the story is understood among a legion of interpreters, there may be some 'variation in detail and emphasis, but the overall consensus is that David deceived Ahimelech at Nob and that the priest therefore replied in innocence to Saul's interrogation and went guiltlessly to his death'. Antithetically, Reis argues that David and Ahimelech together are in 'collusion' against Doeg the Edomite (and by extension, King Saul), and therefore Ahimelech the priest is an *accomplice in deception* with David. When this assumption is made, David and Ahimelech's transaction of dialogue throughout 21.1-10 can be viewed as an attempt by both Ahimelech and David to beguile Doeg the Edomite, an ally of Saul detained in Nob... (Bodner 2005: 25).

Just like Michal in chap. 19 and Jonathan in chap. 20, Ahimelech uses deceptive language to protect David from Saul and his allies.

Ahimelech demands to know why David is alone, and his short queries are met with an effusive response from David, fraught with circumlocutions. David begins by stating that he is on clandestine business for the king, who has charged him with a matter. The secret nature of the operation is dramatically enhanced by a quotation from the king, supplied by David, asserting that nobody should know about this mission. Quotations such as this, of course, are hard to verify, and this is the point. Furthermore, 'no man' is with David because he assigned a *rendezvous* with his men at 'such and such a place' (NRSV). In biblical narrative, this Hebrew expression (פלני אלמוני) is used to designated an intentionally ambiguous place or person (e.g. 2 Kgs 6.8). Again, like the (alleged) quotation from the king, it would be hard to verify David's story, since locating 'such and such a place' would befuddle even the most innovative biblical cartographer.

After explaining why he is alone, David then changes his tune, and asks: 'So now, what is there under your hand? Give five loaves of bread into my hand, or whatever can be found'. This is an underhanded way of coming up with a pretext for this visit, as David abruptly makes it sound as though he needs supplies for his men. If David really needed food and supplies, it is puzzling why he would go to the sanctuary at Nob. The request for bread is a bogus excuse: David has no men, but he needs this diversion because he realizes that danger is lurking in the sanctuary, and that Ahimelech the priest is trembling because one of Saul's retainers is present, as the reader will soon discover. David's request for bread is thus aimed at this other audience.

On the surface, the words are *addressed* to Ahimelech, but they actually have another listener in mind.

21.4-5

The duplicitous dialogue continues, as the priest picks up David' ruse about food. Ahimelech is willing to comply, but only has 'holy bread' on hand. This bread can be released on the condition that David's 'young lads' have restrained themselves from women. One assumes that 'restrain' in this context has a sexual nuance, and commentators often point to passages in the Torah (e.g. Exod. 19.15; Josh. 3.5) to clarify Ahimelech's qualification on partaking of the bread. There is a slight irony here: Saul has recently been obsessed with David's 'unclean' state, whereas here the priest is concerned about any uncleanness in David's men. Nonetheless, I am arguing that Ahimelech's dialogue with David 'glitters with guile' in order to deceive Doeg the Edomite (Reis 2002: 133). Thus the priest is helping David in a *cultic* way, just as Michal hoodwinks Saul's agents by means of *teraphim* and Jonathan misleads his father with the fake excuse about the family sacrifice in Bethlehem. David's rejoinder to the priest in v. 5 may have a bit of ribald, but he certainly stresses his history of loyalty to the king as a veteran of numerous campaigns. This kind of statement will have a boomerang effect later in the storyline, as Kyle McCarter (1980: 349) remarks: 'David reminds the priest that no pious Israelite soldier will touch a woman while he is on active duty (cf. esp. II Sam 11.11)'.

21.6-7

The narrator abruptly interrupts this dialogue between David and Ahimelech with a pair of asides. The first (v. 6) aside describes why the 'bread of the Presence' can be taken away from the sanctuary 'before the LORD', while the second aside (v. 7) introduces a new character who is restrained in the sanctuary on that day 'before the LORD'. To start with v. 6, there are at least two reasons why the narrator inserts this aside at this particular point in the narrative. First, we notice that the (ostensible) concern for proper ritual activity in this sanctuary at Nob contrasts with the flippancy of Hophni and Phinehas at Shiloh. Even though Ahimelech is in collusion with David, there is a still a higher degree of concern for the sanctuary than was the case in Shiloh. I would argue that this detail about the holy bread is included to give a positive portrayal of Ahimelech. Second, we notice that a certain *point of view* is refracted in this aside: the 'camera angle' of v. 6 is from the perspective of someone who is watching. The deliberate actions of the priest are viewed from someone present in the sanctuary, which is why the narrator immediately introduces that 'watcher' in the next aside: a new character whom the reader belatedly discovers has been watching (and hearing) the interaction between the priest and the fugitive.

The second aside (v. 7) is the more foreboding of the two, as it formally introduces a new character into the drama, one who will play a menacing role in the forthcoming narrative: 'Now a man from the servants of Saul was there on that day, restrained before the LORD. His name was Doeg the Edomite, overseer of Saul's shepherds.' I would label this aside as delayed exposition, since the reader is informed about Doeg's presence sometime after David's arrival in Nob. Yet the two interlocutors are aware of Doeg from the outset, and their entire conversation is influenced because Doeg is at hand. The reader now reviews the earlier dialogue between David and the priest; different echoes are heard when we discover that Doeg is eavesdropping. At the same time, the reason why Doeg is 'restrained' (עצר) before the LORD in Nob is obscure. Some scholars posit a cultic reason—meaning that Doeg is unclean. The only other use of the root (עצר) also occurs in connection with Saul's kingship: in chap. 9, God says to Samuel, 'Behold, the man of whom I spoke to you! This one will restrain (עצר) my people.' Notably, the name Doeg means 'worry', and Ahimelech is worried about him.

Doeg himself is one of Saul's senior management team: the 'mightiest' (or chief) of Saul's shepherds. One would assume that Doeg has a vested interest in the Saulide regime, and in all probability a non-Saulide king in Israel would threaten such interests. There are now two shepherds in Nob, David and Doeg. As Diana Edelman (1991: 165) explains, 'Doeg's position as head shepherd of Israel parodies the use of this occupation to describe the office of kingship; a foreigner has been put in charge of "minding the flock" instead of Yahweh's chosen candidate, the trained shepherd David (16.11; 17.15)'. Furthermore, Doeg's status as an 'Edomite' is a reminder of the most famous Edomite so far in the biblical story: Esau (Gen. 25.30). The mention of Edom reinforces the idea that the struggle between David and Saul is like the earlier struggle between Jacob and Esau. Just as Esau was deceived by Jacob, so Doeg (Saul's employee) will be deceived by David and Ahimelech

21.8-10a

The dialogue resumes after the narrational aside about Doeg, and David's words have a slightly different nuance. Now David asks if a weapon is on hand; notwithstanding the zeal of Phinehas in Numbers 25, this a rather odd item to request from a priest. More odd, however, is that David is a military leader who is on a secret mission from the king, yet the business is so urgent that David has no weapon. My point is that immediately after the (delayed) introduction of Doeg, David asks for a weapon, confirming that the Edomite is a palpable threat. While David simply asks if a 'sword or spear' is available, I will suggest in a moment that David *already* knows that a certain weapon is housed in the sanctuary of Nob.

If David's request for a weapon is motivated by Doeg's presence, then surely Ahimelech's reply is equally aimed at the Edomite: 'The sword of Goliath the Philistine—who you struck in the valley of Elah—behold, it is wrapped up in robe behind the ephod'. Why would Goliath's sword be hidden in Nob? The last time the sword of Goliath is mentioned is 17.54, when David takes the head of Goliath to Jerusalem, but the weapons he put in his own tent. At some point, the sword was transferred to Nob and placed under the ephod, and under the stewardship of Ahimelech the priest, confirming the notion that Ahimelech and David are allies. Moreover, Ahimelech speaks deliberate words that are *not* designed to remind David of his previous triumph over Goliath in the valley of Elah, but rather to intimidate Doeg and emphasize David's monumental achievement in hand-to-hand combat. As a side note, the ephod will emerge as a vital piece of oracle software as the story continues. Here the ephod is mentioned in the context of a Saulide threat: its power is hinted at, as it conceals a sword and is guarded by a priest.

Ahimelech offers the sword of Goliath to David, and the episode in Nob moves to a conclusion with David's acceptance of the offer: 'There is none like it', he says to the priest, 'give it to me'. Throughout David's dialogue with the priest, the threat of Doeg has been the motivating factor. The threat of Doeg is underscored in the first part of v. 10, as we are told: 'And David arose and fled on that day from the presence of Saul'. Hence Doeg becomes a proxy for Saul in this episode, and when David flees from Nob, he is running from the king. David is beginning to run out of allies, so in the next scene he will flee even farther. David's next destination, as we will see, is entirely unexpected.

21.10b-15

> And David arose and fled on that day from the presence of Saul, and came to Achish king of Gath. The servants of Achish said to him, 'Is this David, king of the land? Is it not *this one* they sing to each other about in their dances, saying, "Saul has struck his thousands, David his ten thousands"?' David put these words his heart, and he was very afraid in the presence of Achish king of Gath. And he changed his judgment before their eyes, and acted madly while he was in their hand. He put marks on the doors of the gate, and slimy juice ran down to his beard. Achish said to his servants, 'Look at this madman! Why would you bring him to me? Am I lacking in madmen that you would bring this one to behave madly before me? Must *this one* enter my house?'

David's post-Nob destination results in a short and eminently comic scene: David, armed with the sword of Goliath, journeys to Gath, the hometown of Goliath himself! Taking flight from Saul, it is not clear why, of all places, David chooses Gath, where his popularity rating is no doubt low. David's audacious arrival is met with a certain incredulity on the part of King Achish's servants, and one is not sure how they recognize him. Maybe the fact that he is wielding the sword of their fallen champion gives his identity away. Presumably none of Achish's servants were part of David's two hundred operations in chap. 18.

David somehow makes his way right into the royal court of Achish, where the king's servants bemoan his arrival by quoting the same lyrics that the Israelite women sing in 18.7, celebrating the triumph of David against the Philistine giant. Back in chap. 17, Saul interprets the lyrics from his own royal perspective, and arrives at a negative conclusion. The same thing happens in Gath: the lyrics are again interpreted in a manner that threatens the establishment. Ironically, the servants of Achish label David as 'king of land', whereas in reality he is fleeing from the official king of the land. Of course, their statement has an (unintentionally) prophetic resonance in light of the larger storyline.

It is curious that David hears the servants quote the lyrics of the song, and becomes 'very afraid'. The reader might have thought that Achish and his court would be afraid of David, since he has walked into town armed with the sword of Goliath. Perhaps David's fear is augmented by the memory of his past surgical exploits in Philistine territory (18.27). Regardless, this Philistine organ-grinding strikes fear into David, providing an inside glimpse into David's heart for the first time in the story. He who knew no fear before the biggest Gathite is now afraid of other Gathites. David's strategy for survival in Gath gives a preview of how he will respond to other stressful situations in this phase of his career. During this fugitive period, Robert Gordon (1986: 169) notes that David will be forced to 'live by his wits'. In order to survive in Gath, David makes it look like he has lost his wits.

David's puckish behavior in Gath has raised many an eyebrow among commentators, just as it did among the servants of Achish. For the second time in this chapter, David dissembles in front of foreigners: the first time (with Ahimelech) he deceives Doeg the Edomite, and here he deceives Achish and the Gathites. With all the insight of an amateur forensic psychiatrist, it is King Achish who delivers a verdict on the spittle and scratching: madness. Achish also uses this occasion to deliver a mildly insulting remark to his servants, by asserting that there already are enough lunatics in his court already without adding this salivating scribbler. This foreshadows later divisions between Achish and his servants over David, when there will be further arguments as to David's fitness for service. Furthermore, Barbara

Green (2003: 351-52) suggests that this scene in Gath functions as a commentary within the larger narrative:

> ...this little episode raises the question of who fools whom, who baits whom, who sees through whom. It is, I think, another *mise-en-abyme*, the stand off of two kings: one of them feigning madness, one of them misreading it; one of them is shrewd, one clueless; one powerful, one wily. But who plays each of these roles in our more central drama is for the reader to sort.

David is faking madness in Philistine territory, while back in Israel Saul is experiencing the real thing.

1 Samuel 22

On the run from an increasingly manic father-in-law, King Saul, the fugitive period of David's career continues. In the previous chapter, David ventures to the city of Nob, where he encounters both Ahimelech the priest and Doeg the Edomite, mightiest of Saul's shepherds. David then journeys to Gath, where Achish and his servants marvel at his madness. While Achish will not appear in the narrative for some time, both Ahimelech and Doeg have important scenes here in chap. 22. The main episode of the chapter is enveloped with two short scenes. First, David is joined by his family and a motley crew of disenfranchised followers, as he moves to the cave of Adullam and then travels to Moab. The main part of the chapter is a violent sequel to the Nob episode, as King Saul interrogates Ahimelech, spurred on by the eyewitness testimony of Doeg the Edomite. The citizenry of Nob is almost entirely liquidated, but in the final scene of the chapter, a single survivor is able to escape to David and give the latter a full report about the destruction of Nob by the Edomite. The reader then discovers that David was fully aware of Doeg's presence on that day in Nob, and he invites the survivor to remain with him.

22.1-2

The insanity of Gath is only temporary, as David escapes from Philistine territory and journeys to the 'cave of Adullam'. The name 'Adullam' reminds the reader of David's ancestor taking similar refuge. In Genesis 38, Judah himself pitches his tent with Hirah the Adullamite in order to separate himself from his brothers after deceiving their father about the fate of Joseph. Here in 1 Samuel 22, Adullam is a place where David is re-connected with his brothers: 'his brothers and all the house of his father heard, and they went down to him there'. It is not immediately clear why David's brothers join him in the cave; perhaps they are in danger, but the text does not mention any particular reason. One assumes that Eliab must be included, despite his harsh words in chap. 17. Further, according to the reward list of 17.25, the victor's family was supposed to be 'free in Israel'; such does not seem to be the case in the cave of Adullam.

David's brothers and household members are not the only ones who gather around him in the cave; he is also joined by every man who was 'in hard straits, in debt, or bitter of soul'. Of these terms, Hannah is earlier described as 'bitter of soul' when pouring out her heart in prayer (1.10), and Kyle McCarter (1980: 357) notes that the same term also occurs in Judg. 18.25. McCarter summarizes: 'The point of the present passage, then, is that David becomes the leader of all those men who have suffered some kind of loss or deprivation that has left them embittered; he is now champion of the discontented, the disenchanted, and the mistreated'. Evidently, David is not the only one with Saulide problems—perhaps there have been other (unreported) targets for the king's javelin. David becomes the captain of these 400 men, and glancing ahead in the story, one assumes that from this disparate group will emerge some of the key players in David's later administration.

22.3-5

The sojourn in the cave of Adullam is brief, as David moves from there to Mizpeh of Moab to take refuge with *yet another* foreign potentate. Of course, David is not the only Bethlehemite in the biblical record to venture into Moabite territory: during the days of the Judges as narrated in the book of Ruth, Elimelech from Bethlehem in Judah takes his wife and two sons to sojourn in Moab during the days of a famine. David's words to the king of Moab continual the familial tone of this chapter: 'Let my father and mother come out to you, until I know what God will do for me'. While it is conceivable that David's parents are somehow in danger (while their son is a fugitive from the king), one senses that this is more a case of forging a political alliance. Presumably David is *not* drooling and scratching doorposts in Moab, but instead is acting sanely in the midst of these negotiations. One recalls that Saul has inflicted some disaster on Moab (14.47), so maybe the king of Moab is glad to sponsor an opponent to the incumbent king, hoping for a better deal in the event of usurpation. The servants of Achish refer to David as 'king of the land'—perhaps the king of Moab realizes the same thing. J.P. Fokkelman (1986: 374) remarks that it is as though David is speaking to an equal, and the fact that there is no recorded response from the king of Moab leaves the impression that David enjoys the upper hand in this transaction.

Without any formal introduction, the prophet Gad bursts into the narrative with a prophetic utterance for David: 'Do not dwell in the stronghold. Go, get yourself to the land of Judah.' Robert Gordon (1986: 173) suggests that a degree of respectability is conferred on David's company because of the prophet's presence: if so, one hopes that Gad is *not* part of the group of 400 men who are 'bitter of soul' or 'in debt'. The reader knows that there are other prophets in 1 Samuel (see 10.5,11; 19.20), but Gad's affiliation with these other groups is unknown. Either way, Gad's instructions to David are aggressive and apparently unsolicited. The prophet's word also contains a measure of risk: David left the promised land to flee from Saul, but now he is ordered to return to Judah, and be a good deal closer to the king. Nonetheless, David is obedient to the prophet's word and heads to the 'forest of Hereth'—a place otherwise unattested, but apparently located in Judah. There is an immediate comparison here with Saul, who has only bad experiences with the prophetic word. Still, Gad only provides a tactical imperative and a 'constructive' command to David; there is no waiting 'seven days', no testing, and no sacrifices. It is intriguing that 'divine inquiry' occurs here, since this will be a key component of the royal tribunal in the next episode of this chapter. Saul will accuse Ahimelech of 'inquiring' for David, but here in 22.5, the divine word is mediated through a prophet, not a priest.

22.6-8

As soon as David returns to Judah, Saul hears a report of his whereabouts, and that 'men are with him'. Saul's intelligence network has been active before—as in 16.18 when he is told about a certain Bethlehemite, and in 18.20, when it is reported that Michal loves David. Just like Doeg in Nob, one gains the impressions that Saul has 'eyes and ears' throughout the land. Notably, Saul does not hear that David is in Gath or interacting with the king of Moab, but rather David becomes 'known' *after* entering the forest of Hereth, and closer to his ostensible power base in Judah. As for Saul himself, he is ensconced at Gibeah, sitting 'under the tamarisk'. The only other mention of 'tamarisk tree' in the Deuteronomistic History occurs in 1 Sam. 31.13, the place where Saul is eventually buried.

The description of Saul sitting in Gibeah is reminiscent of 14.2, where Saul was sitting 'in the outskirts of Gibeah under the pomegranate tree that is in Migron'. In that episode, Saul has a very long and frustrating day, and a priest from the house of Eli features on a couple of occasions. Here in chap. 22, Saul is sitting with his 'spear in his hand', and the reader knows from past experience (as David and Jonathan also know), that this spear will be hurled at someone before long. Standing around the king are 'all his servants'; according to Samuel's speech in chap. 8, such officials are supposed to be the objects of royal affection. One recalls Samuel denunciation of kingly patronage: 'He [the king] will take the best of your fields, vineyards, olive groves and give them to his servants' (8.14). To this assembly, Saul now thunders:

> 'Listen up, Benjaminites! Even to all of *you* will the son of Jesse give fields and vineyards? Will all of *you* be placed as captains of thousands and captains of hundreds? Indeed, all of *you* have conspired against me, and there is no

one who uncovers my ear when my son cuts a deal with the son of Jesse! No one becomes sick for my sake, and uncovers my ear. Indeed, my son has caused my servant to rise up against me, to set an ambush this day!'

There has been no explicit mention of Saul distributing lands and favors to his family members and fellow Benjaminites. Still, we recall Saul's uncle and his questions about Samuel's words in 10.14-16, and in 14.50 the narrator records that Abner is over the army. Yet from this speech we get the impression that the king *has* rewarded them with fields and vineyards, and he expects loyalty in return. Saul's words are juxtaposed with the preceding report in 22.1-4 about the group who stands around David, as Walter Brueggemann (1990: 158) explains: 'Perhaps verse 2 stands as a counterpoint to verse 7. In verse 2 it is the marginal and indebted, those without land, who gather around David.' Here in this speech, Saul appeals to those with vested interests in the present regime. Will they get a better deal with the son of Jesse? Saul's point is rhetorical: David—should he reign—will surely reward his own inner circle rather than any Benjaminite, and tribal rivalry is highlighted here. So why, Saul asks, are they all guilty of a conspiracy of silence by not informing him about his son's actions? There is an overlap with Saul's earlier threat to Jonathan in 20.31, 'For all the days that the son of Jesse lives on the earth, neither you nor your kingdom will be established'. Similarly, Saul is arguing that the Benjaminites are working against their own interests, and hurting their political and economic interests. In this speech, Saul is formally addressing his fellow Benjaminites, although we will soon discover that there is at least one non-Benjaminites present in this assembly.

22.9-10

Saul's wordy rant does get an answer, but not from any member of the tribe of Benjamin. Doeg the Edomite is the one who speaks up—Doeg who was previously 'restrained' in Nob. Doeg's rejoinder is prefaced with a description: he is 'standing over (עַל) the servants of Saul'. Thus when Doeg speaks, it is as an entrenched member of the Saulide retinue. Based on his testimony, it is now confirmed that Doeg caught sight of David entering Nob, and he observed David's transaction with Ahimelech the priest: 'I saw the son of Jesse come to Nob, to Ahimelech son of Ahitub. He inquired of the LORD for him, and gave him provisions, and gave to him the sword of Goliath the Philistine.' So far, only Saul has used the name 'son of Jesse', but here Doeg also uses the patronymic in a condescending way. Like Wormtongue in Tolkien's *Lord of the Rings*, Doeg imparts some insidious counsel to an already worried king.

Doeg's speech merits careful analysis. He begins by intimating that David and Ahimelech are allies, and (correctly) notes that David received provisions and the sword of 'Goliath the Philistine'. Diana Edelman (1991: 176) comments that Doeg's thrust is rhetorical, and his emphasis 'on the nationality of the former owner of the sword that Ahimelech gave to David—not merely Goliath, whose name alone would have been enough to establish identity, but Goliath the Philistine—seems designed to drive home to the king his personal failure to deliver Israel from the hand of the Philistines in contrast to David's successes in this area'. But surprisingly, Doeg also claims that the priest 'asked' (שאל) of the LORD for David, a fact that is nowhere corroborated in the preceding narrative of chap. 21. There is mention of an 'ephod' by Ahimelech, but no hint of any inquiry, and one would have expected such an important action to have been mentioned by the narrator (who goes to great length to describe the bread in the sanctuary). It is entirely possible that Doeg—realizing he was hoodwinked by David and Ahimelech—concocts the business of the inquiry in order to rile Saul and further indict the priest.

More startling than the inquiry, though, is Doeg's further information on the priest: he is called 'Ahimelech son of Ahitub'. Through Doeg, of all sources, the reader learns that Ahimelech is a member of the house of Eli:

> Ahimelech is now associated with the doomed house of Eli, and it is rather haunting that the one who is subsequently commanded by Saul to destroy 'the house of priests'—Doeg the Edomite—is the one who first reveals to the reader that Ahimelech is connected with Eli's ill-fated lineage. Assuming Doeg is unaware of this charged significance, he is being caricatured as a conduit for purposes that certainly transcend himself, and while his vengeance on the city of priests may be motivated by personal reasons, at the same time he unwittingly participates in the fulfillment of the prophetic word of 1 Sam. 2.27-36 (Bodner 2005: 33-34).

Furthermore, Ahimelech's brother Ahijah has already appeared with Saul in chap. 14, where his cultic work is not altogether successful. Doeg's incendiary statement would no doubt fuel Saul's fire.

22.11-15

Saul does not ask Doeg for further details, but straightaway sends a dispatch to Ahimelech, for the first time now called 'son of Ahitub' by the narrator. Ahimelech is not the only one sent for: the summons also includes 'all his father's house', a house the reader already knows is hanging under a prophetic sentence. After dispensing with the formalities, Saul's interrogation begins with the charge of conspiracy. Notably, Saul accuses Ahimelech of collusion with David: 'Why have you [plural] conspired against me, you and the son of Jesse?' Saul then moves from accusation to evidence, based on the testimony of Doeg the Edomite (who is not mentioned). Further, Saul changes the wording from Doeg: instead of 'provisions' he says 'bread', and reduces Doeg's 'sword of Goliath the Philistine' to 'sword'. Saul seems less interested in these details and more concerned about the (alleged) oracle. Doeg claims that Ahimelech 'inquired of the LORD' for David, but Saul enhances this deposition and charges that *Ahimelech's inquiry* has incited David to lie in ambush. In 22.14, Saul blames Jonathan for inciting David; now, Ahimelech's 'inquiry' is to blame. Saul's fury over this 'inquiry' from a member of the house of Eli is probably heightened because of his previous experiences of inquiry from Ahimelech's brother Ahijah in chap. 14, where there was 'no answer' (14.37). As he answers the king (22.14-15), Ahimelech's task is not enviable:

> 'But who—among all your servants—is like David: faithful, the king's son-in-law, captain of your bodyguard, and held in honor by your household? Did I today begin to inquire of God for him? Far be it from me! Do not let the king set anything against his servant—or the house of my father—for your servant does not know anything in all of this, small or great!'

In terms of word count, Ahimelech's defense is considerably longer than Saul's accusation, and it takes on different contours than one might expect. Had he been deceived, I would have expected Ahimelech to plead his case: David came to him *claiming* to be on a secret mission from the king, and as the priest of Nob, he had no choice but to aid this highly respected servant of the court. However, Ahimelech does not proffer such an excuse, since he has been caught in collusion with David over and against the king. So, instead, Ahimelech launches into a long defense of David *rather than* his own actions. He tacitly admits collusion on the grounds of David's credentials (I am following a slight emendation of the Hebrew text to yield 'captain' rather than the verb 'to turn aside', as in the NRSV). Ahimelech does not address the matters of bread and sword, but he does deny the oracle. Diana Edelman (1991: 178) wonders why the priest focuses on this particular charge; is it 'because it is the only one that he knows to be untrue and to be the least damning of the three now that he has found out the truth of the situation?' At the same time, Ahimelech bravely implores the king not to set anything against 'the house of his father', an ominous note for this priestly line under a sentence of doom. In Ahimelech's final line, when he claims to know nothing of all of this, whether 'small or great', it surely pertains to the irrationality of Saul's fury against his own soldier and son-in-law. As Robert Polzin (1993: 199) sees the matter, Ahimelech's phrase 'great or small' is reminiscent of Jonathan's similar comment in 20.2. Jonathan's reward for defending David in chap. 20 is a spear aimed at his head; it may be that Ahimelech is destined for similar treatment.

22.16-19

The punishment for the priest—who is allowed no further defense—is death, and Saul also includes Ahimelech's entire house in the death sentence. The king issues the execution order to the 'runners' standing around him, and to them he outlines the specificities of the charge: their 'hand' is with David, because they knew he was fleeing and did not report it to the king. Saul is charging Ahimelech with collusion, and in this accusation, the king is correct. At the same time, when Saul informs Ahimelech 'death you will die' (מוֹת תָּמוּת), it is not the first time he has used such a locution. In 14.44, Saul says the same thing to his son Jonathan, 'death you will die' (מוֹת תָּמוּת). On that occasion, Jonathan is 'ransomed' by the people. On this occasion, there is a glimmer of hope for Ahimelech, as Saul's servants have an adverse reaction to the lethal command: they are unwilling to stretch forth their hand and 'reach out' against the priests of the LORD. The fatal difference between the ransom of Jonathan in chap. 14 and the priests of Nob in this episode is one man: Doeg the Edomite.

To paraphrase Antony Campbell (2003: 233), just as Doeg is the one who breaches the Benjaminite reluctance to speak up against David, so once more Doeg breaches the Benjaminite reluctance to turn against the priests of God. Obedient to the king's word, Doeg slaughters 85 priests on that day (this is the number translated in the standard English translations, although the Greet text reads '305'). The priests are not the only ones destroyed, as Doeg also puts the entire village of Nob to death, including women and children and livestock. Unlike Saul in chap. 15, Doeg does not 'spare' the best of the sheep and cattle for sacrifice—everything is put to the sword. The clothing note—the priests are wearing 'the linen ephod'—is a reminder of the young Samuel, his customary garment while he was attending Eli in Shiloh. Perhaps this is what Samuel is wearing when God calls to him in chap. 3 and reiterates the word spoken against the house of Eli (2.27-36) that is even now finding its dismal fulfillment.

The dreadful events of Nob need to be read against the background of the prophetic word articulated in chap. 2. As Walter Brueggemann (1990: 161) reminds us, the past and future of the house of Eli now find a day of reckoning: 'We have seen in 2.31-36 three elements of the history of the priesthood: (1) The house of Eli will be terminated (v. 31); (2) one man of that priestly house shall be spared, but he shall end in grief (v. 33); and (3) there will be instituted a new faithful priestly house'. The third element will not see fulfillment until 1 Kings 2, but the other two are visible here in chap. 22. Saul's culpability in the massacre should not be overlooked, but there is more going on than just royal madness. Other themes are available here: just as the house of Eli has been rejected (and now virtually destroyed), so a not dissimilar fate awaits the rejected house of Saul. Just as the house of Eli will be replaced with an enduring priestly house, so the house of Saul will be replaced by an enduring royal house. Within the demise of Eli's house, an important subplot emerges: the courage of Ahimelech. When David enters the sanctuary of Nob, he enters as the future king and future of the narrative; by contrast, Ahimelech is the scion of a hopeless priestly line. Yet Ahimelech sides with David, and in so doing risks the royal wrath of Saul. The events of chap. 22, one should not forget, happen after David returns to Judah, prompted by Gad's prophetic word. Gad's word intersects with the earlier oracle spoken in chap. 2; by returning to Judah, the destruction of Nob is set in motion, sealing the fate the house of Eli.

22.20-23

According to the prophetic word of the unnamed man of God in 1 Samuel 2, there will be a survivor of the house of Eli. Any 'remainder' (יתר) of Eli's line will live to witness the fall of the house, and survive only to beg for a priestly office from the successor. In 22.20, the reader discovers that Doeg put to death *almost* every priest of Nob. However, a single son of Ahimelech is able to escape the sword of the Edomite, and the line of Eli survives. In a rather dismal sense it is appropriate that the sole survivor is named 'Abiathar' (אביתר), since the name contains the words 'remainder' and 'father'. As the last remainder of Eli's house, Abiathar's name carries with it a reminder of the prophetic word of judgment visited upon his father's line.

Just as David 'escapes' (מלט) and 'flees' (ברח) from Saul in chap. 19, so the same verbs are ascribed to Abiathar in 22.20. There is no stated reason as to why Abiathar flees specifically to David—is he aware of his father's collusion in the previous chapter, and thus that David is a natural ally? Either way, Abiathar continues the 'league' with the son of Jesse, and this is precisely Saul's accusation. Upon arriving to David (still in the forest of Hereth?), Ahimelech informs David what 'Saul' did. We note that Ahimelech's speech is only reported *indirectly*, an appropriate mode of discourse, since Abiathar will not be afforded a single word of direct speech in the story. Despite a number of narrative appearances, Abiathar will not actually say anything. To be sure, he will be ordered around by David—and accompany him on many a sojourn—but does not speak a word. Ironically, it is Abiathar's garrulous son Jonathan who will announce to Adonijah that the feast is over in 1 Kings 1. What seems to matter, therefore, is not what Ahimelech says but rather what David says to him:

> And David said to Abiathar, 'I knew on that day that Doeg the Edomite was there, that he would surely report to Saul. I have turned over every life in your father's house. Stay with me. Do not be afraid—indeed, the one seeking my life seeks your life—but you will be under guard with me.' (vv. 22-23)

David's acknowledgment here is stunning: he obviously knows Doeg the Edomite, because he recognized him 'on that day' in Nob in chap. 21. Furthermore, he must know about Doeg's capabilities (and utter lack of conscience), and that Doeg would inform Saul about the transaction with Ahimelech. The reader now discovers that David was fully cognizant of Doeg's presence in the sanctuary, and the danger he represented. If David was aware of the danger, then certainly Ahimelech was also conscious of this threat. When David thus says to Abiathar that he is 'responsible' for the deaths in Nob, it amounts to a confession of the (ultimately unsuccessful) duping of Doeg. David quickly changes the subject, and moves from the past to the clear and present danger: abide with me, he instructs Abiathar, and be safe from further Saulide purges. Abiathar will be closely watched, and no doubt David is driven by heaps of guilt and humanitarian compassion. But, as it turns out, Abiathar's arrival is also helpful for David. The reader will shortly discover that Abiathar does not arrive into the camp of David empty-handed: in his possession is a very powerful instrument, the details of which emerge in the next chapter.

1 Samuel 23

In the aftermath of Nob's destruction, David is still on the run with the manic Saul still in dogged pursuit. Circumventing Saul has required a certain amount of creativity on David's part, but also the help of key allies along the way. While Saul has his own pockets of loyalty, one senses that David is gaining the ascendancy. In this chapter the pursuit will continue, and the struggle often involves *information technology*: knowledge and the control of knowledge increasingly takes center stage in this 'hide and seek' phase of the narrative. This chapter is structured in three main parts. The first part features David's response to the crisis in the town of Keilah, and in this episode *divine inquiry* plays a prominent role. In the second part of the chapter, the town of Keilah is willing to betray David: local informants are crucial to Saul, who draws near and almost catches David. This section of the chapter includes a fascinating interlude: an appearance by Jonathan with some further data to assist the Davidic cause. After Jonathan's cameo, the third part of the chapter starts with the Ziphite group as their intelligence efforts (on David's whereabouts) are presented to the king. Armed with the Ziphite testimony, Saul closes in on David, but at the last moment a breathless report of Philistine incursion pulls Saul away. This is *another* close shave for David, and Philistine sorties bracket the chapter. In terms of character development, one notices the *speech patterns* of Saul and David in this chapter. Saul is overtly conniving, and speaks lots of words that reveal a divided consciousness. By contrast, David is far more subtle; in fact, the only words David speaks in this chapter are in the context of oracular consultation.

23.1-2

Although he is within the borders of Judah, perilous circumstances continue to pose challenges for David at this juncture in the narrative. In the absence of any chronological marker, one assumes that the events of this chapter begin after the destruction of the priests of Nob (with the sole exception of Abiathar). A report comes to David about a Philistine raid on the town of Keilah. The only other mention of this town (Josh. 15.44) locates it in Judah, perhaps close to Philistine territory. The report comes through anonymous sources, and it is not clear why David is told this news, and not the king. The king, after all, is supposed to save his people from the grip of the Philistines. In light of recent events, there is bizarreness here: while Saul is busy destroying the priestly city of Nob, the Philistines—according to this report—are 'looting the threshing floors' of an Israelite town.

David's response to this report is quite innovative: he 'asks' (שאל) the LORD, 'should I go and strike these Philistines?' Now this is a curious turn of events, since Saul has just liquidated the priests of Nob for allegedly 'asking' (or 'inquiring' of God) on David's behalf. Other than Doeg the Edomite's biased accusation, David is certainly not reported to have inquired of God previously. While David does not inquire of Abimelech at Nob, he does inquire now, and the reader wonders: How and why does David inquire *here*, but not earlier in the story? We will discover the answer to this question in v. 6, but meanwhile, the LORD indeed responds to David's inquiry: 'Go, strike the Philistines, and save Keilah'. Other things being equal, this must be construed as a very favorable answer.

23.3-6

Despite the divine encouragement to save Keilah, David's men baulk at the idea because of 'fear'. Their demurral is not unreasonable. David recently sojourned to Achish king of Gath, and out of fear he played the madman. Here, his men complain that they are afraid within the Israelite region of Judah (in all likelihood because of Saul), and so how much more to take on the battle-ranks of the Philistines! David responds to this mini-crisis by 'again inquiring' of the LORD, and this time there is an *even more* encouraging divine answer: 'Arise, go down to Keilah, for I am giving the Philistines into your hand'. This further raises the technical question of exactly how David is inquiring; some commentators—along with Saul and Doeg—assume that such inquiry takes place by means of a priest, whereby questions are posed and the answer is 'binary' in nature. So, the 'inquirer' will usually pose straightforward questions that receive the equivalent of a yes/no answer. If this is the case, it is notable that David inquires and gets a *long* and favorable response: more than a binary 'yes', David receives a lengthy sentence full of divine encouragement. We recall that Saul 'asks' and obtains no answer. By contrast, David asks and gets a long chat. Not surprisingly, the mission is a success: Keilah is saved, the enemy neutralized, and David requisitions the Philistine livestock.

All of a sudden—in a piece of delayed exposition—the narrator returns to the matter of Abiathar the priest. It would appear that when Abiathar departed from Nob, he carried with him an important item from the sanctuary, only now revealed in the storyline: 'It came to pass when Abiathar son of Ahimelech fled to David, to Keilah, an ephod came down in his hand'. By means of this flashback, the reader makes a few belated discoveries. Since the ephod is an instrument for ascertaining the divine will (wielded by the priest, and giving a binary answer when questions are posed), it now becomes clear that *this* is how David has been 'asking' throughout this chapter so far. Furthermore, when David says to Abiathar 'abide with me' in the final line of the previous chapter, surely the assistance of the ephod is not lost on the fugitive. In the fracas with Saul—where *information technology* is becoming increasingly prominent—the oracle software of the ephod is not without utility.

By revealing the ephod in a flashback, the narrator heightens the political benefit that has accrued to David, as he gains a considerable advantage over Saul in the matter of 'inquiry'. As this juncture in his career, the Elide priesthood (or at least what remains of it) is a useful political ally for David. For the next few chapters, David uses such inquiry at opportune moments. Saul, by contrast, has not enjoyed much success with such priestly matters, as chap. 14 memorably illustrated. Furthermore, Saul has just obliterated an entire village of priests, a move that will not improve his oracular consultations. J.P. Fokkelman (1993: 426-27) notes an irony: Saul destroys a host of priests who wear the 'linen ephod', but in so doing facilitates the escape of the priest with *the ephod* to the camp of David. It would be wise to keep in mind that Abiathar and the ephod will only have a short season in the sun, soon to be replaced by other things in the royal administration. For the moment, though, Abiathar and the ephod will enjoy fifteen minutes of fame, and give David an edge in eluding Saul. As Barbara Green (2003: 360) summarizes:

> whatever construction we may place on the events of chap. 22, Saul's alienating the last priest with his ephod conspicuously facilitates David's communication with God. The ephod, brought by the priest whom Saul has alienated, helps David to anticipate the outcomes of his plans. It is an edge Saul has never had, not from the priests, not from his prophet Samuel, not from God, not from any.

23.7-8

Saul may not have the advantage of priestly consultation, but he still has a network of informants. Most likely, it is a member of this network who informs Saul that David has entered the city of Keilah. Upon receiving the report, Saul utters a statement (ויאמר, 'and he said'), but in the absence of any interlocutor I assume that Saul is talking to himself. Such soliloquies occur often in Saul's life, and this is not the first time the king's internal discourse has been somewhat delusional. I would hazard a guess that Saul is by far the most 'transparent' of royal characters in the Deuteronomistic History; that is, more than any other king, it is the thoughts, intents, and inner musings of Saul's mind that are revealed more often than any other monarch.

Here, Saul is convinced that God has 'alienated' (or 'delivered') David into his hand, because David has closed himself in by entering a city with doors and bars. Saul thinks that God is working in his favor, whereas the opposite is the case. In fact, God will be active in this chapter, but most overtly when consulted by David (who has the ephod-wielding Abiathar in his camp, the priest who narrowly escapes Doeg's purge). In the next few chapters, priestly consultation will prove more valuable than many a human informant. But for the moment, Saul is confident, and prepares to launch an offensive; instead of protecting Israelite towns from the Philistines, Saul is now attacking an Israelite town because of David. He summons all the troops for battle, and goes down to 'besiege' David and his men at Keilah. For a second time, Keilah is on the brink of invasion: first from the Philistines, now from their own king.

23.9-12
'Chapter 23 illustrates', remarks Robert Polzin (1993: 200), 'the epistemological disadvantage under which Saul operates in his quest of David. The contrast between David's knowledge and Saul's makes it crystal clear that David has the upper hand throughout.' Polzin's contention is amply demonstrated in 23.9, where the reader is told simply that David 'knows' that Saul is devising mischief (מחרש) against him. Although the NRSV translates the line with a temporal dimension ('When David learned that Saul was plotting evil against him...'), the Hebrew text is more evasive: David knows of Saul's intentions, but the reader is given no clues as to how he finds out. Quite simply, David 'knows' that there is a problem: he is in a barred city, with a manic king poised to lay siege. This appears to be an unenviable situation.

Unlike Saul, David cannot yet summon an entire army. But he can call forth Abiathar the priest, a luxury Saul has forfeited. David issues an efficient imperative to the priest: 'Bring forth the ephod'. Since the reader now knows that Abiathar wields the ephod, it becomes a new kind of character in the chapter. David's directive to the priest triggers an allusion to Saul's earlier consultation of an Elide—Ahijah—in chap. 14. In that chapter, Saul has been successful against the Philistines, and has his opponent on the ropes, as it were. However, when he 'asks' of God, there is no answer, and a bad day for Israel's first king gets even worse. Like Saul, David poses careful questions in 23.10-12, but his formal inquiry is prefaced with a lengthy account of his circumstances in v. 9. The divine answers, in good binary fashion, are terse. In this case, they are also 'negative'. Saul will 'come down', and the leaders of Keilah will 'enclose' David and his entourage into Saul's hand.

One might have expected some gratitude from Keilah's inhabitants—not least the threshing floor owners—for David's saving of their town. Through the ephod, however, God says such gratitude will not be forthcoming. The motives for surrendering David are not stated; given that Nob has just been destroyed by royal decree, their reluctance to harbor a fugitive (accused of treason) might be understandable. But whether the residents of Keilah are acting out of loyalty to or fear of the king, the ephod is not silent, and thus David at least knows what his options are.

23.13-14

Prompted by the negative prognosis of the oracle, David and his 600 men arise and march out of Keilah; even though the town was just saved from the Philistines by David and his men, the residents are now prepared to hand them over to Saul. David's band of insolvent rakes seems to have swelled: it is listed at about 400 at the beginning of the previous chapter, but has now grown considerably. More debt-dodgers perhaps? Regardless, after departing from pusillanimous Keilah, David's group wanders aimlessly; the Hebrew verb construction is a double hithpael, stressing a lack of direction.

Once more the Saulide intelligence network reports David's activity to the king, informing him that the latter 'slipped away' from Keilah. At this, Saul desists from 'marching out', but he certainly does not give up the chase. While David stayed in the wilderness strongholds in the hill country of the Ziph desert, Saul was seeking him 'all the days'. So, despite being foiled in the Keilah siege campaign, Saul continues relentlessly to search for David. The last clause of v. 14 is a key theological appraisal: God does not give David into Saul's hand. As Walter Brueggemann (1990: 163) reflects, 'Many other readings of the matter might have been possible; the narrator, however, wants to score the single, crucial point. David's future is to be understood theologically'. If this is the case, then Saul's failure (and future) also needs to be understood in terms of 'the divinity that shapes his ends' (*Hamlet*, V.2). God's refusal to hand David over to Saul is a profound contrast with Saul's earlier thought, 'God has surrendered him to me' (23.7). Not for the first time, Saul suffers from delusion.

23.15-18

David's meandering takes him to 'the wilderness of Ziph, in Horesh'. It is here that David 'sees' that Saul has marched out to seek his life. Translators struggle with the verb 'see' (וַיַּרְא) in this context. The RSV adjusts the vocalization of the verb in order to read 'fear', while the NRSV opts for the strange rendering, 'learn'. To be sure, David will be told 'fear not' in a moment, but those are the words of a character, one who might have something at stake in the conversation.

The character who says 'fear not' is Jonathan. After a long interval—the last occasion we see Jonathan is at the end of chap. 20, where he emotionally parts from David after reminding him of the 'oath' sworn in the name of the LORD—Jonathan now returns to the narrative stage. Jonathan's cameo comes at an interesting time for the reader: Saul has just destroyed almost every Elide at Nob, and so the issue of 'survival' after wiping out an entire house is fresh in the reader's mind.

In contrast to his father, Jonathan *actually finds* David, at Horesh. The name 'Horesh' forms a wordplay: Saul is 'devising mischief' (מחרש) against David in 23.9, with the result that David flees to 'Horesh' (חרש) to avoid such machinations. While David is in Horesh, Jonathan arises to 'strengthen his hand in God'. This strengthening happens, I assume, through Jonathan's virtually prophetic utterance about David's present circumstances and great expectations: 'Do not fear, for the hand of Saul my father will not find you. But you will reign over Israel, and I will be to you as a second-in-command—even Saul my father knows it is thus.' It is thematically appropriate that Jonathan begins his speech with 'fear not': if David is in a state of fear, then the rest of his speech will be even more effective.

As for the rest of the speech, there are several elements that need to be mentioned. Not only will David be safe from Saul's hand, Jonathan says, but also David will reign. So far, not much is new. The next two utterances, though, are novel. Jonathan asserts that David will reign, and that he himself will be the number two man in the reign; the 'vice-president', as it were. This idea has not been previously raised by Jonathan. Graeme Auld (2003: 225) wonders if Jonathan's words 'spell out what is already his understanding with David, though we readers have not yet been told? Or does Jonathan here make a new bid, not just to preserve his family but to become David's second in command? Or possibly to preserve his family by becoming the new king's designated lieutenant?' Even more startling is Jonathan's last line, stating that *even Saul* knows this! One is not sure whether Saul knows that David will reign or that Jonathan will be his lieutenant, or both. Regardless, Jonathan's words underscore his father's divided consciousness. On the one hand, Saul knows about David's destiny; yet, on the other hand he (irrationally) pursues *someone he will not find*. Saul knows that he will be succeeded by 'one better than him', yet he threatens his son with words like 'as long as the son of Jesse lives, your kingdom will not be established'. Nowhere will Saul's divided consciousness be more on display than in the next chapter.

Meanwhile, David wordlessly acquiesces to Jonathan's proposal. Once more, Jonathan does all the talking, and David goes along with the stated transaction: 'And the two of them cut a covenant before the LORD'. And thus there is an envelope structure to David and Jonathan's relationship: the first time we see them together at the beginning of chap. 18 there is a covenant, and now another covenant is cut at the end, in this, their last recorded face to face meeting. The final clause of v. 18 is translated by the NRSV as 'Jonathan went home' but we could also render it 'Jonathan went to his house'. The term 'house' is fitting because the survival of Jonathan's house—as we gather from earlier conversations and covenants with David— is his preoccupation. It is also a house, we learn later in the story, that evidently shelters a young son, Mephibosheth (2 Sam. 4; 9). As Jonathan departs for his house, the reader should note that these are his last words and his last formal appearance in the narrative. Jonathan will never live to be David's second-in-command. The next time he is mentioned by name will be as a casualty of war, as Israel's first royal scion is killed on the battlefield in the last chapter of 1 Samuel.

23.19-23

In v. 14 we are told that David was dwelling in the wilderness of Ziph taking refuge among the 'strongholds' in the region's hill country. The local Ziphites must have gotten wind of this, for they now travel to Saul at Gibeah to deliver a report on David's whereabouts: 'Is not David hiding himself with us', the Ziphites ask Saul, 'among the strongholds in Horesh, on the hill of Hachilah that is on the south side of Jeshimon? So now, should your soul desire to come down, O king, then come down, and we will hand him over into the king's hand.' According to Josh. 15.55, Ziph is located in Judah, in the general vicinity of Carmel (a place that will be prominent in chap. 25). Consequently, there is an intriguing juxtaposition here: right after Jonathan of Benjamin shows loyalty to David, the Ziphites of Judah show 'loyalty' to Saul. As with Keilah, there is no stated motive as to why the Ziphites should be loyal to Saul. On the one hand, a reader might have expected that a place in Judah would welcome David. On the other hand, Robert Gordon (1986: 177) suggests that the Ziphites 'may not have welcomed the idea of such a large contingent of freebooters in their neighborhood'.

The Ziphites might be motivated by disinterested affection for the king or they might be seeking to ingratiate themselves in hopes of reward—either way, Saul is delighted to see them. In a dramatic departure from his usual modes of discourse—royal fulmination or brooding soliloquy—Saul sounds positively buoyant as he responds to the Ziphites: 'Blessed are you by the LORD, because you have spared (חמל) me!' Of all the terms Saul could have chosen, 'spare' (חמל) is laced with a great deal of irony, since this is the keyword of chap. 15 when Saul 'spares' Agag and the best of the Amalekite plunder. I assume Saul's use of the verb is unintentional, but this recycled language creates a comparison: just as Saul spares the sheep and cattle instead of (immediately) destroying them, he now blesses the Ziphite for sparing him by bringing information that will lead to David's destruction. Saul's allusion to this earlier downfall in the Amalekite affair underscores his present vagaries and strange priorities in the hunt for David.

Saul's language of blessing does not last very long. His euphoric moment is followed by a good deal of prattle, as he carefully instructs the Ziphites to be *especially* certain of David's location and lurking place. This sprawling and digressive response is not without a moment of raw humor for the reader. Saul cautions the Ziphites to be careful because David is 'very crafty' (ערום יערם), and this forms a homonymic wordplay with the term 'naked' (ערום), as in Gen. 2.29 and 3.1 (when the man and the woman are naked and without shame, and the snake is very crafty). As Ora Horn Prouser (1996: 34) has observed, there is a similar wordplay here: Saul says David is very crafty, yet he himself was rolling around naked at the end of chap. 19. As for other parts of the speech, it is difficult to be sure about some of the details. For example, when Saul concludes his long speech to the Ziphites with the following: 'And I will go with you, and if it should be that he is in the land, then I will search him out among all the thousands of Judah'. Commentators are not altogether sure what Saul means, and, in my opinion, Saul does not seem overly sure either. Most of this speech is violent banter that illustrates a lack of confidence on the king's part. This is why Peter Miscall (1986: 143) suggests that Saul's entire response stresses the themes of assurance and clarity (or the lack thereof), and thus bring to the fore the *information technology* edge that David is gaining.

23.24-28

After Saul concludes his long address, the Ziphites arise and head for their homeland, and sure enough, David and his men are in the neighborhood. Presumably there is a message sent to Saul, because he and his men go forth 'to seek'. When David receives a report about Saul's visit, there follows a drawn out description of the chase. The dramatic narration of colliding paths—as David circles around one side of a mountain while Saul and his colleagues are circling around the other side—leads the reader to believe that the two parties will crash into each other. However, there is a sudden interruption (quite literally, as it is the only spoken line in this whole stretch): 'But a messenger came to Saul, saying, "Hurry and come, for Philistines are making a raid on the land!"' For the second time in this chapter, something unexpected happens, just in the nick of time, which allows David to elude Saul. Previously, it was a report from the ephod; now, moments before the (fatal?) collision with the king, an unnamed messenger brings a report about the Philistine incursion. Saul dutifully forsakes the individual pursuit of David and attends to his national responsibilities: 'And Saul returned from pursuing after David, and went to meet the Philistines. Therefore they call that place "Slippery Rock".' The name *Sela-hammahlekoth* is variously translated; some opt for 'Rock of Escape' while others prefer 'Rock of Portions'. I am understanding the root as 'smooth' (חלק), and notably, it is the same root used in the Jacob and Esau narrative, when Jacob complains to his mother in Gen. 27.11, 'Behold, Esau my brother is man of hair, but I am a smooth (חלק) man'. Jacob and David are elect, just as Esau and Saul are not. Still, 'Slippery Rock' represents a close shave for David.

1 SAMUEL 24

David's exile from Saul's court shows no signs of ending, and thus his status as a fugitive in the wilderness continues. To this point in the narrative, direct confrontation between the king and his son-in-law has been avoided. The events of 1 Samuel 24 report a extraordinary change, as Saul and David come face to face (in rather embarrassing circumstances, as we will see), and have their longest direct conversation thus far in the story. This *tête-à-tête* is the focal point of the chapter, with significant speeches from both major characters. David will speak first, and the reader is impressed with a subtle political genius in this *public* discourse of David. There is both scatology and eschatology in this chapter; that is, after an awkward lavatory moment, the future (and the destinies of two houses) is a central topic of discussion. Both David and Saul are in various degrees acquainted with what the future holds for each of them. But whereas Saul is portrayed as struggling against this destiny, David seems to be able to exercise a measure of self-control, although surely he gets the better deal of the two. A few years ago, H.W. Hertzberg referred to chap. 24 as a 'beautiful' and 'vivid' story. I certainly agree that it is vivid—Saul's detractors have accused him of many things, but incontinence cannot be one of them.

24.1-2

The final line of the previous chapter (in most English versions) begins a new chapter in the story: 'And David went up from there and stayed in the strongholds of En-gedi'. Through this sentence (23.9 in the NRSV, 24.1 in the Hebrew text) we have both closure to the episode of Saul's pursuit at Slippery Rock, and a new scene in a different locale. After a messenger interrupts Saul's pursuit of David to announce the Philistine invasion, Saul then departs to face the Philistines as David moves to a new region, probably looking for a more secure domicile after the narrow evasion at *Sela-hammahlekoth*.

There is no report about the outcome of Saul's fight against the Philistine raiders, but the reader can at least be certain that the king is still alive. No sooner does Saul 'return' from the fight than yet another report is transmitted: 'Behold, David is in the wilderness of En-gedi'. That the narrator does not share details about the skirmish with the Philistines but *instead* returns to the pursuit of David must be a comment on Saulide priorities. We are not sure who reports to Saul that David is in En-gedi—or how this messenger finds out—but Saul responds by mustering 3000 chosen men. Notably, the last time Saul chooses this number of men is at the beginning of chap. 13, an episode where Samuel informs him that his dynasty will not be established, and that another has been chosen in his place. Since Saul's confession at the end of this chapter will confirm as much, the intertext with chap. 13 should be kept in mind.

With his pack of 3000 soldiers, Saul heads in the direction of the 'Cliffs of the Wild Goats' to seek his prey. Virtually every serious commentator feels obligated to make some remark about the terrain of this area, usually informing us about the topographically distinctive features of the En-gedi landscape. From these serious commentators the reader learns that this region is (theoretically) ideal for a fugitive, since the cliffs and rocks are perforated with caves. In the symbolic lexicon of the narrative to this point, a 'cave' is highly appropriate spatial setting. As Peter Miscall (1986: 144) reflects, 'At this point of the story, we can say that Saul's career has been marked by seeking and not finding or by seeking one thing and finding another. Here Saul finally finds David, but the outcome of the encounter is not what he sought.' It may not be significant, but 'wild goat' (יָעֵל) in Hebrew is spelled the same as Jael (יָעֵל) in Judges 4. Aside from this orthographic similarity, there are other interesting parallels between the two stories: in both narratives (1 Sam. 24 and Judg. 4.17-21), a powerful figure moves indoors where he thinks he is safe, but is not—because an enemy with a weapon is lurking within. In Judges 4, Sisera seeks the tent of Jael because he is motivated by survival; in 1 Samuel 24, Saul enters a random cave of En-gedi because of different primal urges.

24.3-4

At some point during this journey to seek David, Saul arrives at a place where 'sheepfolds' (or pens) are by the road, and there is a cave nearby. Naturally, Saul chooses this particular cave as a makeshift latrine, and turns aside from the road. The king of Israel is thus completely alone—only the most foolhardy soldier would accompany him on this campaign, since the object of this mission is to 'overshadow his feet', a euphemism for using the men's room. The next line is one of the most serendipitous in the entire Deuteronomistic History: while the Saul is indisposed, the narrator then reveals *this is the very cave where David and his men are hidden!* Over the past few chapters, Saul's pursuit of David has been one of uncommon assiduity. He has looked high and low for David and his men; now he finds them, but he is completely unaware that they are concealed in the 'thighs' (בְּיַרְכְּתֵי) of the cave. By means of the olfactory sensations tingled by this scene, one is reminded of Eglon king of Moab in Judges 3, the same Eglon who is stabbed with a sword of 'two mouths' (שְׁנֵי פֵיוֹת) by Ehud, the left-handed man from the right-handed tribe (Benjamin). Here in 1 Samuel 24 it is a man of Benjamin who is on the throne, and many of David's men would like to thrust a double-mouthed sword into his royal belly.

The awkward (verbal) silence in the cave is ended by David's men. With a forceful avowal, the men urge David—probably in some sort of troglodyte glottal whisper—to *carpe diem*: 'Behold, the day that the LORD said to you, "Behold, I am giving your enemy into your hand, and you can do to him whatever is good in your eyes!"' On the one hand, there is a wide assortment of body parts here: Saul overshadows his *feet*, David and his men in the *thighs* (or sides) of the cave, the men claim that God has given the enemy into David's *hand*, and so David is told to do what is good in his *eyes*. But on the other hand, what the men are urging is very serious: Saul's unexpected entrance must be God's design, since they claim that God has previously spoken words that justify regicide. This would all be well and good, and the men certainly plead with compelling immediacy, except that God is recorded as having said no such thing. As Graeme Auld (2003: 226) explains, this is an *unverified quotation*: 'We readers have never been told of this promise; David has never spoken of Saul as his enemy'. In other words, the narrator has never disclosed God's words that give David a license to act as people did in the days of Judges: 'do whatever is good in your eyes, and there will be no king in Israel'.

The reason why such an oracle is not recorded is because it never existed. To discharge a popular saying, David's men are full of—how shall I put it—the same *foul refuse* that Saul is presently evacuating from his person. In the cave, the men fabricate God's words, but what is their motive? The group that gathers around David, we recall from 22.2, are distressed, discontent, and in debt. These are men, therefore, who have every reason to want Saul liquidated—and given their various states of debt and distress, probably they are not above fibbing. If Saul is destroyed, so are their criminal records. In fact, this is not the last time the reader will see a manipulation of divine speech (in 2 Sam. 3, Abner will show himself an adroit master of this genre). Meanwhile, when Saul shows up in the cave unaccompanied, the men are no doubt gleeful as the odds suddenly change in their favor: 3000 against 600 now becomes 600 against 1.

Under pressure from his men to act, David arises from a squatting position toward the king of Israel. He sneaks up and cuts off *not* the king's head (as his men desire), but rather a corner of Saul's robe (מְעִיל). This sartorial moment reminds us of another damaged robe, that of the prophet Samuel in 15.27, 'As Samuel turned to leave, Saul took hold of the corner of his robe (מְעִיל), and it ripped'. For the second time in his ill-starred career, Saul is involved in a robe-ripping incident. In chap. 15 Saul unintentionally tears

Samuel's robe, and is subject to a bitter prophetic indictment. This time, it is David who cuts Saul's royal robe, and all the symbolic resonance of losing the kingdom in chap. 15 boomerangs with interest here. In 15.28, Samuel announces, 'The LORD has ripped the kingdom of Israel from you today, and given it to your friend, one who is better than you!' In chap. 24, Saul unsuspectingly enters a cave where that 'friend' is concealed, and his own robe is severed by the one to whom the kingdom is transferred.

A legion of commentators panegyrize David's conduct in the cave, noting that his self-control is a model of piety and restraint. No doubt such commentators are right, but for the author of 1 Samuel, this is also a moment where larger issues of kingship are parabolically brought into the dialogue. At the risk of turning this episode into an *allegory of the cave*, it should at least be mentioned that Saul's robe is not the last such garment to be damaged in the Deuteronomistic History. I would argue that in the context of the larger storyline, this robe-cutting incident becomes an eschatological moment for David, since his own son shortly will be on the wrong end of a ripped-robe illustration by a prophet from Shiloh. In 1 Kings 11, Jeroboam is walking out from Jerusalem dressed in a 'new robe' (שלמה). He is met on the road by the prophet Ahijah of Shiloh, who seizes the new robe (the syntax is ambiguous, but in my view Jeroboam—like his ancestor Joseph—is the one wearing the new robe). Ahijah tears the robe into pieces, anticipating the kingdom of David's son Solomon (שלמה) being torn apart. The reader of the Hebrew text notices a wordplay on robe (שלמה) and the name Solomon (שלמה). One function of wordplay is to draw attention to a reversal of fortune, and there is hardly a more dramatic reversal than the great Solomonic kingdom being dismantled. In 2 Samuel 1, David eulogizes a king's death with the words, 'How the mighty have fallen'. With some *double entendre* these words may be a requiem for his own house as well. Consequently, when Saul turns aside to a cave and gets his royal robe trimmed, neither he nor David have any inkling of the long-term symbolic dimensions.

24.5-7

After slipping back to his hiding place with his men, suddenly 'David's heart struck him' because he had cut off a corner of Saul's robe. The same expression is used in 2 Sam. 24.10 when David is conscience-stricken after performing a census. However, taking the census will be a comparatively serious transgression, whereas excising Saul's robe here seems commendable. I am not altogether sure why David's heart 'strikes him' after returning from Saul to his men, but it is certainly to David's rhetorical advantage—given his next speech—to have his men see him in a conscience-stricken state.

As it turns out, David rather quickly recovers from his cardiac arrest, and proceeds to address his men with some searing words: 'Far be it from me by the LORD, that I should do thing to my lord—to the LORD's anointed—to stretch out my hand against him! For the LORD's anointed is he!' This speech, I would submit, cannot be understood apart from the audience to whom it is delivered. After all, David is speaking to a group who have just *invented* a divine rationale for regicide. Quite conceivably, this same group might be tempted to dream up a divine rationale for doing away with another 'anointed one'.

We note that the epithet 'LORD's anointed' is twice enunciated by David. To be sure, David seems to have a deference for Israel's royal office that is conspicuously lacking among other characters. Yet it is possible that a hint of self-interest might also be here, since David himself is *also* the LORD's anointed. There is an intrinsic advantage, therefore, for David to emphasize this doctrine of never stretching a hand toward the LORD's anointed in any circumstances. This is a refrain that the reader will hear again before long, not surprisingly uttered by David himself.

David's speech effectively restrains his men from carrying out their insidious wiles, and with these words David 'tears into' (שסע) his audience. The entire sentence makes it sound as though David is holding his men back from rising up and destroying Saul themselves, and he accomplishes this restraint through words rather than physical intervention. Meanwhile, Saul has not been privy to this discourse. With his temporary mission accomplished, Saul rises up and returns to the road that hopefully leads to David, oblivious to the damage inflicted on his royal accoutrement by the very hands of the one he resumes seeking.

24.8-15

In an unexpected turnaround, the hunted now marches out after the hunter, and calls out 'My lord, O king!' For Saul, this must be a moment of incredulity, as he simply 'stares behind him' and beholds an image of David nose-diving to the ground, doing obeisance in the vicinity of the cave lately departed. During the moment that Saul is stunned and silent, David begins his longest speech to this point in the story. It might be his best speech to date as well, and my guess is that David is addressing an audience that is bigger than Saul. The reader might have expected David to begin with his customary 'What have I done now?' tirade, but the occasion demands something rather more original than this. David begins as follows: 'Why do you listen to the words of man, saying, "Behold, David is seeking your evil"?' For two reasons, this line marks an effective beginning to the speech. First, David asks Saul why he is listening to human urgings, since David himself (as he will stress), has *not* listened to such homicidal voices. Second, taking a rhetorical cue from his cavemen, David supplies an 'unverified quotation' of his own, since no one has yet been recorded as saying to Saul 'Behold, David is seeking your evil'. Such a quotation sounds effective, and a bit of hyperbole serves to enhance David's point.

Rather than lingering over this unverified quotation, David rather efficiently moves from the theoretical to the practical by stressing *the cave*. Without commenting on the irony of the *rendezvous*—Saul is left to ponder that one on his own—David instead moves to a more probing issue: while Saul was in the cave, 'someone' urged him to kill the king. Telling Saul about his refusal of this offer, David quotes himself in the cave as saying, 'I will not stretch out my hand against my lord, for the LORD's anointed is he'. With the piece of Saul's clothing in hand, the moment is tailor-made to proffer the evidence of the cut robe, emotionally enhanced with the tender title 'my father'. The term 'hand' (יָד, *yad*) thus becomes a keyword in the speech, as Diana Edelman (1991: 195) reflects: 'The motif *yad* appears twice in David's speech, emphasizing his potential physical power over Saul, but indicating his acknowledgment that such power must be exercised properly, even when the opportunity for improper use arises, as it had in the cave'. According to David's argument, Saul has been abusing his power. David stresses that there is no 'evil or rebellion' in his hand, yet the king has been stalking his life.

The final movement in this long speech looks to heaven above and invokes the divine Arbitrator. Not only does David call on God to adjudicate this dispute, but he also calls on God for vengeance, since 'my hand will not be against you'. One barely notices David's quick shift from divine agency to ancient wisdom, as he quotes a proverb of the east: 'From the wicked proceeds wickedness' (מֵרְשָׁעִים יֵצֵא רֶשַׁע). In the three Hebrew words of this (probably verifiable) quotation David is outwardly addressing *himself* rather than Saul, but no doubt a discerning listener can sense an application to Saul and his pursuit. After the proverb, David turns to metaphorical self-deprecation, commenting that Saul is chasing a dead dog—or worse, a parasite on an unclean carcass—which must be construed as a waste of royal time and resources.

24.16-21

David rounds off his speech with a plea for God to judge in his favor, and then—as he finishes speaking 'these words'—Saul speaks for the first time in the chapter: 'Is this your voice, my son David?' While David's 'my father' finds its immediate counterpart with Saul's 'my son', there may be other echoes heard in Saul's troubled question. Walter Brueggemann (1990: 171) wonders if by means of this question the Deuteronomist is evoking an allusion to the story of Isaac, Jacob, and Esau in Genesis 27, a story that is about the transfer of blessing:

The language is powerfully reminiscent of Isaac, who was feeble and could not identify his son (Gen. 27.18, 32). Is the question placed in Saul's mouth intended to recall Isaac? Is Saul, like Isaac, old and feeble? Is Saul afraid of being duped? Is Saul dealing with a David who is as swift and crafty and unprincipled as the stealthy Jacob? Is David, in this forceful encounter, about to seize something from Saul that is not rightly his, as Jacob seized from Isaac and Esau?

When Saul asks the question 'is this your voice, my son David?', he already knows the answer, and hence there is only one response: 'Saul lifted up his voice, and wept'. Like Esau, Saul weeps when confronted with his future, and the bleak house wherein he now dwells. As we will see in the next chapter, the allusions to Genesis continue.

Saul has been subject to many emotions in the narrative thus far. Israel's first king has had many bad days, but this is the first—and indeed the only—time that Saul weeps. As we reflect on *what is represented* on the narrative canvas here, it should be noted that kings do not often cry in the Deuteronomistic History. In fact, the king who weeps the most of any royal figure in the story is none other than Saul's interlocutor here, David himself. Saul's teardrops for a lost kingdom anticipate David's weeping on numerous occasions, including the loss of his (potential) successor, Absalom, in 2 Samuel 19. I am not sure whether Saul's expression of grief here is cathartic, but after weeping he finds his voice again, and utters a remarkable confession to David:

> 'You are more righteous than I, because you dealt me good, but I have dealt you evil. For *you* have reported today that you have done good to me; how God closed me into your hand but you did not kill me. For what man finds his enemy, but then happily sends him on his way? May the LORD requite you with good today on account of what you did for me. And now, behold, I know that you will *surely* reign, and the kingdom of Israel will be established in your hand. And now, swear an oath to me by the LORD, that you will not cut off my seed after me, and that you will not destroy my name from my father's house.'

In his classic work of literary criticism *Aspects of the Novel*, E.M. Forster opined that a fully developed literary character is one with a *capacity to surprise*. Through this speech—the most articulate of his career—Saul meets Forster's criteria by exhaling words that are in turn humble, thoughtful, and even deferential toward his rival, whom he now faces in the most surprising of circumstances. Saul begins with an acknowledgment that David is in the right, and he is not the first character in biblical narrative to say 'you are more righteous than I'. In Genesis 38, Judah makes a similar confession to his daughter-in-law Tamar, after he has just said 'Bring her out and let her be burned' as a penalty for harlotry. Saul declares that even though God 'closed him' (סגר) into the hand of David (the verb occurs five times in the previous chapter), David does not choose to kill him. In return for this unexpected mercy, Saul quotes, if not a proverb, then certainly a rhetorical question that sounds like a popular expression: 'who ever heard of someone letting an enemy go?' Such an act, Saul says, deserves a divine reward.

Not only does Saul acknowledge that David is in the right, but he also confesses—replete with enhanced syntax—'reigning you will reign'. After hearing the song lyrics in 18.8, Saul darkly whispers to himself that only the *kingdom* remains for David. This muttering precipitates Saul's downward spiral into jealously, as he 'eyes' David from that day onward. Yet on this day, in the aftermath of the cave, the king now publicly affirms that the same kingdom will be established in David's hand. Some commentators argue that in these declarations Saul gives a great deal away. For all his words in vv. 8-15, David really does not ask for very much. In a series of rhetorical questions, though with an eye to his wider audience, David only asks Saul to stop pursuing him. In his rejoinder, Saul concedes far more: righteousness, reign, and an established kingdom.

On one level, it certainly appears as though Saul caves in. But on another level, it is possible that Saul makes the most of a bad situation, and through his initial concessions, he is actually positioning himself for a petition that would be hard to deny. Through his long series of opening words, Saul is setting up David such that the latter cannot but 'swear an oath' as Saul requests. With this, Saul sounds like his son Jonathan, who on numerous occasions has asked David to swear an oath. Like Jonathan, Saul moves from the present to future, calling on David to promise that he will not 'cut off' (כרת) his offspring, and poignantly it is the same verb that is used for David's action in v. 5; Saul has had his royal robe 'cut off' symbolizing his loss of the kingdom to David, whom he now asks for a oath so that his family and *his own name* will not be cut off when David becomes king. Saul has not made a plethora of politically astute moves in the past, but it could be argued that securing this oath is his smartest move so far.

24.22

This 'vivid' chapter—as Hertzberg describes it—draws to a close as David swears the oath. What king has an enemy's house in his hand, yet allows that house to live? In Judges 9, Abimelech does not shy away from destroying the house of *his own* father, and later kings in the Deuteronomistic History will efficiently destroy rival houses. But an oath is sworn by David, and one wonders if the oath will be sorely tested in the days to come. After securing the oath, Saul then goes 'to his house', the same house that will never produce a successor to Saul, and the same house that David has sworn an oath not to exterminate. Rather than accompanying his father-in-law, however,

David and his men go up 'to the stronghold'. Is David rather less sanguine than one might have expected after such a stunning (public) endorsement from Saul? Does David not quite trust Saul? The final line of the chapter suggests that David's fugitive period is not yet over. The next time 'stronghold' is mentioned in the story will be 2 Sam. 5.7, when David captures the stronghold of Zion, and renames it 'the city of David'. Jerusalem is the very place where David will reign, just as Saul confesses.

1 Samuel 25

This chapter begins with a funeral and ends with a wedding. In between, there is a considerable amount of dialogue. The conversation is mainly carried by three characters: a man woefully named 'Nabal', his clever wife Abigail, and David. The bulk of the action in this chapter takes place on one eventful day and the morning after, with the plot revolving around revenge—or the lack thereof—and some timely intervention that averts bloodshed. Like chap. 24, the central topics include harassment, self-control, and (in a strange way) 'sonship'. In fact, one could argue that chap. 25 functions as a kind of commentary on some of the themes raised in chap. 24. Nowhere is this more clear than in the portrayal of Nabal as a representation of Saul. Barbara Green (2003: 393) observes that both Nabal and Saul are the subject of numerous 'nameplays', and she proceeds to ask: 'what is to be made of a story of a man who is at one level clearly not Saul but who is drawn by the author in such a way that the analogy with the king is difficult to miss, even begs to be taken up? How can the angle of representation be identified so that its play within the chapter can be appreciated?' Thus in the configuration of this story, Nabal as a character becomes something of a surrogate for Saul, the reader can immediately discern a certain narrative wisdom in operation here. By means of the thematic links with chap. 24 (and chap. 26, as we will have occasion to see), we are provided with a new lens that opens our eyes to nuances of the story that we may otherwise have missed. Consequently, this chapter becomes an important one for both the overall storyline and the unfolding characterizations of both Saul and David.

25.1

The chapter begins with an entombment: 'And Samuel died, and all Israel gathered and lamented for him, and buried him at his house in Ramah'. A similar report occurs later in chap. 28, and so the reason for this mention is somewhat befuddling. Of course, as Kyle McCarter (1980: 388) intones, this obituary notice of Samuel anticipates the story in chap. 28, but the question of placement remains: 'But why, especially since it *does* appear in c 28, has it been inserted here? Perhaps we are to assume that it was at this time that Samuel died and that the notice in 28.3 is not an independent announcement but merely a reminder, included as part of the preparations for the strange story that follows.'

Three short points can be raised in light of this death notice. First, the description of Samuel's death and burial establishes in the reader's mind—beyond a doubt—that the man is dead, and with few exceptions, dead people remain such. While seemingly obvious, this point needs to be stressed since Samuel makes a post-mortem appearance in chap. 28. Thus the present notice at the outset of chap. 25 confirms that by the time we reach chap. 28, Samuel will have been dead for quite some time.

Second, for most readers the death of Samuel is sad. We have known Samuel since before he was born, suffered with him in the sty of Shiloh, and admired his flowering in the mud puddle of Hophni and Phinehas. We perhaps have been maddened by his irascibility, sympathized with his view of kingship, and have been ambivalent about his corrupt and wayward sons. Whether the reader thinks that he shafted Saul or whether he was an austere champion of orthodoxy, the death of Samuel surely marks the end of an era, and represents a moment of transition in the narrative.

Third, I assume that the narrative chronology is intentional—that is, Samuel dies at this particular point in the story, and is duly noted by the author for a particular reason. It is not a mere twist of fate that *immediately* after Saul's confession, Samuel gives up the ghost. Saul's confession—that David will reign and the kingdom will be established in his hand—echoes the very words that Samuel has thundered to Saul. As soon as Saul gives voice to these words, Samuel expires, as though his work is now complete. Although the relationship between these two major characters has never been straightforward, at least Samuel's death is reported at a symbolically appropriate moment in the story.

All Israel gathers for the prophet's state funeral, and the occasion—complete with corporate lamentation—is reminiscent of Jacob's funeral in Genesis 50. But right after the notice that Samuel is buried at his house, the last half of 25.1 is strange: 'And David arose and went down to the wilderness of Paran'. It is possible that the syntax of this verse implies that David is *present* at the funeral, and then departs on his way. If this the case, then David pays his last respects to his anointer, and then departs for the wilderness of Paran, the dwelling-place of Ishmael in Genesis 21, and last mentioned as a stopover in Numbers 13. Some scholars struggle with the location of Paran, since in geographic terms it is considerably south. The next episode of 25.2-42 takes place in Maon, which is further north, and hence some are led to emend the text (following the Greek Μααν). However, both the RSV and NRSV follow the MT and opt for 'Paran' as the preferred rendering. Taking a cue from these venerable translations, the reader is inclined to think that David is traversing a very wide area at this point in his fugitive existence. At times David attempts to get as far away from Saul as possible (e.g. Paran in the south), while at other times he is content to advance his cause closer to home (e.g. Maon in Judah), as we see in the next sentence.

25.2-3

A new episode begins with the introduction of a new character: a man from Maon, whose 'work' is in Carmel. According to Josh. 15.5, Maon is located in Judah, in the neighborhood of Carmel. We recall from 1 Sam. 15.12 that Carmel is the place where Saul erects a monument, so one wonders if Carmel/Maon is a spatial setting that represents pro-Saul interests. Furthermore, at the end of 1 Samuel 23 it is in the wilderness of Maon where Saul *almost* catches David, so the reader might be expecting a resumption of Saulide hostility.

The reader is also informed that this new character is a great flock-master, with three thousand sheep and one thousand goats. The man is called 'Nabal' (נבל), an unusual name since the standard definitions of נבל are either 'fool' or 'wineskin'. As we will see, both of these meanings are exploited in the narrative, but in the first instance, the name 'Nabal' functions as a kind of 'character assassination' right from the start (Levenson 1978: 13). Not only is the man named Nabal, but he is further defined as 'rude, and evil in practices' (קָשֶׁה וְרַע מַעֲלָלִים). It is striking, therefore, that his wife Abigail should be sketched in such antithetical terms: she is woman of good sense (a quality that is mentioned in biblical wisdom literature, e.g., Prov. 16.22) and lovely in appearance (like David in 16.12). All of these qualities come into play in the forthcoming narrative.

The only patronymic associated with Nabal is 'Calebite' (כָּלִבִּי, *qere*). In the Torah, one recalls, Caleb is a celebrated figure: along with Joshua, he brings a positive report about the promised land to the community of Israel (Num. 13–14), and later dislodges the indigenous giants of Hebron to secure his allotted domicile (Josh. 15). The designation 'Calebite', at least on the surface, is certainly not pejorative. Yet Nabal, although he is tribally affiliated with the Calebite clan, is characterized as crude and harsh, qualities that are not readily aligned with the legacy of Caleb. At the same time, the name Caleb shares the same consonants as 'dog' (כלב), and there may be some intentional *double entendre* suggesting that Nabal will be a figure who rages with canine ferocity (this is the way that the Greek translators understood the description). There is an ironic intersection with the previous chapter, where David labels himself 'dead dog'; before the end of 1 Samuel 25 there will be a dead Calebite.

A further detail in this paragraph should be noted. Nabal's considerable holdings in sheep necessitates a sheep-shearing event, a festive occasion that has a curious antecedent in biblical narrative. The reader first encounters sheep-shearing in Gen. 31.19-20. When Laban the Aramean goes to shear his sheep, Rachel steals his gods and Jacob steals his heart by not telling his father-in-law that he is about to flee. Now, commentators are most helpful when they point out that the name Nabal (נבל) is Laban spelled backwards (לבן). At a minimum, such nomenclature presents the reader with the very real possibility that Nabal is about to get fleeced.

25.4-8

While David is in the wilderness, he somehow learns that Nabal is sheep-shearing, and dispatches ten of his lads to deliver an emphatic greeting of *shalom* to Nabal. At first it is unclear why ten young men have to be sent to deliver such a peaceful greeting, but as the instructions continue, one begins to sense some possible reasons. Perhaps ten are sent as a sign of respect, or as a show of force, or even (as Peter Miscall suggests) for practical reasons, as David is expecting a substantial gift that requires a great deal of heavy lifting. David's men are to inform Nabal of David's benevolent activities, such as not humiliating the shepherds and not taking anything. Furthermore, David's protection has been so good that Nabal might not even know about, in which case he simply has to ask his own lads. In light of such humanitarian aid, David requests that Nabal, from his abundance, supply him and his entourage with provisions. He concludes the message with 'your son David'; given the fact that he and Nabal have not been recorded as spending much time with each other, this is a surprising term of endearment.

At first sight, this message may seem well and good, but some deeper probing reveals a more disconcerting side to the memo from the ten lads. For one, it is almost as if David is *expecting* an objection from Nabal, which he pre-empts in the message by encouraging Nabal to ask his own shepherds about what happened in the wilderness. Several commentators note the possibility that David is running the ancient Near Eastern equivalent of a 'protection racket'. The problem, I gather, is that such operations have a peculiarly mafia-like aroma, and this would not envelop David in a positive fragrance. For Mark Biddle (2002: 637), any negative strains would actually be part of a larger narrative strategy. Biddle argues that

> 1 Sam 25 undercuts and deconstructs the surface-level portrayal of David found in 1 Sam 24 and 26. After all, Nabal actually owed David nothing. He had not contracted for David's protection. It is difficult to escape the conclusion that, in fact, the only threat to Nabal's flocks had been David himself. Surely, Nabal did not owe David payment for a theft not committed.

In terms of David's message to Nabal, Barbara Green (2003: 397) likewise asks: 'Is this the humble presentation of a bill, or is it an extortionate demand for payment which had better not be refused?' If Biddle and Green are on the right track, then there are hints in this chapter of a murkier side to David than explicitly has been seen to this point in the story.

25.9-11

For the second time in the story, David asks for provisions. Back in chap. 21, David asks Ahimelech for supplies, and a massive disaster results as an entire household is destroyed (see Polzin 1993: 211). One hopes that the present situation here in chap. 25 will be more peaceful. David's lads duly deliver their message—frontloaded with *shalom*—and apparently sit down and wait (NRSV, 'and then they waited', וַיָּנוּחוּ). After a while, the reader gains the distinct impression that the lads are being ignored, especially since Nabal's eventual rejoinder ('Who is David? Who is the son of Jesse?') does not exactly present him as a paragon of ancient Near Eastern hospitality. The fact that Nabal uses the term 'son of Jesse' is interesting, since the lads are carefully instructed to deliver their message in the name of David, Nabal's 'son'. How does Nabal—who asks 'who is David'—know that David is the son of Jesse? It seems that Nabal knows more than he lets on. Further, by barking the name 'son of Jesse' he certainly sounds like Saul, or Doeg for that matter, both of whom use the patronymic in a derogatory manner. It is possible that Nabal is pro-Saul, and hence his comments are meant as a slur. In essence, Nabal calls David a rogue and a runaway servant, and he adamantly refuses to share his provisions. While many readers in the past have taken offense at Nabal's churlish dismissal, Joel Rosenberg (1986: 150) contends that something more may be happening than simply a 'benighted cynicism' of Nabal: 'This is the first recorded protest in the narrative against Davidic taxation'. Following Rosenberg's lead, we are encouraged to look for other signs of David's future reign in this chapter.

25.12-13

Having been thoroughly rebuffed by Nabal, the ten lads return to David as bearers of churlish news (rather than provisions, as requested). Like the earlier transactions with Saul, the contact between David and Nabal is indirect: they only converse through intermediaries. What is rather different here, though, is David's reaction. Having received the news, he immediately orders his men to arm themselves for battle, and he too straps on his sword. Several commentators note that David includes three greetings of *shalom* in his message to Nabal, whereas now the 'sword' is mentioned three times, as an antithesis. The sword is exactly what David does *not* use in the wilderness. He claims that nothing belonging to Nabal was harmed, but now the opposite situation is poised to take place. This violent reaction illustrates that David is certainly capable of revenge, making his restraint in the cave (in chap. 24) all that more intriguing. With 400 of his men David sets out toward

Nabal's compound, but there is an odd notice that two hundred men are left behind 'with the supplies' (הַכֵּלִים). This detail suggests, as Diana Edelman (1991: 209-10) argues, that David has considerable holdings himself, causing one to wonder how desperately David needs provisions from Nabal:

> His motives concerning Nabal now become suspect. Has he deliberately forced a confrontation in order to seem to have a legitimate grievance and basis for gaining control over Nabal's flocks and wool? Has this been a long-standing plan, formulated months ago in Carmel when Nabal's shepherds first appeared on the scene? Has David set up Nabal?

If the answer to any of these questions is affirmative, then this chapter hardly qualifies as an apology for David's conduct.

25.14-17

The disjunctive syntax in the Hebrew text of v. 14 indicates a moment of simultaneity: while David is strapping on his sword, something else is happening at Nabal's house. One of the 'lads'—who evidently is privy to the conversation between Nabal and David's messengers—gives an eyewitness report of the transaction to the prudent Abigail. This is a key moment in the chapter, for without the intervention of this young lad, the story would surely have turned out differently. When 'one from the lads' (אֶחָד מֵהַנְּעָרִים) speaks, we are immediately reminded of an earlier speech by 'one from the lads' (אֶחָד מֵהַנְּעָרִים) in 16.18, when 'one from the lads' gives effusive testimony about a son of Jesse in Saul's court. In 16.18, the servant lad tells Saul about a gifted young man, with the serendipitous result that David is brought before Saul. Now, here is another 'one from the lads' who, at a timely moment, proffers vast information about David's good actions, and likewise appears well-informed, opinionated, and deeply sensitive to David and his cause.

The lad begins his long speech to Abigail with a summary of recent events: messengers were sent by David from the wilderness to 'bless our master', but Nabal screamed at them. These opening words, we should note, assume Abigail's basic familiarity with David and his residence in the area. The lad then proceeds to launch a defense of David and his men's activities. His testimony squares with David's message (about not embarrassing anyone or stealing anything), and is enhanced by saying that the men were 'good to us' and by use of the 'wall' metaphor. The lad then counsels Abigail to act, and he denigrates his master by referring to him as a 'son of Belial'. By any measure, these are rather scathing words from an underling, and Nabal is thus indirectly connected with other 'Belial' men of the story (notably the sons of Eli in chap. 2 and those who despise Saul in chap. 10). The most intriguing aspect of the lad's speech is his forecast of evil: 'So now, know and see what you should do, for evil has been determined against our master and against all his house'. While the servant lad argued that David has been a man of blessing, his warning implies that David is capable of extreme action as well.

At the end of this extensive speech the reader is left with a substantial irony. As Jon Levenson (1978: 16) has observed, Nabal earlier says that many slaves are breaking away from their master, and now here is a slave breaking away from *his* master, Nabal himself! Listening to the lad's speech, the 'protection racket', as it were, appears rather more benevolent. Robert Alter (1999: 155) concludes that the lad's speech does not reveal everything: 'He thus makes emphatically clear that David's men really provided protection faithfully, whether in the simple sense or in the racketeering sense'. Still, despite the lad's energetic defense of David and his commendation of the latter's 'wall' of security, what is not clarified is the *motive* for such guarding. One still suspects that something unsavory might be going on.

25.18-19
Abigail wastes no time either thanking the lad for his report, or rebuking him for his negative remarks about her husband. Instead, she is pictured as simply 'hurrying'. In contrast to her husband (who seems to make the messengers wait), she quickly assembles a considerable amount of provisions. Earlier in the chapter, Nabal refuses to share his 'bread and water'; here, Abigail gives a good deal more, and the commodities (including dessert items like clusters of raisins and cakes of figs) border on luxurious. As well as loaves and ready-dressed sheep, Abigail also includes a pair of 'wineskins' (נְבָלֵי־יַיִן), forming a wordplay on her husband's name. The pun on Nabal is all the more poignant since Nabal himself is oblivious to his wife's activity. There is no reason stated as to why she is so secretive, although the lad's testimony (highlighting that Nabal is notorious for his lack of reasonable behavior) may give a necessary clue. In terms of Abigail's larger role in the story, Barbara Green (2003: 400-401) makes a very interesting comparison with Jonathan. Just as Jonathan equips David and supplies him with weapons and clothing at an important juncture in his career, so Abigail likewise equips him with provisions here. Both Jonathan and Abigail can be seen as working against the interests of their respective households (Jonathan against his father, Abigail against her husband). And in both cases, one has to ask if there is not an element of self-interest. With Jonathan, he clearly has David's future prominence in mind when he secures an oath for his family's survival and his own position as 'number two' in the nation (23.17). It remains to be seen if Abigail will make any such request, and whether *she* has David's future house in mind. It seems, therefore, that Abigail is a more complex character than one may have thought. She is not content merely to

send the provisions with the young lads; she herself mounts a donkey and follows after them.

25.20-22

With Abigail guiding her donkey down the slopes in the shadow of the mountain, David and his men are *en route* to destroy Nabal's kennel. The reader knows that destruction is on David's mind because the narrator provides a glimpse of such thoughts in v. 21. The next two lines should be understood in the 'pluperfect' sense, suggesting that just as Abigail loads up the provisions and herself on a donkey, David is breathing out murderous designs. For Jon Levenson (1978: 23), there is a stunning contrast between the presentation of David in earlier chapters (as an 'appealing young man of immaculate motivation and heroic courage') and the David presented here in the Nabal incident: 'But the David of chapter 25 is a man who kills for a grudge. The episode of Nabal is the very first revelation of evil in David's character. He can kill. This time he stops short. But the cloud that chapter 25 raises continues to darken our perception of David's character.' Consider David's words as translated in the magisterial KJV:

> Surely in vain have I kept all that this fellow hath in the wilderness, so that nothing was missed of all that *pertained* unto him: and he hath requited me evil for good. So and more also do God unto the enemies of David, if I leave of all that pertain to him by the morning light any that pisseth against the wall.

To be sure, this is a side of David the reader has not yet seen.

There is a significant interchange of language here with chap. 24, most notably David's complaint of 'evil in place of good'. In the previous chapter, Saul acknowledged to David, 'You have dealt me good, but I have dealt you evil'. The reversal here implies that David abandons the self-control that marks his conduct in the previous chapter. Moreover, David's scatological language (inimitably expressed in the KJV) is also reminiscent of Saul 'overshadowing his feet' in the cave. According to most scholars, David's phrase here refers to a uniquely male endowment, and most often occurs in the context of an imminent extermination of a (northern royal) house (e.g. 1 Kgs 14.10; 2 Kgs 9.8). But this is the first time that the phrase has occurred in the Bible so far. In the future, it will be used in the context of eliminating rival houses, and one cannot escape the conclusion that an element of personal vendetta may also be involved. David is earlier characterized as 'sensible of speech' (16.18), and thus far in the story he has distinguished himself as an orator. Yet this particular speech—about annihilating Nabal's house—presents a contrast. Joel Rosenberg (1986: 151) is equally puzzled: 'David, who in other situations is the consummate pauser and pronouncer, here is shown cooking up his reasons in a distracted, improvised, and hurried manner as he rushes toward confrontation, and his language is notably blunt, colloquial, and crude'. Finally, one should note that David swears an oath about Nabal's house just as he swears an oath in the previous chapter. Of course, earlier he swears *not* to destroy the house of Saul, whereas now he swears *to destroy* the house of Nabal. If David breaks his vow to destroy Nabal's house, then we wonder about the long-term viability of the oath sworn to Saul.

25.23-31

The last time David was near a 'mountain setting', the arrival of an envoy prevented conflict with Saul; in chap. 23, we recall, just as Saul is rounding the mountain with hostile intent, a messenger arrives to announce a Philistine incursion. Here in chap. 25, the spatial setting of a 'mountain' is where Abigail encounters David, and her (many) words have the efficacy of dissuading David from his violent resolution and his oath to destroy Nabal and his entire house. H.W. Hertzberg (1964: 203) finds her speech bubbling with 'feminine charm and exceptional sagacity'. One certainly would have a hard time claiming that the lady protests *too little*. As it stands, this speech has to rank as one of the longest between a woman and man who are not married (to each other) in the entire Deuteronomistic History. Although Abigail is not married to David at the time of this speech, I am arguing that the purpose of the long speech is to change that very situation. In other words, Abigail's speech has an ulterior motive and a personal agenda: it is marriage proposal of sorts. As Diana Edelman (1991: 214) comments:

> Abigail's self-characterization also carries with it deliberate sexual overtones associated with being a mistress or concubine, which, in light of Abigail's earlier description as physically beautiful, would seem to imply an invitation to David to settle any remaining debt or 'punishment' through sexual favors.

I would suggest that Abigail is not content with mistress status, but rather she is interested in becoming a royal wife and, by extension, a queen mother.

Abigail arrives with an elaborate fall, and, while prostrate at David's feet, implores him to assign the 'guilt' to her. She then encourages David not to 'set his heart' on matters concerning Nabal, whom she vilifies. If one thought that the servant lad was a tad out of order when speaking about his master in disparaging terms, then Abigail goes a step beyond. She provides an interpretation of Nabal's name, and her exegesis is not charitable: 'Fool is his name, and folly is with him'. She claims not have seen David's messengers, followed by an oath of her own that deals with refraining from bloodguilt. This is rather serious oath-language, especially since Abigail wishes for all David's enemies to 'be like Nabal'. Since Nabal is alive and well, such an utterance is nothing short of scandalous. Noting this problem, Kyle McCarter (1980: 394) concludes that v. 26 is 'clearly out of place', and rearranges the text such that v. 26 comes at the end. Other scholars, though, resist emendation and opt for the dramatic currency generated by Abigail's mortal thoughts. For instance, consider David Jobling's (1998: 154) appraisal:

> What does she mean when she wishes that David's enemies may 'be like Nabal'? Presumably she does not wish them to be 'surly and mean'. What she means is 'dead'—she is using a conventional expression (cf. 2 Sam 18.32). But Nabal is not yet dead! What Abigail lets slip out, surely, is her wish that he is dead.

If Jobling's reading is plausible, then it fits well with my proposal; namely, that Abigail is making a declaration of alliance with David. Her words are pregnant with thoughts of the future, and this future does not include Nabal.

The speech continues as Abigail mentions the 'blessing' (הַבְּרָכָה); what her husband Nabal was reluctant to give, she now hand-delivers. The announcement of the gift is a useful prelude to what comes next. When Abigail wishes that David's enemies 'be like Nabal', it is a dramatic forecast to say the least. But it pales in comparison to her next utterance: after yet another plea for forgiveness, she asserts that the LORD will make for David 'an established house'. In this stunning prediction, Abigail goes a step beyond the words of Saul in the previous chapter. Saul says 'you will reign', whereas Abigail envisages a 'sure house', that is, a long-lasting dynasty. I have no idea how Abigail knows this, but she is looking more like Jonathan all the time. The rationale for God granting David a 'sure house' is that he fights the battles of the LORD (מִלְחֲמוֹת יְהוָה). There is an (unconscious) echo of Saul's deceptively flattering remark in chap. 18, in the context of betrothal negotiations. Saul tells David simply to be a brave warrior and fight 'the battles of the LORD (מִלְחֲמוֹת יְהוָה), the only other place in the Deuteronomistic History where the phrase occurs. Abigail further declares that 'evil will never be found' in the hand of David. I assume she says this without blushing, but surely the reader cringes, since this staggering thesis will not be borne out in the text. At this point, a brave argument might be that Abigail's conduct here prefigures the Bathsheba dalliance later in 2 Samuel 11, when David acquires another man's wife and *certainly does* incur bloodguilt in the process. Not only is evil found in David's hand in 2 Samuel 11, but events are set in motion that result in someone other than Abigail becoming the queen mother.

For the time being, though, Abigail highlights the virtue of restraint in light of David's expectations of a sure house (בַּיִת נֶאֱמָן). Her words intersect with those of the man of God in chap. 2, who talks about the miserable future of Eli's house in contrast with the sure house (בַּיִת נֶאֱמָן) of a rival (2.35). Eli's house falls because of gross misconduct; David's house, so reasons Abigail, needs to kept from needless bloodshed. 'One could hardly imagine the later crowning of David at Hebron', says Bruce Birch (1998:

1168), 'if he had wiped out the entire household of a prominent Calebite'. In effect, Abigail counsels David *not* to be like Saul, and indeed, David's pursuit of Nabal seems about as rational as Saul's pursuit of David. This is yet another way this chapter functions as a commentary on the former: by framing a series of analogies. David would have wiped out a house here just like Saul did in chap. 22 if not for Abigail's timely intervention. Diana Edelman (1991: 215) makes a poignant observation about the spatial setting of this episode: it is, after all, the same neighborhood where Saul is said to erect a monument to himself in 15.12, raising the issue about 'the need for the king to rely upon Yahweh to kill Israel's enemies instead of taking personal responsibility (or credit) for the task'. David needs to be interrupted from traveling a 'Saul course' at this point in his career—again, a stark contrast to his restraint in the previous chapter.

Along with her counsel to refrain from incurring bloodguilt, Abigail includes a flattering allusion to David's triumph over the Philistine with a sling. Nabal earlier asks 'Who is David?', yet Abigail seems to know quite a bit about his past history, such that she is able to create a nice metaphor. But more than this obsequiousness, I am intrigued by her final imperative in v. 31: 'So now, when the LORD has done good for my lord, then may you remember your maidservant!' I assume that by 'remember' she is referring to an alliance between them, and in the event, it will be sooner rather than later that Abigail is remembered by David. In terms of the broader storyline, Abigail affirms that David will rule Israel, and her description of a 'sure house' implies that she sees herself as having a future in this house. David earlier refers to himself as Nabal's 'son', yet now Abigail alerts him to a rather different destiny as Nabal's replacement. Any parallels with Saul are entirely intentional.

25.32-35
Compared with Abigail's verbosity, David's rejoinder is rather pedestrian in terms of length and self-disclosure. Nonetheless, Peter Miscall (1986: 153) notes that 'David replies to Abigail's entreaty with a pomposity befitting most of the speeches of the chapter'. Along with several invocations of the divine name, David compliments Abigail's 'taste' (טעם), the same thing that he 'changed' before Achish in 21.14 ('And he changed his taste [טעם] in their eyes, and played the madman in their hand'). He also blesses Abigail for preventing him from shedding blood with his own hand. Such beneficent language, however, is partially offset with a reiteration of his crude remark above, stating that had she not come, 'surely there had not been left unto Nabal by the morning light any that pisseth against the wall' (KJV). One wonders if David simply cannot pass up a moment for bravado before a beautiful woman. I am not sure if this is the best language to use on a first

date, but with that, he accepts her gift and tells her to go home: 'See, I have listened to your voice and lifted up your face'.

After Abigail departs, the reader ruminates on the fact that David really does not say that much in his rejoinder to a very long speech full of optimism for his future. For instance, David does not contest her forecasts, and proffers no interrogation about her relationship with Nabal. This is certainly not the last time in the story that David will accept a woman's quasi-judicial 'plea', and thus the reader is alerted to the idea that David is quite susceptible to being swayed by a persuasive female orator (see 2 Sam. 14). However, as far as any immediate intentions with Abigail, he discloses little. But when David takes the gift, he may well see it as a mere deposit, without any direct response to her invitation to 'remember me'. One recalls his words to Saul's servants at 18.23, 'Is it a light thing in your eyes to become the king's son-in-law?' It appears that David is showing the same reticence with Abigail.

25.36-38

During Abigail's long conversation with David, her husband Nabal has not been idle. While his wife has been conversing with a man threatening to destroy his house, it turns out that Nabal has been 'feasting in his house'. Indeed, Nabal's party is no ordinary feast, for the narrator further describes it (by means of a simile) as 'like the feast of a king' (כְּמִשְׁתֵּה הַמֶּלֶךְ). There are several reasons why the author might deploy this particular image. First, the picture of a feasting Nabal implies that he would have been ill-prepared for armed conflict; that is, as David is marching toward his house, Nabal is partying. Second, the image of Nabal feasting highlights the fact that David (who has been anointed by the recently deceased Samuel) has not been invited, and reminds the reader of Nabal's snub. Either way, it is hard to escape the biting irony: Nabal has been feasting *like a king* while his wife has been asking a future king to remember *her* when he comes into his kingdom!

In the Deuteronomistic History, it is usually not a good idea for kingly figures to over-imbibe on the fruit of the vine. For instance, in 1 Kings 20, Ben-hadad and the 32 kings allied with him are getting drunk at high noon. When he is told that men are advancing from Samaria, Ben-hadad orders—without a great deal of coherence—the following: 'If they have come out for peace, take them alive, but if they have come out for war, take them alive!' Unwisely, Nabal is in the same general category as Ben-Hadad; not only is he feasting like a king, but a lengthy description is provided of Nabal's inebriation: 'the heart of Nabal was good upon him, and he was drunk, very much so' (וְהוּא שִׁכֹּר עַד־מְאֹד). It is while Nabal is in such spirits that Abigail returns from her Davidic dialogue, where she has just been discoursing on the long-term future of David's house, and telling him that she wishes all his enemies to 'be like Nabal'. Notably, Abigail refrains from telling Nabal anything 'whether great or small, until the morning light'. This is the exact phrase that David has just used, and to see it recycled as part of Abigail's consciousness already illustrates her solidarity with David even at her husband's expense. Otherwise, why would she wait, or why for that matter would she have to tell him anything at all?

After delaying and letting Nabal enjoy his feast, Abigail chooses the cold light of day to approach her husband with some rather sobering news. In general terms, she picks the morning (בַּבֹּקֶר), but in specific terms, she picks an arresting moment for conversation. The NRSV translates the next clause in 25.37 as 'In the morning, when the wine had gone out of Nabal' (בְּצֵאת הַיַּיִן מִנָּבָל), inferring that Nabal is now clear-headed after a night of debauchery. However, Peter Leithart (2001: 525-27) argues that the Hebrew infinitive construct could well be understood as happening *at the same time* as the main verb of the sentence, thus yielding the following translation: 'while the wine was going out from Nabal, his wife told him'. Aside from the obvious earthiness of the moment, there are two immediate advantages in Leithart's translation. First, it exploits the nameplay between 'Nabal' (נבל) and 'wineskin' (נבל). When Abigail chooses to approach Nabal, it is while the wineskin is bursting, so to speak. Second, the translation provides a further connection with Saul in the previous chapter (where Saul is 'overshadowing his feet'). Saul could have been destroyed in the cave during his outhouse break, and Nabal learns while urinating that his house could have been destroyed by David during the feast. Nabal had been flushed with much wine on the previous evening; now, on the next morning (as the wine is being flushed from his person) Abigail imparts some news.

In such awkward circumstances, Abigail tells Nabal 'all these things'. Curiously, the reader is only indirectly informed of Abigail's communication with Nabal; after we hear one of the longest speeches from a woman in the entire Deuteronomistic History, we are not privy to what she says to Nabal! Whatever she says, it has a fatal effect: 'his heart died in his midst, and he became like a rock'. Earlier Abigail wishes that anyone who seeks David's life should be slung away, as from the hollow of a sling. It appears as though her husband—now stone-like—has fulfilled that prophetic utterance. Even so, one wonders what *in particular* Abigail says that induces this kind of cardiac arrest in Nabal. Diana Edelman (1991: 219) reflects, 'The audience is left to decide whether his condition resulted from fear over what he had narrowly escaped at David's hands, reaction to loss of his wife's support and guidance, or reaction to the loss of a small fraction of his vast possessions'. One cannot know for sure, but it could be a combination of all three.

It has been an eventful 24-hour period for Nabal. On the day before, his heart is 'good', but on the next morning his heart is 'dead'. Nabal lasts for another week-and-a-half in this state of suspended animation, until the reader is next informed: 'About ten days later, the LORD struck the heart of Nabal, and he died'. In times past, commentators speculated on the manner of Nabal's stone-like condition and subsequent striking by God, and suggested a coma, stroke paralysis, or some similar affliction. For me, the point seems to be a comparison with Saul, and the death of Nabal somehow prefigures the death of Saul. Like Nabal, Saul is 'dead' as a king for quite some time, until the final day of his death. As Barbara Green (2003: 403) points out, both Nabal and Saul will enjoy a final meal on the night preceding their demise, and like Saul, 'Nabal will not see his line wiped out, but he will know that those on whose loyalty he presumed to count have gone over to his disdained (if justified) opponent'. As for Abigail, there is no mourning reported when she learns of her husband's death (cf. Bathsheba in 2 Sam. 11.26). Hopefully Abigail undergoes a period of mourning, but the author does not linger on such detail.

25.39-44

The rest of the chapter seems to unfold without any undue drama, at least on the surface. Somehow, David hears of Nabal's demise—presumably from a similar source from whom he hears of Nabal's sheepshearing in the first place. Once acquainted with the news, David speaks: 'Blessed be the LORD…' I have no idea who David is addressing, and in the absence of any stated listener, one can only assume it is his men, or perhaps whoever brings him the news. After the initial language of blessing, David then recounts how God has taken up his legal cause, and expresses gratitude that his hand has been restrained from doing evil. Most poignantly, he asserts that God has turned evil on Nabal's own head, and again the words echo the previous chapter (see 24.17). At the end of his self-vindicating speech, David then sends messengers to Carmel—for the second time in the chapter. This time the message is for Abigail, and the messengers report David's interest in marriage. Abigail obliges, proffering a now characteristic speech. Her loquaciousness with David (or his emissaries) contrasts with her reticence to her husband, as her dialogue with Nabal is never recorded. For the second time in the chapter she 'hurries', and as she once more rides on a donkey, this time she has a queenly retinue of maidservants along with her. This might imply that she is also bringing some wealth and status as well. Abigail becomes David's wife, who has certainly 'remembered' her just as she asked.

Below the surface, however, the formal denouement of the episode can be read two ways. On the one hand, it can be read as a straightforward vindication of David's restraint (greatly aided by the prudent Abigail). Commentators who argue that this section of text is a 'Davidic apology' are especially wont to argue this line. In such thought, David's line about divine vindication is an apt evaluation of the entire scene with Nabal. Nabal is a churl who has insulted the anointed king, and thus deserves to die. Yet on the other hand, it is possible to feel a more negative sub-current in this episode. Several scholars draw further attention to the connection between this chapter and 2 Samuel 11. Jon Levenson (1978: 24) observes that in both of these chapters 'David moves to kill a man and marry his wife. In the instance of Nabal, as the story-teller would have it, Abigail's arguments and an act of God frustrate the murder and legitimate the marriage. With Uriah, such luck is not to be David's. 1 Samuel 25 is a prophetic glimpse, within David's ascent, of his fall from grace'. Mark Biddle (2002: 637) is another reader who rejects the 'Davidic apology' line of reasoning, noting that in numerous instances David's 'innocence' is the result of people in his inner circle working for him (whether Abigail here, or, more infamously, Joab later in the story). 'If this is a Solomonic era defense of David's purity and thus of the integrity of Solomon and the Davidic dynasty', Biddle says, 'it is perplexingly cynical'. Furthermore, the darker side of this episode becomes more apparent when the final lines of the chapter (vv. 43-44) are considered:

> But Ahinoam David had taken from Jezreel, and they were, even the two of them, wives for him. But Saul had given Michal his daughter, the wife of David, to Palti son of Laish who was from Gallim.

These last verses describe two antecedent actions in the narrative. First, David has taken—sometime prior to chap. 25—Ahinoam from Jezreel. One recalls the words of Moses in Deuteronomy 17, stating that the king should not take many wives. Of course, David is not *officially* king yet, but the acquisition of Ahinoam looks suspiciously like multiplication. Ahinoam herself is the subject of a statistical anomaly: as several commentators point out, there is only one other Ahinoam in the Hebrew Bible: the wife of Saul. A number of recent studies are taking the view that, at some point, David appropriates Saul's wife. Such an inference can help to explain Saul's outburst at Jonathan in 20.30 (where Jonathan's mother is referred to in unbecoming terms, including 'perverse, rebellious woman'), and Nathan's prophetic indictment of 2 Sam. 12.8 ('I gave your master's house to you and your master's women into your bosom'). The notion of David marrying Saul's wife remains speculative, but the very fact that Ahinoam is mentioned right after marriage to Abigail may well leave a bad taste in the mouths of some readers. According to Jon Levenson (1978: 27), 'Saul's action in v 44 is a *quid pro quo* to David's in v 43'. At the very least, the name of Ahinoam and David's multiple marriages serves to foreshadow the negative way women will be treated as objects of political maneuverings (indeed, it is

David's wife Ahinoam who gives birth to Amnon, who himself will have his share of sexual struggles). So, even if the identity of Ahinoam remains indeterminate, it functions as one more open-ended matter that conspires against a superficial reading of this chapter as a Davidic apology.

The second antecedent action—again occurring sometime prior to chap. 25—is that Saul has taken Michal and given her to Palti. The reader is not sure whether David marries Ahinoam before or after Saul's action. No motive is ascribed for Saul's action (or its legality, for that matter), but it does not seem to be the brightest move. If David is on the rise, would it not be better for Saul to be in a position of marriage alliance? Such a strategy is exactly what David will adopt in the future, if he has not already done so. This marital strategy no doubt would be something of a downer for Abigail: if she harbors any ambition of being a queen mother, the chapter ends with a note that it will be a very competitive business. If David's fall from grace in 2 Samuel 11 is hinted at in this episode, then, equally, one gathers that the succession to the Davidic throne might not be entirely straightforward either. At any rate, the drama with Michal is far from over. The last we heard she lets David out of a window, through which he does not return. Michal will be heard from again in due course, as will her new husband Palti (see 2 Sam. 3).

1 SAMUEL 26

Despite being freshly married to Abigail, David is still a fugitive from Saul's court, and this chapter shows the reason why there is no honeymoon. In view of Saul's affirmation in chap. 24, it is moderately surprising that he continues his pursuit of David. But then, at the end of chap. 25, Saul has just been described as having given Michal away; so now, the pursuit continues in an episode that carries a host of similarities with chap. 24. Once upon a time it was fashionable to see chaps. 24 and 26 as doublets of the same episode. But fashions have changed, and recent scholars are more interested in the shades of difference and development of character and theme in the two chapters, intentionally sandwiched by chap. 25. In fact, above I referred to chap. 25 as a commentary on chap. 24. I should now like to go a step further and say that chaps. 24–26 function as a unit. David Jobling (1998: 92) argues that chap. 25 'stands in an allegorical relation' to chaps. 24 and 26, and I will be alert to such nuances in my analysis below. The chapter itself has two major sections. In part one, there is a build-up to another confrontation between Saul and David, complete with a nocturnal setting and plenty of witnesses. The second part of the chapter features a lengthy dialogue between David and Abner/ Saul. There is further development of David and Saul, but also a couple of other significant characters feature in this episode—Abishai and Abner. Since both of these military figures have prominent roles in 2 Samuel, the reader should be alert as to how they are characterized. Both figures fulfill a certain role in the story, and both fade from view around the same time as the chapter unfolds. Since Abishai and Abner will be rivals later in the story, their respective appearances here merit attention.

26.1-4

Once again the Ziphites make an appearance in the narrative. On the previous occasion in chap. 23, they go up to Gibeah and present Saul with intelligence: 'Is not David hiding himself with us?' Here the language is nearly identical, as they once more approach Saul at Gibeah and present similar information: 'Is not David hiding himself on the hill of Hachilah, on the face of Jeshimon?' The Ziphites' motive is obscure in chap. 23, and there is no further indication here as to why they make the effort of traveling to Gibeah to reveal David's presence. Since Saul is in Gibeah (rather than in the wilderness), maybe he has not been intent on chasing David, and perhaps the Ziphites are the ones who replant the idea of resuming pursuit. It is as though Saul cannot resist one more attempt on the son of Jesse. Like Nabal, the Ziphites do not favor David, and instead choose loyalty to Saul. The communiqué here is a little different from chap. 23, though. They provide Saul with the same address of David's whereabouts (Hachilah, Jeshimon), but there is no deferential 'according to all your soul desires, O king' (23.20). This time the Ziphites are more terse, probably because Saul's pursuit did not come to a successful resolution last time.

When the Ziphites approached Saul with information on David in chap. 23, Saul responded with glee ('May you be blessed by the LORD!'), and then asked a myriad of questions. This time when the Ziphites approach, Saul does not respond with the language of blessing; in fact, no response whatsoever is given. Saul does, however, gather 3000 troops, and usually when he takes this number he has Davidic destruction on his mind (see 24.3). Saul follows the Ziphites's directions, and apparently camps for the night in the desert of Ziph. This is something of a contrast with chap. 14, when Saul urged an all-night pursuit of Israel's enemies (14.36). Here in chap. 26 he camps for the night, and it will prove frustrating in the end. Furthermore, Saul's campsite itself will play into David's hand, and the spatial setting of the 'hill' will actually prove to benefit David. But the Ziphites are quite right: David is in the neighborhood, and he is closer than Saul realizes. There is a switch in narrative point of view, as now David 'sees' that Saul is in the area, and his presence is doubly verified as David sends spies to confirm Saul's advance. It is evident that David is acting in a proactive manner. There will not, it seems, be a random encounter this time, as in the cave of En-gedi.

26.5-6

Accompanied by a small group, David himself now arises and scopes out Saul's campsite. David's visual perspective is refracted in the narrative, as he sees the spot where Saul is lying, at the center of the camp. In close proximity to Saul is Abner, commander of the army. Saul is well-protected, a rather different situation than his solo venture to the outhouse-cave in chap. 24. David then addresses 'Ahimelech the Hittite' and 'Abishai, the son of Zeruiah, the brother of Joab', and inquires: 'Who will go down with me to Saul, to the camp?' There are not many Hittites in the books of Samuel; in fact, Uriah the Hittite will be the only other one, and we never hear of Ahimelech the Hittite again. One senses, therefore, that the real object of this speech is Abishai, who is carefully introduced as the son of Zeruiah

(David's sister), and 'Joab's brother'. The sons of Zeruiah, as we will have occasion to see in 2 Samuel, forge quite a reputation for themselves as hard men. When David addresses Abishai here, there must be a larger strategy in mind. Peter Miscall (1986: 158) asks: 'Why does David want an accomplice and only one at that? David may want someone, especially a man like Abishai, to go down to Saul's camp with him to serve as his "straight man" by proposing to kill Saul on the spot'. Miscall's proposal is attractive because we assume that David knows Abishai well, and probably anticipates a prominent position in the army for him and his brothers in the days ahead.

To be sure, David's invitation here seems rash: who is willing, he asks, to walk with me right into the heart of the enemy camp, and approach Saul? Yet Abishai is game—which says a lot about him—and off they go. Such willingness to accompany David is why H.W. Hertzberg (1964: 209) refers to Abishai as 'a real daredevil'. At the same time, there are other reasons why it is appropriate for Abishai to volunteer for this duty. For one, Abishai is the counterpart of Abner, who is sleeping in close proximity to the king. Just as Abner is the commanding officer of Saul, so Abishai is part of a family that will become the most powerful military leaders in David's court. Moreover, in view of the larger portrait of Abishai that eventually emerges from the narrative, James Ackerman (2006: 14) reflects: 'More than any other character Abishai is depicted as David's alter ego, the consistent voice of his dark side, who advocates use of violence to advance David's honor and self-interest'. The recruitment of Abishai for this particular mission serves a wider purpose in the storyline, and provides a first glimpse of the violent propensities of the sons of Zeruiah.

26.7-8

As David and Abishai stealthily move down toward the sleeping Saul—who is surrounded by his troops—a key component of Saul's weaponry is mentioned: his spear, thrust into the ground at his head. David is intimately acquainted with this spear, since it has been thrust at *his own head* on numerous occasions. But such nostalgia is not on Abishai's mind. He sees this as an ordained opportunity that requires a deft touch: 'God has closed (סגר) your enemy into your hand today! So now, let me strike him right through the earth with the spear one time, and I won't need a second!' The reader immediately recognizes a similarity to the cave-talk in chap. 24. When Saul is in the vulnerable state of overshadowing his feet, David's men say to him, 'Behold, the day that the LORD said to you, "Behold, I am giving your enemy into your hand, and you can do to him whatever is good in your eyes!"' Both Abishai and the men in the cave advocate the destruction of Saul, but there are a few differences in Abishai's plan. In the first place, Abishai provides no alleged divine quotation giving some sort of rationale, like the men in the cave do. Furthermore, Abishai does not encourage David to approach Saul, but offers to do it *himself*. In the cave, of course, David refrained from cutting off anything except Saul's robe. Abishai does not quite trust David with the deed, it would seem. One senses that Abishai intends to miss neither Saul nor this particular opportunity. As far as the deed itself, Abishai proposes to use Saul's own spear to strike him. Maybe this is something of a badge of honor, for both David (17.51) and Benaiah (2 Sam. 23.21) snatch a bigger opponent's weapon and turn it against the man. Abishai has every intention of joining this elite fraternity.

26.9-11
For all of Abishai's willingness, he runs into a brick wall of Davidic obstinacy. Abishai is the one David wants to accompany him, because in all likelihood Abishai will want to kill the king, and thus David can speak this line: 'Do not destroy him! For who can send out his hand to the LORD's anointed and be unpunished?' The reader has already heard David talk about the inviolability of 'the LORD's anointed' in the cave, where it has a self-serving element. But in this context it is not an identical utterance because of the different audiences involved. In the cave David is addressing his group of men, a group of brigands who need to hear the message that David will *never* strike the LORD's anointed; by extension, neither should they (despite any personal advantage that might be gained). In chap. 26, though, David is only addressing Abishai, and the reader should keep in mind that Abishai will be a military commander (akin to Abner) once David is on the throne. David wants Abishai to hear this message, and subsequently filter it down to the rest of the troops. Notably, the idea of respect for the house of Saul will not be rigidly adhered to by Abner; later in 2 Samuel 3 he appears to position himself for a run at the (northern) throne.

Probably flabbergasted, Abishai does not respond to David's utterance of v. 10. In fact, Abishai does not speak again for the rest of the chapter. David is far from finished, though, and he continues in a similar vein: 'As the LORD lives, surely the LORD will strike him down, or his time will come and he will die, or he will go down to battle and be swept away'. As Graeme Auld (2003: 227) notices, David appropriates some lessons learned from chaps. 24 and 25: 'At their previous encounter David called on Yahweh to avenge him on Saul. Since then he has seen Yahweh avenge him on Nabal. He is now more explicit about wanting Saul dead, one way or another—but not by his hand.' With one more comment about the LORD's anointed, David then instructs Abishai to grab the spear and the water jug at Saul's head, and depart. The spear, as mentioned above, reminds us of some earlier encounters between Saul and David. Saul's water jug, though, makes its first appearance in the story. Some commentators are wont to see some symbolic imagery at work here (such as water as a life-giving force, or something similar). I prefer to see the water jug as practical evidence: Saul will know the jug was at his head, and that David had a lethal opportunity to strike—just like in the cave.

26.12

Having ordered Abishai to retrieve the spear and jug, v. 12 reports that *David himself* proceeded to take the articles at Saul's head. Robert Alter (1999: 165) comments on this oddity: 'David takes them himself, after having ordered Abishai to do it. The medieval Hebrew exegete David Kimchi offers a shrewd explanation: "He changed his mind and didn't want Abishai to approach the king, lest he prove unable to restrain himself and kill Saul".' Because David takes the spear and jug, there is a nice symmetry with chap. 24, as once more David creeps up to Saul in the darkness. Still, the reader may wonder how all this is possible—by any standard, it is incredible that two unarmed men should be able to walk up to a king surrounded by large contingent of soldiers. As it turns out, the daring feat is facilitated by some divine intervention: not a single member of Saul's battalion is afflicted with insomnia, because a 'deep sleep of the LORD' (תַּרְדֵּמַת יְהוָה) had fallen over them. The term for 'deep sleep' is not common in the Hebrew Bible, and often signals a supernatural agency. It is first used when a deep sleep falls upon Adam (in order to procure a wife from his side), and again in Genesis 15 when Abram has the same experience (a prelude to his vision of the covenant ratification ceremony). I am not sure how cognizant David and Abishai are of this divine activity, but it does add an unmistakable element of providence to the whole scene.

26.13-16

Armed with the souvenirs taken from Saul, David removes himself from the middle of the camp, and heads for the top of 'a hill far away'. The text is careful to mention that a great distance stands between David and the camp. With a voice loud enough to rouse them from their deep sleep imposed by God, David addresses both the army, and specifically, the commander: 'Will you not answer, O Abner?' Abner may not have been the expected interlocutor, especially since he has not been seen for quite some time. Abner's is last mentioned at Saul's feast of chap. 20, when he takes his place beside Saul (who discoursed on the son of Jesse and the kingdom before hurling the oft-used spear at Jonathan). After 1 Samuel 26, Abner will not resurface until 2 Samuel 2, when he takes Saul's son Ishbosheth to be crowned king of Israel in Mahanaim. We assume, therefore, that by addressing Abner David is making some sort of political statement, the nature of which is partially revealed as this nocturnal conversation continues.

To this point in the story, Abner has only spoken on one occasion. At the end of chap. 17, Saul interrogates him about the parentage of the 'stripling' who is marching out to face Goliath. Unable to supply positive identification, Abner merely responded: 'By your life, O king, I do not know'. Such a response is important to keep in mind for the present episode, because the cryptic words of Saul in chap. 17 reveal a suspicion about David's destiny that Abner does not grasp. Now David is a hunted rival, yet Abner's groggy reply in v. 14 ('Who are you that calls to the king?') does not reveal any greater awareness about David's identity. As Diana Edelman (1991: 227) puts it, 'Just as in 17.55, Abner is unable to identify David; he cannot recognize the king-elect'. Abner will emerge as the most powerful force in the north after Saul's death, but this is not the last time that he will suffer from an acute failure to read a situation correctly (see 2 Sam. 3.27).

In contrast to Abner, David has emerged as a skilled orator. He proved this with his response to the trash-talk of Goliath in chap. 17, and he sounds impressive now in a long speech ostensibly addressed to Abner, but no doubt David has other audiences in mind as well. The main charge is an accusation of gross negligence: the king was not watched closely enough, and could have been attacked. Barbara Green (2003: 389) suggest that this accusation might also contain a jibe against Saul as well: 'The double charge is clear enough: against Abner for serious neglect that would admit an enemy to the king's sleeping place and against Saul for being such a king that someone might wish to assassinate him'. Of course, David does not quite acknowledge the 'deep sleep' issue that contributed to the negligence; but then, he may be in the dark about this divine intervention. Through David's next line ('For one of the army came in to destroy your lord the king'), the reader can see the value of having Abishai along for the ride: he now becomes, as it were, a public foil for David's self-control, much like the words of the men in the cave of chap. 24.

Without actually saying it, David seems to impute another misdemeanor to Abner, in that Abner also did not 'keep watch' over the king while the latter was in the cave overshadowing his feet. Overall, David's assessment of Abner's stewardship of Saul is 'not good' (לא־טוב) in v. 16. For Peter Miscall (1986: 160), there is a forward glance in this statement: 'The statement anticipates the defeat of the army at Mt Gilboa and Abner's absence or escape from Mt Gilboa, where he again fails to keep watch over his lord. Abner is not a proper servant to his lord.' To my mind, this is an important topic that will emerge in the early chapters of 2 Samuel: Saul's general (Abner) will not remain indivisibly loyal to his master's house. By contrast, David characterizes himself as the consummate loyal man. Such loyalty is punctuated as David's words to Abner (and the rest of the troops) move toward a conclusion: 'As the LORD lives, all of you are sons of death

(בְּנֵי־מָוֶת), because you did not keep watch over your lord, the LORD's anointed'. Notably, this is not the last time that David will use the expression 'son of death'. The same epithet occurs in 2 Sam. 12.5, when David vows, 'As the LORD lives, the man who did this thing is a son of death!' Sadly for David, he is the man—but that is a long way off. For now, David closes with a stinging question ('So now, look! Where is the king's spear? What about the water jug at his head?') sealing his indictment for negligence.

26.17-20

> Saul recognized David's voice, and said, 'Is this your voice, my son David?' David said, 'It is my voice, O my lord the king'. He said, 'Why is my lord pursuing after his servant? For what have I done, and what evil is in my hand? So now, please let the king hear the words of his servant. If the LORD has incited you against me, then may he smell an offering. But if this is from sons of men, then cursed are they before the LORD, for they have driven me today from attaching myself to the LORD's inheritance, saying, "Go, serve other gods!" And now, do not let my blood fall to the ground away from the presence of the LORD. For the king has marched out to seek a single flea, like one would chase after a partridge on the hills!'

It is quite possible that David frames his speech to Abner in order to elicit a response from Saul. If so, David's strategy is successful, as Saul speaks instead of Abner. It is curious that Saul recognizes the voice, but then asks the same question that he asks in 24.17, after David's long speech near the entrance of the cave. Saul is not the only one who repeats himself, though, as David also replies to the king with his usual 'what have I done?' On this occasion David *has done* something: taken the king's spear instead of killing him with it. In his analysis of this passage, Robert Polzin (1993: 209-13) talks in general terms about an analogy with chap. 15, where Saul does not kill a king when commanded to. In chaps. 24 and 26, David does not kill a king though on two occasions he has the opportunity. Perhaps it is this twice-revealed self-control that prompts David to ask Saul who 'incited' (סות) him. The next time this verb occurs will be in 2 Samuel 24, where the LORD incites (סות) David to take a census of Israel, with disastrous consequences.

By far the strangest moment in David's speech is when he supplies a 'quote' from some unspecified agitators who are saying 'go, serve other gods'. Since nowhere in 1 Samuel does anyone actually say this to David—or anything remotely similar—it may be that David intends for his hearer to understand the words in a figurative sense. Commentators proffer a number of theories as to what these words mean. Graeme Auld (2003: 227) remarks,

> The fear of being unattached resonates with one further threat in Samuel: where the unnamed man of God (1 Sam 2.36) warns Eli that the remnants of

his house will seek attachment to another of the hereditary priesthoods. Being unattached to Yahweh's heritage also implied serving other gods: Yahweh the High God, who allotted lands to peoples, also allotted each their god (Deut 32.8-9).

In contrast, Robert Gordon (1986: 189) suggests that David's words do not exactly represent mainstream theology in the Hebrew Bible, so the reader is still left wondering why David uses this kind of speech (assuming he is not trying to baffle Saul and the army encamped below the hill). As far as leaving the boundaries of the promised land, Peter Miscall (1986: 160) notes that David will be on the move in the next chapter: 'Does David already have the latter move in mind and now is attempting to blame it on Saul and to cast it in theological rather than political-military terms?' Indeed, to this point David has made numerous excursions outside the land (even a trip to Jerusalem) all in the interests, so it would seem, of gathering external allies. In the end, it may be that David's rhetoric emphasizes that Saul's pursuit is wholly out of proportion, and by recycling the 'flea' image (see 24.15), implies that continuing this game of hide and seek is a royal waste of time. More puzzling is why David adds the ornithological metaphor of a 'partridge' (קֹרֵא) on the hills—but it does form a clever wordplay with the verb 'call' (קרא), as David stands on the top a hill and calls out.

26.21-25

For the second time in his career, Saul utters the words, 'I have sinned'. Back in chap. 15 Saul pleads guilty before Samuel, and then asks the prophet to 'return' (שׁוב) with him to the elders. Here in chap. 26 the words are remarkably similar. If Saul was trying to make the most of a bad situation with a face-saving measure in chap. 15, I suppose it is possible that something similar is happening here with David. In effect, he confesses his guilt, and then invites David to return with him—making for a good public relations move. Having said that, Saul also makes a promise never to do evil to David again, a promise that is actually kept, whether by default or by design. Furthermore, for the second time in his career, Saul is connected with the verb 'play the fool' (סכל). In chap. 13 Samuel accuses Saul of acting foolishly (סכל) by not keeping the divine commandment, and here in chap. 26 Saul says to David 'Behold, I have played the fool (סכל)'. This idea of 'fool' creates an obvious thematic connection with the previous chapter: Nabal is a fool, and here Saul confesses to be one. Even though two different words are used, it serves to equate further Saul and Nabal, both of whom— in David's estimation—have returned good with evil. At the same time, the reader would be wise to keep in mind that David himself will use the same word (סכל) in a confession to God about his folly in taking a census in

2 Samuel 24. Once more, Jon Levenson's point is apt: even at the height of his 'innocence' David's guilt is presaged.

David's rejoinder to Saul is at least three times as long, beginning with a recommendation that one of the lads come and fetch the king's spear. In effect, David is refusing Saul's invitation to return—much like he refused Saul's armor in chap. 17. One is not sure what happens to the water jug. Perhaps David retains it as evidence for the future (much like the piece of cut robe), should Saul ever be tempted to renege on his promise, 'I will never do evil to you again'. If David is not quite trusting Saul, then this would explain his words in v. 23, where he basically reiterates his self-control ('God gave you into my hand today'), yet out of respect for the LORD's anointed David refused to lift up his hand. After David's final plea for vindication from the LORD, Saul's generic blessing sounds a bit flat. Notably absent in Saul's last words is any reference to David reigning over Israel. Saul says that David will do great things, but the term 'king' is certainly not present.

Saul does, however, use the term 'my son', and with this intimate appellation the narrative now closes a circle. Having kings is like having sons, and David is the 'son' who will succeed Saul. Alongside this personal story of Saul and David is the larger story of kingship in Israel, and so it is poignant that after these last words, the paths of Saul and David will never cross again. Saul will now move toward his final destiny, while David takes refuge outside the land, as captured in the final sentence of the chapter: 'And David went on his journey, and Saul returned to his place'. For Peter Miscall (1986: 161), there is a balance between the first line of the chapter and the last: 'This contrasts with the geographical details at the opening of the story and anticipates the continuing narrative of David's "way" to kingship and Saul's "place" on Mt. Gilboa'. David has several times alluded to Saul's death. We have already seen one rejected leader plunge to his death (Eli), and the question now for Saul is *when*, not *if*.

1 SAMUEL 27

The *spatial setting* for this chapter—fitting in the light of 26.25b—is outside the land of Israel. The main characters are David and (again) the Philistine king of Gath, Achish. Having finished his conversation with Saul, David now moves in with another king, and in this chapter we will pay attention to the portrait of Achish that emerges more fully on the canvas. The reader is privy to some further royal dialogue between Achish and David, and we will try to ascertain if either is looking for an advantage over the other. This short chapter begins with an *internal monologue* of David, followed by his flight to Philistia. The bulk of the action centers on the activities of David during this period, and the corresponding response of Achish. Overall, Robert Gordon (1986: 191) notices a connection with the ark narrative in 1 Samuel 5–6, where the Philistines are 'outwitted' by an exile, so to speak. As in the Nabal episode, another side of David is revealed in this chapter.

27.1

Kurt Vonnegut once said: 'When I used to teach creative writing, I would tell the students to make their characters want something right away even if its only a glass of water. Characters paralyzed by the meaninglessness of modern life still have to drink water from time to time.' At this juncture in the story, the Deuteronomist dips into the well of David's consciousness to serve the postmodern reader an interesting beverage. Having rejected Saul's invitation to 'return' with him, David now has to go somewhere, and such ponderings are presented by means of a rare soliloquy from David himself: 'And David said to his heart' (וַיֹּאמֶר דָּוִד אֶל־לִבּוֹ). This is the not the first internal glimpse of David; back in chap. 21—in Gath, coincidentally enough—David 'put these things in his heart' (the words of Achish's servants), 'and was much afraid before Achish king of Gath'. Here in chap. 27 David's internal deliberations will take him *back* to Achish king of Gath.

As is readily apparent, David's self-talk covers a fair bit of ground: 'Now, I will be swept away (ספה) one day by the hand of Saul. There is nothing good for me, unless I surely slip away to the land of the Philistines. Then Saul will despair of seeking me within the borders of Israel, and I will slip away from his hand.' On one level, these words can be taken quite literally, as an expression of genuine anxiety. For those readers who judge this text to be an elaborate apology for David, such a reading is no doubt attractive. But at another level, could there not be something more complex at work here? Is it possible that even in his *inner thoughts* David is politically astute? It seems unlikely—for a host of reasons—that David should believe these things, unless this internal monologue represents a moment of doubt. More plausibly, David would want his men to know that *this* is what he is thinking. I am reminded here of Gen. 27.41-42, 'Esau bore a grudge against Jacob because of the blessing that his father blessed him, and Esau said in his heart, "the days of mourning for my father are drawing near, and I will kill my brother Jacob". And the words of her older son were reported to Rebekah...' It is possible, based on the Esau model, for inner thoughts to become public knowledge, by whatever means. When David speaks 'to his heart', one cannot help thinking that such thoughts are exactly what he wants his men to hear. David may be speaking in his heart, but he may also be wearing his heart on his sleeve.

Commentators have a variety of views as to why David opts to depart. David Jobling (1998: 235) suggests a practical advantage: 'By having David take refuge in Philistia the narrator forces the Philistines into a peculiar double narrative role. They must bring about the death of Saul and his sons and they must provide David with a refuge from Saul for the last crucial part of Saul's life.' For Robert Polzin (1993: 216), 'David's escape to the land of the Philistines serves a narrative purpose wider than ensuring his physical safety'. One such narrative purpose is revealed by means of the verb 'swept away' (סָפָה). As Polzin discusses, this is a thematically powerful verb that is used—over the course of the narrative—to show the close connection between the fate of the king and the fate of the people. David has just used the same verb in 26.10 (when speculating on the death of Saul in battle), and most famously the verb occurs at the end of chap. 12, in Samuel's angry address: 'But if you keep doing evil, even you and your king will be swept away (תִּסָּפוּ)'. For Polzin (1993: 270), 'Now, the narrator's first clear indication of the inner thoughts and feelings of David (27.1) reveals to us someone whose striving to avoid the fate of Saul and Israel turns out to be prophetically accurate on the personal level but ominously mistaken according to the wider vision of the History' (Deuteronomy to 2 Kings). It is also worth asking whether David's decision to flee to the Philistines (to avoid being swept away) is spontaneous, or whether he had this contingency in mind when he fled to Philistine territory the first time back in chap. 21. Given David's language in the previous chapter ('go serve other gods'), one suspects the latter. The timing should also be considered: David first travels to Philistine territory *after* glimpsing Doeg the Edomite in the sanctuary. Doeg is a useful member of Saul's retinue, as the events at Nob in chap. 22

illustrate. In light of David's activities with his men in Nabal's neighborhood, it is conceivable that David is interested in transferring his protection racket elsewhere, and (re)applying for a position as a foreign mercenary.

27.2-4

Immediately following the internal monologue about slipping away to Philistine territory, the reader is informed that David 'passes over' to King Achish son of Maoch of Gath, accompanied by his six hundred men. While the verb 'pass over' (עבר) seems harmless enough, Diana Edelman (1991: 233) notes that it is 'a term that carries with it overtones of betrayal or transgression as well as the movement across physical space'. But this fugitive is not alone: ever since chap. 23 David has had a sizeable group of men with him. Unlike other occasions (such as 23.9-13), there is no consultation of the ephod this time. So, one is not sure if this proposal to relocate to Gath was a tough sell to his men or not.

During his fugitive period, David has made a few trips outside Israel. For instance, in 22.3 he ventures to Moab, and there deposits his parents for safekeeping. Apparently David has an ally in the Moabite king, so it is conceivable that he could have gone there to slip away from Saul. When we recall David's last trip to Gath, he made a strange first impression: he changed his taste, scratched doors, allowed spittle to drool down his beard, and looked decidedly unhinged. On the surface, it would seem less likely that David would return to Gath at this point in the story *unless* he has been planning such a trip all along (or at least keeping it as an option). In chap. 21, David feigns madness before Achish and court of Gath. This time he will play a rather different game of dissembling, as the reader will have occasion to witness.

Unlike in chap. 21, there is no reception for David recorded here in 27.3. When David first shows up in the presence of Achish, the king of Gath directs some quasi-insulting remarks toward his own servants. In other words, David's arrival in Gath creates some division between Achish and his court. To be sure, no such division is mentioned in chap. 27, but I daresay it is festering, and indeed will come to a climax in the coming days. Yet for all his deprecating comments in chap. 21, Achish was actually rather ambivalent about David himself. I suppose one could argue that Achish was playing the role of a consummate politician: not showing his hand and only asking questions. Again, it is notable that no reaction of Achish is recorded when David shows up for the second time.

A major difference, though, is that David is not flying solo this time. Not only is David attended by his six hundred men, but also every man and his household roll into Gath. Rather tersely, the narrator reports: 'And David dwelt with Achish in Gath, he and his men, each man and his house'. It is hard to disagree with H.W. Hertzberg (1964: 213) on this score: 'The most important difference is that in the earlier narrative David appears as a forsaken fugitive, whereas here he comes as the head of a powerful, indeed, much-feared, band'. Included in this domestic assembly are David's two wives, Ahinoam of Jezreel (no further indication is given whether or not she is the Ahinoam of 14.50) and Abigail. The NRSV renders the end of v. 3 as 'Abigail of Carmel, Nabal's widow'. However, the Hebrew text could just as easily be translated 'Abigail wife of Nabal the Carmelite', perhaps implying a subtle censure. David's marriages create another contrast with his former visit. In 21.12 he is referred to as 'the king of the land'; now he has two wives of political import (see Levenson and Halpern 1980: 507-18). Moreover, a group of this size—full of men alienated from Saul—would no doubt be attractive to Achish as a fighting force or a raiding unit.

A brief notice is attached at the end of this paragraph: 'It was reported to Saul that David had fled to Gath, and he did not continue again to seek him (לְבַקְשׁוֹ)'. Once more (see 23.7) Saul is informed about David's actions, but an informant is not specified. It is also not clear *why* Saul thinks David has fled to Gath, such that he abandons pursuit. Does he think that David politically defected, and thus has a new cause with a new royal patron? Or does he think that David has forfeited his inheritance, and, resigned to his fate, has now become a theological exile, one who 'serves other gods'? Could it be that the Philistines—so often on the wrong end of David's sword—have given David a better offer? It is impossible to know exactly why Saul calls off the chase, but there is something of an incongruity here: David *could have been* far more dangerous to Saul when he was with the Philistines, for he could have gone into battle against him! This is, in one sense, the *worst* time to give up the pursuit. But even though Saul will no longer pursue David, he will 'seek' (בקשׁ) in the next chapter, and the object of his seeking there will be the witch of Endor.

27.5-7

Having lodged with Achish for an indeterminate length of time, David approaches the king of Gath with a proposal: 'If I have found grace in your eyes, let a place be given to me in one of the cities of the field, so I can live there. Why should your servant live in the royal city with you?' David's request is framed in a deferential manner, but a quick glance ahead in the chapter reveals an ulterior motive. While he sounds submissive (with expressions like 'your servant' and 'the royal city'), most readers agree that David wants to be away from the watchful eye of Achish, and plundering. David's speech in 27.5 is indicative of the way he will communicate with Achish from now on: flattering, with leading questions, and fraught with equivocation.

> On that day, Achish gave to him Ziklag. Therefore, Ziklag has belonged to the kings of Judah until this day. The length of time that David dwelt in the country of the Philistines was a year and four months. (27.6-7)

To this point in the chapter Achish has not been afforded any direct speech. There is no dialogue surrounding his 'gift' of Ziklag to David, so the reader is left to puzzle over the choice of the town, and any motive Achish may have. As far as location, Robert Bergen (1996: 261) situates Ziklag 'about twenty-five miles southwest of Gath in what was technically territory assigned to both the tribes of Simeon (cf. Josh 19.5) and Judah (cf. Josh 15.31). Though the city was allotted to the Israelites, they had never conquered it.' Ziklag certainly seems to be under Philistine control, otherwise it would not make much sense for Achish to assign it to David.

In terms of genre, the reader can immediately discern a different kind of speech accent in vv. 6-7. First, the notice about Ziklag being in possession of the kings of Judah 'until this day' stands out. Incorporating the work of J.P. Fokkelman, Robert Alter (1999: 169) notes, 'This seemingly technical geopolitical notice serves a function of historical foreshadowing, as Fokkelman observes: David, the Philistine vassal and fugitive from Saul, is destined to found a lasting dynasty, "the kings of Judah"'. Second, in terms of chronology we are give a fairly precise record of the time that David spends in Philistine territory. Of course, this notice adds a dash of historical verisimilitude to the account and, to pick up on Bergen's point above, illustrates how David is successful in 'conquest' unlike his Judahite forbearers. But in terms of irony, we note that David is about to accumulate a large amount of plunder—some of which he will send as 'gifts' to the people of Judah in chap. 30—that will facilitate him being crowned as the first 'king of Judah' before too long. By giving Ziklag to David, Achish sends him closer to (what will soon be) his own power base.

27.8-11

Having established himself at Ziklag, David now gets down to serious business: raiding various settlements. The Davidic practice involves attacking Geshurites, Girzites, and Amalekites, and commentators refer to these groups as hostile to Israel. Thus David, one could say, is multi-tasking. With one hand he is playing the pirate (and presumably giving some of the spoils to Achish), and with the other hand he is helping out southern Judah and Simeon. The most infamous group in recent memory is the Amalekites. The fact that the Amalekites are included in David's sorties glances back to Saul's failure (of course, there should not be any more Amalekites in 1 Samuel), and also looks ahead to chap. 30, where they themselves conduct a raid on Ziklag. Most striking, though, is the difference between David and Saul, since David takes of Amalekite plunder, and benefits from it: 'When David would strike the land, he would leave neither man nor woman alive, and he would take flocks, herds, donkeys, camels and cloths, and he would return and come to Achish.' The contrast with Saul's plunder experience could not be more stark.

The Hebrew text is problematic at the beginning of 27.10, but reconstruction of the Qumran text suggests that Achish asks the question, 'Against whom did you raid today?' (see Cross 2005: 93-94). Nonetheless, the reader is still not sure how—or why—Achish interrogates David with this question. Is he suspicious, or merely curious? If there are suspicions, they seem to be allayed by David's response, as he lies to Achish by asserting that his raids have been conducted against Judah and related southern regions friendly to Judah. Furthermore, there are no witnesses that can testify to the truth, as Graeme Auld (2003: 228) summarizes, 'No prisoners survive to become slaves and tell tales in this grim transaction; apparently neither the animals nor the clothing betrays its real origin to Achish'. Indeed, a great cloud of witnesses could supply an inconvenient truth to Achish, but David eliminates them: 'But neither man nor woman David would leave alive, to bring to Gath, saying, "Lest they report on us, saying, 'Thus David has done!'"' For the second time in as many chapters, David furnishes an unverifiable quotation. In 26.19, he quotes the line 'go, serve other gods', and here he supplies the hypothetical testimony of those who would have reported on his customary practice. Several scholars make a further point: David intends to kill all the males of Nabal's house in chap. 25, but he is no respecter of gender in chap. 27, as both male and female perish at David's hands.

27.12

Whatever Achish was thinking when he asked where David raided, he is sufficiently persuaded by the latter's response. In fact, Achish's credulity is expressed in a strong way by the narrator: 'Achish believed in David' (וַיַּאֲמֵן אָכִישׁ בְּדָוִד). In this expression, Victor Hamilton (2001: 283) notices an interesting intertext: 'The phrase "Achish trusted David" uses the same Hebrew construction (*'aman be*) as Gen. 15.6, "and he [Abram] believed the LORD". Abram put his faith in a God of truth. Achish put his faith in a master of duplicity.' Such duplicity, though, might be a two-edged sword. Robert Polzin (1993: 217) questions whether David's dissembling strategy is restricted to Gath:

> One continues to wonder whether David's dealings with various Israelites might not conceal similarly self-serving motives. However successfully David is shown escaping the clutches of Saul, he cannot escape the scrutiny of the reader. The story of David's rise to power is contrived as much against him as for him.

Such nuances, though, are surely not part of Achish's concern right now. For him, David is believable, and thus for the second time he is duped by the son of Jesse. Achish functions in the story as someone who really does not know how to read David, and who only hears his words in good faith. I daresay there are a few of Achish's hermeneutical descendants still floating around today.

The final line of the chapter gives a hint of Achish's agenda, as he discloses in an internal monologue: 'He utterly stinks among his people, in Israel, and he will be a slave for me forever!' Achish has not said a word of direct speech in this chapter, but now he speaks, and it is to himself. Nabal earlier said that many slaves are breaking away from their masters, and now Achish is convinced that David is his slave. In structural terms, several commentators note an envelope structure to the chapter, in that it opens with an internal slice of David's mind, and closes with the internal speech of Achish. There are a number of reasons as to why the chapter would conclude on such a note, but the key point would be that Achish is emerging as something of an alter ego of David himself. Achish is guilty of royal bifurcation, in that his court is skeptical of David while the king is gullible. David himself will suffer from similar lapses of judgment later in his career, and thus Achish is used to introduce themes in the story that will be appropriated as the narrative continues. Here David is the swindler, but later he will be the one hoodwinked.

1 SAMUEL 28

In the context of mounting war between Israel and the Philistines, the strangest episode in the entire book of 1 Samuel is set to unfold. After their final parting, Saul and David have been journeying on different roads. David traverses back to Achish, whereas Saul is about to battle the very same Philistines with whom David is ostensibly allied. The chapter begins with dialogue between David and Achish, but then switches to Saul, along with the reiteration by the narrator that the prophet Samuel is dead. The bulk of the chapter takes place during a dark night, as Saul travels to Endor to consult a necromancer after repeated attempts to ascertain the divine will have failed. Since the contributions of this chapter to the plot—notwithstanding the forecasts of doom that are surely realized in due course—are actually quite minimal, the analysis below will pay particular attention to the matters of characterization that arise during this episode. For Saul, this must represent the nadir of his fortunes, as his increasing desperation leads to the illegal trek to the witch's lair. As for the prophet Samuel, he was buried way back in chap. 25, yet he makes a very surprising appearance, and he is larger than life (after death). I am also interested in the presentation of the witch of Endor in this story, as there are some unexpected twists during her memorable appearance in this stretch of Deuteronomistic History. Commentators have long struggled with this haunting episode, as the specter of the long-dead Samuel is raised in the presence of the prostrate king. At the outset of my analysis it would be wise to consider Walter Brueggemann's (1990: 196) careful theological reflection on 1 Samuel 28 as a whole:

> This scene is filled pathos and anguish. Its vibrant narrative details have the potential of seducing us in our interpretation. The matter of summoning ghosts is an act sure to fascinate the religiously curious. A theological interpretation, however, must hold to a steady discipline against such fascination. The narrative has no real interest in the summoning of spirits or in the role or capacity of the woman. The speech of Samuel keeps the narrative thoroughly and insistently Yahwistic. It is Yahweh and Samuel with whom Saul must come to terms. The narrative invites reflection on the vocation of royal power in a context where God's singular power will not be mocked. To diffuse the narrative into a pluralism in which other powers have force or significance is

to misread the story and diminish its voice for our own demanding religious situation. The narrative is a reflection on how hard and dangerous is the single voice to which Saul failed to give heed.

28.1-2

The opening verses of this chapter recount a conversation between Achish and David. A quick survey of major commentaries indicates that some scholars prefer to include 28.1-2 with the preceding chapter. Of course there are some good reasons for such inclusion: we are dealing with the same characters, engaged in similar dialogue, and there are natural points of connection and development between chap. 27 and 28.1-2. Having said that, there are other reasons to infer that 28.1-2 signals a new narrative unit. For one, it seems that some time has elapsed due to the temporal marker 'In those days' (וַיְהִי בַּיָּמִים הָהֵם) at the outset. As we will see, conflict between Israel and the Philistines is brewing, and the next few chapters will exhibit some chronological displacement as the narrative switches back and forth from David to Saul. Further, the first six verses of chap. 28 illustrate something of a contrast between the two kings, Saul and Achish. While Achish is plotting his battle strategy, Saul is full of fear and desperately seeking supernatural signs. The reader will also see the motif of 'dissembling' continue in chap. 28. Not only does David continue to deceive Achish, but Saul himself will disguise himself with other raiment. The object of Saul's deception, however, is less clear.

At the beginning of the chapter, the Philistines are gathering their camp for battle, and Achish approaches David with an apparent directive: 'You *know* that with me you will march into the camp—you and your men'. Since Achish believes David when he claims to have been raiding in Judah and allied settlements, Achish now issues a call of duty to his 'forever slave' (27.12). David's rejoinder merits careful attention: 'Therefore you will know what your servant will do!' On the one hand, David's words can be construed as a pledge of allegiance to Achish and his cause. But on the other hand, there is yet again a measure of equivocation in the language. The reader certainly knows what David has been doing: raiding non-Judahite villages, and lying to Achish. Whether David is planning to destroy the Philistines from within their own camp cannot be determined.

The conversation between Achish and David bears some resemblance to the earlier transactions between Saul and David (see 18.17-27), replete with posturing and masked agendas. I assume that Achish is not calling David's bluff with his reply: 'Therefore I will appoint you as the keeper of my head forever!' Achish is seduced once more by David's language, and buys the pretence of loyalty. Of course, Achish's reply misses something else as well. Though the NRSV translates David's appointment as 'bodyguard', the more literal rendering 'keeper of my head' (שֹׁמֵר לְרֹאשִׁי) should at least be considered, not least because David has kept other Philistine heads before. One recalls David carrying the head of Goliath from Gath in chap. 17—a point that seems now lost on Achish. Through this reply, as Robert Gordon (1986: 193) quips, 'Achish himself comes dangerously near to unconscious irony'.

28.3

There is a chronological interruption at this point in the narrative. By means of a flashback, the reader is told two things: one has already been reported in chap. 25 (the death of Samuel), but the other is new information (Saul's expulsion of the necromancers). The Hebrew syntax suggests that both should be rendered as pluperfects: 'Now Samuel had died, and all Israel lamented for him, and they buried him in Ramah, in his city. Now Saul had turned aside the mediums and the spiritists from the land.' We recall that the first notice of Samuel's death (25.1) precedes an episode where David hears about his future from a prudent woman. Now the second time there is a notice about Samuel's death, Saul will hear a message about his future by means of medium. As Peter Miscall (1986: 167) summarizes, 'Saul's dealings with a knowledgeable woman are to have a radically different outcome from David's'. There certainly is some literary currency in the repetition of Samuel's death notice here in chap. 28 that coincides with the reader (belatedly) being informed that at some previous time Saul expelled witches and warlocks: the flashback becomes an instrument of foreshadowing.

No motivation is stated for Saul's actions, but a number of texts in the Torah that address issues of the occult are often invoked by commentators. Among these, a suggestive intertext is Deut. 18.11, 'Let no one be found among you who causes his son or daughter to pass through the fire, or who practices divination, soothsaying, auguries, sorcery, casting spells, or makes inquiry of a ghost (שֹׁאֵל אוֹב), spirit, or seeks the dead'. It is conceivable that Saul purges necromancy from the land out of zeal for orthodoxy. We have seen examples of Saul's cultic activity before, and he appears upright in this regard (e.g. chap. 14). Glancing further ahead in the story, a similar expulsion will be sponsored by Josiah (2 Kgs 23.24). But for Saul in 1 Samuel 28, the whole affair is threatening to lapse into a bad irony: having expelled the necromancers, he is now on the threshold of violating his own ban.

28.4-7

After the flashbacks, we return to the main storyline of battle preparations. Further specifics about geography are given, as the Philistines gather their camp and assemble at Shunem. Last mentioned in Josh. 19.18, Shunem is a village in the northern tribe of Issachar, in the vicinity of Jezreel. In response to what apparently is a Philistine initiative, Saul pitches his camp at Gilboa.

In contrast to Shunem, Gilboa is a site *not* mentioned in Joshua—this is the first mention of the place. In fact, the only times Gilboa is ever mentioned in the Hebrew Bible is in connection with Saul's last fall.

Following the locations of the respective armies, the narrative focus shifts to Saul's internal perspective, as he 'sees' the camp of the Philistines and 'his heart trembled greatly'. It has been a while since Saul is described a fearful; not since chap. 18, where he is afraid of David. Here Saul sees the camp of the Philistines—a camp that may well include David—and along with a trembling heart he is also manifesting some cultic anxiety: 'And Saul asked of the LORD, and the LORD did not answer him, even by dreams, even by Urim, even by the prophets'. There is no specific reason stated as to why Saul is inquiring, or indeed, what he is asking. The context of battle with the Philistines reminds the reader about the technological upper hand that they enjoy with respect to Israel (see 13.19-21). Yet in chap. 13, Saul is never the object of the verb 'fear'. Saul has his faults, but he never succumbs to fear until after he is rejected by Samuel. Now, because of a stressful situation, Saul asks of the LORD (וַיִּשְׁאַל שָׁאוּל בַּיהוָה) and the wordplay should be noted: Saul's name means 'asked', but he asks of the LORD who does not answer. Indeed, unanswered questions follow Saul throughout his career (see Craig 1994: 221-39). One also recalls the divine silent treatment of chap. 14. At least Saul had the service of the Elide priests there. Now, Saul inquires of the Urim, and surely it would have helped Saul's cause had he not exterminated all the priests at Nob. No wonder such inquiry is proving fruitless. Like chap. 3, the word of the LORD is rare in these days.

Through all this inquiring, Saul certainly is not 'doing what his hand finds to do'. The reader is drawn into a comparison of Saul and Achish. Achish makes David a bodyguard, whereas Saul has debarred his former armor-bearer; Achish makes preparation for battle by enlisting David and his men, whereas Saul seeks signs and signals. At the same time, even the most vitriolic anti-Saul critic has to admit that this is a sad moment for Israel's first king. Notwithstanding the prior removal of witches and warlocks from the land, Saul seeks a ghost-wife. Desperate times lead to these desperate measures of illegal consultation. But the reader will certainly wonder how it is possible to find a witch if all of them have been banished. Does Saul suspect that occult arts are still practiced, despite his apparent efforts to eliminate them? The king's imperative to his servants—commanding them to find a woman who is a medium—is immediately met with the servants' response, stating matter-of-factly that such a woman is to be found in Endor. Of course, the servants are *not* supposed to know this, since Saul has prohibited all such practitioners. But this issue is not raised. Just as in chap. 16, where Saul's servants have an answer for Saul's problem of torment by the evil spirit, so they have a solution here for their master's oracular woes.

28.8
Unluckily for Saul, Endor is inconveniently situated. Most scholars position Endor several miles northeast of Shunem, meaning that the medium's village is located *behind* enemy lines. Thus any visit would be a dangerous one; that Saul is willing to take the risk says a great deal about his desperation. Endor's location may help explain Saul's unprecedented actions: 'And Saul disguised himself, and dressed in other clothes'. As one recalls, Saul is a head taller than all the other Israelites (9.2), so any costume would need to be particularly creative. No doubt there are a number of practical reasons why Saul dons a disguise, such as concealing himself from the Philistines (near whose ranks he must traverse) or even hiding from his own people (lest they spot him en route to Endor and start asking uncomfortable questions). It is also possible that he is desirous to conceal himself from the medium, lest she refuse to co-operate out of fear.

There is a symbolic dimension to Saul's disguise as well. When Saul removes his (royal) garments and replaces them with 'other clothes', the reader recalls other instances where clothing has marked a pivotal moment in Saul's career. As Robert Alter (1999: 173) summarizes, 'his disguise also is the penultimate instance of the motif of royal divestment. As we have seen, clothing is associated with Saul's kingship—the torn or cut garment is the tearing of his kingship, and among the ecstatics surrounding Samuel, Saul stripped himself naked. Now, in an unwitting symbolic gesture, he divests himself of his royal garments before going to learn of his own impending death'. In the present context, Saul voluntarily lays aside his kingship raiment in pursuit of the occult, but in the wider context of Israel's monarchic history, Saul is not the only king to undress, as it were. Richard Coggins (1991: 55-62) notes that other royal figures also don a disguise—including the wife of Jeroboam, Ahab, and Josiah (in Chronicles)—and for all of them, 'God's will is conveyed in a form which is liable to be quite unacceptable to the one seeking it'. For later royal figures, the disguise is ultimately ineffective; Saul will shortly be the prototype.

The spatial setting for the rest of the episode is inside the witch's house, but the temporal setting is also worth noting, as Saul sets out (along with two men) after darkness falls. One of the more poignant interpreters of this chapter in Saul's life is Elie Wiesel. It is particularly fitting that Wiesel (2003: 136-37) brings out the temporal setting of *night* in his reading of this episode. 'Three men', he writes, 'walk quietly in the night: the king and his bodyguards, silent shadows moving breathlessly so as not to make a sound. The enemy, powerful and bent on vengeance, has established a camp nearby, at Shunem. To reach Ein-Dor, a tiny village in the foothills of Harei-ephraim, they must follow a narrow path bordering on the Philistine encampment.' By so focusing on this journey by stealth, Wiesel foregrounds the ambience of the nocturnal in this episode. Over the course of his career, one recalls that Saul often does things under the cover of darkness; here, the temporal setting symbolizes a lack of spiritual perception, just like the nearly blind Eli in chaps. 3 and 4.

Face to face with the witch in Endor, Saul begins this nefarious interview with an imperative: he instructs the woman to use divination (קסם) and call up a particular person whom he will specify. One senses that Saul's opening remark is slightly cautious, as though he is feeling out the woman, so to speak. Alternatively, maybe Saul is hesitant to invoke the prophet's name too early in the negotiation phase, lest the medium refuse to comply. Saul's imperative also includes the term 'ghost' (אוֹב). Some scholars surmise that the word 'ancestor' (אָב) is a related term, indicating that an ancestral figure is being summoned. The Hebrew word is also related to the noun 'skin-bottle', perhaps revealing the divination instrument used by the medium. On this point, Graeme Auld (2003: 228) has a useful discussion:

> The implement itself may have been a 'bottle' made of skin or a bladder—at least the word is identical to the one Elihu uses when he is bursting to speak, like a new bottle ready to spill its wine (Job 32.19). In disguise Saul asks her to use her 'bottle' to 'divine' for him—and the last time we met that word in Samuel was when the Philistines needed advice about how to handle Yahweh's ark (6.2). Saul is desperately using Philistine means to cope with his Philistine foe.

The most recent occasion when Saul has heard the word 'divination' (קסם) is at 15.23, where he is told 'rebellion is like the sin of divination'. Ironically enough, it is the prophet Samuel who utters these words, and, as we will see, it is Samuel himself whom Saul seeks through the bottle of divination.

28.9-11

Before agreeing to undertake any divination, the woman issues a caveat: 'Behold, *you* know what Saul has done, how he cut off the mediums and spiritists from the land! So why are you laying a snare for my life, to cause my death?' On the surface, Saul has made a fairly straightforward—if slightly guarded—request, in the context of the witch's occupation and the expected mode of business transaction. But the witch's reply is equally circumspect, and she draws attention to the risks of her work during Saul's administration. This risk factor is highlighted by a particular use of language. Pamela Reis (2002: 154) notices that the narrator reports Saul 'turning aside' (הֵסִיר) necromancers from the land, whereas the witch employs the more lethal verb 'cut off' (הִכְרִית) in her own account. Along with image of 'laying a trap to bring about death', the witch stresses the more violent side of the equation. On the one hand, the woman might be suspicious of this late-night visitor, whose stature is head and shoulders above his companions. On the other hand, the witch too might be feeling out her client. If so, then her words have a great deal of dramatic irony, since she is addressing none other than Saul himself.

From Saul's vantage point, the witch evidently has sufficient concerns, and he proceeds to allay such concerns by means of an oath sworn in the name of the LORD: 'As the LORD lives, no guilt will encounter you in this matter'. Thus Saul reassures the medium by swearing an oath by the divine name—incidentally, this is the same God who outlaws necromancy (in both Leviticus and Deuteronomy) and who has not 'answered' Saul, which brings him to the witch's hovel in the first place. As the LORD lives, Saul swears, the woman will not be punished for summoning the dead.

Presumably set at ease by the oath, the medium asks who Saul wants 'brought up'. While this query from the witch might be expected, Saul's choice is surprising: he wants Samuel brought up. Why, of all people, does Saul want Samuel? Over the course of the narrative, Samuel has rarely had any good news for Saul, but only doom and gloom. On a structural level, I can appreciate Bruce Birch's (1998: 1182) remark: 'the fates of Samuel and Saul have been intertwined from the beginning. Even Samuel's birth story (chapter 1) was filled with allusions to Saul's name. It seems only fitting that the two should appear together at the end.' Still, it is hard to know exactly why Saul is so keen to communicate with Samuel—by means of a witch, no less—since hitherto the prophet has not been a source of much practical advice for Israel's first monarch. According Elie Wiesel's (2003: 138-39) reading, there is a more deep-seated psychological angle captured at this narrative juncture:

> Could it be that he [Saul] came to Samuel fully aware of the futility of his move? Could it be that he knew that it was for nothing—that nothing could or would change after their meeting? Is it possible that he came to Ein-Dor in order to be defeated once more? To be humiliated again? To attract Samuel's anger and the old witch's pity? To illustrate his downfall and accelerate its pace? And bring to a climax the process of self-destruction?

It must be a sign of extreme desperation if Saul *has* to summon Samuel in this his (virtual) last hour. Thus, the one who warns Saul that rebellion is like the sin of divination in 15.23 now himself becomes the object of divination, as Saul seeks to be part of a dead poet's society.

28.12-14

There have been a few surprising twists and turns already in this chapter, but the strangest event is the woman's moment of recognition: 'And the woman saw Samuel, and she cried out in a loud voice, and the woman said to Saul, saying, "Why have you deceived me? You are Saul!"' I find it utterly baffling how the woman perceives Samuel the prophet, and then immediately is able to identify Saul. For Kyle McCarter (1980: 481), the confusion is a result of some redactional malfunction, and a few earlier scholars had a similar appraisal. One can appreciate that strange things are happening in this episode, but source-critical solutions do not seem overly convincing in this stretch of text. After many years of studying these questions, Antony Campbell (2003: 282) tersely concludes that textual emendation 'does not help', and Campbell confesses that he has yet to discover any learned suggestions that illuminate these nocturnal mysteries. Somehow, Saul's disguise is rendered superfluous with a mere glimpse of the prophet, and educes a loud cry from the witch (who I assume is well-versed in her trade, yet is genuinely startled here). If the witch is troubled, then scholars can be forgiven for having the same reaction. My guess is that the witch's initial reaction indicates that the prophet is the one who will carry the day (or the night, in this case), and the first hint that the interview will not go well for Saul.

After seeing Samuel, the witch accuses her client of deceit. This is a correct diagnosis: the witch is certainly correct about Saul's intentions, and she now sees through the disguise. Further, the witch's charge of deception intersects with earlier moments in the story. Robert Polzin (1993: 270-71) observes that Saul himself makes an almost identical accusation in chap. 19, when he demands of his daughter, 'Why have you deceived me?' In both cases, clothing is the instrument of deception: Michal uses clothing (בגד) to deceive Saul's agents, and now Saul uses other clothing (בגדים) to mislead the witch. As Polzin points out, the root for 'treachery' (בגד) is thus exploited by means of the clothing in both episodes. This instance of symmetry between chaps. 19 and 28 serves as a 'measure for measure' moment in the king's life, and illustrates how far the mighty king is about to fall. Clothing and *teraphim* are used by Michal to deceive Saul, but when Saul tries to deceive with clothing (in the context of divination) he is categorically unsuccessful.

Despite Saul's earlier oath of amnesty, the witch appears to be fearing for her life. It is not incidental, therefore, that 'the king' speaks the next words. Indeed, this is the first and only time in this chapter that the narrator refers to Saul as king; thus, when he says 'do not fear' to the witch of Endor, we assume it carries the weight and assurances of his royal office. After commanding the woman not to fear, Saul asks her what she sees, to which she reports: 'I see gods (אֱלֹהִים), ascending from the earth'. In her use of the term 'gods', the witch is taking what seems to be the party line, as Isa. 8.19-20 might illustrate: 'Now if people say to you, "Consult the ghosts and the familiar spirits that chirp and mutter; should not a people consult their gods, the dead on behalf of the living, for teaching and for instruction?" Surely, those who speak like this will have no dawn!' (NRSV). Whether or not Saul is encouraged by this preliminary report is not stated, but nevertheless he presses for further details by asking 'What is his outline?' If the woman is a bit vague when she says 'gods', she is far more specific in describing the appearance of the figure she sees: 'An old man is ascending, wrapped in a robe (מְעִיל)'. Of any garment that distinguishes the prophet Samuel, it is surely his robe. We recall that the robe has marked Samuel from an early point in his career, as his mother Hannah would make him a 'little robe' and deliver it to him every year in Shiloh. Most dramatically, Saul (accidentally) tears Samuel's robe in chap. 15, which the prophet immediately transforms into a ripping illustration of how the kingdom has been torn from Saul. The witch's description of an old man wrapped up in a robe conjures up an image of Saul's regal loss, and Samuel's words of rejection.

Moreover, when the woman sees the robe, she provides the reader with a symbolic insight. As Robert Polzin (1993: 218) summarizes,

> In this shadowy outline the reader sees an outline of the entire book of 1 Samuel: Samuel's birth and death encompass the book and express its central topic, the birth and death of kingship in Israel. Nothing clothes Samuel and Saul alike in kingship better than the robes they wear throughout the book.

One guesses, therefore, that Samuel is appropriately attired for the occasion, and by wearing his (ripped) robe, the reader suspects that once more Samuel enters the narrative stage for judgment. Saul seems to infer the same thing: 'And Saul knew that he was Samuel, and he bowed down—face to the ground—and did obeisance'. Thus, for a second time in his ill-starred tenure, Saul is disrobed and prostrate before Samuel, bringing to mind the ecstatic affair at the end of chap. 19. While Saul has abandoned his royal robe for the journey to Endor, Samuel refuses to relinquish the robe of his authority, despite the fact that he has been dead for quite some time now.

28.15-19

Although dressed for the occasion, Samuel is not in the best of humor, and post-mortem existence has evidently not tempered his general state of irritation with his former protégé. Even the most casual hearing of his question to Saul ('Why have you agitated me, to bring me up?') reveals that his displeasure is starkly apparent. One hopes that this is a sincere request for information, because otherwise—that is, if it is a rhetorical question—then the prophet might be guilty of humiliating his floundering protégé. Saul understands the question as a request for information, which he duly provides. He explains that his stress is great because of the Philistine offensive, and God has not answered through two forms of inquiry, prophets or dreams. And so, Saul concludes, he has summoned Samuel for advice, to 'cause him to know' what to do.

Saul's speech can be heard in a couple of different ways. On the one hand, he certainly puts his own spin on the affair. Saul refrains from mentioning the 'Urim' mode of divine inquiry, perhaps to avoid any unpleasant questions about Nob's fate. Second, as Kenneth Craig points out, Saul implies that divine silence is a rather new phenomenon, whereas the reader has been aware since chap. 14 that Saul has received the silent treatment from God. Craig adds that Saul also is selective in his use of language. He earlier tells the witch to 'bring someone up' (עלה) but in the presence of Samuel he softens the illegality by using the verb 'call' (קרא)—'I have called you'. Craig (1994: 233) concludes that this shift in verbs 'underscores once again the duplicity of his actions. Just as he must change clothes, he must also change words when he finds himself in Samuel's presence.'

On the other hand, the speech must evoke some pity, as Saul sounds as desperate as he must look. Elie Wiesel (2003: 137) paraphrases Saul's words as follows:

> 'I need you', says the unhappy king. 'I need help. I am going to war tomorrow without knowing whether God is with me or against me. I am afraid. Help me; you can, you alone can. Tell me God's will—only you can do that since God refuses to speak to me or even notice my presence. It is as though I don't exist for Him. You, the prophet and defender of God's first king, you must come to my aid.'

For Wiesel, Saul's discourse is a speech that merits some compassion from the prophet. But Samuel, having been unseasonably disturbed, is not moved by Saul's words, as is evident from his lengthy response:

> Samuel said, 'So why are you asking me? The LORD has turned away from you and has become your enemy. The LORD has done for himself just as he spoke by my hand: the LORD has ripped the kingdom from your hand and given it to your friend, to David! Inasmuch as you did not listen to the voice of the LORD and did not execute his fierce wrath against Amalek, therefore this thing the LORD has done to you today. And the LORD will give Israel—with you—into the hand of the Philistines, and tomorrow you and your sons will be with me. Even the camp of Israel the LORD will give into the hand of the Philistines.'

If Saul was hoping for some sympathy from Samuel, he badly miscalculates. Similarly, if the scholarly reader is hoping to get some insight on the murky mysteries of existence in Sheol, any hopes are dashed with Samuel's opening wordplay—'Why do you ask (שאל) me?'—punning once more on Saul's name. This is not a warm welcome from the prophet, and his news gets worse, asserting that God has become Saul's enemy. Samuel emphasizes his own prophetic role, and summarizes Saul's career by alluding to one incident: the ripped robe. There is a unique twist, though. While Samuel reiterates the familiar 'succession by friend/neighbor' theme, the identity of the successor was never identified. Here, for the first time, Samuel explicitly mentions the name 'David' to Saul. The reason for this succession by David, as Samuel explains, is because of the Amalekite fiasco of chap. 15. Surprisingly, there is no word of Saul's faulty sacrifice in chap. 13, the first moment where the prophet brings a stinging word of rejection. Of course, it could be that the Amalekite affair is simply mentioned as a summary of Saul's failed reign. Alternatively, Samuel stresses the Amalekite debacle because Saul's culpability is less ambiguous than in chap. 13. But, of course, this would mean that Samuel—much like Saul—is putting his own spin on things in this dialogue at Endor.

Speaking of condemnation, a reader may have thought that Samuel would rebuke Saul for violating Torah, but rather than indicting the king for the shady business of trafficking with the dead, Samuel is angry for being 'agitated'. Then again, maybe such condemnation is self-evident and hardly needs to be mentioned. This might be why Samuel aims for an efficient condemnation: massive casualties will be inflicted on Israel, and *tomorrow* Saul will die. There is nothing vague or hazy about this—Saul's hope is extinguished. The announcement of Saul's imminent death—along with his sons—aligns with earlier narrative events. Peter Miscall (1986: 170) points out that Saul and his sons will die on the same day just like Eli and his sons died on the same day earlier in the story (chap. 4). This suggests that Eli's backward fall (from his throne) anticipates the fall of Saul, and the demise of both their houses. Samuel's grave words transport the reader back to the future, as the two dynastic houses of Saul and Eli will play no part in Israel's long-term leadership.

It is difficult for the reader to know how best to respond to the prophet's severity here. In general terms, commentators are divided. Some state that Saul—the disobedient sinner—gets exactly what he deserves, while other are more sympathetic, and feel that Samuel might have been more helpful to Israel's first king during what must be a very trying time. Elie Wiesel (2003: 137-38) asks a series of mediating questions: 'It is impossible for a student of biblical literature not to feel shock: how could a prophet of the God of Israel treat another human being so heartlessly, especially when that person is in such distress? Even if his nocturnal visitor were not a king, even if he had not waged heroic battles on behalf of his people, even if he had not brought honor and security to the land of Israel, how could God's messenger inflict such pain on Saul in his darkest hour?' Irrespective of one's interpretation, these are Samuel's words in the story, and at the very least, one can be sure that Saul is not comforted by this dire forecast. In the end, Saul has not found what he was looking for when summoning Samuel through the witch of Endor. Saul wanted advice for what do, but Samuel tells him only what will soon take place. Tomorrow, Samuel says, Saul will be with him.

One can hardly imagine a worse fate for Saul than the prospect of spending an eternal length of time with Samuel.

28.20-22

With uncommon celerity, Saul falls down 'to the fullness of his height' as Samuel's speech comes to an end. Saul's height is the distinguishing characteristic by which he is first introduced in chap. 9, and it physically sets him apart—so the reader thinks—as a king who can lead his nation into battle. Now, Saul's height marks how far he has fallen, as he hears the news about an impending battle with the Philistines, a battle from which he will not return. Saul's fall here in chap. 28 functions as a(n) (un)dress(ed) rehearsal for his fall on the next day.

Not only does Saul collapse because he is filled with fear, but also because he is famished: 'Moreover, strength was not left in him, for he did not eat all that day or all that night'. It should not really come as a shock when the reader belatedly discovers that Saul has been fasting and thus is without strength, since ritual blunders have followed him ever since the ill-fated *rendezvous* with Samuel at Gilgal in chap. 13. The narrative purpose for the delay in reporting Saul's fast, I suppose, is to give us one more example of Saul's cultic dysfunctionality; the consultation in Endor was doomed from the start, just like Saul's other fasts and sacrifices have been without efficacy. Face down on the floor, Saul does not even see Samuel exit the narrative stage, as the prophet once more bids the world farewell.

However, the departure of Samuel opens the door for another character to take center stage. With Saul prostrate in her house, the witch approaches him. Several commentators feel that the witch leaves the room during the transaction between Saul and Samuel, and only now returns. I am inclined to suggest the opposite: based on her words, the woman has been privy to the entire exchange between dead prophet and (soon to be dead) king, and thus she is acquainted with Saul's dreadful expectations. But before she speaks, we are given her perception of the king, as she sees 'that he was greatly disturbed' (כִּי־נִבְהַל מְאֹד). The phrase could also be translated 'he was thrown into a great panic'. The last time the rare verb בהל occurs in the Deuteronomistic History is Judg. 20.41, where the tribe of Benjamin see that the tide of battle has turned against them. Their reaction to this disastrous turn of events is the same verb בהל, 'they are thrown into a panic'. Here in 1 Samuel 28, a later member of the tribe of Benjamin is also thrown into a panic as he realizes how badly things have turned against him.

> Behold, your maidservant listened to your voice, and I set my life in my hands, and I listened to your words that you spoke to me. So now, please listen—even you—to the voice of your maidservant, and I will set before you a morsel of bread to eat. It will give strength for you, because you will go on the journey.

The medium's message for the fallen king begins with a reminder of the risk she took by obeying Saul's voice, and now she implores him to return the favor by listening to her voice. It is hard to miss the connection with Samuel's speech above: Saul did not 'listen' and now he is on the verge of death. As Kenneth Craig (1994: 235) summarizes,

> The woman who is obedient to the king sounds an ironic note, and the repetition is certainly not accidental. The king, whose not listening to the Lord has already been an issue at Gilgal (13.13), reinforced subsequently in the Amalekite incident (chap. 15), is now not even obeying his own edict (28.3)!

The ironic intertextual links do not stop here, as several commentators observe. When the medium offers Saul 'a morsel of bread' (פַּת־לֶחֶם), there is an echo of another prophetic denunciation: in chap. 2, the man of God forecasts that the house of Eli will be reduced to begging for 'a morsel of bread' (פַּת־לָחֶם). Thus Eli's last descendant and Saul are pictured as needing a last meal to stay alive just long enough to bring fulfillment of the prophetic word spoken against both rejected houses.

The medium's desire to serve the last meal to Israel's first king has piqued the curiosity of a number of scholars, who speculate on her motives. When she tells Saul this handmaiden's tale, is she motivated by disinterested compassion, or is she a life-saving opportunist? In my view, the key line is her last, when she says that she will set food before Saul so he can eat, and then walk 'on the journey'. Having heard Samuel's words (and indeed, witnessed Saul's horizontal response), the medium of Endor knows full well that the bell tolls for Saul. That Saul is offered a crust of bread by an illegal practitioner of the dark arts—a character drawn with surprising sympathy, given her heterodoxy—is a sad way to begin his final journey.

28.23-25

Saul initially refuses the medium's hospitality, and speaks his last words of the chapter: 'I will not eat'. Yet, after repeated urges from the woman and the two members of his constabulary who attend him, Saul wordlessly succumbs: he listens to their voice, and rises from the ground to sit on the bed. Saul's stubborn resistance—and eventual relenting—have a parallel of sorts in chap. 15. At least, that is how Saul presents the matter. In chap. 15 he tells Samuel that he feared the people 'and listened to their voice'. Here in chap. 28, though weary and terrified, he listens perhaps to the voice of reason and accepts the nourishment. However, it is rather more than a 'morsel of bread' that the woman prepares:

> Now the woman had a fattened calf in the house. She hurried, and sacrificed it. And she took flour and kneaded it, and baked unleavened bread. She brought it near Saul and his servants. They ate, and arose, and walked into the night.

Saul's last supper is as close to a royal meal as can be expected, given the circumstances. I am following Pamela Reis in translating the term 'sacrifice' (זבח) rather than 'slaughter' as in the NRSV, since it catches the nuance that has been a subtext of the entire exchange with Samuel: a (faulty) sacrifice drives Saul to rejected despair in the first place, and now an aberrant sacrifice is his last meal. One recalls Saul's coronation dinner in chap. 9, when the cook says 'Eat, for it has been kept safe for you until this appointed hour'. We could guess that the medium's portion carries the same label, and along with the unleavened bread, the feast becomes a pale parody of a Passover celebration. But at the same time there may be some hints of divine grace: in the midst of Saul darkest hour, God will yet be faithful to the unwise Israelites who demanded 'Give us a king!' Having been once more rejected by the prophet who anoints him, Saul's final banquet is prepared by a witch, yet it is a meal—replete with unleavened bread—that evokes memories of the greatest moment in Israel's story so far, the exodus from Egypt.

There is an envelope structure to this episode: it begins with Saul's journey into the night, and ends with the night. This structure dovetails with Saul's whole hapless career as Israel's first king. Peter Miscall puts it this way: 'As seeking and eating, particularly at night, marked Saul's beginning, they mark his end'. For all intents and purposes, Saul has asked his last question, and finally received an answer. If the reader is wondering why on earth such a strange chapter would be included in the Deuteronomistic History, then surely the words of Samuel and the response of Saul provide the clues. This chapter graphically illustrates the ultimate sterility of divination, a practice that cannot reveal anything new but only point to the veracity of the prophetic word. As the witch serves the last meal, the reader is given a taste of an enduring truth: necromancy is a self-consuming artifact, while the prophetic word provides sustenance beyond the grave.

Saul's two falls in this chapter certainly prepare the reader for one final collapse on the slopes of Mt Gilboa. As Julius Wellhausen described many years ago in his *Prolegomena*, 'No proof is wanted to show that this is the prophetic shadow cast before the fall of Saul in his last fight with the Philistines. His turning to the witch to call up to him the departed Samuel suggests in the most powerful way his condition of God-forsakenness since Samuel turned away from him.' At the end of the chap. 28, Saul departs into the same darkness from whence he came; none the wiser, but far more acquainted with grief.

1 Samuel 29

After all the nocturnal strangeness of Endor, the reader is now given a flashback to an earlier day, in the spatial setting of the Philistine camp as they prepare to engage Israel in battle. Following a bad night in the coven, this short chapter comes as something of a comic relief. The purpose of the chapter is straightforward enough: while Saul is hearing news about the imminent battle by means of divination, David also hears news that determines his future with respect to the same battle, courtesy of the Philistine commanders who are deeply skeptical of the man's loyalties. The chapter is constructed as a series of efficient dialogues between the various characters (David, Achish, and the Philistine captains), and the entire episode can easily be imagined as having transpired within an hour of real time. Although David said to Achish 'Now you will see what your servant will do' in 28.2, this chapter actually provides the reasons why David will not do anything for Achish, as it were. Because of 1 Samuel 28, the reader knows that Saul *will* be going to battle; because of 1 Samuel 29, the readers knows that David *will not* be present on the occasion.

29.1-3

The chapter opens with the Philistines gathering their forces together at Aphek, while Israel is camping by the spring in Jezreel. As we recall, the Philistines have gathered at Aphek earlier in 1 Samuel 4. Near the end of Eli's ill-fated tenure, the Philistines muster their troops at Aphek, and are successful in the battle that eventually results in the loss of the ark and Eli's two sons, Hophni and Phinehas. In the aftermath of the battle that begins with a muster at Aphek in chap. 4, the ark is taken to an idolatrous temple of Ashdod. Similarly, in the aftermath of the battle that begins with a muster at Aphek in chap. 29, the corpse of Israel's first king is going to be taken to an idolatrous temple of Beth-shan. Just as a gathering at Aphek marks the beginning of the end for Eli—and the fulfillment of the prophetic word spoken against his house—Saul will have a not dissimilar experience.

The Philistine 'overlords' (סַרְנֵי פְלִשְׁתִּים) have not made an appearance in the narrative since chap. 7. These political heavyweights now return to lead the procession of troops, while Achish is marching at the back of line along with David (the recently appointed 'keeper of his head') and his men. This otherwise serene tableau is interrupted with some internal dialogue among the Philistine senior leadership, as the presence of David and his men elicit disparate reactions. Notably, it is the military commanders (as opposed to the political overlords) who entertain some misgivings: 'What are these Hebrews?' My guess is that the military captains are less than thrilled with Achish's motley crew; just as David created tension when he first enters Gath (when his beard was covered with spittle and the doors were scratched), so the same tension resurfaces here in the battle preparations.

During his Philistine sojourn, David has been sailing very near the wind, as a mariner might put it. But he has secured the trust of Achish, who now leaps to his bodyguard's defense: 'Is this not David, the servant of Saul king of Israel, who has been with me these days or these years? I have not found anything in him from the day he fell in with him until now!' Achish's argument is certainly passionate enough, but it lacks something on the tactical side. For one, referring to David as the 'servant of Saul' may not be the wisest appellation under the circumstances, and alluding to David's loyalty 'since he has been a traitor' could also be ill-advised. Achish is certainly not above using a bit of hyperbole: he claims that David has been with him for 'years' when in fact the reader knows that the time is closer to one year and four months (27.7). One wonders why Achish does not opt for honesty with his Philistine peers, and explain that David has been raiding villages in Judah (so he thinks) and thus has made himself odious. But then, perhaps Achish is not sharing the wealth with his colleagues, and so avoids the raiding issue altogether.

29.4-5

Achish's apology for David only succeeds in generating anger from the military leaders, as evidenced by the comparative size of their two speeches. Their first question (in Hebrew) has only three words (מָה הָעִבְרִים הָאֵלֶּה, 'What are these Hebrews?'), whereas their speech in vv. 4-5 is a lengthy and vociferous outpouring. The anger of the military commanders initially is conveyed through an imperative: 'Make the man return, that he might return to his place, where you assigned him there'. There is an allusion to Ziklag—the place that Achish has apportioned for David—although there are no further hints of whether it is generally known about David's activities there. Furthermore, the military commanders insist that David is *not* to accompany them on this campaign: 'He will not go down with us into battle, so that he may not be an adversary against us in the battle'. Their fear is that David is a double agent of sorts, and in the thick of battle will become a 'satan' (שָׂטָן, the term I have translated 'adversary'). It is becoming obvious that the military captains view David as a miscreant, and any about-turn would actually serve to reconcile him with his master (Saul): 'How can this one make himself acceptable to his master? Would it not be by heads of these men?' In light of David's previous Philistine activity, there is a bit of humor here: the Philistine captains are suggesting that by the heads of these men David might return to his master's favor, just as he secured his master's daughter by means of their foreskins.

At the outset of chap. 27, David thought 'One of these days I will perish at the hands of Saul', and this rationale drives him (back) to Achish. But the Philistine commanders are not the least bit convinced. They are sensing rascality. Rather than a Trojan horse, perhaps they think David is like another 'ark', who will *internally* damage them. Consequently, the capstone of their argument is David's past reputation: 'Is this not David, of whom they answer in their dances, "Saul has struck his thousands / David his ten thousands"?' The women who first sang these lyrics in chap. 18 should be getting international royalties, as this is the second time the song is quoted in Philistine ranks. If the military captains are arguing that David is a leopard who cannot quite change his spots, then they quote these lyrics to remind Achish of David's previous triumph over another Gathite. It is the lyrics of this song that first drive a wedge between Saul and David back in chap. 18; now the song *continues* to keep them apart (at a most opportune moment for David, it must be said). There is an intentional narrative design here: in chap. 28 David hears from Samuel that David will be king, and in the very next chapter the same lyrics are quoted that first hinted to Saul, 'what could be next [for David] but the kingdom?' In the end, the lyrics are the lynchpin of the military commanders' case for disallowing David to march with them. As Diana Edelman (1991: 256) summarizes, 'The generals presume that David's loyalty to Saul is permanent and that the apparent break in relations is temporary at best. From experience at the Michmash pass, they know that Hebrews can be turncoats during the heat of battle and cannot be trusted.'

29.6-8

The verdict of the military leaders is final, and so Achish—who acquiesces to their counsel without a parting shot—is left with the task of sharing this news with David. His tone is almost pastoral. Achish begins swearing in the name of the LORD that David is upright, and 'good' in his eyes. Numerous scholars have paused over the language here, finding it intriguing that a Philistine king is using Israel's covenant name for God! No doubt Achish uses the name in an attempt to convey deep solidarity with David, and as a preface to his commendation of David's honesty. Indeed, Achish asserts that he would have been quite willing to fight alongside David, since he has yet to find any 'evil' in him. This is quite an endorsement from Achish. In chap. 27 I compared Achish and Saul, tilting toward the former as more organized heading into battle. But their reading of David could not be more different.

Saul has been far more wary of David's guile, as when he informed the Ziphites 'I have heard he is very crafty' (23.22), whereas Achish praises David for being bolt upright. This represents quite a contrast between these two monarchs. Of course, Achish may yet have one eye on the plunder that David is adept at accumulating, but his deferential tone makes it sound as though he is wary of offending David.

After the flattery, Achish eases into the wrinkle. I like you, says the king of Gath, 'but in the eyes of the overlords, you are not good'. This is not entirely accurate, since it is the military captains who officially register the complaint, not the overlords. Achish makes it sound as though it is a political, not a military issue. And so, politely, David is invited to return (presumably to Ziklag), for he will not be participating in this battle, lest evil be done in the eyes of the overlords. Since David has 'changed his taste' in the presence of Achish before (in 21.14, when he feigns madness), the reader infers that he is capable of doing so again. The dissembling of chap. 21 should be kept in mind, since David may be accused of 'protesting too much' in his rejoinder to Achish. David's begins with his now customary line—'What I have done?'—and proceeds to recycle much of Achish's own language to affirm his innocence. Yet the alert reader notes that, as with all of David's dialogue with Achish, there is some equivocation. For instance, who exactly are 'the enemies of my lord the king' that David is so keen to fight against? Achish might assume that David is referring to Saul and the Israelites, but a potential *double entendre* can be detected here. In the previous chapter, Saul disguises himself with 'other garments'; in this chapter, David disguises himself with 'other words', as it were. At the very least, one must agree that David has an uncanny ability to navigate the tricky waters of deception.

29.9-11

David's remonstration is met with another obsequious speech from Achish, who equates David with 'an angel of God'. On one level, Achish's 'angel' counters the 'satan' used by the military captains, but I suspect there might be a deeper narrative purpose here. First, Achish is falling into the same trap as Samuel before him; in chap. 16, Samuel judges through the 'eyes', and misses the heart of the matter. Second, Achish, as I have suggested earlier, is a kind of *alter ego* for David. It is curious, therefore, that the next time the 'angel of God' simile is invoked will be by the wise woman of Tekoa, who says the same thing to David who has just been duped by his son in a not dissimilar manner as he has duped Achish. I certainly agree with Walter Brueggemann that David has a knack for 'making his way through crises unscathed' at this point in his career, but in the future David may not be so lucky. Like Achish and Samuel before him, David will suffer from depth perception even at the apex of his reign over Israel.

After his angelic metaphor, Achish adds some apparent credibility to his justification by 'quoting' the Philistine opposition for David: 'However, the captains of the Philistines said, "He will not go up with us into the battle"'. This quotation is slightly misleading. For one, there is a contradiction; in v. 6 Achish claims that the overlords have a problem, whereas now in v. 9 he changes the story and says that the captains are complaining. The reader may think that he is merely correcting himself, but from David's vantage point there must seem to be some obfuscation. Moreover, the quotation itself is, at best, an economical précis, for in fact the captains say a good deal more. Achish dilutes the complaint, turning into a rather pedestrian affair. All the while he is avoiding the real reason: the generals fear that David will be a turncoat once the battle is underway.

Achish's final instructions are for David to slip out of the camp discreetly—early in the morning—before anyone wakes up. In the NRSV, Achish's speech in v. 10 is considerably longer, as is evident when one compares it with the RSV:

> Now then rise early in the morning with the servants of your lord who came with you; and start early in the morning, and depart as soon as you have light. (RSV)

> Now then rise early in the morning, you and the servants of your lord who came with you, and go to the place that I appointed for you. As for the evil report, do not take it to heart, for you have done well before me. Start early in the morning, and leave as soon as you have light. (NRSV)

The NRSV is here following the longer Greek text, a reading that includes two additional pieces: Achish instructs David to go the place appointed (Ziklag), and also the exhortation not to 'take to heart' the evil report. My guess is that both lines are a later addition, but at least the second has the advantage of emphasizing the 'heart' issue: Achish tells David not to take the insult to heart, but meanwhile it is the Philistine generals who have a better gauge of David's heart than Achish himself. Either way, this is Achish's last formal appearance in the story; after this dismissal, David will not again interact with the king of Gath. Achish has a brief cameo of sorts in 1 Kings 2—when two slaves of Shimei escape to Gath—but otherwise, his fifteen minutes of biblical fame has expired. David and his men depart at dawn, and the stress on 'the morning light' underscores a symbolic difference: the 'morning' of David contrasts with the previous 'night' of Saul. The idea of daybreak vs. darkness must signify the contrasting destinies, as David has strength for today, but Saul has no hope for tomorrow. Still, the next day will be troublesome enough for David. He might not fight against Saul and Israel, but the next chapter shows that he will have to fight a war of his own upon returning to his temporary home of Ziklag.

1 Samuel 30

The Philistine captains do not want David to go down to battle against the Israelites. As it turns out, David engages in a considerable amount of battle in this chapter, but the opponent is that implacable foe, the Amalekites. Any mention of Amalekites should immediately bring to mind the words of Samuel in chap. 28, and Saul's rejection that stems from his dealings with that group. The very fact that the narrative detours here in chap. 30 with an 'Amalekite interlude'—instead of heading straight to Gilboa where Saul takes his last stand—lends credence to the idea that this chapter is designed as something of a counterpoint. Indeed, the numerous similarities of language and theme with the surrounding material make it evident that this chapter subtly works as a study in contrasts. Issues such as succession and future leadership are raised in this chapter, which is structured in three main parts. First, David and his men make a fearful discovery upon returning to Ziklag: their village has been raided, and their families taken captive. The second part of the chapter is a build-up to the recovery, with an inquiry of God and the unexpected discovery of a discarded slave who provides vital information for the pursuit. The third part of the chapter brings a sense of resolution, and also includes the distribution of some newly acquired plunder. In general terms, one gets the sense that *at roughly the same time* as Saul is destroyed along with most of his house, David is rescuing his house from the Amalekites—who provide a principal occasion for Saul's rejection, as Samuel has just reminded him in chap. 28.

30.1-5

Taking their leave of Achish, David and his men make the three-day journey back to their 'place', Ziklag. However, given that Achish informed David that he *and his men* would be marching out with the Philistines, Ziklag would be particularly vulnerable in the absence of all the fighting men (28.2). During David's return journey, the reader is parenthetically informed of a raid (פשט) by the Amalekites. Since the same verb is used of David and his men in 27.8—when they raided, among other places, Amalekite villages—it is not hard to imagine some retribution: despite his contrary claim to Achish, David earlier raided the Amalekites, and now they have returned the favor.

However, David's strategy was to leave no one alive, whereas the Amalekites here in chap. 30 keep all the women and children alive, from the least to the greatest. Yet one suspects that the Amalekite intentions are not charitable, a situation that does not augur well for the captives.

Verse 3 is refracted from the visual perspective of David and his men, as they enter Ziklag: 'But behold, it had been burned with fire, and their wives, sons, and daughters taken captive!' At this point, David and his men probably assume there are no survivors; their own practice is to put everyone to death (lest someone report 'This is what David has done, and such is his custom'), so they may well think that the raiders of Ziklag subscribe to the same tactic. Consequently, the loss of every man's family occasions much lamentation, and the group weeps until all strength is gone. David himself is not exempt from this grief, since his 'two wives' have also been taken. Once more, Abigail is referred to as 'the wife of Nabal' (אֵשֶׁת נָבָל). In chap. 25, David was about to invade Nabal's house, and was prevented by a providential intervention from Abigail. If Abigail is to survive, another providential intervention is needed here.

30.6-10

This bad day in Ziklag gets worse for David: not only is he grieving the loss of his family, there is also some grumbling among the people. When David's men are first introduced they are described as 'bitter of soul' (מַר־נֶפֶשׁ). The men are in no better frame of mind now that their families have been abducted. All of them are bitter of soul (מָרָה נֶפֶשׁ), and they are talking seriously about 'stoning' David. It is hard to know exactly why the men are blaming David. Are they angry because the march with Achish was a waste of time—with the result that they left their sons and daughters unprotected? Or are they angry because they are 'empty fellows' and simply look to ascribe blame? Either way, their muttering is audible, and this kind of discourse serves to increase the Davidic stress level.

Speaking of stress, the RSV and NRSV render the verb צרר differently. The RSV renders the beginning of v. 6 'And David was greatly distressed', but the NRSV opts for 'David was in great danger'. In my view, the RSV is preferable. No doubt the danger is palpable, but 'danger' misses the connection with 28.15, where Saul says 'I am in great distress' (צרר). The fact that David and Saul both have a stressful experience provides a moment for comparison. In great distress, Saul dresses in other raiment and inquires of the witch of Endor, but David 'strengthens himself' in God and inquires of the ephod. To facilitate this inquiry, Abiathar is called (he who escaped the sword of Doeg during the purge of Nob, and fled to David). We have not heard from Abiathar for a while, but is he is ready when called upon, and this inquiry—again, in contrast to Saul—is highly successful. When David asks 'Should I chase after this band? Will I overtake it?', the answer is astounding: 'Pursue! For you will surely overtake and surely succeed!' The oracle goes well beyond what David asks, and even implies that there are survivors. For Saul, the result of his inquiry in chap. 28 is silence, whereas David gets more than he asks (שׁאל) for. The contrast between legitimate and illegitimate inquiry could not be more dramatic.

Encouraged by the loquacious ephod, David and his entourage set out in pursuit of the raiders. Yet, at the Wadi Besor, something happens that might be conceived as putting a damper on the mission: a full one-third of David's men are 'dead' tired and give up at the river. The language is not perfectly clear in v. 9—especially the participle 'those remaining'—but together with v. 10 the stress falls on the 'left behind' idea. As Robert Polzin argues at length, the narrator is here drawing attention to the fact that David is also 'left behind' from a major battle, and this theme will continue as the chapter unfolds.

As far as David and his men are concerned, two hundred men have remained with the 'baggage' previously in chap. 25, so this is not particularly unique. However, the raiders may well prove a bigger challenge than Nabal's house would have been, and so to lose one-third of the soldiers is a considerable loss. Diana Edelman (1991: 266) notes that the entire group is probably tired at this point, not just the two hundred: 'By implication, then, the 400 who pursue the raiders with David are also extremely worn out and not particularly in the best condition for the rescue effort underway'. Edelman continues, 'The resulting image of a ragtag group of physically and emotionally exhausted men heightens the importance of the divine reassurance given in v. 8 that victory against the raiders will be forthcoming; there is no way that such a group would be able to prevail on their own'. Perhaps the reader is intended to recall the unlikely victory of Gideon over the Midianite army with only three hundred men—another situation where God guaranteed a triumph against considerable odds.

30.11-15

The beleaguered pursuers get an unexpected boon when they chance upon someone else who is too exhausted to continue on a march. As it happens, the two hundred exhausted men from David's retinue are not the only ones left behind: an Egyptian lad is 'found' in the field, and subsequently brought to David. The lad needs sustenance, and so they patiently nourish him; he has not eaten for three days (and nights), just like David and men had traveled hard for three days. Unlike Saul near the end of chap. 28, this Egyptian does not need to be urged to eat; instead, the sense is that he has a ravenous appetite. Eventually, after a main course followed by dessert (a slice of fig-cake and a bunch of raisins) he revives, and upon David's inquiry, begins to tell his sorry tale:

> I am an Egyptian lad, the slave of an Amalekite man. My master abandoned me three days ago because I was ill. We raided the Negev of the Cherethites, and around that which is to Judah, and on the Negev of Caleb. And Ziklag we burned with fire.

The combination of a three-day time period and the burning of Ziklag confirms that this Egyptian lad must have been a part of *the* raiding party that David is pursuing. Thus David now knows that he is dealing with Amalekite raiders. Should one guess that this slave was captured on an earlier raid in Egypt? If this is how they treat their slaves (this fellow was merely 'ill'), what are the implications for the captured families? But still, the testimony of the Egyptian lad at least gives David and his men a reason to carry on. In his own raiding practice, David would leave no one alive, lest they report 'this is what David has done!' The Amalekites may have wished they followed the same custom. They leave someone alive, who happens to report 'this is what the Amalekites have done!' According to the Egyptian lad's testimony, an extensive southern region has been raided, and this might well suggest a good deal of plunder is also on offer.

There is a curious historical twist here as well. 'Remember what Amalek did to you on the journey, when you were coming out from Egypt', Moses intones in Deuteronomy 25, 'when they encountered you on the road, and attacked all those who were shattered at the back of the line, when you were faint and weary, and he did not fear God'. In the earlier account, the Amalekites first attack the 'weak' when Israel is coming up from Egypt; now in 1 Samuel 30 they leave a weak Egyptian alive after an attack on Israel/Ziklag. Notably, David and his men revive this weak Egyptian slave, whereas this is *exactly* the kind of person who the Amalekite would have preyed on when Israel was marching up out of Egypt. It is clear that David views this abandoned slave as an opportunity, and hence he questions the lad in v. 15, to determine whether he is able to lead them to this raiding party. The lad is sufficiently conscious to be quite articulate about his terms: 'Swear an oath to me by God that you will not kill me or close me in to the hand of my master, and I will lead you down to this troop'. The request for an oath uses similar language to Saul in chap. 24. While no response from David is recorded, the reader assumes that the oath has been sworn, since the next sentence shows the lad leading David's group toward the Amalekite raiders.

30.16-20

The recently revived Egyptian lad duly leads David and his men toward his (former) master and the Amalekite band. If the slave has been abandoned on the journey, I have no idea how he knows where to find them; perhaps his run of good luck merely continues, or perhaps his master had earlier tipped his hand as to the next destination. Either way, his efforts are successful, and the Egyptian lad—with his life secured by an oath—guides David to the required destination. Just as the entrance to burned Ziklag is refracted from David's perspective in v. 1, so the visual perspective is again filtered from the same angle in v. 16: 'Behold, they were dispersing themselves all over the face of the ground, eating, drinking, and partying with all the great plunder that they had taken from the land of the Philistines and the land of Judah!' The participle that I have translated 'dispersing themselves' (נְטֻשִׁים) entails a sense of reckless abandon, as though the Amalekites are celebrating (aided by their international plunder) in a riotous manner. Some scholars argue that term 'partying' (חגג) has a more religious nuance here, but the immediate context may rather suggest that David is witnessing pagan revelry rather than festal observance. Either way, this celebration is about to be abruptly terminated.

As an uninvited gatecrasher to this party, David takes advantage of this wanton state by launching an immediate offensive. Thus he catches his opponent unawares, since the Amalekites, like Nabal in chap. 25, have probably drained a few wineskins. Other than the time frame, there is virtually no description of the battle. But clearly it is a rout, since the reader is informed that 'no man was able to slip away from them'. David's conduct in battle will later be likened to a 'bear in the field, robbed of offspring' (2 Sam. 17.8), and quite conceivably it is occasions such at this where his reputation is forged.

In this comprehensive victory—just as the oracle forecasted—there is only a slight qualification, as four hundred young lads mount up on camels and flee. Several commentators note the significance of '400', since it is equal to the number of David's fighting men. This statistic would underscore the breadth of David's triumph, and how victory is secured despite being, by extension, severely undermanned. Of course, the survival of four hundred Amalekites alerts the canonical reader to the fact that Amalekites will surface again in biblical history, as early as 2 Samuel 1, and as late as the postexilic book of Esther (where the rivalry with this ancient foe is replayed, centuries later, in the cosmopolitan court of the Persian empire).

The offensive is successful in two ways. First, all the families are recovered, including David's wives. This must be good news for David, not least because those rocks now can be tossed aside, rather than at his person. Second, a considerable spoil is also appropriated, and this spoil takes a prominent place on the stage. In the victory parade described in v. 20, the captured herds are driven in front of all the other livestock, with the chorus ringing out: 'This is David's spoil!' The talk in v. 6 was about stoning David;

but now the chatter is about the procession of plunder. A youthful reader—one reared in a modern democracy—could be forgiven for wondering if this is the ancient Near Eastern equivalent of a campaign trail.

30.21-25

Meanwhile back at the wadi, those who were 'left behind' now come forward to meet the conquerors. David's conflict in this chapter is not quite over: victory brings in a hitherto unforeseen problem, and exposes some tension within the ranks. Although David takes initiative by extending a greeting of *shalom*, the conversation between him and those left behind is interrupted by a subgroup within his entourage who are 'evil and Belial'. This subgroup were part of the larger contingent of four hundred who had chosen to follow David and attack the Amalekites, though they were suffering from fatigue as well. 'Since they did not go with us', these men of Belial say, 'we will not give them any of the plunder we rescued. Each man can have his wife and sons, and drive them off and go!' This scene brings to mind an earlier disruption, where some sons of Belial were *themselves* almost destroyed. But back in chap. 11, Saul intervened by stating that no one would be put to death on that day, 'because the LORD has done salvation in Israel'. How will David resolve this crisis involving men of Belial?

The serious rupture in David's camp is assuaged with some good leadership. This is mostly the same group, after all, that rallies around David as long ago as chap. 22, when he became their captain. Here, David intervenes with a passionate and persuasive speech, and—like Henry V after the battle at Agincourt—ascribes the victory to God: 'You must not do this, my brothers, because of what the LORD has done for us: he guarded us, and gave the troop who came against us into our hand!' But in v. 24 David goes for the jugular, and concludes this important speech with a virtual royal fiat: 'So who should listen to you in this matter? Indeed, the portion of the one who goes down into battle is the same as the one who stays with the supplies. Alike they will share!' The plunder is to be equally divided. Just as the Egyptian slave who is left behind is given provisions, so the members of David's retinue who are left behind are also given 'provisions' from the plunder. Far from a one-time deal, David transforms this moment into a speech-act of lasting significance, and this principle becomes a 'statute and custom for Israel until this day'. Bruce Birch (1998: 1194) describes David's conduct as follows: 'The declaration of new laws for the basis of distributing economic goods is an action we would expect of a king. David boldly decides the issue and claims an authority that anticipates his kingship.' Earlier, the prophet Samuel warned that the king would take a tenth of everyone's grain and vintage and give it to his eunuchs and servants (8.15). Here, at least for the time being, David suggests that the opposite policy would be far more politically correct: all subjects, from the smallest to the greatest (as it were), will share in the spoils of victory that God gives. Yet, as Robert Polzin (1993: 223) points out, there is another level of meaning here. The Egyptian, the two hundred 'dead' men, and, momentarily, the elders of Judah, all share in the spoil without participating in the battle. In this they have something in common with David: he will share the spoil of Saul's death (and reap the benefits) without actually participating in the battle.

30.26-31
The final event of the chapter involves a further distribution of the plunder. Not only do those 'left behind' benefit, but so also do large portions of the Judahite population. Upon returning to Ziklag, David sends part of the spoil to the elders of Judah, 'to his neighbor'. The term 'neighbor' should be interpreted liberally, since the list of villages who profit from Davidic beneficence extend beyond the tribal borders of Judah. All the places have a generally southern locale, and the reader may wonder if some of the plunder was stolen by the Amalekites from these places in the first place. Since the Amalekite raids (according to the Egyptian lad) included the 'Negev of Judah', David could be returning what was previously taken. A brief look at the list of towns reveals that the list begins with Bethel and ends with Hebron, and in between are a host of places presumably friendly to David during his freebooter period. Hebron is the last place mentioned, and this will be his first seat as king of Judah, where he is initially crowned as king.

Thus David's *last activity* during his long period as a fugitive in the wilderness is generously to dole out gifts to his future constituents, and it is something that surely paves the way for being crowned king of Judah in the early days of 2 Samuel. Connecting this event of plunder distribution within the chapter as a whole, it is surely wise to agree with H.W. Hertzberg (1964: 226) that the Amalekites have a fateful significance in the early history of Israel's monarchy: Saul's expedition against the Amalekites—despite the *military* success—leads to his rejection as king on account of the plunder, whereas David's expedition against the Amalekites will lead to his acclamation as king on account of his dealing with the plunder. Overall, there is no more telling contrast than the inquiry of the ephod: Saul's campaign against the Amalekites is ultimately unsuccessful whereas David gets a guarantee of success before he even knows that his campaign is against the Amalekites. At this late point in the narrative, the only thing that Saul knows for certain is that he will be with Samuel 'tomorrow'. With Saul's reign almost over, David's reign is already beginning.

1 Samuel 31

After the prolonged Davidic interlude of chaps. 29–30, the reader finally returns to Saul's much-anticipated last campaign. During David's successful skirmish against the Amalekite raiders, Saul has been in a state of suspended animation in the narrative, awaiting the realization of Samuel's mortal prediction. It is the slopes of Mt Gilboa that provide the spatial setting where Samuel's final prophetic utterance is enacted. This brief final chapter of the book has three parts. In the first part, the action opens abruptly as the reader is taken directly into the heat of the battle, where the tide quickly turns against Israel. There is an incremental narrowing of focus: from Israel in general, then to Saul's sons, then to Saul himself and his hard-pressed predicament. The second part then outlines Saul's limited options—with literally nowhere to run or hide—and records Saul's last words with his armor bearer before falling on his sword. The third part of the chapter brings some resolution as to fate of the royal corpse: will it remain in enemy hands? The last event of the chapter—involving some brave men from Jabesh-gilead—is a poignant reminder of Saul's first act of national leadership, when he liberated them from certain optical peril at the hands of Nahash the Ammonite. That Saul's final hour should recall his finest hour provides a useful opportunity for some sympathetic reflection on the beginning and the end of Israel's royal trailblazer.

31.1-2

There has been a long build-up to this battle, and it seems that the troops have been amassing for quite some time. Indeed, three full chapters have come and gone since the first hints of impending conflict at the start of chap. 28. Any sense of delay is dispensed with at the beginning of chap. 31, and it feels like the reader is parachuted into the midst of the fray, only to experience an immediate momentum shift in favor of the Philistine army. Israel flees, and many fall slain. The opening line begins with a participle that gives a sense of non-linear time sequence (וּפְלִשְׁתִּים נִלְחָמִים בְּיִשְׂרָאֵל, 'But the Philistines were battling against Israel'). Diana Edelman (1991: 279) explains the syntax: 'Grammatically, the phrase has the force of a circumstantial clause and represents an action that occurred simultaneously with the previous action, so that the Philistine–Israelite battle is thereby placed on a contemporaneous chronological plane with David's Amalekite operation'. If the purpose of such sequencing is to compare Saul and David, then the results could not be more disparate: David embarks on a successful search and rescue mission to recover his 'house', while Saul is battling along with his house, with no hope for survival.

The Philistines enjoy the upper hand in this clash, to the point that the Israelite troops have either fled or fallen slain on Mt Gilboa. Furthermore, the Philistines are tenacious in pursuit of Saul and his sons. The NRSV translates the opening clause of v. 2 as 'The Philistines overtook Saul and his sons', but the verb דבק could also be rendered 'cling', with the sense of 'keep close'. The verb last occurs in 14.22, when the Israelites relentlessly pursue the Philistines; now the tables are turned, and there is a full-scale reversal. Hitherto the Philistines have not targeted Saul himself, but in light of Samuel's prophetic word in chap. 28, one senses that the Philistine army—like the cows of chap. 6—are driven by some unseen hand. Maybe Saul can be recognized because of his royal robe, which he presumably puts back on after the séance of Endor.

The Philistines are partially successful in their pursuit of Saul and his sons, as they strike Jonathan, Abinadab, and Malchishua. Jonathan's death is surely a sad occasion for most readers, especially as his earlier confidence and heroism in battle against the Philistines is recalled: 'Come now, and let us cross over to the outpost of these foreskinned ones. Perhaps the LORD will act for us, for there is nothing that can restrain the LORD from saving whether by many or by few!' Here in chap. 31 Jonathan is wordlessly killed by the same foe against whom he was previously so triumphant. Earlier in the story Jonathan informed David that he would be second in command, a post that he will obviously never attain. At least Jonathan has secured an oath from David for the survival of his line, an oath that will generate a subplot of its own in the courtly atmosphere of 2 Samuel 9 and following. Alongside Jonathan are two other deaths: Malchishua is otherwise only mentioned in passing in 14.49, while Abinadab is listed here for the first time. On this anomaly, Graeme Auld (2003: 229) notes an affinity with another Abinadab who is also passed over for election, as it were: 'It is interesting that Samuel reports both Saul and Jesse as naming a son similarly to the ill-fated sons of both Aaron (Num 3.1-4) and Jeroboam (1 Kgs 14.1,20)'. So, Saul's sons have been destroyed in battle, just as Samuel predicted on the previous night in Endor.

It might come as a mild surprise, but Saul's house is not *completely* destroyed on the slopes of Mt Gilboa. We will discover early in 2 Samuel that another son survives: Ishbosheth, whom the narrator has not so much as even mentioned (foreshadowing, perhaps, his ultimate irrelevancy in Israel's monarchic experiment). On this note of Saul's family and inner circle, the reader could well wonder: Where is Abner? David's scathing words in 26.15 immediately spring to mind: 'Why did you not keep watch over your master, the king?' While it might be a stretch to accuse Abner of dereliction of duty (or intentionally *not* protecting the LORD's anointed), Abner is conspicuous by his absence in this battle. Unlike Jonathan, Abinadab, and Malchishua, Abner will live to fight another day, and in fact will have a very prominent role in the days ahead, as he makes a play for the Saulide throne by appropriating the concubine Rizpah and undermining his (new) master at several turns. But all that remains in the future. For this day in chap. 31, much has gone wrong for Saul. While David has just rescued his house from foreign attackers, Saul enjoys no such good fortune, as most of his house has just been destroyed by foreign attackers. At least this chapter follows the basic lineaments of Saul's aborted reign: first his dynasty is rejected in chap. 13, then he himself is rejected in chap. 15. In chap. 31, first his house is destroyed, then he himself follows suit.

31.3-4

Back in the early chapters of 1 Samuel, the verb 'heavy/honor' (כבד) was a keyword used in the chronicle of Eli's fall. For instance, in 4.18 Eli hears the report of the ark's capture and he 'fell backward from his throne beside the gate; his neck was broken, and he died, because the man was old and heavy (כבד)'. It is a signal moment, therefore, when the verb recurs here in this context of Saul's last stand: 'The battle was heavy (כבד) around Saul, and the archers found him'. Just as the root 'heavy/honor' (כבד) is thematically important in the fall of the house of Eli, so now the verb recurs in this context of the fall of the house of Saul. Eli fell backward because he was 'heavy'; it remains to be seen whether Saul will fall forward because of the 'heavy' battle.

Presumably injured by the arrows (the Hebrew text describes Saul as 'writhing'), Saul speaks for the last time in his life: 'Draw your sword and run me through with it, lest these foreskinned ones come and run through me, and abuse me'. Notably, these are the only words of direct speech in the entire chapter, so it would appear that the narrator isolates Saul's words in order to emphasize their significance. In the first instance, there is an intersection between Saul's last words and his first words back in chap. 9. As one recalls, Saul's first words in the story are an imperative directed to an underling; similarly, his words in the story are an imperative directed to an underling. Furthermore, in both cases Saul's command is not obeyed, as such. In chap. 9, Saul issues an imperative to his servant lad—'Come, let us go back'—but his words are met with a creative refusal, and the ensuing events lead to a meeting with Samuel, in search of a prophetic word. Here in chap. 31, Saul's imperative is likewise met with a refusal—'But his armor bearer was not willing, because he was very afraid'—leading to fulfillment of the dead Samuel's most recent prophetic word. One could argue that the first and last words of Saul form an appropriate envelope structure for a king whose name means 'asked for' yet whose requests are rarely heeded. Saul often 'asks' throughout his ill-fated career, yet seldom is he given a favorable response.

When Saul orders his armor bearer to 'run him through', a number of commentators are reminded of an analogous episode in Judges 9, where Abimelech—crowned as king of Shechem—suffers a terminal head injury courtesy of a woman who drops an upper millstone and cracks his skull. Fearing eternal embarrassment, Abimelech then utters his own last words (9.54) to his armor bearer: 'Draw your sword and kill me, lest they say of me, "A woman killed him!" And his lad ran him through, and he died.' It is evident that there are a number of similarities between the story of Saul's death and the earlier narrative of Abimelech, the account in Judges that Barbara Green (2003: 441) calls 'that prior story of monarchy born out of time'. Any connection with Abimelech—that antitype of true kingship in the Deuteronomic worldview—is not complimentary, and no doubt many readers could view this is as a negative appraisal of Saul. Yet Saul's situation, for all the points of comparison, is different. In Judges 9 Abimelech is on the offensive, whereas in 1 Samuel 31 Saul is on the defensive. Abimelech is a *bona fide* hoodlum, whereas Saul—for all his faults—has far more national legitimacy. Moreover, Abimelech makes a fatal miscalculation, as far as his reputation is concerned: it *is* said that 'a woman killed him', and Abimelech's legacy is to become an ignominious proverb. 'Who struck Abimelech?' (2 Sam. 11.21) develops into a byword for foolishness in battle.

That the author is drawing an affinity between the deaths of the first experimenter in kingship and first actually anointed king is obvious enough, but what is the ultimate point of the connection? On the one hand, the invocation of Abimelech in 1 Samuel 31 implies a judgment, not so much on Saul himself, but rather on the political decision to opt for a monarchy. The choice of Israel's elders to institute kingship—based on the model of the surrounding nations—is ultimately a suicidal enterprise. But, on the other hand, to my mind there is a deeper moment of narrative reflection here. I would argue that the Abimelech analogy produces an unsettling piece of foreshadowing, since this is *not* the last time that Abimelech's ignoble death will be invoked by our author. As mentioned above, in 2 Sam. 11.21 Joab sends a report to the king about events during the siege of Rabbah—the key piece of information, of course, pertains to the death of Uriah the Hittite. Putting words in David's mouth, Joab refers to the death of Abimelech, a warrior who dies at the hand of a woman because he drew too close to the wall. The reader can appreciate the allegorical point: David—with a recklessness that rivals Abimelech—got too close to the wall, as it where, and was dealt a serious blow by a woman. In light of the overall narrative, therefore, the allusive account of Saul's fall in 1 Samuel 31 contains hints of another fall—that is, the serious head injury suffered by David in 2 Samuel 11. The longer-term value of the Abimelech analogy in 1 Samuel 31 is that it prepares the way for another analogy, when David is explicitly compared with that heedless 'king' in Judges 9. So, even as Saul falls on his sword, the audience is warned that Israel's first king will not be the last king to be compared with Abimelech. The mighty will be lacerated in 2 Samuel 11 as well.

In light of his armor bearer's non-compliance, Saul is left with few options in these grave circumstances: 'And Saul took the sword, and he fell on it'. Ostensibly, Saul fears that he will suffer abuse (עלל) at the hands of the Philistines. The same verb occurs in Judg. 19.25, with the unpardonable treatment of the Levite's concubine happening, in all places, *at Gibeah of Benjamin*. Saul is genealogically acquainted with this kind of grief, and not interested in partaking of a similar fate. To my mind this makes Saul's reaction of sword-falling more understandable, since such abuse—if the Judges text is read alongside—is surely worth avoiding. On a related trajectory, Bruce Birch (1998: 1198), argues that the issue of Saul's death is not suicide (in the modern Western sense), but rather a leader's responsibility in a military context: 'He did not have the choice of life or death, only the choice of further humiliation for Israel through his capture and execution or a kingly act that brought an end to this moment of Israelite defeat'. At the same time, there is an earlier use of the verb 'abuse' or 'make sport of' (עלל) that might be instructive. Robert Polzin (1993: 224) points out that the Philistine diviners warn their compatriots in 6.6 not to harden their hearts like the Egyptians who were 'made sport of' to the point that they had to let Israel go. When 6.6 and 31.4 are taken together, Polzin reasons, a message for the exiles emerges: the only hope for the nation lies in a God-ordained 'new exodus'. Polzin concludes with this intriguing possibility: 'As the ark was returned leaderless to the land of Israel (chapter 6), so might Israel one day return kingless to its own land'.

To his credit, Saul at least picks the right weapon, in that he falls on his sword instead of his spear. There are practical reasons why the spear is not the best instrument for this skewering task, but one cannot resist the conclusion that had Saul chosen to fall on his spear, no doubt he would have missed (as the cranially intact David would testify). But fall on his sword he does, and so, as J.P. Fokkelman (1986: 625) points out, both Saul and Goliath finally perish by means of their own swords. In fact, Saul falls the same direction as Goliath (face forward, cf. 17.49), and immediately the lyrics of Hannah's song spring to mind—'O tall one, O tall one!'—where those who are set on lofty perches coming crashing down.

31.5-6
Having declined Saul's appeal to run him through, the armor bearer sees that Saul is dead, and promptly falls on his own sword. By showing terminal loyalty his master, Saul's armor bearer recalls the brave exploits of Jonathan's servant in chap. 14. Both armor bearers persevered with their masters in spite of considerable odds against the Philistines, but while Jonathan's armor bearer survives, Saul's does not. Saul's unnamed armor bearer in chap. 31 prompts a recollection of another holder of that office in chap. 16, David himself, who of course is not present on Mt Gilboa. Speaking of David, this might provide a clue as to why the armor bearer is afraid and refuses to obey the king's order: one suspects he was privy to David's words in chap. 26 about the sacrosanct nature of the LORD's anointed, and, like many a commentator in the years to come, he interprets Davidic speech quite literally.

The end result of Saul's last campaign is summarized in v. 6: 'So Saul died, and his three sons, and his armor bearer, even with all his men, on that day together'. Once again, the Philistines are agents of fulfillment of the prophetic word; just as in chap. 2, when the anonymous man of God brings the message about the imminent fall of another chosen dynastic house. A fateful day is decreed for the house of Eli, a word that comes to fulfillment because of the tenacity and manly discourse of the Philistine troops in chap. 4. In that account, Eli falls backwards, and now Saul falls forward. Eli and his sons all die on the same day, just like Saul and his sons in 1 Samuel 31; similarly, the birth of Ichabod prefigures the deaths of Saul's sons. Both houses fall by the hand of the Philistines, and while there have been other adversaries (Ammonites, Amalekites), the exigencies of plot demand that the Philistines be the agents of fulfillment in chap. 31. The man of God speaks the word of judgment at the beginning of the book, and the prophet Samuel speaks the prophetic word that guides the final events of the book: the doggedness of the Philistines—pressing hard against Saul and his sons—is merely in service of the prophetic word already spoken. Later in the Deuteronomistic History, Ahab will be pierced by a 'random' arrow as he tries to thwart the prophetic word (1 Kgs 21.34), but Saul makes no such attempt. I am not necessarily implying that Saul dies like a martyred hero, but I would say that at least—unlike Ahab—he does not try to circumvent his grim destiny. Indeed, Diana Edelman (1990: 284) believes that Saul's manner of death illustrates that Saul embraces his fate, and he goes down fighting. Obviously there are hints of a tragic story here, but even beyond the personal tragedy of Israel's hapless inaugural monarch, one senses an urgent national message. For Barbara Green (2003: 444), the portrait of Saul serves as a cipher for the entire royal experiment in Israel, with the specific utility of prompting 'reflection on the non-viability of monarchic leadership for the future. That is, the characterization of Saul has needed to, and managed to, suggest succinctly the inherent weakness of the institution as experienced over time, primarily (though not exclusively) in the long tenure of the Davidic line.' Although David himself will enjoy far more personal success that Saul, his own royal line will not be re-established in the same way after the exile.

Saul's exit from the narrative stage reminds me of his first appearance on the public stage: the lot-casting ceremony (chaired by Samuel) in chap. 10. I can appreciate why some scholars invoke another lot-casting ceremony when trying to come to grips with the Saul story, that of the (e)scapegoat in Leviticus 16. When the lot falls on Saul in chap. 10, he seems vaguely aware of his impending journey. As we reach 1 Samuel 31, it would appear that there are two goats, so to speak. One goat (the house of David) is on the way to the temple, where atonement will be made. The other goat (the house of Saul) is doomed to wander in the wilderness. When the elders of Israel make the unwise request for a king, there is collateral damage, and that damage is from the tribe of Benjamin. I have heard some recent scholars contend that Leviticus 16 is a post-exilic composition (see Pinker 2006: 21-22), but I have yet to hear anyone suggest that the inspiration for that ceremony is the Saul story. In his final moments, Saul is not hiding among the baggage, but rather he stands tall, and falls in a battle where he really does not have a fighting chance. On the previous night, Saul fell to the fullness of his height, a prostration that served as a dress reversal (*sans* royal attire) for this full-length fall, just as Samuel choreographed from beyond the grave. On that previous night in Endor, the ghostwife made a sacrifice; in chap. 31, Saul becomes something of a sacrifice himself, just as David intones in his lament of 2 Sam. 1.19-27, where he appropriates sacrificial imagery in his royal requiem for the house of Saul. With Saul's death comes the formal end of a character who never applied for a job that should never have been created in the first place. It is a sad yet not undignified end for an overwhelmed and woefully under-equipped character, and I think Elie Wiesel (2003: 140) is poignant in his appraisal:

> No wonder that [Saul] has captured the fancy of the great among poets, painters, composers. Rembrandt and Holbein, Byron and Rilke, Lamartine, Handel, D. H. Lawrence and André Gide, all were inspired by the tragic nobility, the romantic gravity of his singular yet exemplary destiny. More than any figure that followed, Saul intrigued creative spirits. More even than David, whose impact was greater both historically and metaphysically, Saul attracts anyone who approaches Judaism from an aesthetic or ethical viewpoint. David and his conquests make us proud; but it is Saul and his

failures that intrigue us. More complex than David, more tormented, more tortured, Saul pulls you along to mountain heights and then drops you into the abyss. Few ever experienced as many metamorphoses, as many dramas, as many breakdowns, as he did; few destinies ever followed as fast a rhythm, or had as many ups and downs in rapid succession. Few men knew such glory and few lost it for reasons as absurd.

31.7

After the summary notice of Saul's death and the death of his sons, a kind of panoramic view from an Israelite perspective is given: 'And the men of Israel who were across the valley and across the Jordan saw that the men of Israel had fled and that Saul and his sons were dead, they abandoned their cities and fled. And the Philistines came and dwelt in them.' The immediate purpose for this particular detail is twofold. First, the eyewitness-type report of Israelites in the valley and beyond the Jordan 'seeing' that Saul is dead brings an element of despair into the chapter. The retreat of the general population (following the defeat and retreat of the army) signals a loss not only of leader, but also of land. Robert Gordon (1986: 203) notes that 'the Philistines have, by their defeat of Saul, made deep inroads into Israel'. The whole point of having a king was to rescue them from oppression of groups like the Philistines, something that emphatically has not happened here. In chap. 8 the people ask for a king to lead them in battle; the king falls, and they abandon their towns. But, second, there is also a kernel of hope in 31.7. Even after the death of the king in battle, and even after invasion and foreign occupation, there yet remains a remnant of survivors. One senses a message for an exilic audience: even after the death of kingship, there is still a remnant that survives *on the other side of the Jordan*. The death of the monarchy, in other words, is not the end of the story.

31.8-10

The first part of this chapter deals with the living Saul's last moments. The second part of this chapter revolves around the dead king's corpse. It is curious that the Philistines—so keen on aggressively pursuing Saul in v. 2—only stumble on the dead king and his sons on the next day, when they arrive to plunder the slain soldiers. This contributes to the notion sketched above that an unseen hand guides the Philistine army and their archers. The verb 'strip/plunder' is used numerous times in 1 Samuel, most notably when Jonathan strips off his robe and hands it to David in 18.4, and then in 19.24 when Saul divests himself of his royal robes and rolls around naked in prophetic ecstasy. Here in chap. 31 it is the Philistines who finally disrobe Saul for the last time, bringing a literal and symbolic climax to the intricate subplot of the king's royal garments. Saul has been continually losing clothes, while David gradually has been collecting them. Indeed, in 2 Samuel 1, several accoutrements of Saul's royal attire will once more be handed to David, unofficially completing the long transfer of power that begins with David's entrance to Saul's court.

Encountering the dead Saul, the Philistines proceed to cut off his head. Robert Polzin often remarks that in the Deuteronomistic History, 'head' is symbolic for leadership and authority. In chap. 17, for instance, David removes the head of Goliath and takes this grizzly trophy to the Canaanite fortress of Jerusalem as a sort of deposit, and a guarantee that he will be back (to assume the mantle of leadership and authority there). Here in chap. 31 the Philistines amputate the head of Israel's king, in what must be an attempt politically to dissect their opponents.

Events such as the beheading Israel's king and the stripping of his weapons are worthy of publication. This is duly undertaken by the Philistines, as they send word not only to their people, but in the first instance to the 'house of their idols' (בֵּית עֲצַבֵּיהֶם). I suppose the construct noun 'house' can be construed as a plural (adopted by a number of English translations), but the point would be that Saul's death is not just a political or military triumph, but represents a religious victory as well.

We should note, furthermore, that the verb used for sending the message of this triumph is 'to bring good news' (בשר). This verb is last used in chap. 4, where the man of Benjamin brings the good news of Israel's defeat (again at the hands of the Philistines) that prompts the backwards fall of Eli. As mentioned in our analysis there, the verb בשר usually occurs in the Former Prophets when the news is good *for the house of David*. So, the deaths of Eli and Saul in the short term do not seem good for Israel, but in different ways the news *is* good for the house of David. There is some great irony here, consequently, when the Philistines think the death of Saul is good news worth proclaiming in the temple of their gods, because it will be bad news just a short time from now. In 2 Sam. 5.21 the Philistines will be defeated by David, and will 'abandon their idols' such that David and his men are able to carry them off. When the Philistines abandon their idols in 2 Samuel, it effectively marks the Philistines' exit from the narrative stage.

2 Samuel 5, however, lies in the future. Meanwhile, the Philistines consign Saul's armor to the house of goddess Ashtaroth (עַשְׁתָּרוֹת, rendered as Astarte in the NRSV), but his corpse is impaled on the wall of Beth-shan. To begin with Beth-shan, both C.F. Keil and Kyle McCarter locate it within the northern borders Israel (referring to Josh. 17.16). If this is the case, then it must be particularly grating that an occupied city now boasts the carcass of the slain king. The mention of the Ashtaroth house is curious, not least because there is no mention here of Dagon. The parallel passage in 1 Chronicles 10 *does* specify the house of Dagon, so I would hypothesize that in

1 Samuel 31 the absence of Dagon must be playfully polemic, and fraught with dark comedy: the corpse of headless Saul cannot be mounted in Dagon's house because the latter is busy convalescing from his own cerebral amputation when the ark came to visit back in chap. 5.

31.11-13
Saul's story could have ended in many different ways. Why does the author select this particular event for the last word?

> Then the inhabitants of Jabesh-gilead heard what the Philistines had done to Saul. And all their men of courage arose, and walked all night, and took the corpse of Saul and the corpses of his sons from the wall of Beth-shan. They brought them to Jabesh, and burned them there. Then they took their bones and buried them under the tamarisk in Jabesh, and they fasted for seven days.

It seems like twenty chapters since we have last visited Jabesh, but that dramatic episode has naturally left a lasting impression: a small town on the wrong side of the Jordan is under siege by no less than Nahash ('Snake') the Ammonite, yet this hopeless situation is remedied by a daring rescue operation led by a newly installed king who combines strategic acumen with uncommon valor. In the last few verses of 1 Samuel 31 there are a number of allusions to chap. 11, so I assume that the writer wants the reader to think about the connections, along with all that has transpired in the meantime. Peter Miscall (1986: 182) captures the occasion:

> Saul's end is ignominious, yet the book of 1 Samuel closes by putting aside allusions to Saul's dark and clouded days. It closes with an act that is not a power play, a calculated show of restraint, a deception, or an attempt to buy someone's loyalty; it closes with pathos, with a memory of Saul's finest hour.

This account of the Jabeshites rescue of the king's corpse elicits a bit of overdue sympathy for the pitiable Saul by rehashing his own liberation of Jabesh at the outset of his reign.

The hazardous mission to recover Saul's corpse is set in motion when the residents of Jabesh 'hear' what has been done to the king by the Philistines. The hearing of Jabesh stands in contrast to the 'seeing' by the Israelites of the valley in v. 7. It is appropriate that the Jabeshites hear of Saul's posthumous treatment, since Saul 'heard' of their dire predicament those many moons ago. Traveling under the cover of night, the courageous men of Jabesh are able to see so well in the dark is because they have both their eyes, thanks to Saul, who waited all night to launch his surprise attack on Nahash. When the salvage operation in Beth-shan is over, the people of Jabesh burn the corpses to cleanse them from idolatrous contamination; 'to that extent', remarks J.P. Fokkelman (1986: 629), '(a part of) Saul's last wish is still fulfilled, his body is removed from the hands of the uncircumcised brutes'.

After the cleansing, the bones are given a proper burial under the tamarisk, a site that the reader has seen before. Graeme Auld's (2003: 229) comment is worth noting: 'Chronicles has the royal bones buried under an oak, which has many suitable connections in stories of the Old Testament. Samuel has changed the tree to a tamarisk, perhaps to link the burial of David's adversary to the scene at Gibeah where Saul had sought information against David (22.6).' As Auld points out, it is under the tamarisk tree in chap. 22 where Saul sits, and vainly clings to the throne that had already been given to another. 'Under the tamarisk', I would add, contains hints of David's succession, since this is the place where Saul warns the men of Benjamin not to expect any favors from the son of Jesse. Ironically, when the Jabeshites bury Saul under the tamarisk, it reminds the reader that the next occupant of the throne certainly will not be from Benjamin.

Given the contours of Saul's regal career, it is fitting that the phrase 'seven days' should close this chapter of the story. Back in chap. 11, the city of Jabesh is apprehensive: they have boldly asked Nahash for seven days of respite, and they hope that a savior arrives. Before the time had elapsed, Saul arrives with a national muster and saves them. So here in chap. 31 it makes sense that the residents of Jabesh fast for seven days to commemorate this moment of liberation. But the phrase 'seven days' also reminds us of chap. 13, when by contrast a seven-day period *does* elapse. When Samuel does not show up at the appointed time (according to the narrator at 13.8), it marks the beginning of the end for Saul. Those under siege from Nahash were grateful that Saul did show up on time, and saved them from humiliation. Therefore, when the optically intact citizens of Jabesh fast for seven days, it creates an element of symmetry between Saul's first deed and his final honor. The seven-day fast of Jabesh may not finally rehabilitate Saul's legacy, but as the last word of 1 Samuel, the event at least recognizes the best memory of a barren reign.

BIBLIOGRAPHY

Ackerman, James S. 'Who Can Stand before Yhwh, This Holy God? A Reading of 1 Samuel 1-15'. *Prooftexts* 11 (1991) 1-24.
—'Abishai'. Page 14 in *The New Interpreter's Dictionary of the Bible*. I. Ed. Katherine Doob Sakenfeld. Nashville: Abingdon, 2006.
Alter, Robert. *The Art of Biblical Narrative*. New York: Basic Books, 1981.
—*The David Story: A Translation with Commentary of 1 and 2 Samuel*. New York: Norton, 1999.
Amit, Yairah. '"The Glory of God Does Not Deceive or Change his Mind": On the Reliability of Narrator and Speakers in Biblical Narrative'. *Prooftexts* 12 (1992) 201-12.
Arnold, Bill T. *1 and 2 Samuel*. NIV Application Commentary. Grand Rapids: Zondervan, 2003.
Auld, A. Graeme. '1 and 2 Samuel'. In *Eerdmans Commentary on the Bible*. Ed. J.D.G. Dunn and J.W. Rogerson. Grand Rapids: Eerdmans, 2003.
—*Samuel at the Threshold: Selected Works of Graeme Auld*. SOTSMS. Aldershot: Ashgate, 2004.
Auld, A.Graeme, and C.Y.S. Hos. 'The Making of David and Goliath'. *JSOT* 56 (1992) 19-39.
Baldwin, Joyce G. *I and II Samuel: An Introduction and Commentary*. Downers Grove, IL: InterVarsity Press, 1988.
Bar-Efrat, Shimon. *Narrative Art in the Bible*. JSOTSup, 70. Sheffield: Almond Press, 1989.
Bergen, Robert D. *1, 2 Samuel*. NAC; Nashville: Broadman & Holman, 1996.
Biddle, Mark E. 'Ancestral Motifs in 1 Samuel 25: Intertextuality and Characterization'. *JBL* 121 (2002) 617-38.
Birch, Bruce C. 'The First and Second Books of Samuel'. Pages 947-1383 in *The New Interpreter's Bible*, II. Nashville: Abingdon, 1998.
Blenkinsopp, Joseph. 'Jonathan's Sacrilege. 1 Sam 14, 1-46'. *CBQ* 26 (1964) 423-49.
Bodner, Keith. *David Observed: A King in the Eyes of his Court*. Hebrew Bible Monographs, 5. Sheffield: Sheffield Phoenix Press, 2005.
—'Readers of the Lost Ark: Literary Studies of the Ark Narrative in 1 Samuel 4–6'. *Currents in Biblical Research* 4 (2006) 169-97.
Brooks, Peter. *Reading for the Plot: Design and Intention in Narrative*. Cambridge, MA: Harvard University Press, 1984.
Brueggemann, Walter. *First and Second Samuel*. Interpretation. Louisville, KY: John Knox Press, 1990.
Childs, Brevard S. *Introduction to the Old Testament as Scripture*. Philadelphia: Fortress Press, 1979.
Coggins, Richard J. 'On Kings and Disguises'. *JSOT* 50 (1991) 55-62.

Craig, Kenneth M., Jr. 'Rhetorical Aspects of Questions Answered with Silence in 1 Samuel 14:37 and 28:6'. *CBQ* 56 (1994) 221-39.
Cross, Frank Moore, Donald W. Parry, Richard J. Saley, and Eugene Ulrich. *Qumran Cave 4. XII. 1–2 Samuel*. DJD, 17. Oxford: Clarendon Press, 2005.
Cuddon, J.A. *The Penguin Dictionary of Literary Terms and Literary Theory*. London: Penguin, 4th edn, 1999.
Deist, Ferdinand. 'Coincidence as a Motif of Divine Intervention in 1 Samuel 9'. *Old Testament Essays* 6 (1993) 7-18.
Driver, S.R. *Notes on the Hebrew Text and the Topography of the Books of Samuel*. Oxford: Clarendon Press, 2nd edn, 1913.
Edelman, Diana V. *King Saul in the Historiography of Judah*. JSOTSup, 121. Sheffield: JSOT Press, 1991.
Esler, P. 'The Madness of Saul: A Cultural Reading of 1 Samuel 8–31'. Pages 220-62 in *Biblical Studies, Cultural Studies: The Third Sheffield Colloquium*. Ed. J. Cheryl Exum and Stephen D. Moore. Sheffield: Sheffield Academic Press, 1998.
Eslinger, Lyle. *Kingship of God in Crisis: A Close Reading of 1 Samuel 1–12*. Sheffield: Almond Press, 1985.
Evans, Mary J. *1 and 2 Samuel*. NIBC, 6. Peabody, MA: Hendrickson, 2000.
Ewing, W. 'Shiloh'. Pages 2768-69 in *International Standard Bible Encyclopedia*. Ed. James Orr. Grand Rapids: Eerdmans, 1949.
Exum, J. Cheryl. *Tragedy and Biblical Narrative: Arrows of the Almighty*. Cambridge: Cambridge University Press, 1992.
Fokkelman, J.P. *Narrative Art and Poetry in the Books of Samuel. II. The Crossing Fates (1 Sam. 13–31 and 2 Sam. 1)*. Assen: Van Gorcum, 1986.
—*Narrative Art and Poetry in the Books of Samuel. IV. Vow and Desire (1 Sam. 1–12)*. Assen: Van Gorcum, 1993.
Forster, E.M. *Aspects of the Novel*. New York: Harcourt, Brace, Jovanovich, 1927.
Garsiel, Moshe. *The First Book of Samuel: A Literary Study of Comparative Structures, Analogies, Parallels*. Ramat Gan: Revivim, 1985.
Goldingay, John. *Old Testament Theology. I. Israel's Gospel*. Downer's Grove: Intervarsity Press, 2003.
Gordon, Robert P. *1 and 2 Samuel: A Commentary*. Grand Rapids: Zondervan, 1986.
Green, Barbara. *How Are the Mighty Fallen? A Dialogical Study of King Saul in 1 Samuel*. JSOTSup, 365. Sheffield: Sheffield Academic Press, 2003.
Gunn, David M. *The Fate of King Saul*. JSOTSup, 14; Sheffield: Almond Press, 1980.
Halpern, Baruch, and Jon D. Levenson. 'The Political Import of David's Marriages'. *JBL* 99 (1980) 507-18.
Hamilton, V.P. *Handbook on the Historical Books*. Grand Rapids: Baker, 2001.
Hawk, L. Daniel. 'Saul's Altar' (unpublished paper presented at the SBL Annual Meeting, Philadelphia, 2005).
Hertzberg, Hans Wilhelm. *1 and 2 Samuel*. Trans. J.S. Bowden. OTL. Philadelphia: Westminster Press, 1964.
Jobling, David. 'Saul's Fall and Jonathan's Rise: Tradition and Redaction in 1 Sam. 14:1-46'. *JBL* 95 (1976) 367-76.
—*The Sense of Biblical Narrative: Structural Analysis in the Hebrew Bible*. II. Sheffield: Almond Press, 1986.
—*1 Samuel*. Berit Olam. Collegeville, MN: Liturgical Press, 1998.

Keil, C.F., and F. Delitzsch. *II Samuel*. In *Commentary on the Old Testament*. Trans. J. Martin; Grand Rapids: Eerdmans, 1950 (1875).
Klein, Ralph W. *1 Samuel*. WBC, 10; Waco, TX: Word Books, 1983.
Knoppers, Gary N. *I Chronicles 1–9: A New Translation with Introduction and Commentary*. AB, 12. New York: Doubleday, 2003.
Kugel, James. *The God of Old: Inside the Lost World of the Bible*. New York: The Free Press, 2003.
Leithart, Peter J. 'Nabal and his Wine'. *JBL* 120 (2001) 525-27.
Levenson, Jon D. '1 Samuel 25 as Literature and History'. *CBQ* 40 (1978) 11-28.
—*Sinai and Zion: An Entry into the Jewish Bible*. Minneapolis: Winston Press, 1985.
Long, V. Philips. *The Reign and Rejection of King Saul: A Case for Literary and Theological Coherence*. Atlanta: Scholars Press, 1989.
McCarter, P.K. *1 Samuel: A New Translation with Introduction, Notes, and Commentary*. AB, 9. Garden City, NY: Doubleday, 1980.
McConville, J. Gordon. *I and II Chronicles*. Philadelphia: Westminster Press, 1984.
Miscall, Peter D. *The Workings of Old Testament Narrative*. Semeia Studies. Philadelphia: Fortress Press; Chico, CA: Scholars Press, 1983.
—*1 Samuel: A Literary Reading*. Bloomington: Indiana University Press, 1986.
Moberly, R.W.L. ' "God is Not a Human that He Should Repent" (Numbers 23:19 and 1 Samuel 15:29)'. Pages 112-23 in *God in the Fray: A Tribute to Walter Brueggemann*. Ed. Tod Linafelt and Timothy K. Beal. Minneapolis: Fortress Press, 1998.
Mullen, E.T. Jr. *Narrative History and Ethnic Boundaries: The Deuteronomistic Historian and the Creation of Israelite National Identity*. Atlanta: Scholars Press, 1993.
Noll, K.L. Review of *1 and 2 Samuel* by Tony W. Cartledge and *1 Samuel* by Antony F. Campbell, S.J. *Interpretation* 58 (2004) 404-408.
Polzin, Robert. *Samuel and the Deuteronomist: A Literary Study of the Deuteronomic History*. II. *1 Samuel*. Bloomington: Indiana University Press, repr. 1993 (1989).
Pinker, Aron. 'A Goat to Go to Azazel'. *JHS* 7 (2006) www.purl.org/jhs.
Prouser, Ora Horn. 'Suited to the Throne: The Symbolic Use of Clothing in the David and Saul Narratives'. *JSOT* 71 (1996) 27-37.
Rad, Gerhard von. *Studies in Deuteronomy*. Trans. D. Stalker. London: SCM Press, 1953.
—*Old Testament Theology*. I. *The Theology of Israel's Historical Traditions*. Trans. D.M.G. Stalker. New York: Harper & Row, 1962.
Reis, Pamela Tamarkin. 'Collusion at Nob: A New Reading of 1 Samuel 21–22'. *JSOT* 61 (1994) 59-73.
—*Reading the Lines: A Fresh Look at the Hebrew Bible*. Peabody, MA: Hendrickson, 2002.
Reiss, Moshe. 'Samuel and Saul: A Negative Symbiosis'. *Jewish Bible Quarterly* 32 (2004) 35-43.
Rendsburg, G.A. 'Confused Language as a Deliberate Literary Device in Biblical Hebrew Narrative'. *JHS* 2 (1999), available online at <www.purl.org/jhs>.
Römer, Thomas C. *The So-Called Deuteronomistic History: A Sociological, Historical, and Literary Introduction*. London: T. & T. Clark International, 2005.
Rosenberg, Joel. *King and Kin: Political Allegory in the Hebrew Bible*. Bloomington: Indiana University Press, 1986.
—'1 and 2 Samuel'. Pages 122-45 in *The Literary Guide to the Bible*. Ed. Robert Alter and Frank Kermode. Cambridge, MA: Harvard University Press, 1987.

Smith, H.P. *A Critical and Exegetical Commentary on the Books of Samuel*. ICC. Edinburgh: T. & T. Clark, 1899.
Sternberg, Meir. *The Poetics of Biblical Narrative: Ideological Literature and the Drama of Reading*. Bloomington: Indiana University Press, 1985.
Sweeney, Marvin H. *I & II Kings*. OTL. Louisville, KY: Westminster John Knox Press, 2007.
—'Davidic Polemics in the Book of Judges'. *VT* 47 (1997) 517-29.
Watson, W.G.E. *Classical Hebrew Poetry*. Sheffield: JSOT Press, 1986.
Wellhausen, Julius. *Prolegomena to the History of Ancient Israel*. Trans. J.S. Black and A. Menzies. Edinburgh: A. & C. Black, 1885 (orig. 1878).
Weinfeld, Moshe. *Deuteronomy and the Deuteronomic School*. Oxford: Clarendon Press, 1972.
Wiesel, Elie. *Wise Men and their Tales: Portraits of Biblical, Talmudic, and Hasidic Masters*. New York: Schocken Books, 2003.
Yadin, Azzan. 'Goliath's Armor and Israelite Collective Memory'. *VT* 54 (2004) 373-95.

INDEXES

INDEX OF REFERENCES

Hebrew Bible

Genesis
1.2	115
2.29	247
3.1	247
4.7	160
6.6	153
15.6	288
16	16
18.22	40
19	102
21	259
24	84
25	127
25.30	227
27	206, 254
27.11	248
27.41-42	284
28	200
29–30	16, 85
29.1-12	84
31	206-208
31.19-20	261
31.28	122
31.32	207
34	85
35	47
35.8	94
35.16-18	50
37–50	183
38	231, 255
43.31	122
45.1	122
50	259

Exodus
2.16-21	84
7.25	56
15	18
17	150
19.6	71
19.15	226
28–29	132
32	161
32.4	161
32.24	162

Leviticus
16	322
17	142

Numbers
3.1-4	317
6	18
13–14	260
13	259
15.8-10	24
23.19	161
24.7	152
25	227

Deuteronomy
12	142
16.18-20	69
17	73, 75, 272
17.14-20	73
17.17-18	74
17.17	147
17.18-20	73
17.18	100
18.11	292
18.14	56
25	150, 312
28.14	59
29.25-28	116
30.19-20	4
32.8-9	281

Joshua
2	206
3.5	226
6	45
7	99, 150
7.25	140
8	152
9	62
9.27	64
10.13	139
11.22	177
13.3	51
15	260
15.5	260
15.10	59
15.31	287
15.44	240
15.55	246
17.16	324
19.5	287
19.18	292
19.51	33
21.8-16	64
24.23	65

Judges
1.16	151
3	250
3.7	64
4	151, 250
4.17-21	250
6	89, 150
6.8	39
7.16	106, 107
8	132
8.23	71
8.27	199
9	70, 172, 256, 319
9.6	70
9.43	106
9.54	319

Judges (cont.)			47	2.13-17	34
10	65	1.4-5	15	2.15-16	48
10.16	66	1.4	12	2.17	31
11	18, 145	1.5	15	2.18	31
11.35	140	1.6	27, 29	2.19-21	32
13	18, 19	1.7	22	2.20	32
13.2	18	1.8	16, 17, 21,	2.21	34, 69
14.3	133		24	2.22-26	33
15.11	46	1.9	17	2.25	34, 66
16	51, 54	1.10-11	18	2.26	34, 80
17–21	49	1.10	232	2.27-36	34, 36, 235,
17.2	139	1.11	19, 22, 33		237
18–21	14	1.12-14	19	2.28	80
18–19	132	1.13	31	2.29	34, 48
18.25	232	1.15-16	20	2.30	50, 65
18.30-31	14	1.17	20, 21	2.31-36	237
19–21	87	1.18	21	2.31-33	136
19–20	79, 100	1.19-20	22	2.31	237
19	105	1.20	22	2.33	237
19.25	320	1.21-22	23	2.35-36	217
20–21	66	1.21	23	2.35	127, 267
20	196	1.23	24, 47, 76,	2.36	35, 280
20.16	185		94	3	37, 38, 41,
20.27	136	1.24-28	24		42, 44, 65,
20.41	301	1.25	24		132, 153,
21	47, 102,	1.28	8		167, 237,
	104	2	26, 36-38,		293, 295
21.19	13, 45, 47		41, 48, 50,	3.1-3	37
			73, 75, 82,	3.1	38
Ruth			92, 114,	3.2	38, 40
1	11		136, 169,	3.3	38
1.20	18		217, 237,	3.4-10	38, 39
2.4	156		238, 263,	3.5	39
			267, 302,	3.10	39
1 Samuel			321	3.11-14	40, 72
1–12	21	2.1	26, 28	3.13	40
1–3	19, 42, 44,	2.2-5	28	3.15-18	40
	63, 70	2.3	28, 79	3.19-21	41
1–2	33	2.4	29	3.19	41
1	12, 14, 18,	2.5	28, 35	3.21	45
	19, 22, 28,	2.6	171	4–6	43, 44, 57,
	29, 38, 47,	2.8	30, 171,		63
	50, 78, 79,		217	4	17, 21, 34,
	81, 85, 89,	2.10	27, 28, 52		42-44, 46,
	118, 296	2.11-18	30		47, 49-52,
1.1-2	11	2.11-17	31		63, 67, 76,
1.1	79, 81	2.12-17	142		85, 93, 132,
1.3	13, 17, 33,	2.12	20		136, 176,

Index of References

	295, 300, 304, 321, 324	7	5, 44, 63, 64, 66, 67, 98, 112, 114-16, 119		84, 87, 93, 97, 99, 131, 133, 134, 167, 170, 173, 181, 227, 301, 303, 318
4.1	43, 44				
4.2-5	45	7.1-2	63		
4.3	46, 55	7.2	65, 136		
4.4	45, 70	7.3-4	65		
4.6-9	45	7.3	46, 114	9.1-2	78
4.6-7	45	7.4	65	9.1	79, 80, 89
4.8	57	7.5-6	66	9.2	294
4.10-11	46	7.5	66	9.3-4	80
4.12-16	46	7.6	66	9.3	80, 82, 83
4.12	134	7.7-11	66	9.4	80
4.13	47, 66	7.10	67	9.5-9	87
4.16	47	7.12-14	67	9.5	81, 94
4.17-18	48	7.13-14	67, 68	9.6-7	82
4.18	38, 48, 49, 318	7.15-17	68	9.7	94
		7.17	70, 142	9.8-10	83
4.19-22	49	8	13, 19, 69, 72, 73, 75-78, 87, 89, 94, 97, 111, 113, 114, 125, 172, 233, 323	9.9	83
4.21-22	132			9.11-14	83, 86
5–6	38, 283			9.11-13	84, 210
5	51, 52, 55, 56			9.12-13	84
				9.14-17	87
5.1-2	51			9.14	84
5.3-5	52			9.15-17	86, 87
5.5	56, 60	8.1-3	69	9.16	83, 90, 92, 177
5.6-10	52	8.3	69, 110		
5.6	57	8.4-5	70	9.17	133
5.8	53, 54	8.4	45	9.18-20	87
5.10-12	54	8.5	70, 71	9.21	88, 157
5.11	55, 56	8.6	71, 111, 113	9.22-24	89
6	55, 56, 58, 60, 317			9.24	89
		8.7-10	72	9.25	90
6.1	55, 56	8.7-9	72	9.26-27	90
6.2	56, 295	8.7	72, 78, 116	9.27	90
6.3-6	56	8.10-18	74	10	83, 92, 97, 147, 149, 150, 174, 189, 263, 322
6.5	58	8.10	73		
6.6	320	8.11-19	73, 111		
6.7-9	58	8.11-18	73, 74		
6.10-12	58	8.11	100, 120		
6.13	59	8.14	233	10.1	92, 93, 167
6.14-18	59	8.15	314	10.2-6	123
6.15	60	8.19-22	75	10.2	86, 93, 180
6.16	60	8.20	197	10.3-6	94
6.19-21	60	8.21	76	10.3-4	94
6.19	60	8.22	76, 78, 111	10.5	68, 233
6.20	62	9–15	78	10.6	189
6.21	62	9	78-81, 83,	10.7-8	95

1 Samuel (cont.)		12.1-2	110	13.15-18	127		
10.7	95	12.2	111	13.15	127		
10.8	95, 96, 108, 120, 124, 168	12.3-11	111	13.19-22	128		
		12.3	111	13.19-21	293		
		12.11	112	13.19	128		
10.9-12	96	12.12-13	112	13.22	130		
10.10-13	211	12.14-18	114	13.23	129		
10.10	79, 195	12.19-22	115	14	99, 130-33, 135, 136, 138, 144-47, 149, 157, 159, 175, 177, 186, 191, 204, 214, 220, 221, 223, 235, 237, 242, 243, 275, 292, 293, 299, 321		
10.11	94, 97, 233	12.22	115, 116				
10.13-16	97	12.23-25	116				
10.14-16	234	12.23	116				
10.16	98	12.24-25	165				
10.17-19	98	13	7, 40, 86, 104, 108, 111, 118, 119, 124-26, 130-32, 135, 138, 149, 150, 153, 155-57, 160, 168, 177, 221, 250, 281, 293, 300, 301, 318, 326				
10.17	98						
10.20-24	99						
10.24	113						
10.25-27	100						
10.25	74						
10.27–11.1	103						
10.27	104, 106, 113, 186						
				14.1	119, 130, 131, 133, 214		
11	5, 102, 103, 105, 108, 109, 120, 121, 128, 134, 145, 151, 314, 325, 326						
				14.2-3	131		
				14.2	233		
		13.1–14.46	146	14.3	133, 143, 223		
		13.1	118				
11.1	102	13.2-3	119	14.4-7	133		
11.2-3	103	13.3	68	14.6	133		
11.4-5	104	13.4-7	119	14.7	123, 214		
11.6-7	104	13.4	120	14.8-15	134		
11.6	104	13.5	120	14.16-19	135, 136		
11.8-10	105	13.6	128, 138, 179	14.18-19	135, 136, 142		
11.8	119						
11.11	106, 121, 128	13.7	119, 120, 131	14.18	64		
				14.19	136, 143		
11.12-15	106	13.8-9	128	14.20-23	137		
11.12	106	13.8	120, 326	14.20	137		
11.13	121	13.9-10	121	14.21	131, 137		
11.14	113	13.10	121	14.22	137, 317		
11.15	110	13.11-14	121	14.23	137		
12	73, 109-11, 113, 115-17, 165, 168, 284	13.11	121	14.24-26	138		
		13.13-14	122, 146	14.24-25	139		
		13.13	125, 302	14.24	138, 139		
		13.14	2, 125, 134, 211	14.25	139		
12.1-6	111			14.27-30	140		

Index of References

	14.31-35	15.13	163	16.23	175
	141	15.14	162	17	2, 170, 176,
14.31-32	141	15.16-19	157		178, 179,
14.35	142	15.17	158		181, 189-
14.36-39	143	15.18	157		91, 193,
14.36	136, 275	15.20-23	158		194, 196,
14.37	236	15.20-21	158		229, 231,
14.40-44	144	15.23	206, 295,		279, 292,
14.41	144		296		324
14.44	145, 237	15.24-26	159	17.1-3	176
14.45-46	145	15.27-29	160	17.3	177
14.45	145	15.27	193, 251	17.4-7	177
14.46	146	15.28	123, 252	17.4	177
14.47-52	147	15.29	161, 162	17.8-11	178
14.47-48	146, 147	15.30-31	163	17.8	179
14.47	232	15.32-33	163	17.9	179
14.49-52	147	15.32	163	17.10	179
14.49	317	15.34-35	164	17.12-19	179
14.50	98, 189,	15.35	210	17.12	185
	234	16–17	194	17.15	227
14.52	68, 175	16	39, 83, 91,	17.16	179, 180
15	125, 127,		95, 166,	17.17-19	180
	149, 150,		167, 170,	17.19	180
	153, 154,		172-76,	17.20-25	180
	156, 158,		196, 209,	17.20	192
	162, 165,		215, 224,	17.21	180
	166, 168,		293, 307,	17.22-23	182
	174, 237,		321	17.25	231
	246, 251,	16.1	166	17.26	181
	252, 280,	16.2-3	167	17.27-29	182
	281, 298,	16.3	171	17.27	182
	300, 302,	16.4-7	169	17.28-29	213
	318	16.4-5	224	17.28	170
15.1-3	149	16.6-7	83	17.30-37	183
15.4-6	151	16.7	186	17.34-37	184, 187
15.6	151, 152	16.8-11	170	17.35	196
15.7-9	152	16.11	227	17.38-40	185
15.7	152	16.12-13	171	17.40	185
15.8	152	16.12	260	17.41-47	186
15.9	152	16.14	172, 196	17.45-47	186
15.10-11	153	16.15-19	172	17.48-53	187
15.11	153-55,	16.18	83, 184,	17.49	320
	158, 161,		263, 265	17.51	277
	166	16.20-22	174	17.54	187, 228
15.12	154, 260,	16.21-22	197	17.55-58	188, 190
	268	16.21	192	17.55	195, 204,
15.13-15	155	16.22	192		279

1 Samuel (cont.)			238, 247,	20.30	215, 272
17.58	190		297, 298	20.31	234
18	139, 175,	19.1-3	202	20.32-34	221
	190, 191,	19.1	203, 214,	20.34	221
	193, 202,		219	20.35-42	221
	213, 216,	19.2-3	203, 213	21–22	61, 136,
	229, 246,	19.2	205		188
	267, 293,	19.4-7	203	21	128, 188,
	306	19.7	204		223, 224,
18.1-2	191	19.8-10	204		235, 239,
18.2	192	19.8	205		262, 283-
18.3-4	192	19.9	131		85, 307
18.3	215	19.10	196, 205	21.1-10	225
18.4	210, 323	19.11-17	205	21.1	223
18.5	193, 194,	19.11-13	205	21.2-3	224
	197	19.12	220	21.4-5	226
18.6-9	193, 194	19.13	210	21.5	226
18.7	229	19.14-17	206	21.6-7	226
18.8	196, 256	19.17	217, 220	21.6	226
18.10-11	195	19.18-20	208	21.7	226, 227
18.11	196	19.19	216	21.8-10	227
18.12-16	196	19.20	233	21.10-15	228
18.12	196	19.21-24	209	21.10	228
18.13	197	19.22	210	21.12	286
18.17-27	181, 291	19.24	210, 323	21.14	268, 307
18.17-19	197	19.25	213	22	74, 128,
18.18	199	20	183, 212,		231, 233,
18.19	199		214, 215,		237, 238,
18.20-27	197		225, 236,		242, 268,
18.20-21	198		245, 278		284, 314,
18.20	216	20.1-2	213		326
18.21	199	20.2	236	22.1-4	234
18.22-25	199	20.3-4	214	22.1-2	231
18.22	203	20.3	214, 221	22.2	234, 251
18.23	269	20.5-8	215, 216	22.3-5	232
18.25	201	20.5	215	22.3	285
18.26-27	200	20.8	215	22.5	233
18.26	200	20.9-11	216	22.6-8	233
18.27	229	20.11	216	22.6	326
18.28-30	201	20.12-17	216	22.7	234
18.28	201	20.14	217	22.9-10	234
18.29	201, 217	20.16-17	216	22.9	131
19–22	217	20.18-23	218	22.11-19	136
19	164, 202,	20.23	218	22.11-15	235
	206-208,	20.24-26	219	22.14-15	236
	210, 211,	20.25	219	22.14	236
	214, 215,	20.26	219	22.16-19	237
	220, 225,	20.27-31	220	22.20-23	238

22.20	238	25.1	258, 259,	27.5	286
22.22-23	238		292	27.6-7	287
23	243, 260,	25.2-42	259	27.7	305
	266, 274,	25.2-3	260	27.8-11	287
	275, 285	25.4-8	261	27.8	309
23.1-2	240	25.9-11	262	27.10	288
23.3-6	241	25.12-13	262	27.12	288, 291
23.7-8	242	25.14-17	263	28	160, 164,
23.7	244, 286	25.14	263		171, 195,
23.9-13	285	25.18-19	264		258, 259,
23.9-12	243	25.20-22	265		290-92,
23.9	243, 245,	25.21	265		297, 301-
	249	25.23-31	266		304, 306,
23.10-12	243	25.26	266, 267		309, 311,
23.13-14	244	25.31	268		316, 317
23.14	244, 246	25.32-35	268	28.1-2	291
23.15-18	244	25.36-38	269	28.2	304, 309
23.17	264	25.37	270	28.3	258, 292,
23.18	246	25.39-44	271		302
23.19-23	246	25.43-44	272	28.4-7	292
23.20	275	25.43	272	28.8	294
23.22	307	25.44	272	28.9-11	295
23.24-28	247	26	183, 196,	28.12-14	296
24–26	274		261, 274,	28.15-19	298
24	160, 196,		275, 277,	28.15	310
	249-52,		278, 280,	28.17	123
	258, 261,		281, 321	28.20-22	301
	262, 265,	26.1-4	274	28.23-25	302
	274-80, 312	26.5-6	275	29–30	316
24.1-2	249	26.7-8	276	29	44, 183,
24.1	249	26.9-11	277		304
24.3-4	250	26.10	277, 284	29.1-3	304
24.3	275	26.12	278	29.4-5	305
24.5-7	252	26.13-16	278	29.6-8	306
24.5	256	26.14	279	29.6	308
24.8-15	253, 256	26.16	279	29.9-11	307
24.10	196	26.17-20	280	29.9	308
24.15	281	26.19	288	29.10	308
24.16-21	254	26.21-25	281	30	287, 309,
24.17	271, 280	26.23	196, 282		310, 312
24.22	256	26.25	283	30.1-5	309
25	246, 258-	27	283, 285,	30.1	313
	61, 265,		288, 291,	30.3	310
	266, 272-		306	30.6-10	310
	74, 277,	27.1	283	30.6	310
	288, 290,	27.2-4	285	30.8	311
	292, 310,	27.3	285	30.9	311
	311, 313	27.5-7	286	30.10	311

1 Samuel (cont.)		11.11	226	10.1-11	217
30.11-15	311	11.21	319	11.1	217
30.15	312	11.26	271	17	6
30.16-20	312	12	160, 183	23.24	292
30.20	313	12.5	280	25	4, 6, 77
30.21-25	314	12.8	272	25.22-36	98
30.24	314	14	269		
30.26-31	315	17	88	*1 Chronicles*	
31	108, 316-25	17.8	313	6	13
31.1-2	316	18.18	155	10	324
31.2	317, 323	18.32	267		
31.3-4	318	19	255	*Job*	
31.4	320	20	100	2.9	40
31.5-6	321	21.17	38	32.19	295
31.6	321	22	29		
31.7	323, 325	22.3	29	*Psalms*	
31.8-10	323	22.14	29	5.12	27
31.11-13	325	23.21	277	9.3	27
31.13	233	24	142, 282	20.5	123
		24.10	122, 252	68.4	27
2 Samuel				78	61
1	29, 313	*1 Kings*		78.60	61
1.19-27	322	1	238		
1.19	86	2	35, 237,	*Proverbs*	
2	252, 278		308	16.22	260
3	147, 189,	2.26	35		
	219, 251,	3.4	64	*Isaiah*	
	273, 277	11	252	8.19-20	297
3.14	200	11.36	38		
3.18	123	11.38	165	*Jeremiah*	
3.27	279	12	6	3.15	123
4	246	14	42	6.24	15
5	324	14.1	317	7	42, 61
5.2	123	14.10	265	38	158
5.7	257	14.20	317		
5.8	178	15.4	38	*Hosea*	
5.12	126	20	269	3.4	206
5.18-21	46	21	74		
5.21	324	21.34	321	*Jonah*	
6	61, 64, 136,	22	143	4	154
	208	22.22-23	161		
6.10-12	64			*Zechariah*	
7.12-13	126	*2 Kings*		10.2	206
9	246	1	209		
11–12	183	6.8	225	NEW TESTAMENT	
11	124, 267,	8.19	38	*Luke*	
	272, 273,	9	92, 168	1.46-55	27
	320	9.8	265		

INDEX OF AUTHORS

Ackerman, J.S. 61, 95, 156, 276
Alter, R. 18, 19, 40, 79, 81, 85, 110, 123,
    138, 141, 149, 154, 160, 162, 203,
    206, 207, 213, 264, 287, 294
Amit, Y. 162
Arnold, B.T. 125
Auld, A.G. 2, 14, 23, 26, 35, 37, 42, 49,
    61, 66, 76, 79, 98, 107, 116, 118,
    154, 189, 221, 224, 245, 251, 277,
    280, 288, 295, 317, 326

Baldwin, J.G. 65, 72, 129
Bar-Efrat, S. 84
Bergen, R.D. 25, 114, 287
Biddle, M.E. 261, 272
Birch, B.C. 15, 21, 27, 30, 33, 42, 56, 74,
    76, 98, 103, 118, 125, 133, 157,
    168, 170, 174, 193, 209, 267, 296,
    314, 320
Blenkinsopp, J. 130
Bodner, K. 225, 235
Brooks, P. 8
Brueggemann, W. 22, 29, 31, 33, 41, 107,
    111, 116, 121, 153, 157, 173, 185,
    209, 234, 254

Campbell 38, 58, 64, 125, 138, 182, 192,
    237, 297
Coggins, R.J. 294
Craig, K.M., Jr. 143, 293, 299, 302
Cross, F.M. 2, 288
Cuddon, J.A. 86

Deist, F. 83
Driver, S.R. 118

Edelman, D.V. 76, 80, 90, 95, 107, 111,
    131, 133, 136, 152, 158, 160, 180,
    186, 189, 200, 203, 214, 218, 224,
    227, 235, 236, 254, 263, 266, 268,
    270, 279, 285, 306, 311, 316, 321
Esler, P. 89
Eslinger, L. 27, 75, 80, 113
Evans, M.J. 25, 30
Ewing, W. 42
Exum, J.C. 124

Fokkelman, J.P. 21, 33, 35, 44, 66, 81, 83,
    89, 95, 105-107, 114, 177, 210,
    220, 232, 242, 320, 325
Forster, E.M. 255

Garsiel, M. 12, 79
Goldingay, J. 7, 123
Gordon, R.P. 21, 27, 31, 35, 40, 49, 68,
    70, 74, 77, 89, 95, 99, 131, 138,
    141, 178, 199, 217, 229, 232, 281,
    283, 292, 323
Green, B. 32, 50, 55, 70, 78, 79, 94, 96,
    100, 105, 110, 111, 113, 116, 134,
    139, 140, 146, 153, 158, 181, 190,
    195, 205, 220, 230, 242, 258, 261,
    264, 271, 279, 319, 322
Gunn, D.M. 7, 83, 87, 125

Halpern, B. 286
Hamilton, V.P. 112, 128, 157, 161, 288
Hawk, L.D. 35
Hertzberg, H.W. 266, 276, 286, 315
Hos, C.Y.S. 2

Jobling, D. 112, 132, 136, 141, 147, 164,
    267, 274, 284

Keil, C.F. 150, 177, 324
Klein, R.W. 53
Knoppers, G.N. 151
Kugel, J. 96

Leithart, P.J. 270
Levenson, J.D. 85, 260, 264, 265, 272, 286

McCarter, P.K. 137, 141, 146, 151, 178, 194, 197, 226, 232, 258, 266, 297
McConville, J.G. 162
Miscall, P.D. 20, 22, 24, 31, 33, 57, 67, 72, 73, 83, 85, 86, 89, 97, 104, 108, 114, 126, 129, 144, 152, 157, 160, 167, 183, 190, 198, 207, 214, 218, 224, 247, 250, 268, 276, 279, 281, 282, 292, 300, 325
Moberly, R.W.L. 162
Mullen, E.T., Jr. 197

Noll, K.L. 8

Pinker, A. 322
Polzin, R. 13, 16-19, 21, 23, 25, 27-29, 38, 39, 48, 58, 75, 82, 92, 95, 96, 108, 109, 139, 145, 164, 168, 188, 193, 196, 206, 210, 216, 219, 236, 243, 262, 280, 284, 288, 297, 298, 315, 320
Prouser, O.H. 193, 210, 247

Rad, G. von 36
Reis, P.T. 226, 295
Reisse, M. 96
Rendsburg, G.A. 84
Römer, T.C. 4
Rosenberg, J. 29, 262, 265

Smith, H.P. 122
Sternberg, M. 86, 164
Sweeney, M.H. 6, 87

Watson, W.G.E. 35
Weinfeld, M. 4
Wellhausen, J. 222, 303
Wiesel, E. 124, 294, 296, 299, 300, 322

Yadin, A. 178

www.ingramcontent.com/pod-product-compliance
Lightning Source LLC
Chambersburg PA
CBHW052050230426
43671CB00011B/1853